HISTORIC PHOTOS OF LITTLE ROCK

Text and Captions by Kimberly Reynolds Rush

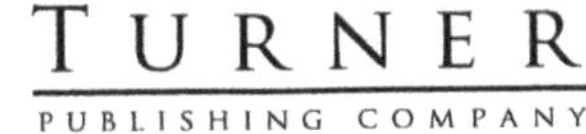

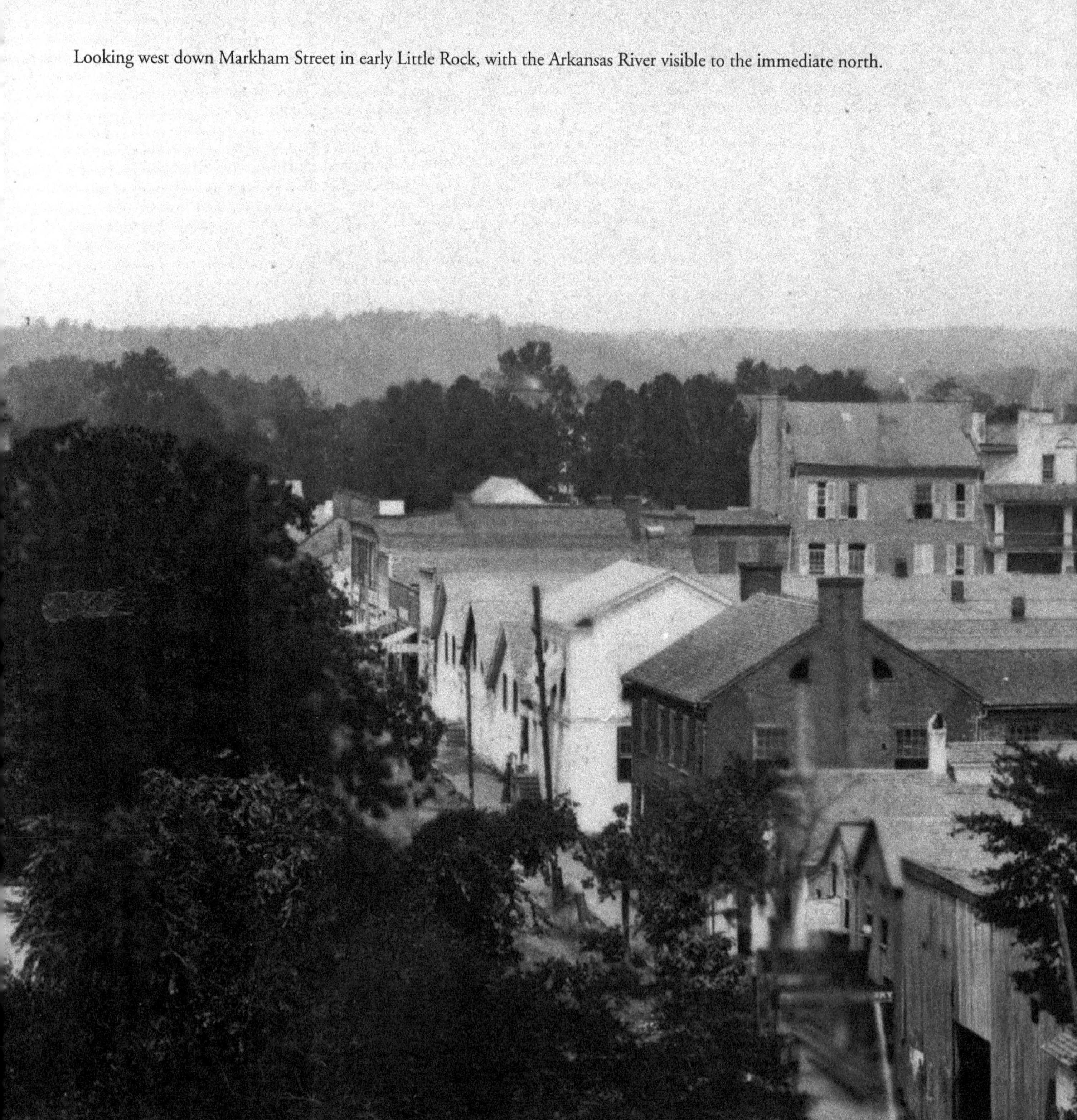

Looking west down Markham Street in early Little Rock, with the Arkansas River visible to the immediate north.

HISTORIC PHOTOS OF LITTLE ROCK

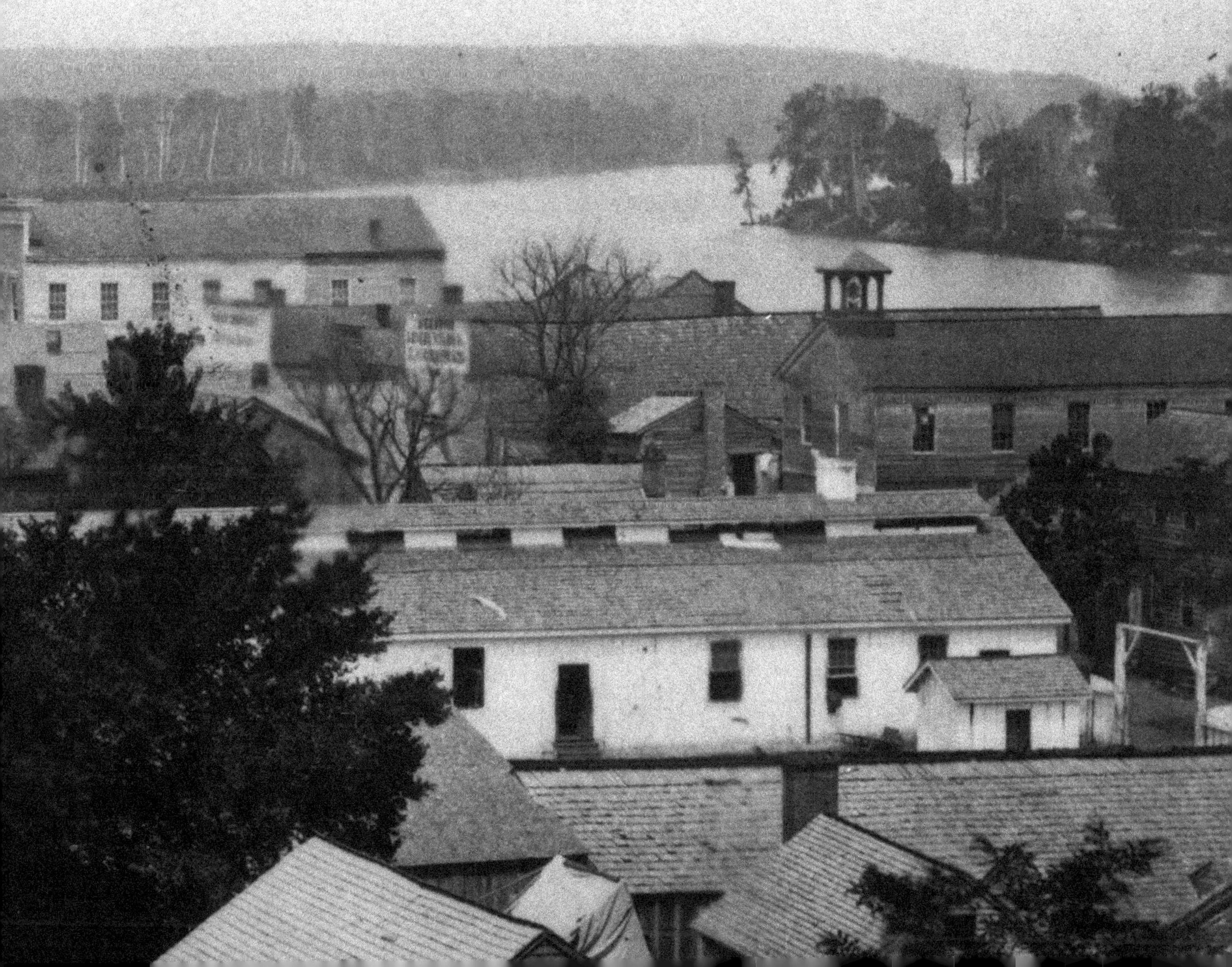

Turner Publishing Company
www.turnerpublishing.com

Historic Photos of Little Rock

Library of Congress Control Number: 2008901852

ISBN: 978-1-59652-379-1

Printed in the United States of America

ISBN 978-1-68336-966-0 (hc)

Contents

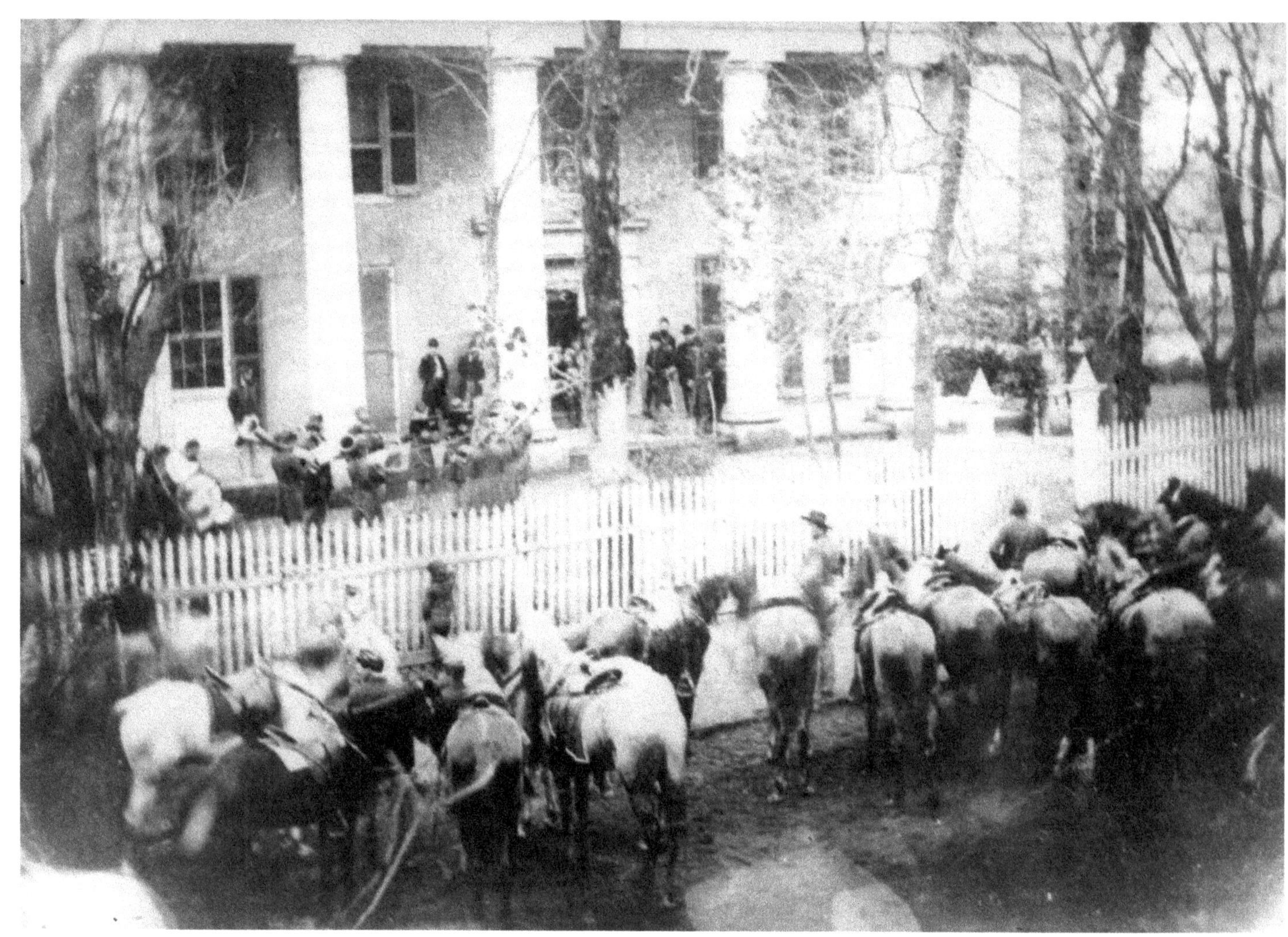

Spectators on horseback watch a band play in front of Major General Frederick Steele's headquarters at Ashley House, around 1865. During the Civil War, General Steele comomanded Union forces in the capture of Little Rock. Chester Ashley, one of the first lawyers to settle in Little Rock and a former United States senator, built the Ashley house in the 1820s. The house was razed in the 1920s

Acknowledgments

This volume, *Historic Photos of Little Rock,* is the result of the cooperation and efforts of many individuals and organizations. It is with great thanks that we acknowledge the valuable contribution of the following for their generous support:

Arkansas History Commission
Butler Center for Arkansas Studies
The Library of Congress
University of Arkansas at Little Rock

The writer would like to thank Ryan Rush and Sandy Reynolds for their invaluable assistance in proofreading the text and Kati Bazzell for taking the writer's photograph.

PREFACE

Little Rock has thousands of historic photographs that reside in archives, both locally and nationally. This book began with the observation that, while those photographs are of great interest to many, they are not easily accessible. During a time when Little Rock is looking ahead and evaluating its future course, many people are asking, How do we treat the past? These decisions affect every aspect of the city—architecture, public spaces, commerce, infrastructure—and these, in turn, affect the way that people live their lives. This book seeks to provide easy access to a valuable, objective look into the history of Little Rock.

Although the photographer can make decisions regarding subject matter and how to capture and present it, photographs, unlike words, are less prone to interpret history subjectively. This lends them an authority that textual histories sometimes fail to achieve, and offers the viewer an original, untainted perspective from which to draw his own conclusions, interpretations, and insights.

This project represents countless hours of review and research. The researchers and writer have reviewed hundreds of photographs in numerous archives. We greatly appreciate the generous assistance of the individuals and organizations listed in the acknowledgments of this work, without whom this project could not have been completed.

The goal in publishing this work is to provide broader access to this set of extraordinary photographs that seek to inspire, provide perspective, and evoke insight that might assist people who are responsible for determining Little Rock's future. In addition, the book seeks to preserve the past with adequate respect and reverence.

With the exception of touching up imperfections that have accrued with the passage of time and cropping where necessary, no changes have been made. The focus and clarity of many images is limited by the technology and the ability of the photographer at the time they were taken.

The work is divided into eras. Beginning with some of the earliest known photographs of the city, the first section records photographs through the end of the nineteenth century. The second section spans the beginning of the twentieth century through World War I. Section Three moves from the 1920s through the 1930s, and the last section covers the World War II era to recent times.

In each of these sections we have made an effort to capture various aspects of life through our selection of photographs. People, commerce, transportation, infrastructure, religious institutions, and educational institutions have been included to provide a broad perspective.

We encourage readers to reflect as they go walking in Little Rock, strolling through the city, its parks, and its neighborhoods. It is the publisher's hope that in utilizing this work, longtime residents will learn something new and that new residents will gain a perspective on where Little Rock has been, so that each can contribute to its future.

—Todd Bottorff, Publisher

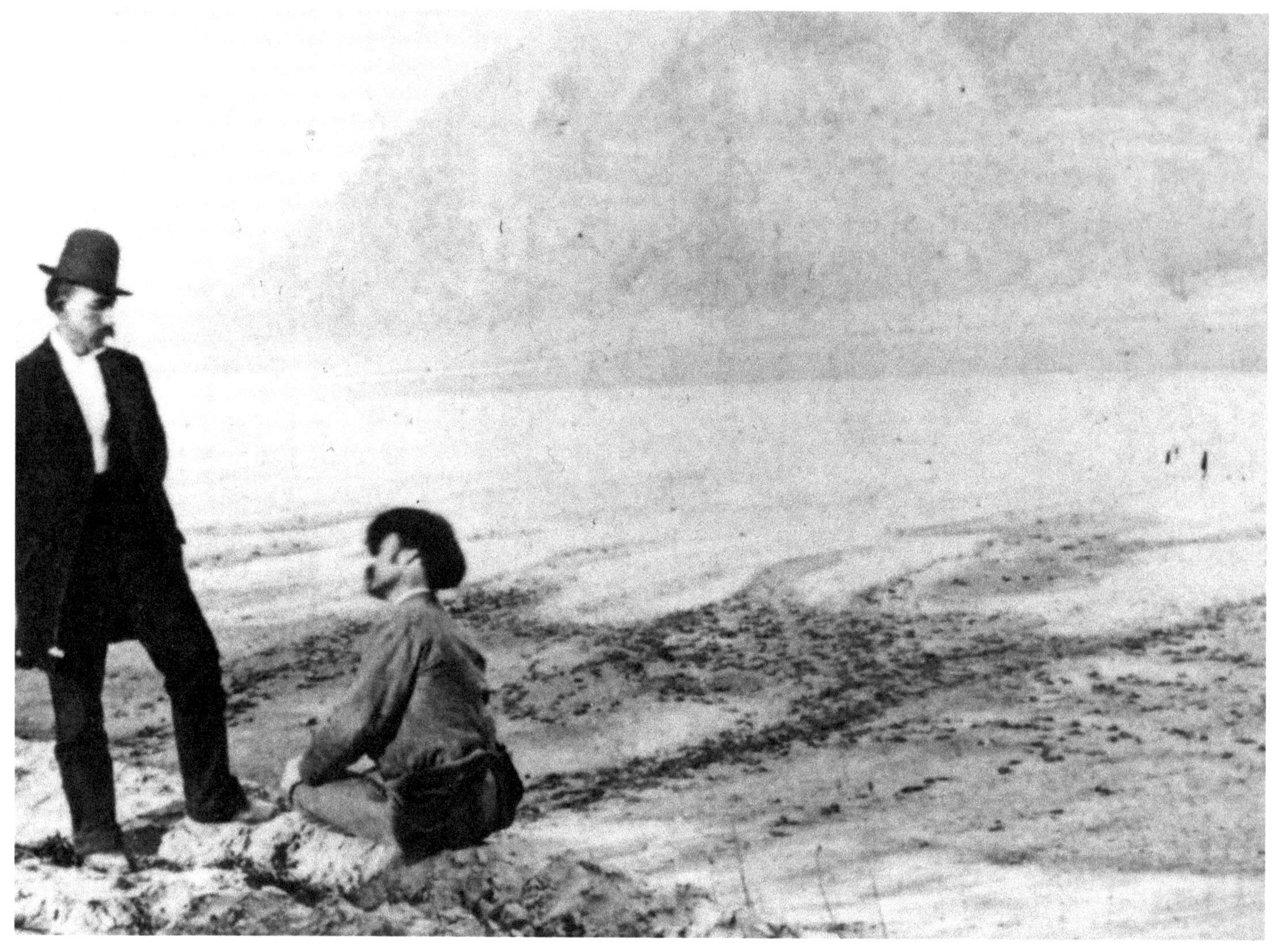

A view of Big Rock Mountain, opposite Little Rock, from around the 1870s.

An Enterprising Spirit

(1860-1899)

The capital of Arkansas is located 12 miles southwest of the geographic center of the state on the south side of the Arkansas River where the Mississippi delta gives way to the Ouachita Mountain foothills. It is named for a small stone outcropping along the bank of the river called "La Petit Roche" by the French explorers who discovered it.

The first settler in Little Rock was William Lewis, who built a log cabin in the spring of 1812 but left the following October. Permanent settlers began to show up by 1820, the year the town was surveyed, and within another year Little Rock had become the capital of the Arkansas Territory. On June 15, 1836, Arkansas was admitted to the Union as the 25th state.

Growth was slow in the following decades until the 1820s, when advances in technology gave the city a boost, including a proposed railroad connecting Little Rock to Memphis, Tennessee, the introduction of gasworks for streetlights; and a telegraph line that connected Little Rock to the rest of the country. With this infrastructure in place, the population began to increase.

In 1860, the United States was facing a crisis that would erupt in civil war. South Carolina seceded from the Union on December 20, followed by other states in 1861, with Arkansas voting to secede in May. Although Little Rock was the site of an arsenal, everyday life in the city did not change much in the early stages of the war. The Civil War did not arrive full force in Little Rock until 1863, when Union troops commanded by General Frederick Steele marched on the city. Little Rock fell within hours and Union occupation began. After the war, conflict reemerged during Reconstruction with the gubernatorial election of 1872. The Brooks-Baxter War was decided by the Grant administration in favor of Governor Baxter.

As the century moved into its final decades, Little Rock's fortunes showed greater promise. The proposed railroad to Memphis was completed in 1873 with the construction of the first Baring Cross Bridge, enabling the railroad to replace steamboats as the most important transportation link between Little Rock and the rest of the country. In 1877 streetcars were introduced to the city, and the first telephone exchange opened in 1879. The streets were soon paved with cobblestones, the first sewer lines were laid, and electricity made its debut. In 1880, an American was born in Little Rock the nation would later come to know as General Douglas MacArthur.

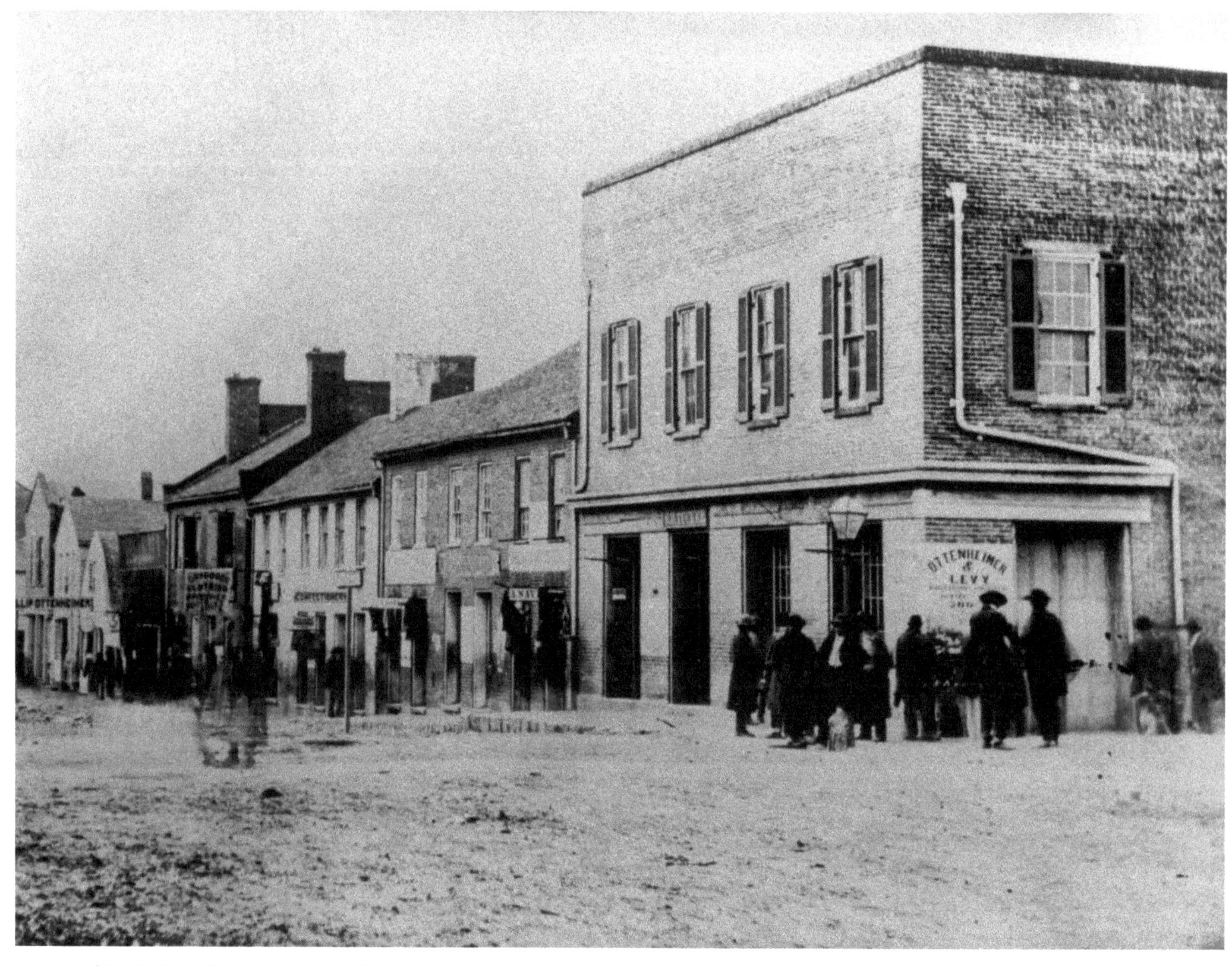

A view of Little Rock from the corner of Main and Markham streets in 1863.

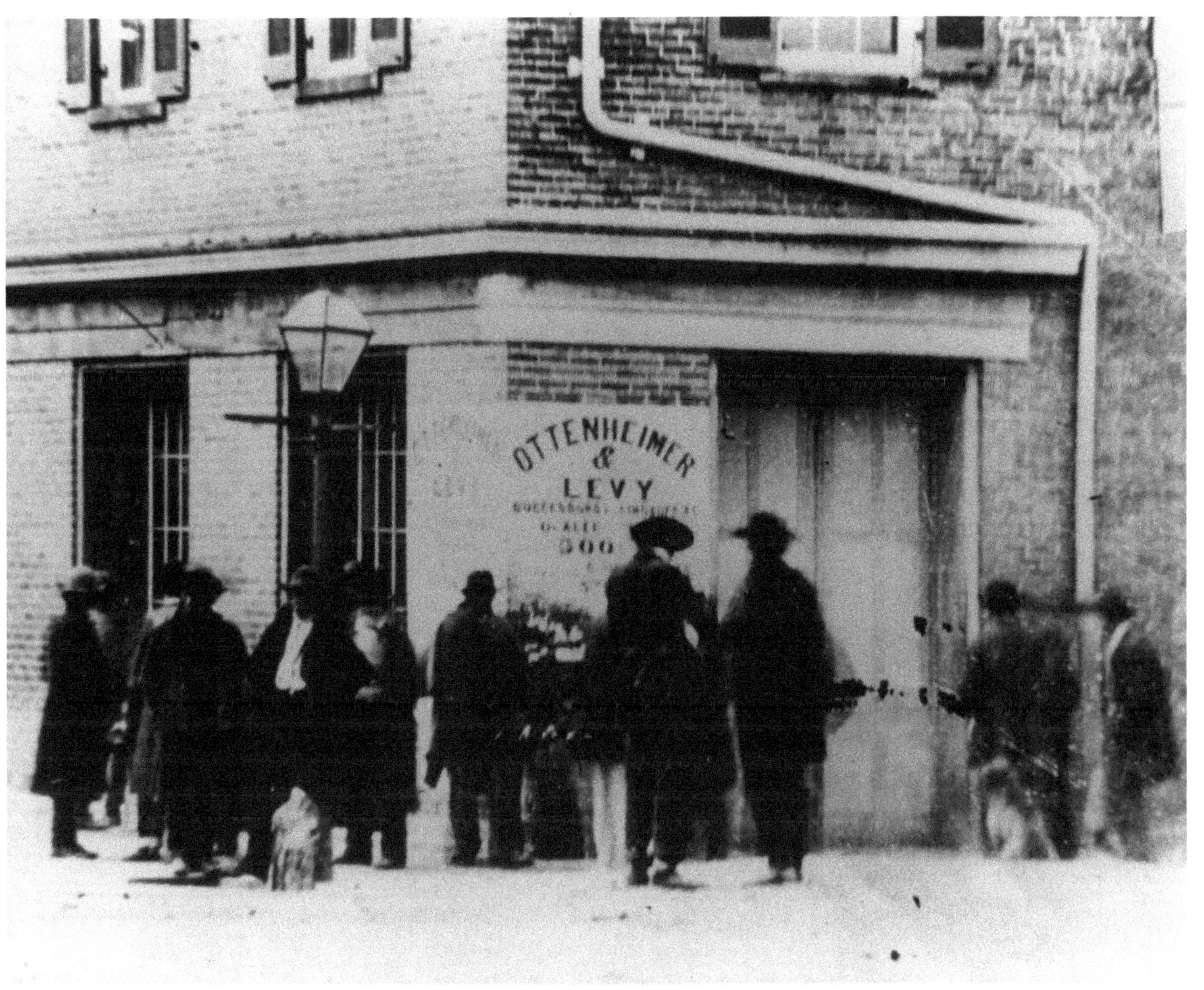

Ottenheimer and Levy Goods, on the corner of Markham and Main streets.

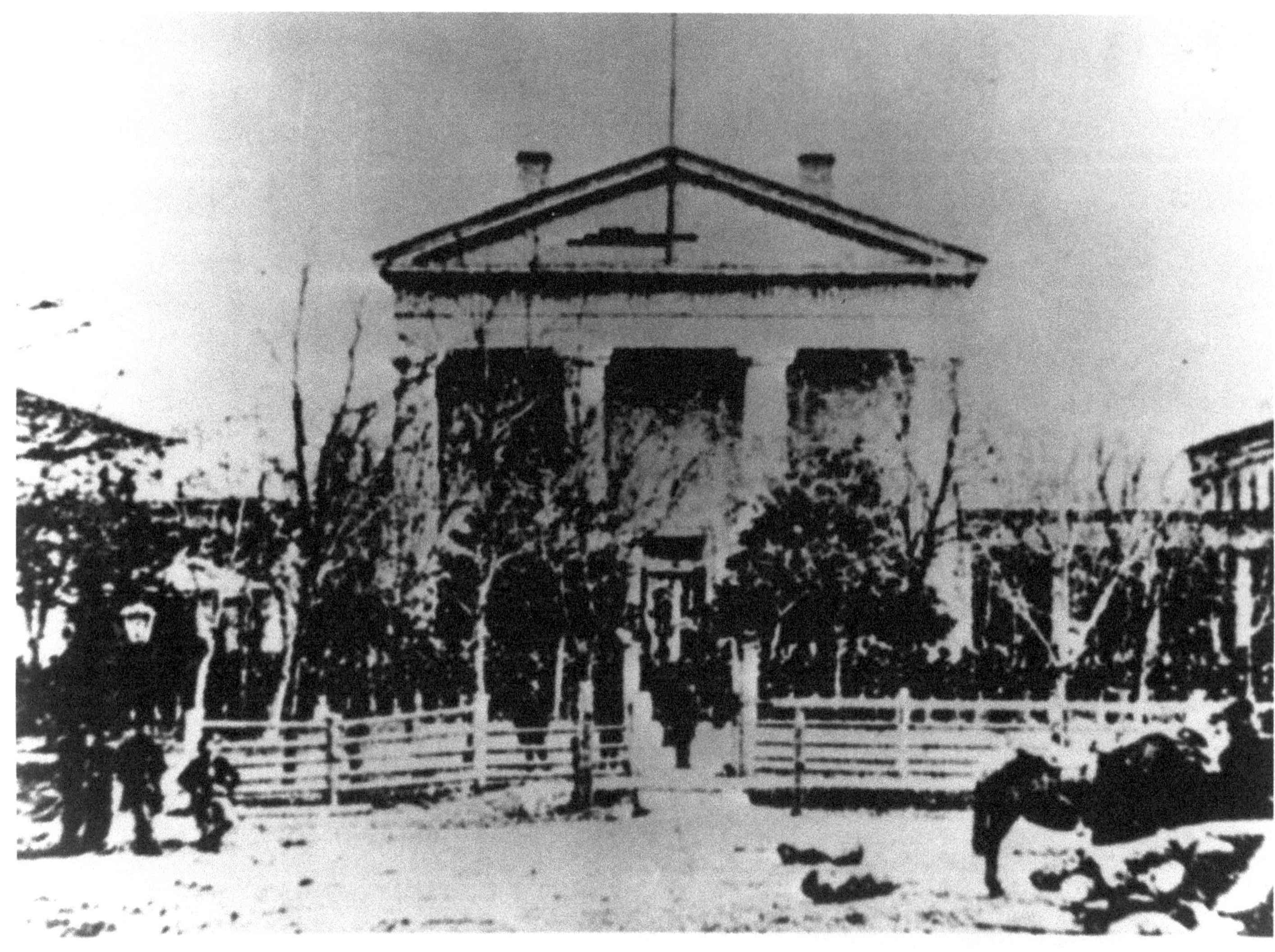

Members of the Third Regiment, Minnesota Volunteer Infantry, stand in front of the Old State House in 1863. The regiment was formed on August 27, 1862. Regiment members participated in Colonel Henry Hastings Sibley's campaign against the Sioux Indians and the Siege of Vicksburg before taking part in teh campaign to capture Littele Rock, where they remained in garrison until April 28, 1864. The infantry was discharged on September 16, 1865.

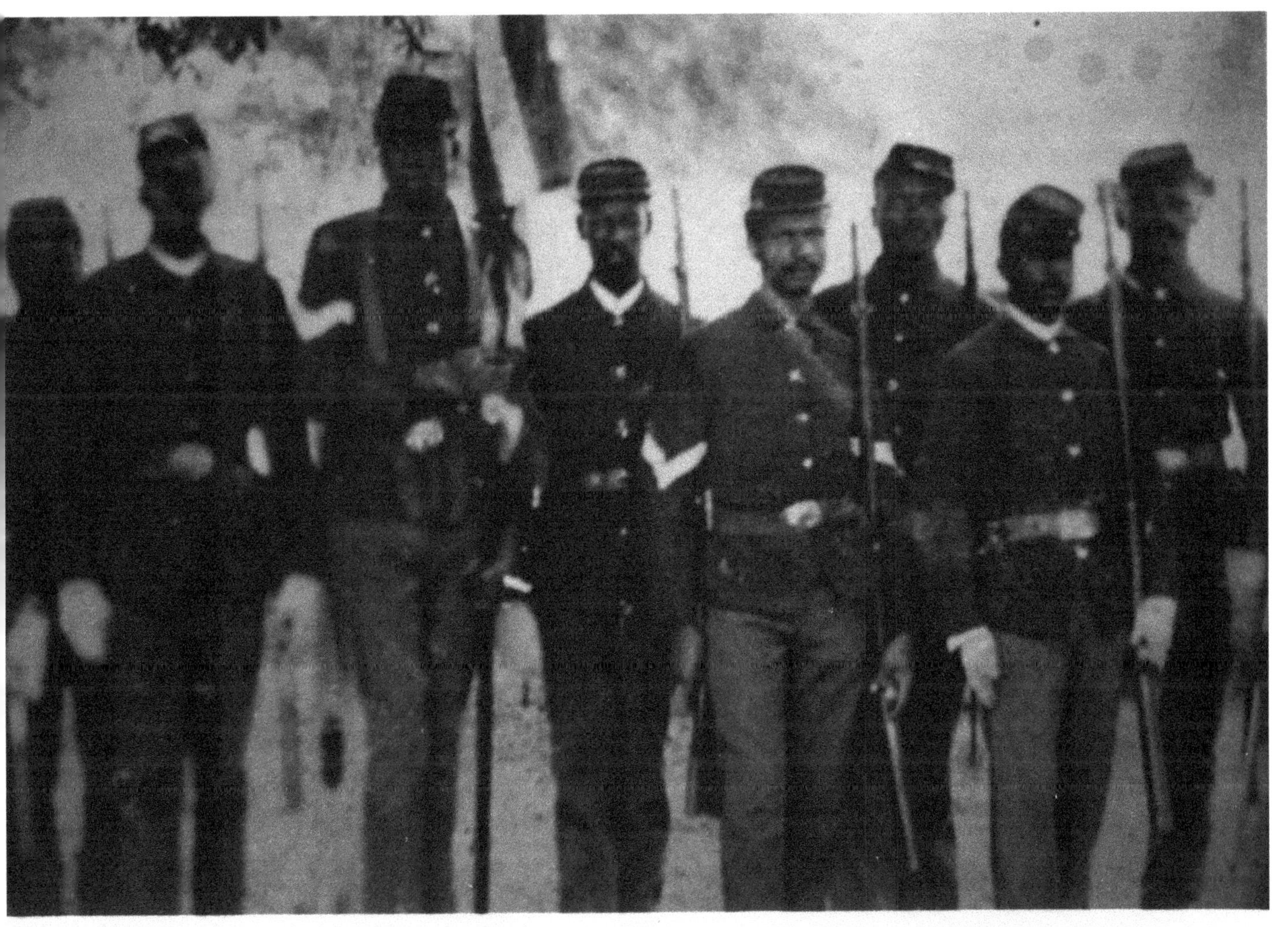

The 57th Regiment Infantry U.S. Colored Troops, Company F, was organized on March 11, 1864. It was originally the Fourth Regiment, Arkansas Volunteers, and attached to the District of Eastern Arkansas, Seventh Corps. Companies in teh infantry were posted at various places around Arkansas, including Little Rock. The regiment mustered out on December 31, 1866

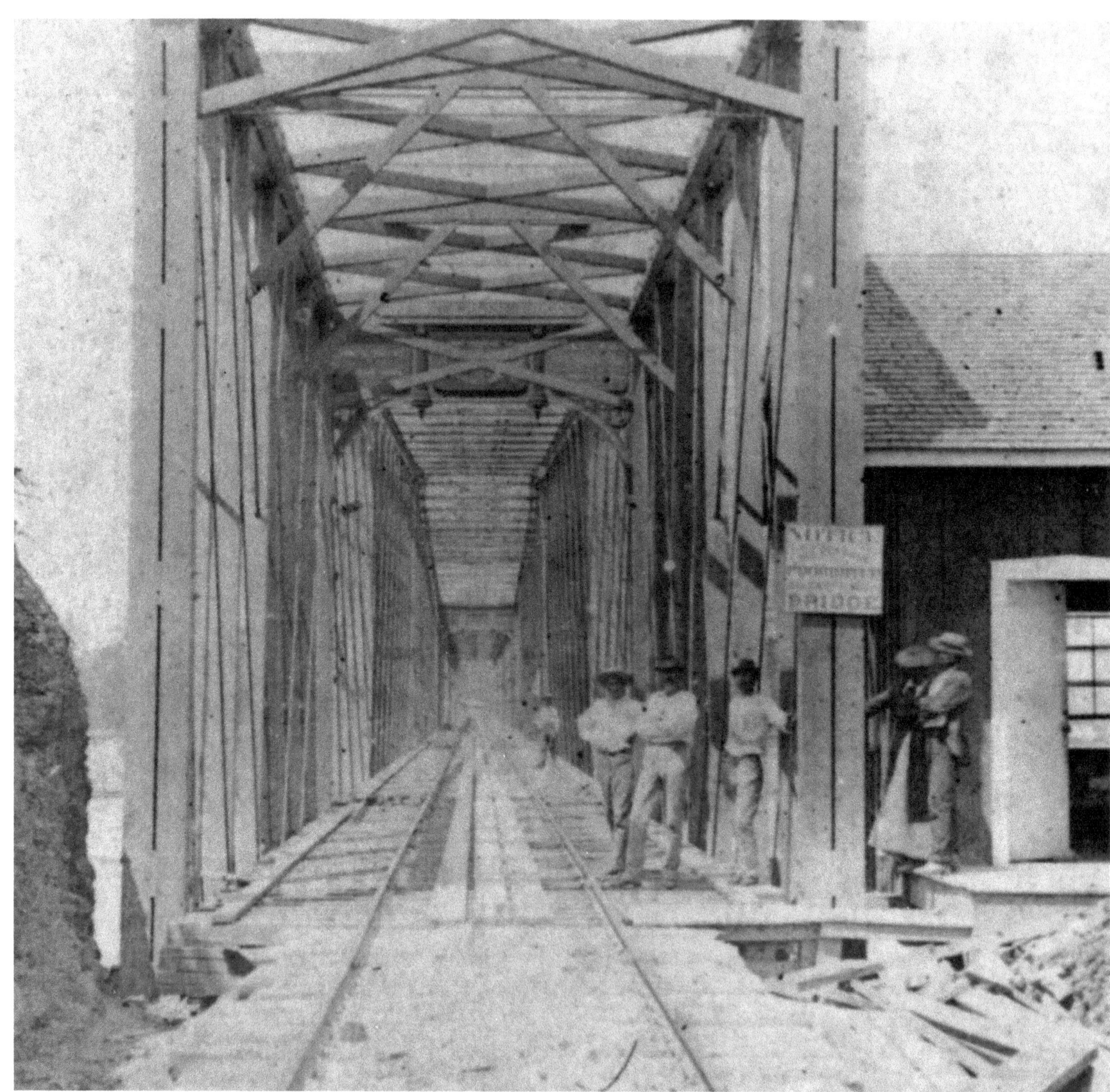

A railway bridge over the Arkansas River from the perspective of those aboard a train.

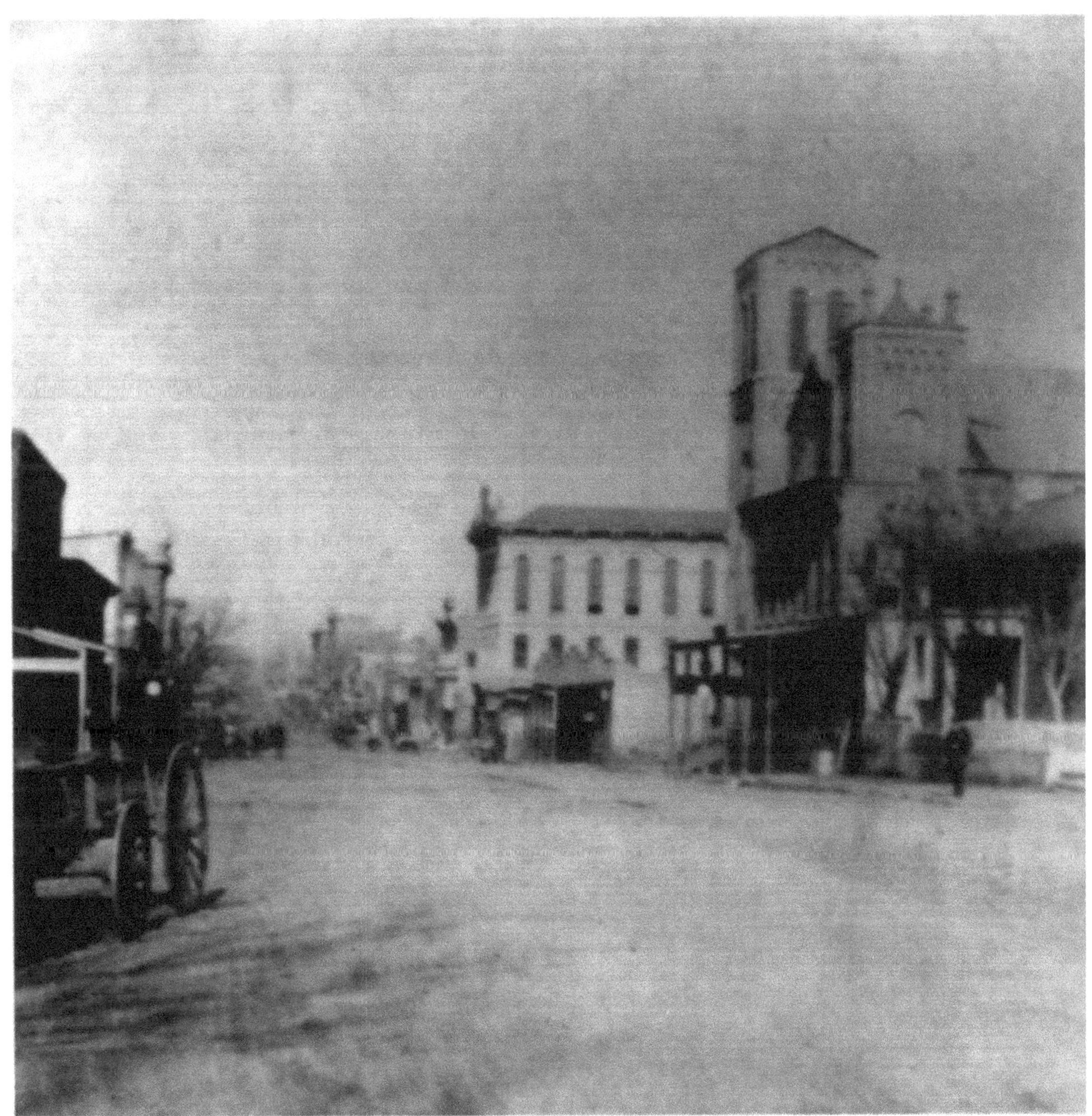

Facing north down Markham Street. To the right are several buildings, including the Northern Methodist Church.

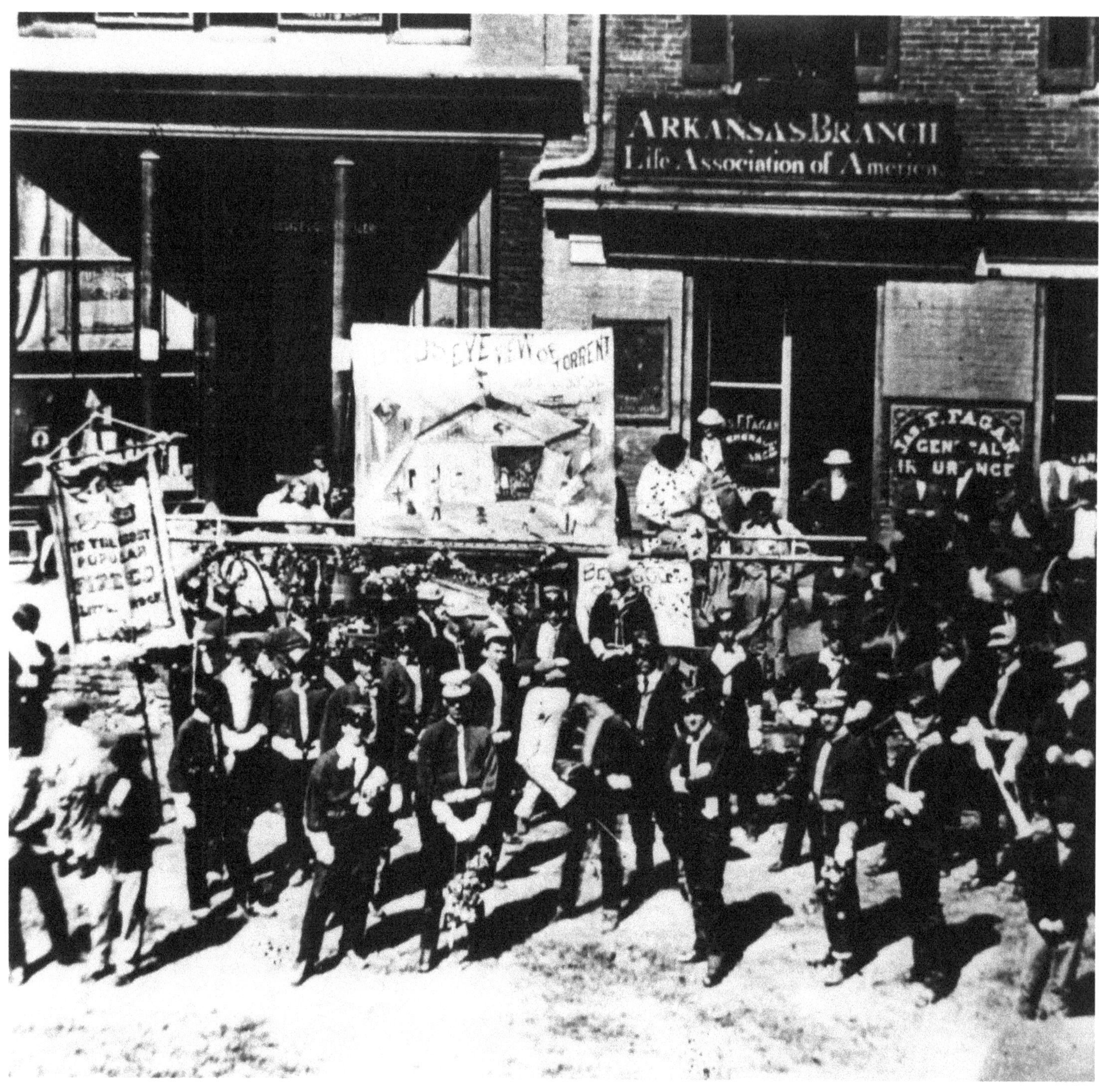

Members of the Torrent Fire Company pose for a group shot in 1872.

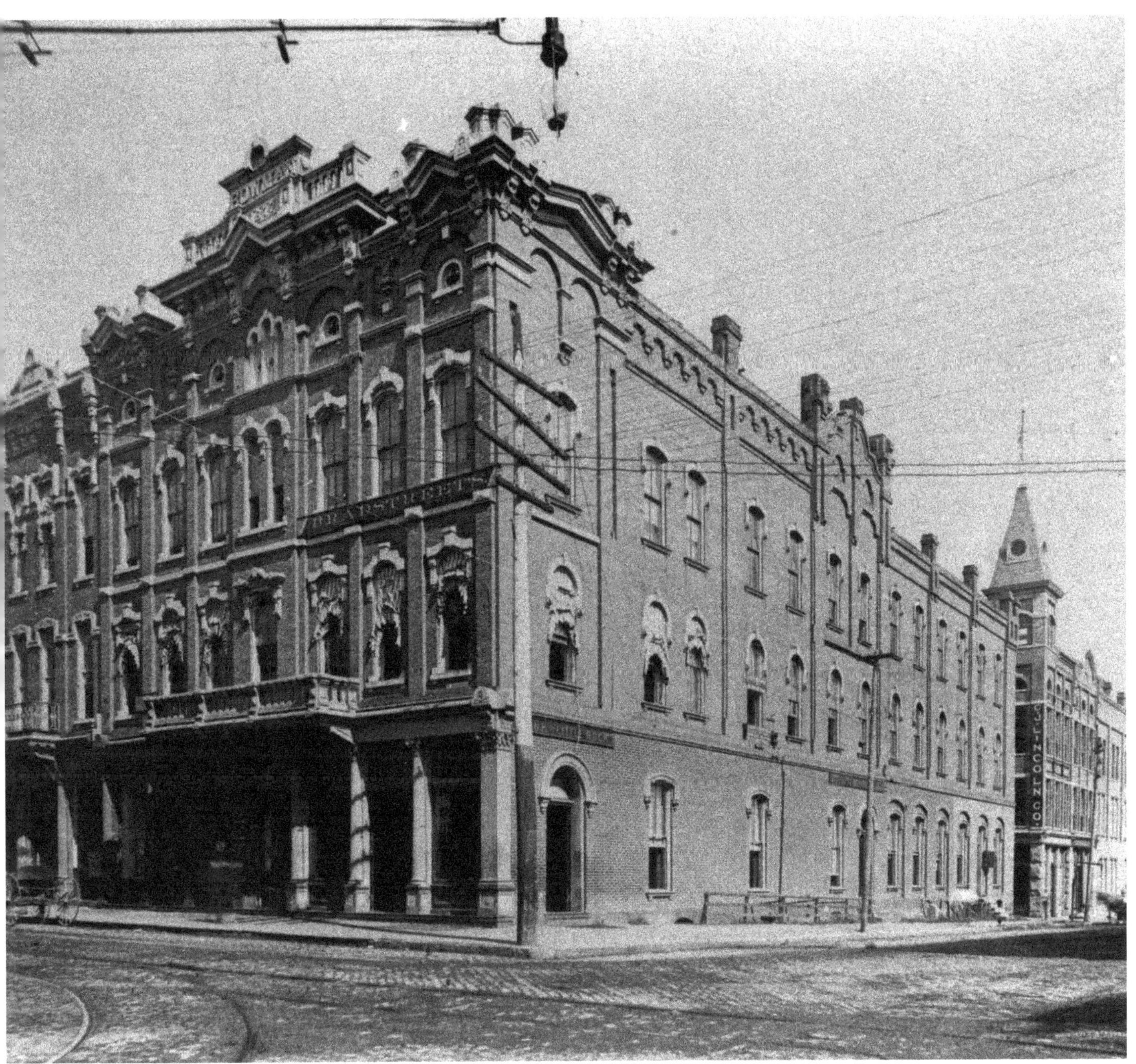

The Bowman block, at the corner of Markham and Main streets. The ill-fated Metropolitan Hotel would open in this building.

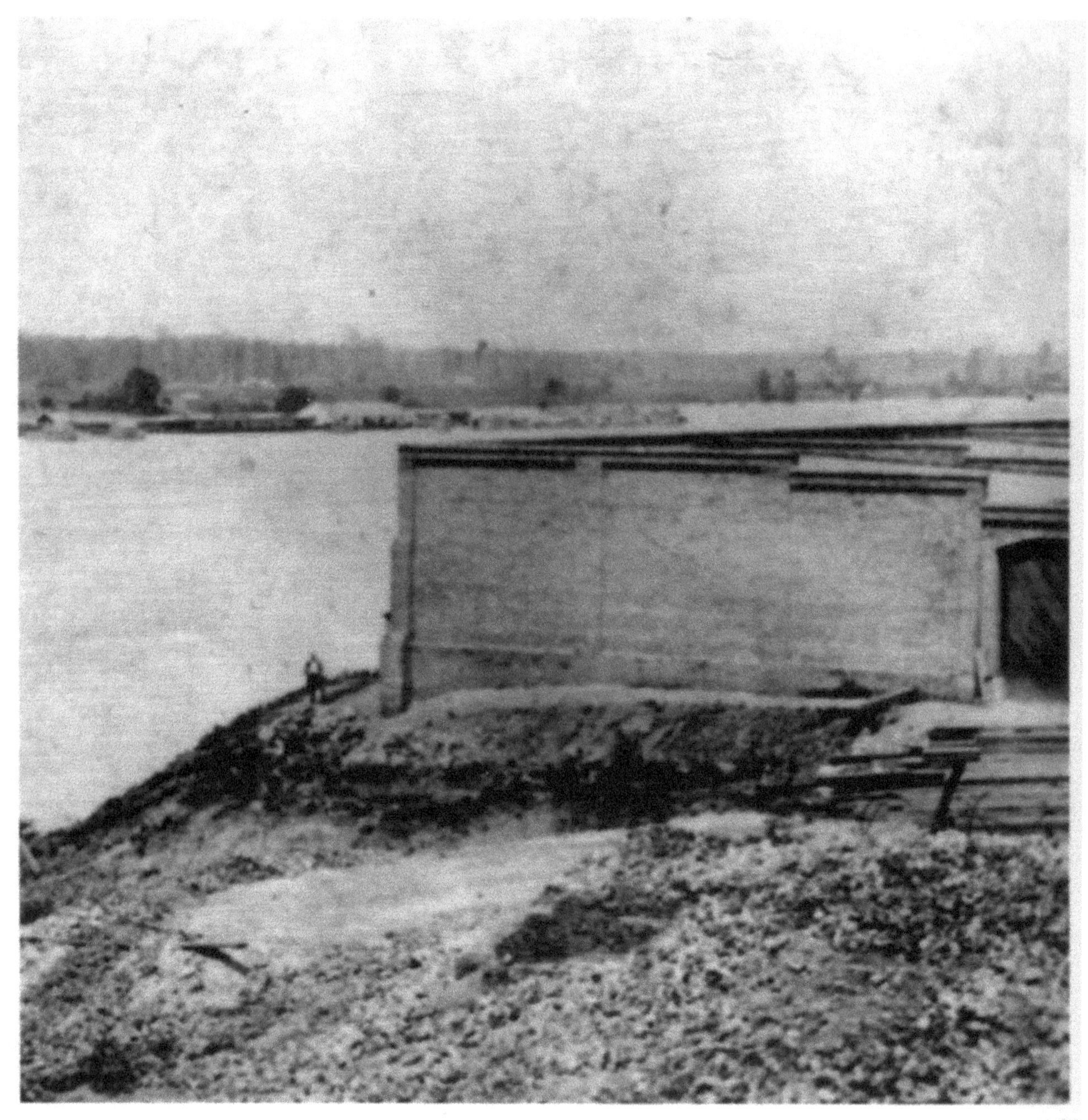

A cotton warehouse at the foot of Main Street near the Arkansas River. Cotton has always been, both before the Civil War and after, an important cash crop to the Arkansas economy.

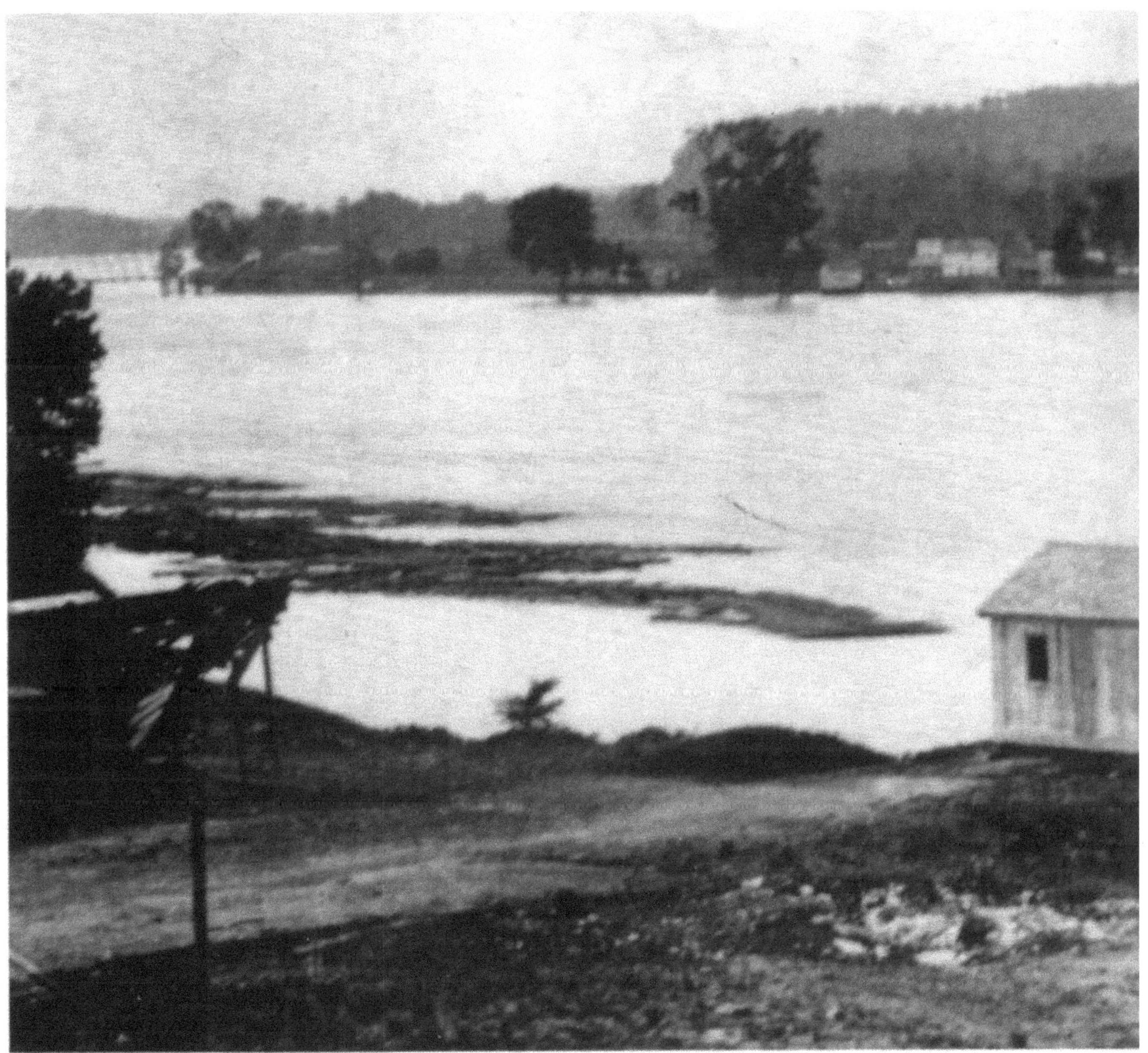

The city wood yard, located on the banks of the Arkansas River. As the sixth-longest river in the United States, the Arkansas flows from its headwaters in the Rockies of Colorado through parts of four states to the Mississippi River. Little Rock would grow to become one of the principal cities along its route.

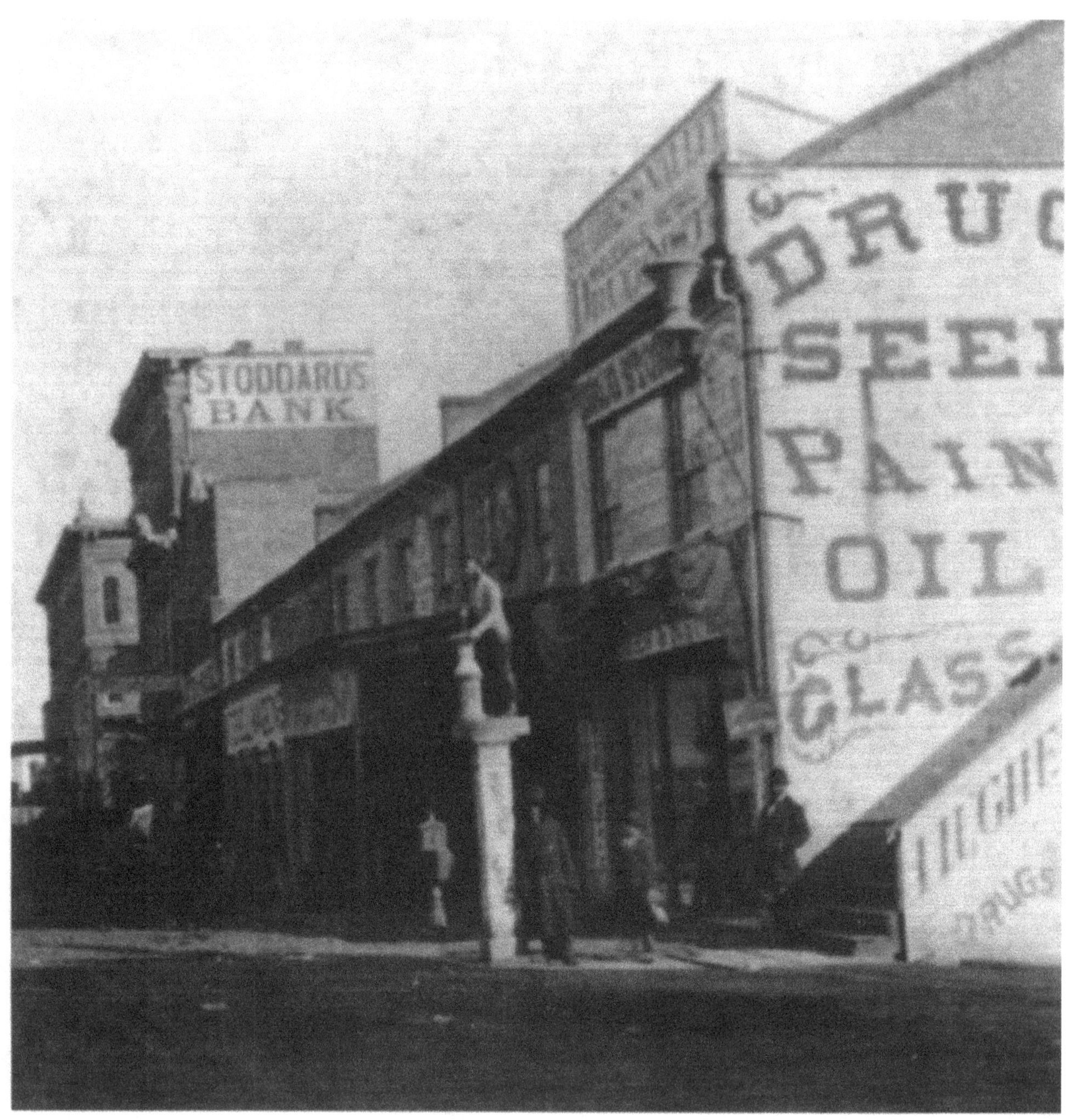

A view of Markham Street, with Stoddard's Bank and a drugstore on the right. Markham was an unpaved thoroughfare during this era. A century before the advent of computers, signage of the day was hand-lettered, a skill that required considerable effort and aptitude to acquire.

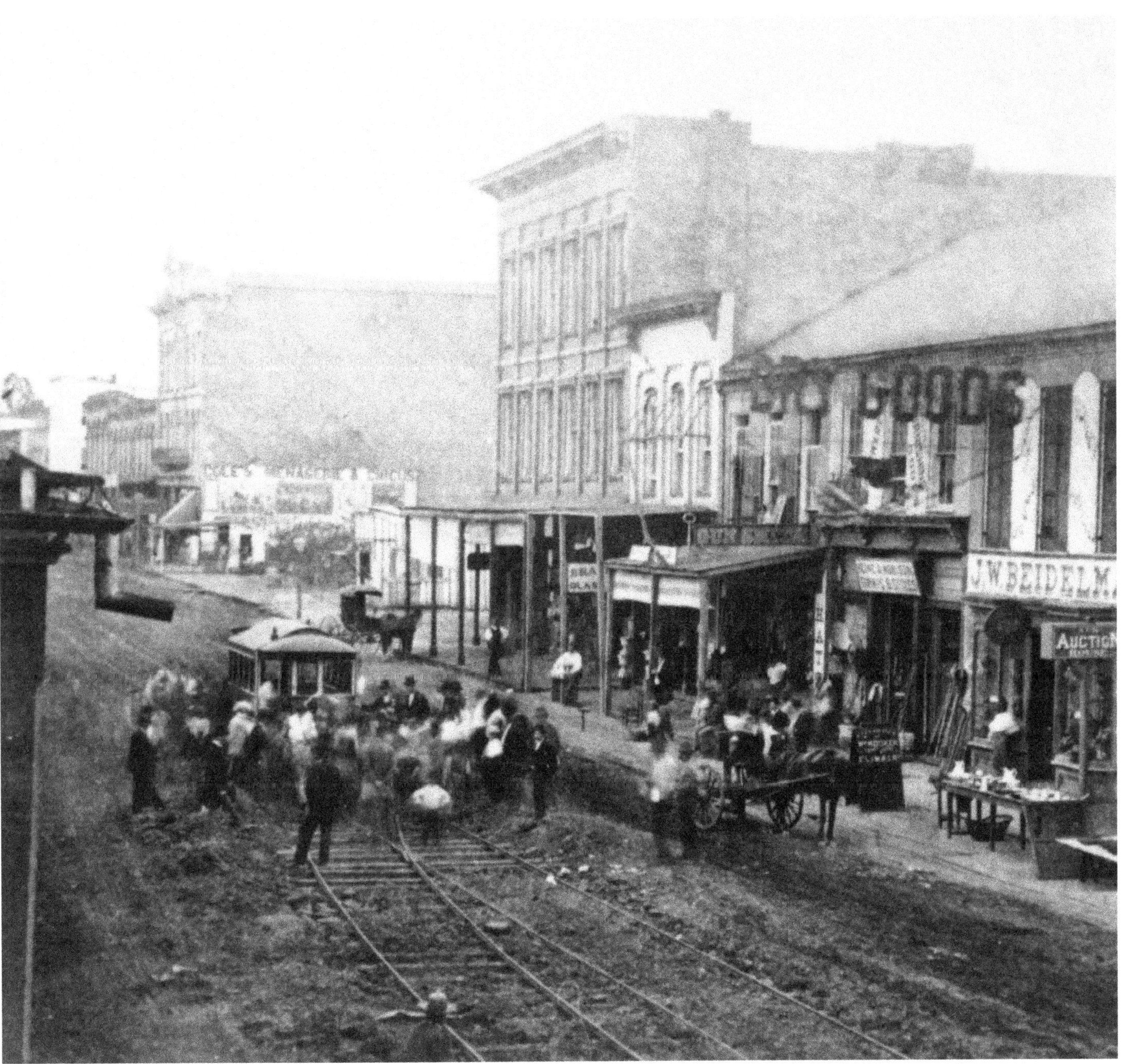

A crowd gathers around a streetcar on Main Street during the inauguration of the city's mule-powered railway in May 1877. By 1891, an electric streetcar system would be up and running. Streetcars were the main form of public transportation in Little Rock until 1947, when they were replaced with bus service.

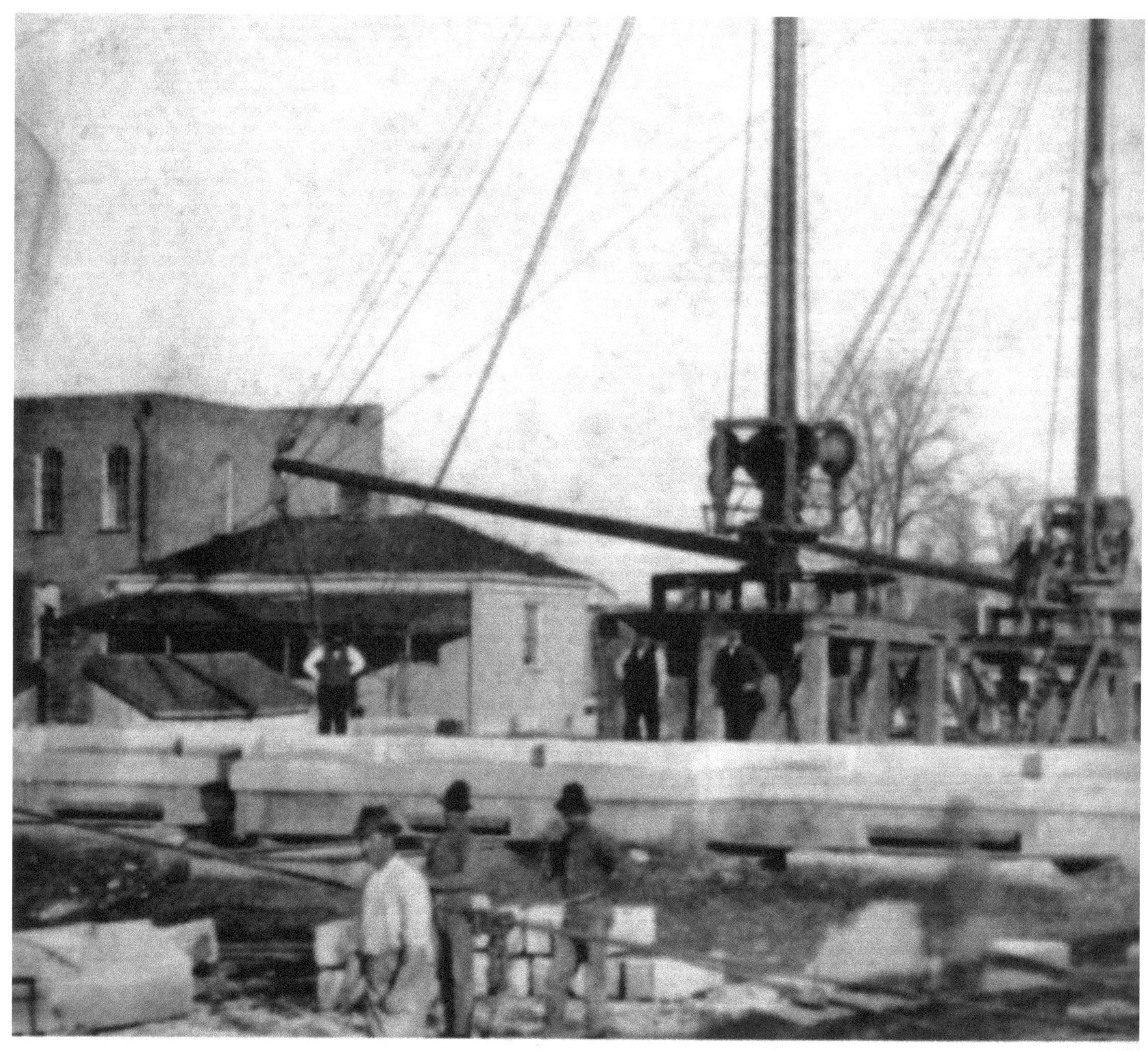

Construction of the Post Office and Courthouse in Little Rock began around 1876. In this view, heavy-lift construction booms are in place and ready to begin raising the blocks of granite and sandstone used in the structure.

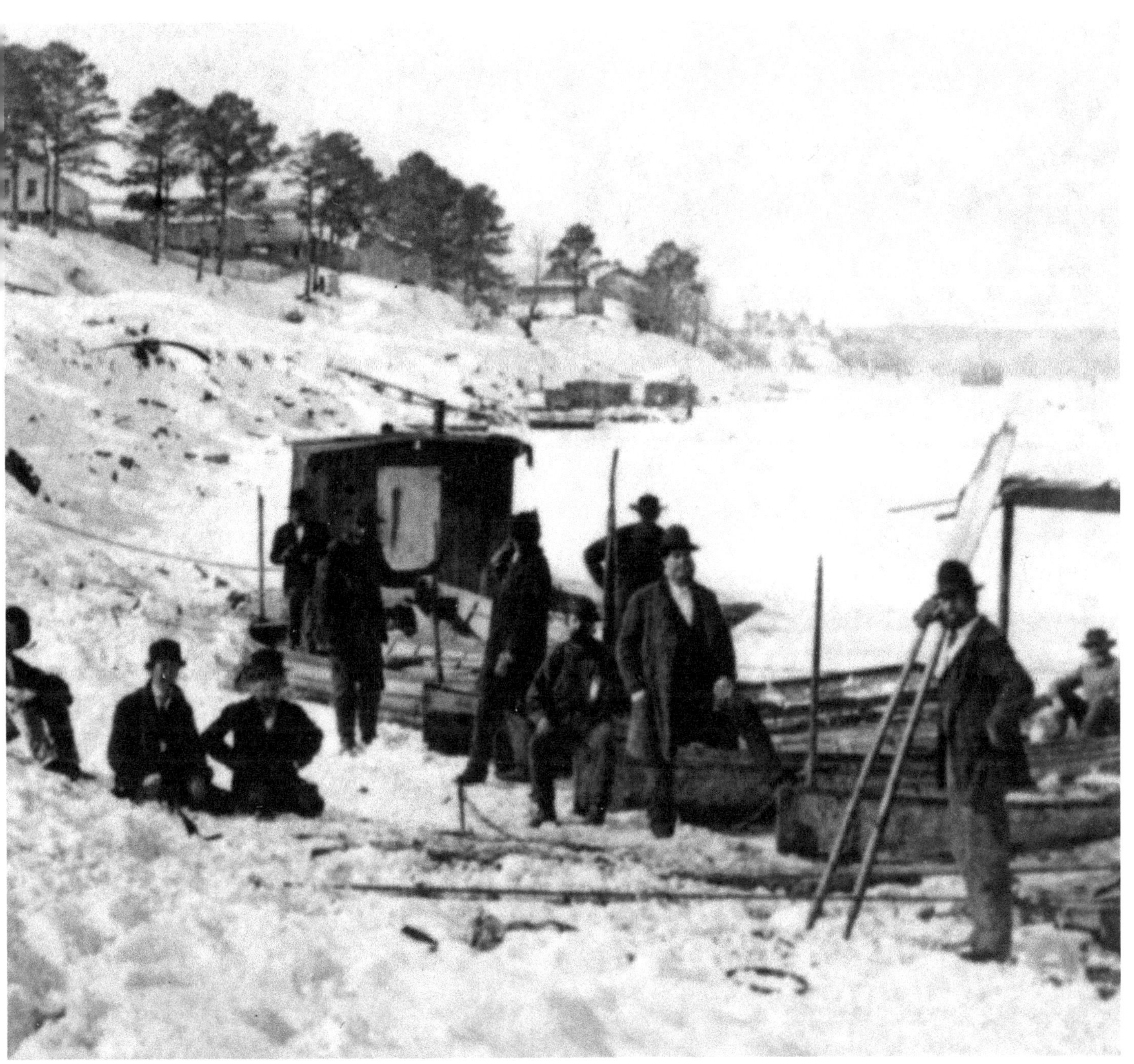

A group of men gathers on the banks of the Arkansas River during the winter of 1876. A blanket of snow carpets the riverbank and the river, which had frozen.

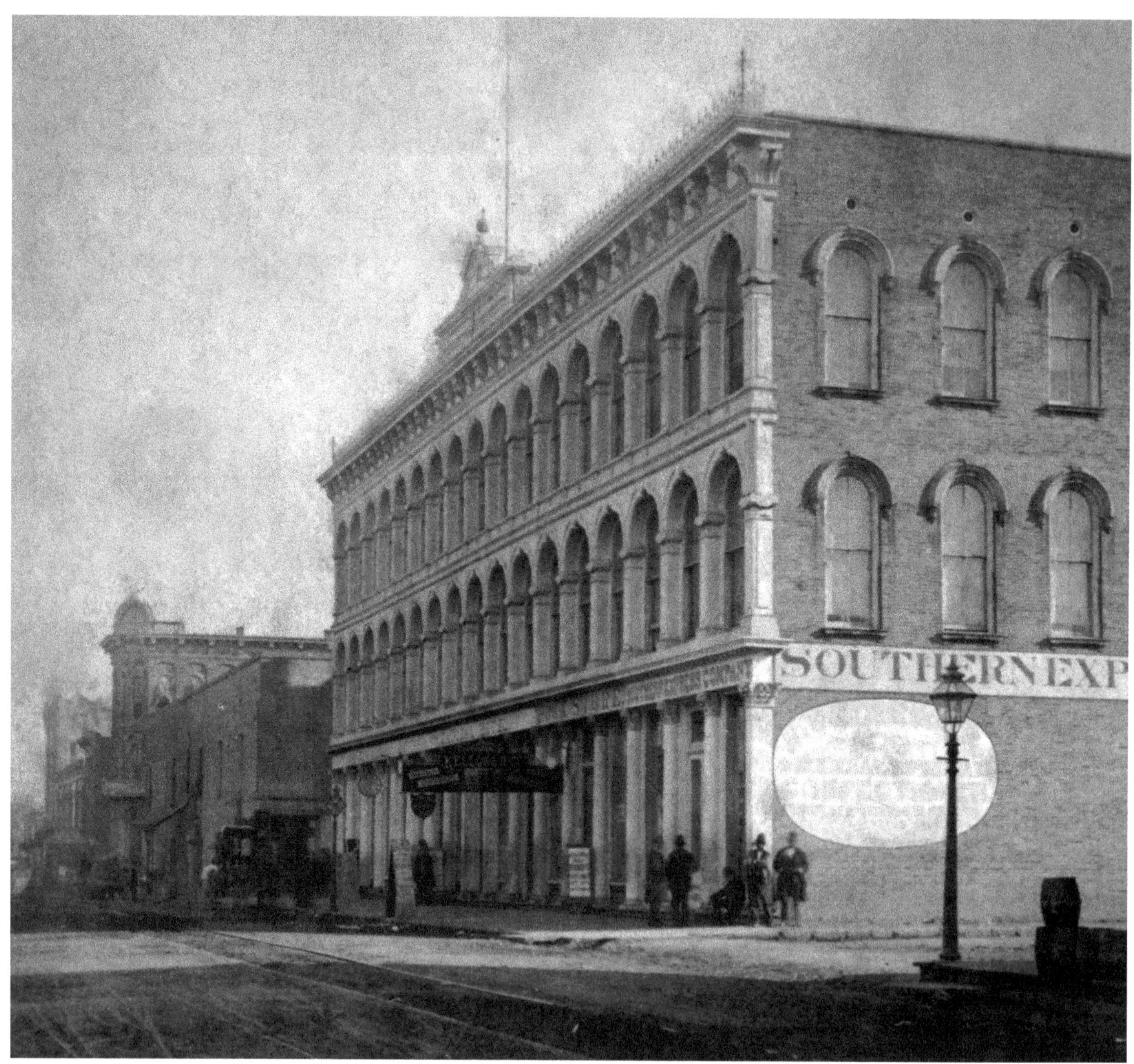

The Denckla Block of Markham Street, built by railroad magnate William Denckla to house downtown businesses, would be refitted in 1877 to become the grand Capital Hotel. In the nineteenth century, "block" was commonly used to denote a building.

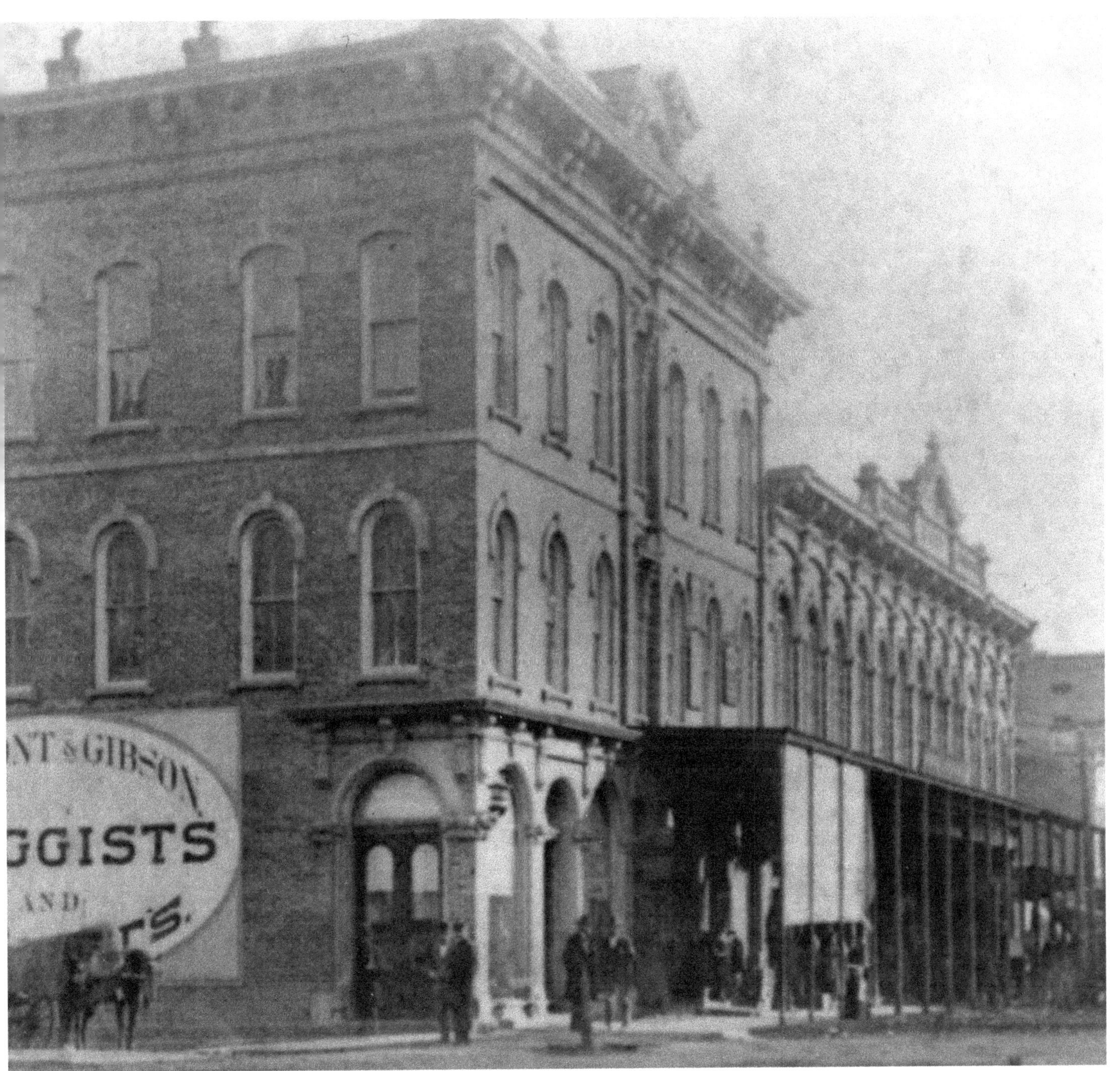

The McAlmont and Gibson drugstore was located on a corner of Markham Street.

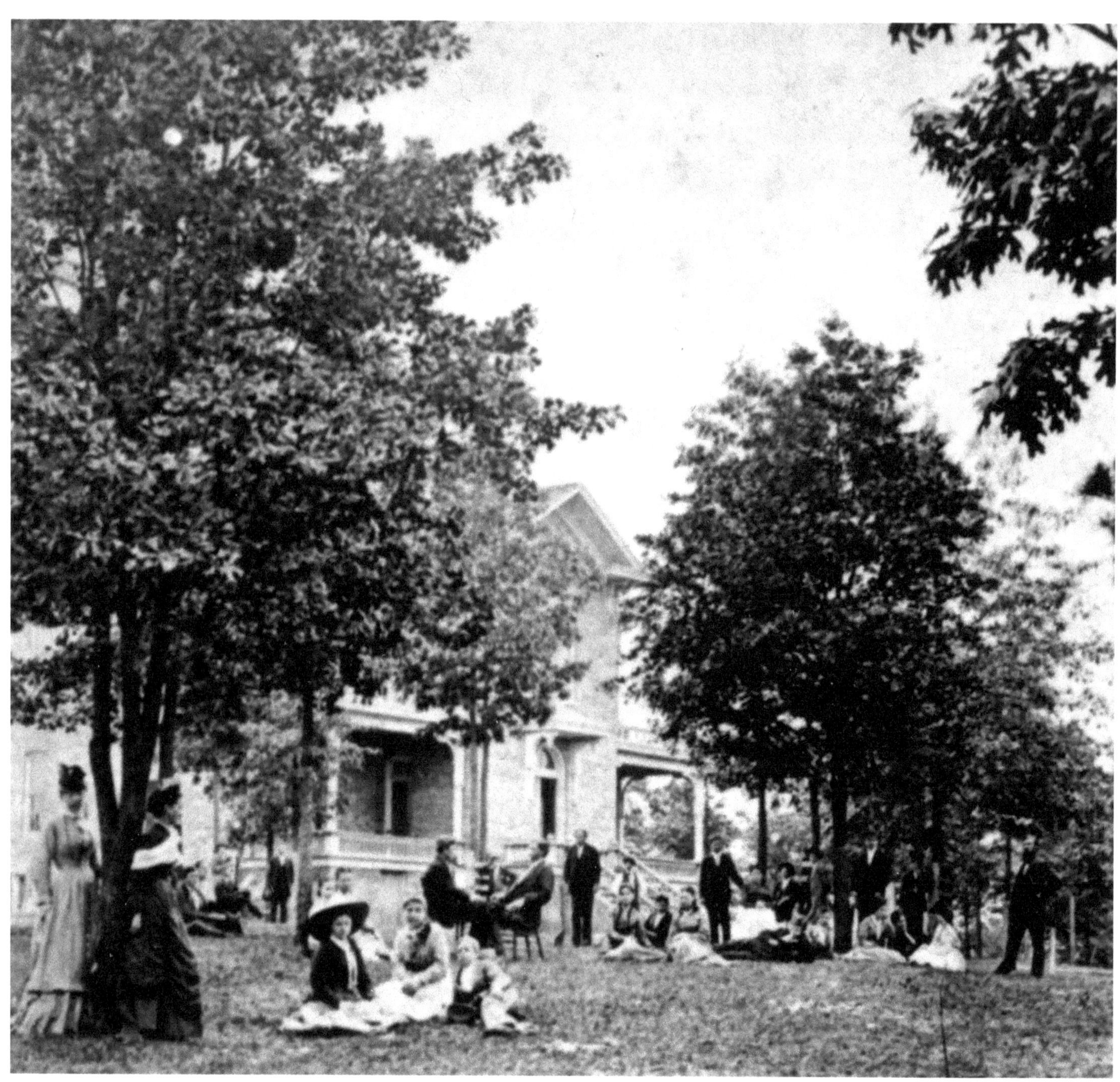

The Arkansas Deaf Mute Institute, around the 1870s. The school opened in 1870, but was destroyed by fire in 1889. A new building was built in the same location and today houses the Arkansas School for the Deaf.

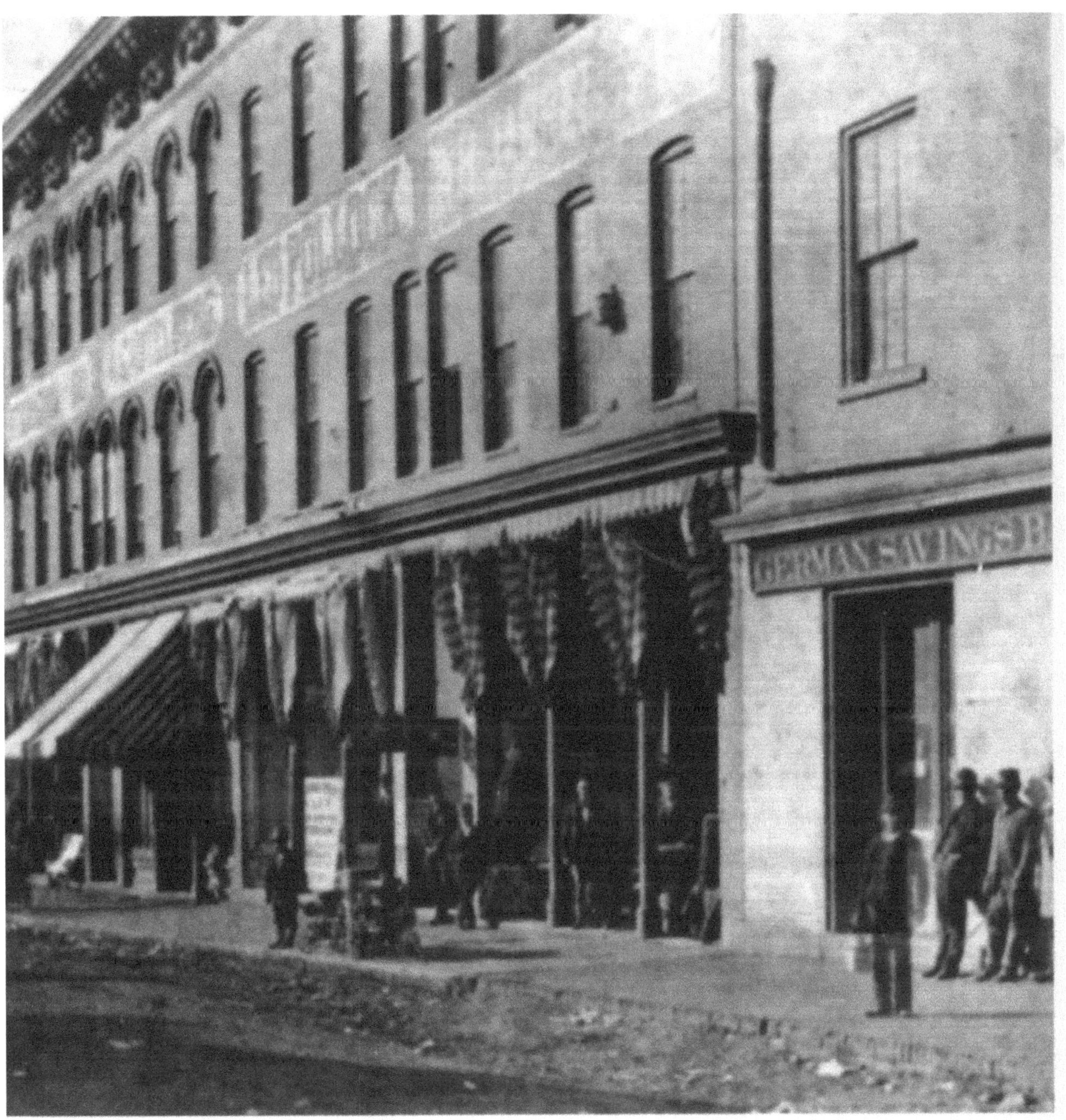

The Equitable block was located on Main Street, where this view from around the 1870s was recorded. Before the days of air-conditioning, most homes and businesses sported retractable awnings, which offered shelter from the sun and helped cool interior spaces in the summer months.

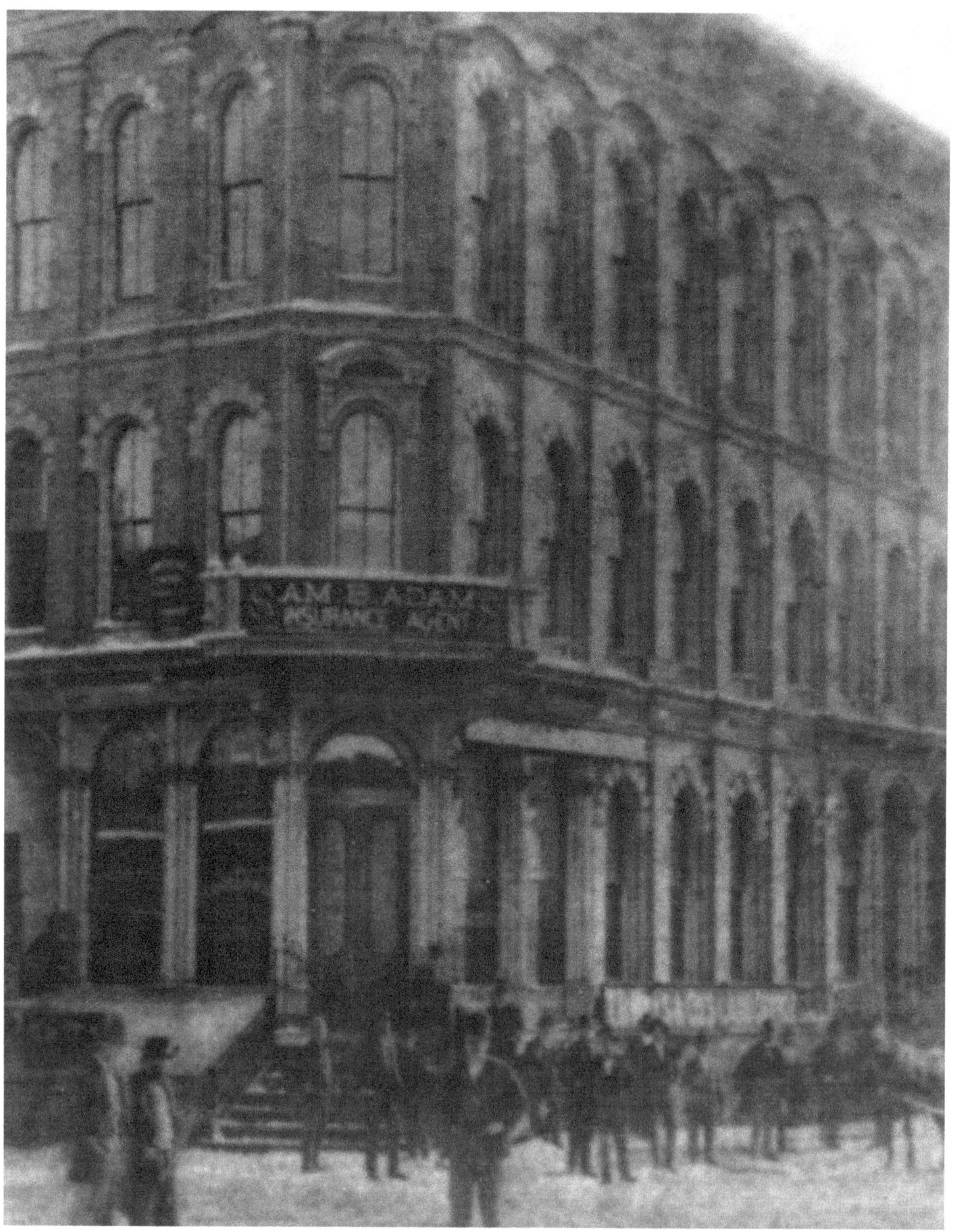

An insurance company is open for business in this stately, three-story brick edifice on Markham Street in 1877. Locals on the street are posing for the photographer. In the early days of the camera, those who wanted their likeness sharply recorded, not blurred, knew that remaining motionless was a requirement.

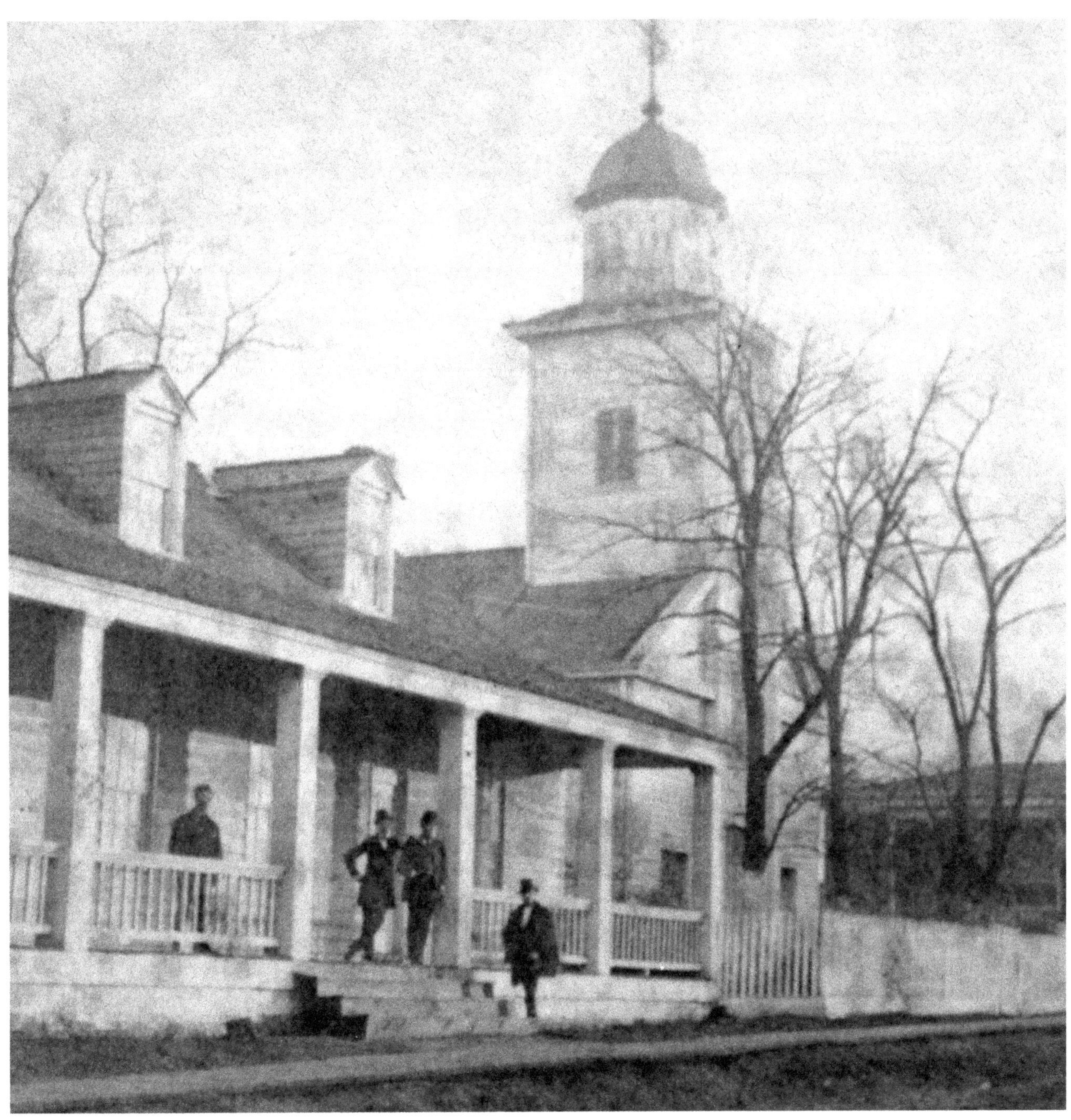

A group of men pose for a photograph around the 1870s. Behind them rises the steeple of the local Catholic church.

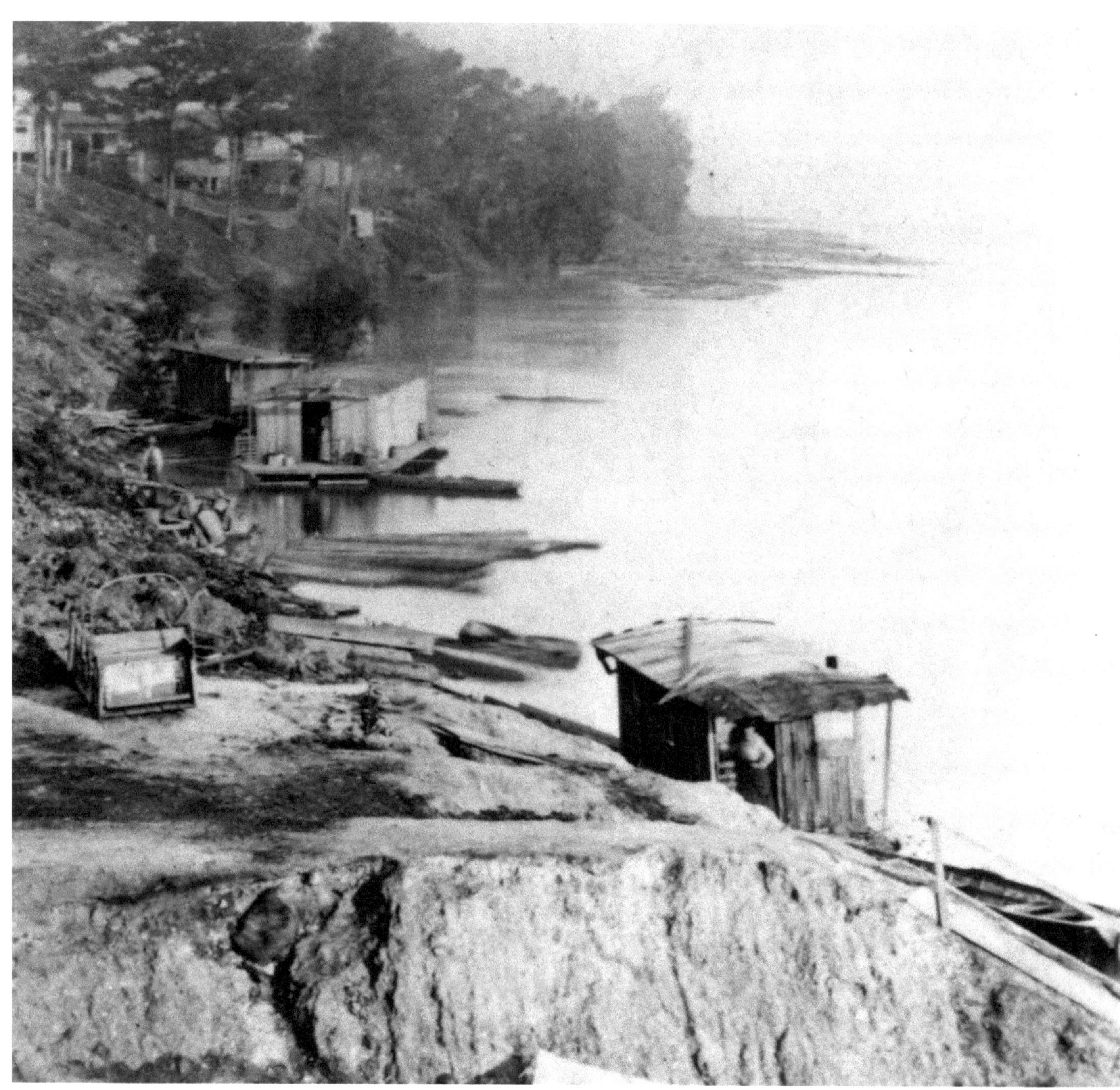

An early-day view of life on the banks of the Arkansas River.

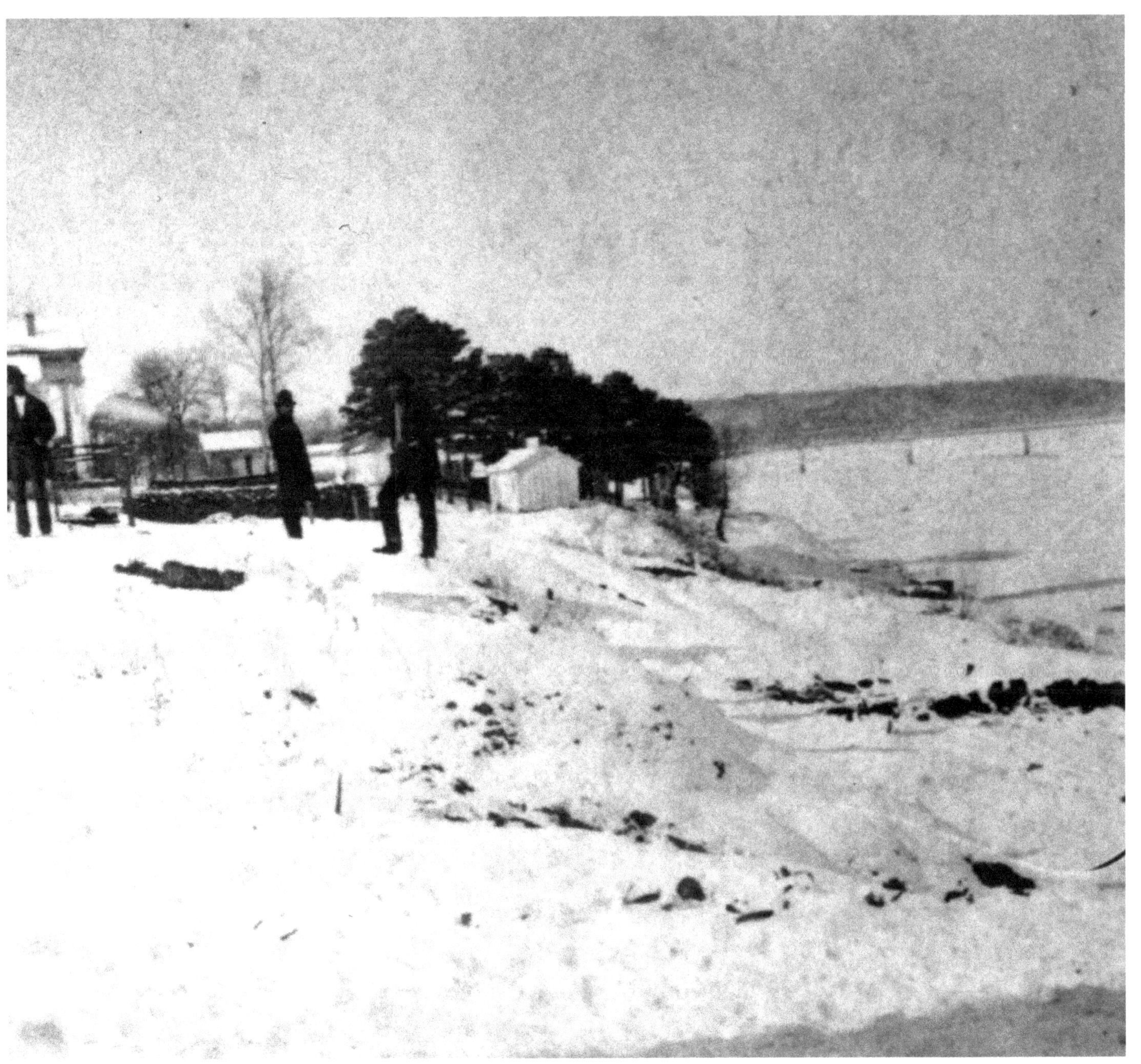

Piney Point on a frozen Arkansas River during the winter of 1880.

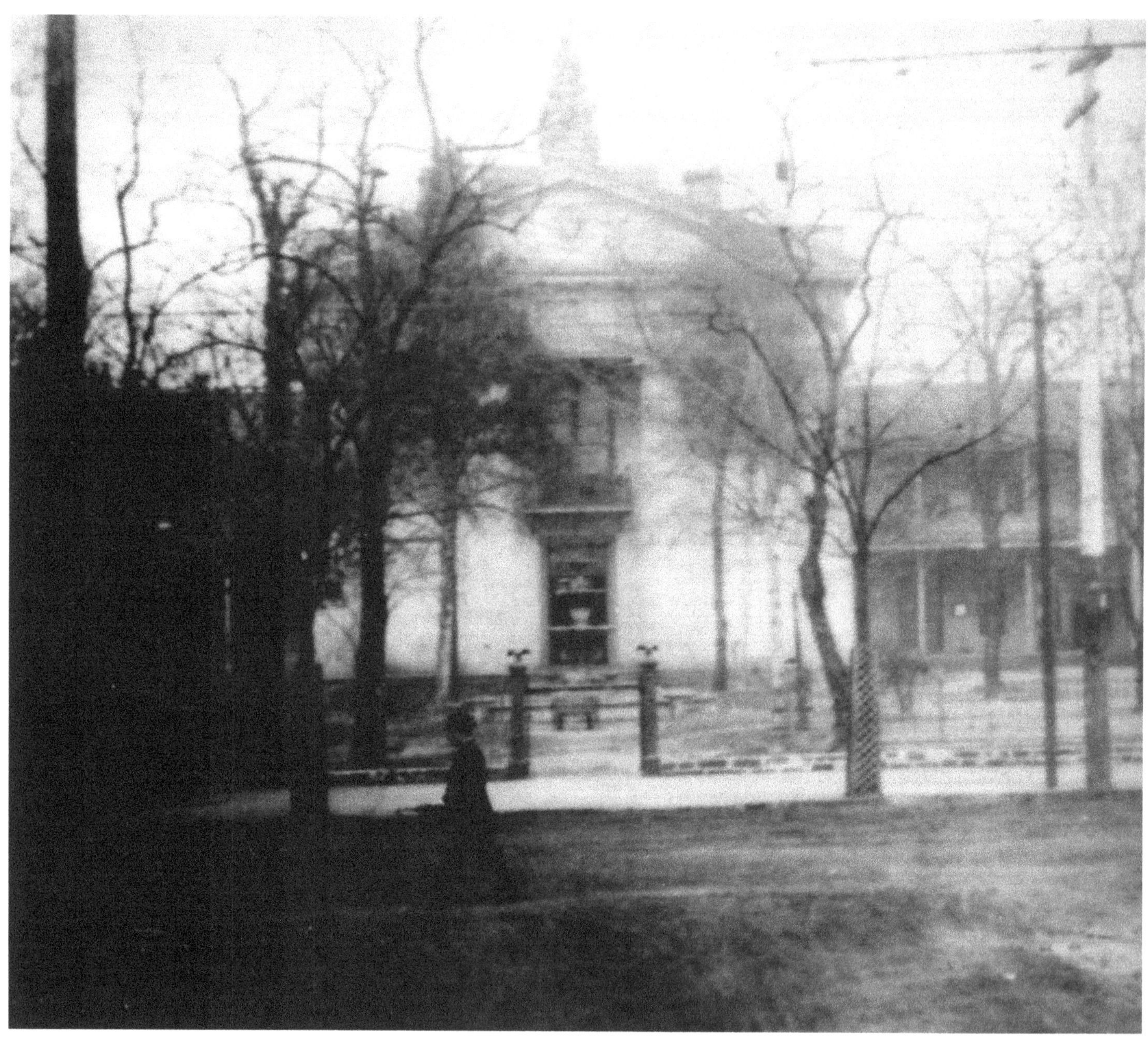

The Old State House, shown here as it appeared around the 1880s, is the oldest surviving capitol west of the Mississippi River. The territorial governor, John Pope, chose Kentucky architect Gideon Shyrock to design the building. Construction began in 1833 and was completed in 1842. The State House, which was occupied by Union troops during the Civil War and figured prominently in the Brooks-Baxter War during the Reconstruction, would serve as the state capitol until 1911. Today it houses a museum decicated to Arkansas history.

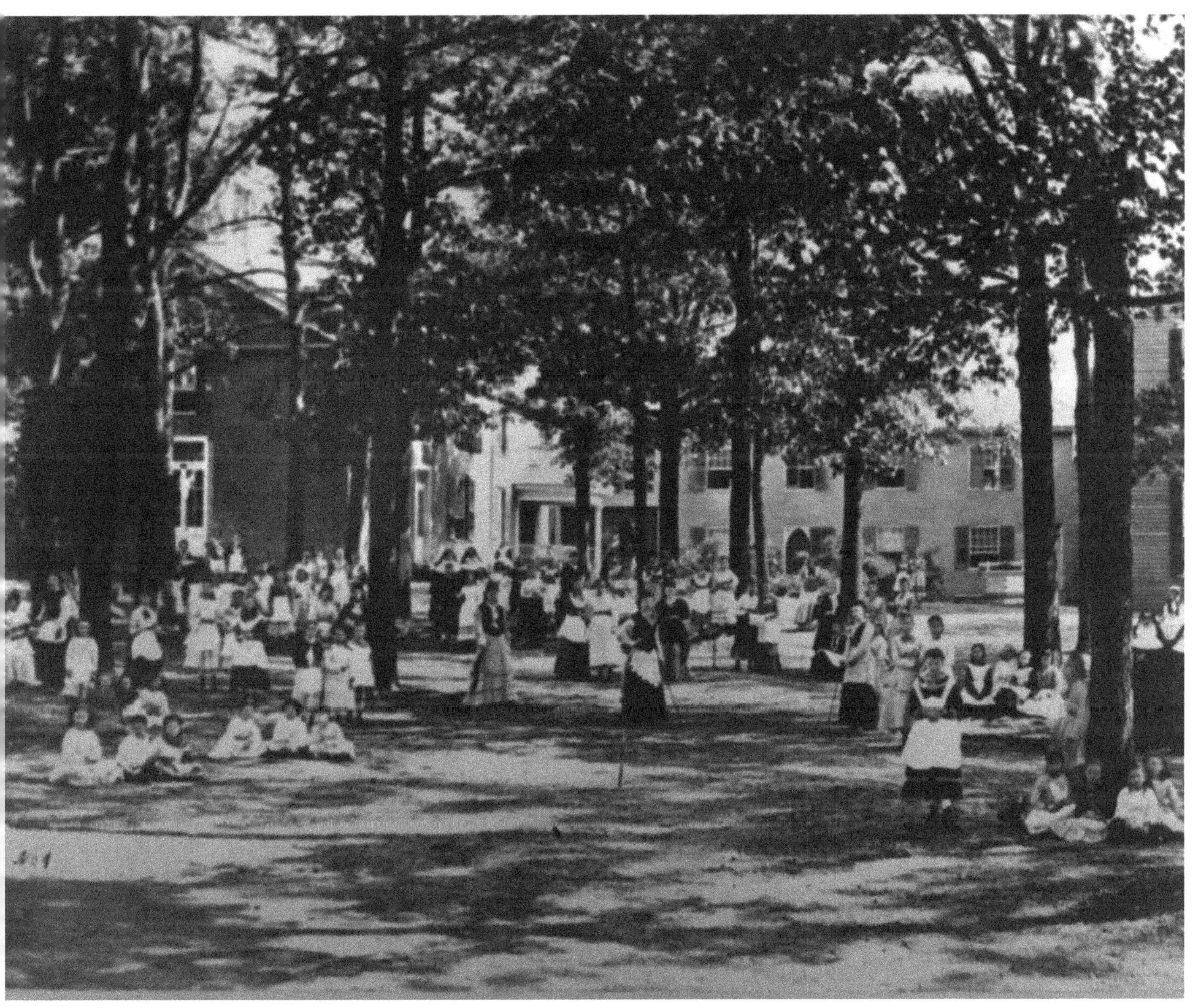

Students and teachers gather on the lawn of Mount St. Mary's Academy around the 1880s. Mount St. Mary's, a Catholic school established in 1851, is the oldest education institution in the state. The school later moved to its current location in Pulaski Heights and today is the only all-girl secondary school in Arkansas.

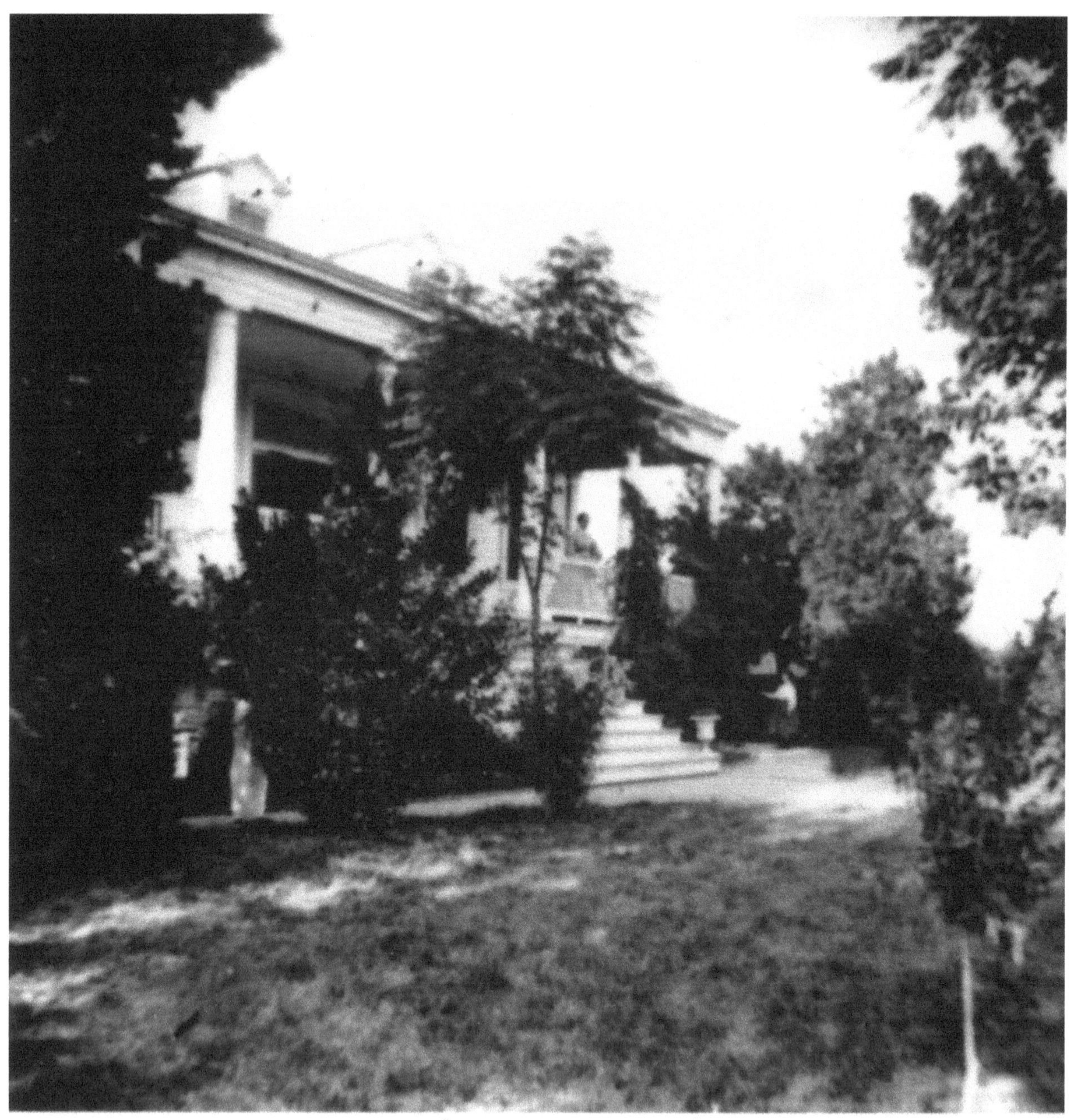

The McDonald-Wait-Newton House (or Packet House), located on Cantrell Road, was built in 1870 by Alexander McDonald, a former U.S. senator and president of Merchant's National Bank (later First National Bank).

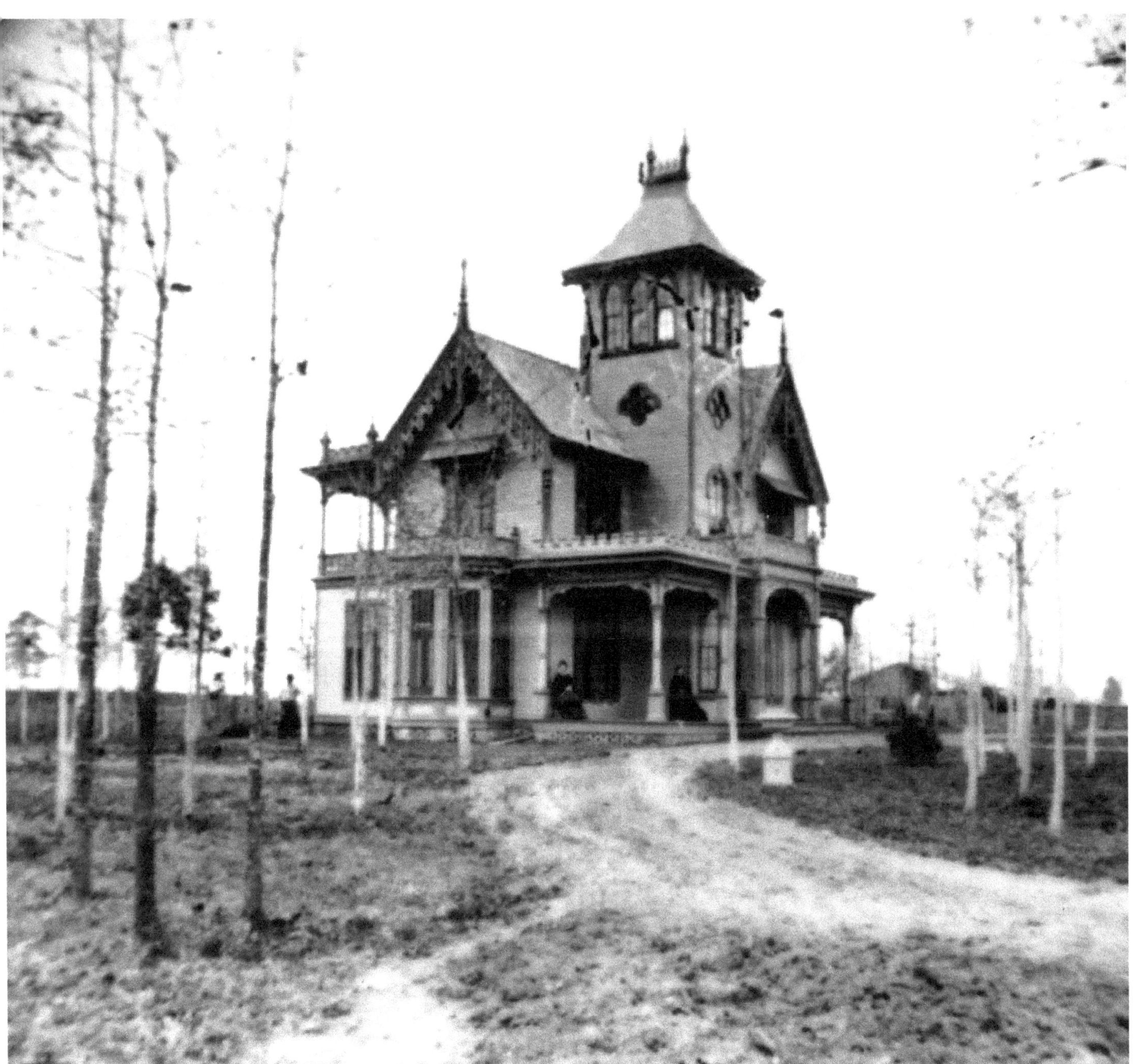

The Milton Rice House on Twentieth Street, around the 1880s. Milton Rice was a state senator, a lawyer, and the president of the Cairo and Fulton Railroad. In 1870, he built this Gothic revival house and named it Oak Grove. Today the Milton Rice House can be found at 2015 South Battery Street.

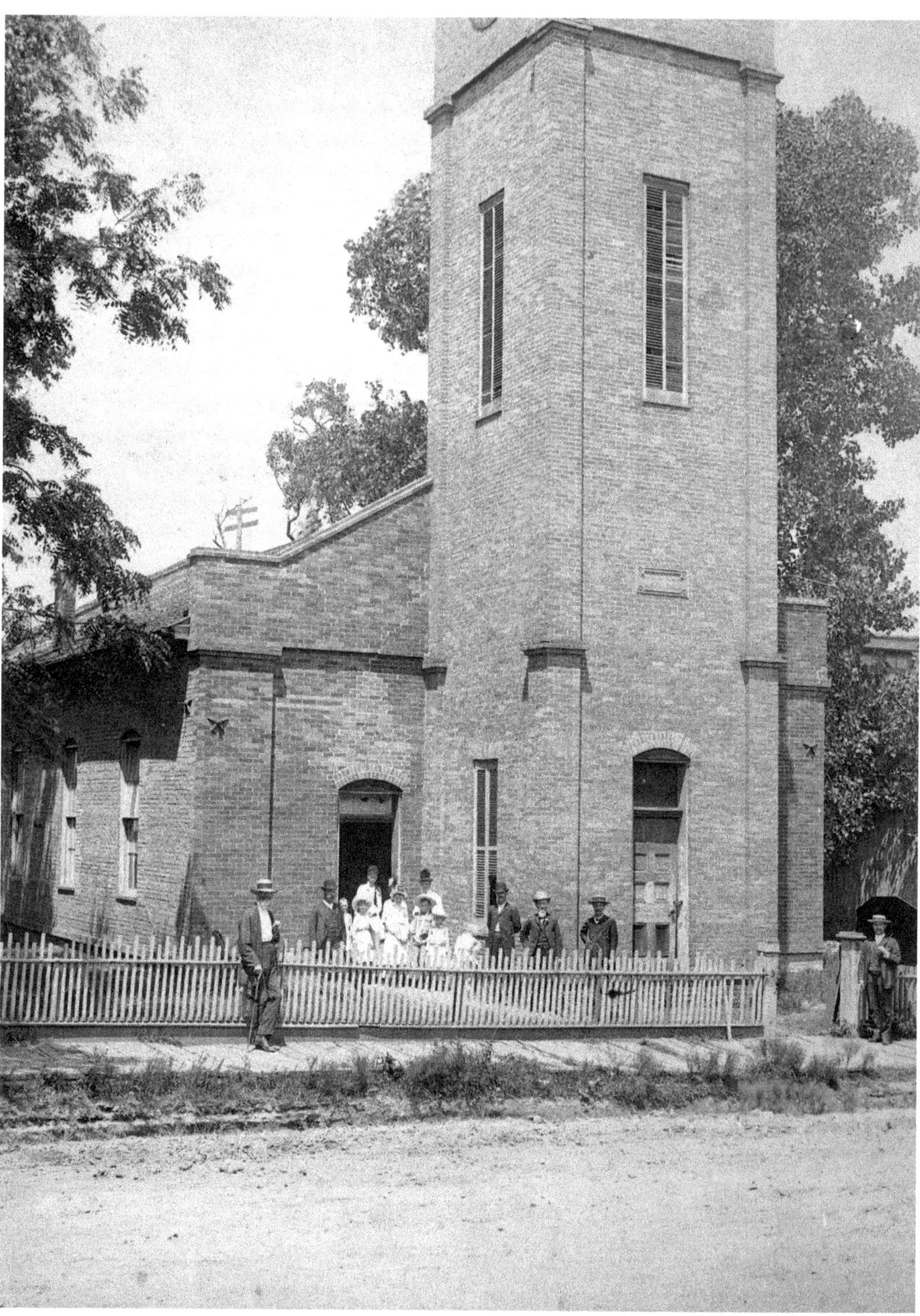

The First Christian Church was located between Third and Fourth streets. These church members are posing for a photograph in front of the building around 1885.

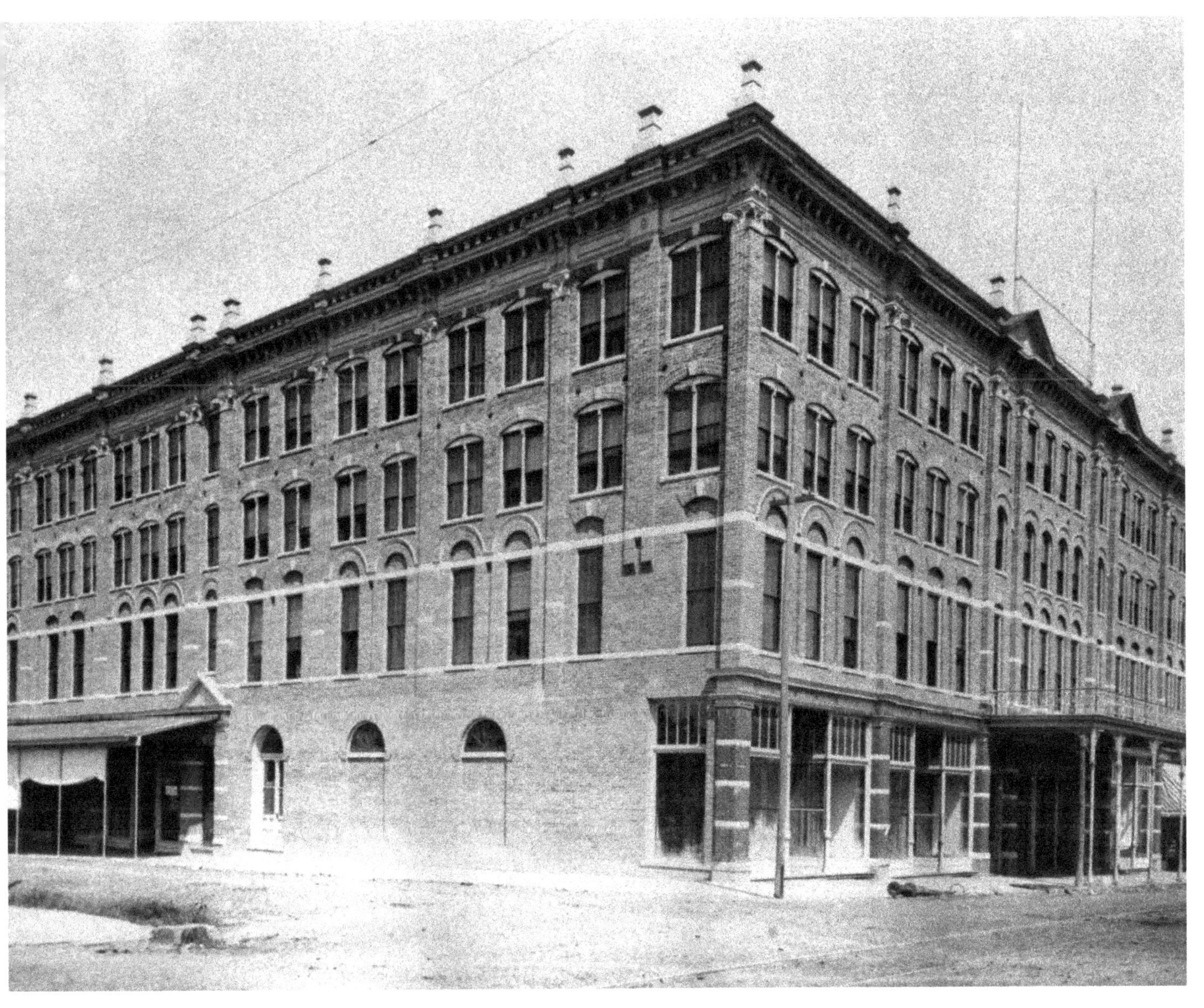

The Hotel Richelieu. In October 1894, a tornado would rumble through downtown, killing and maiming citizens and badly damaging the hotel and most other buildings in the business district, including the Western Union telegraph office and the quarters of Governor Fishback.

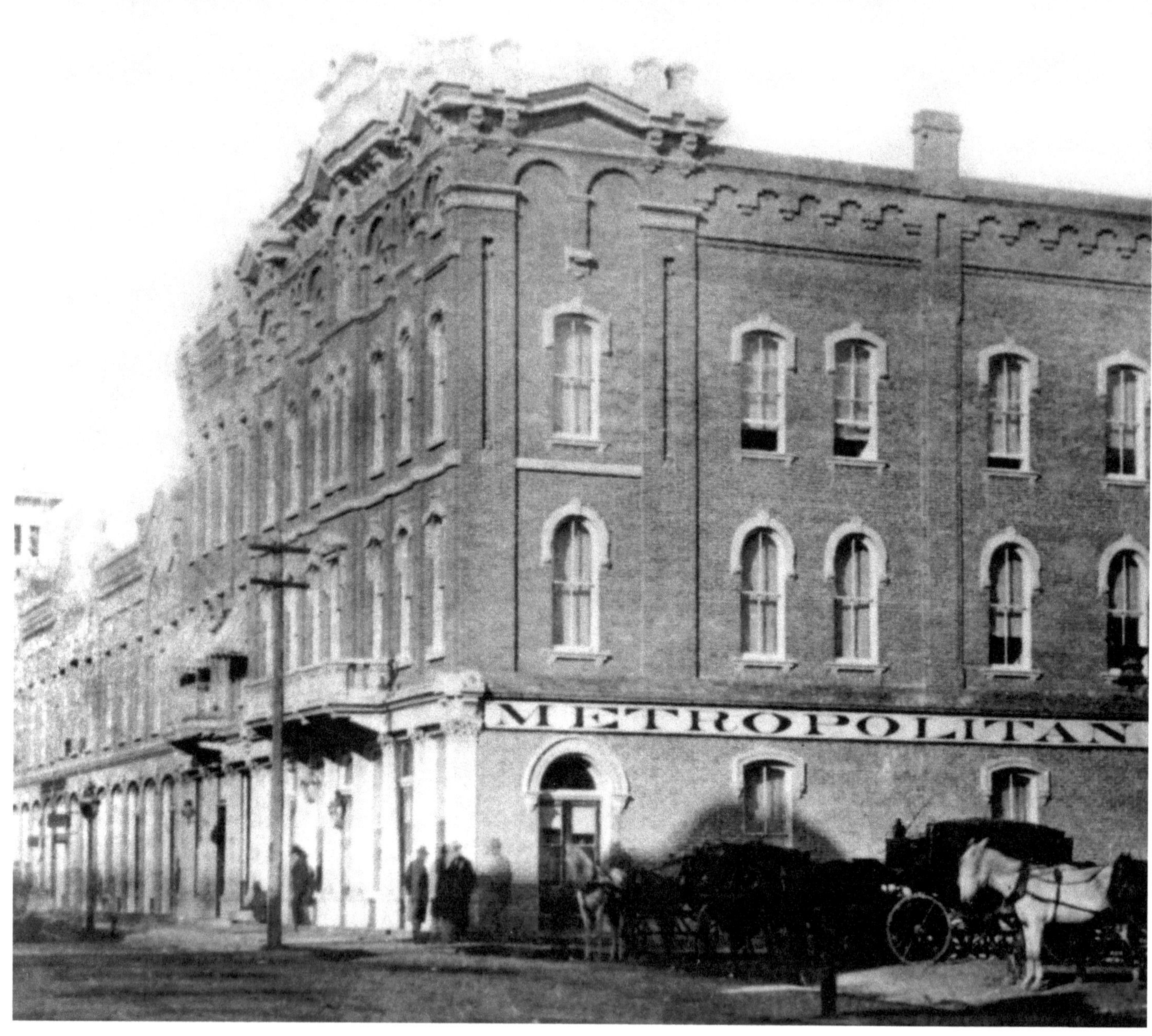

The Metropolitan Hotel on the corner of Main and Markham streets, around the early 1870s. The city's only upscale hotel of the day, it was destroyed by a fire on December 14, 1876. The loss prompted construction of the grand Capital Hotel, a city landmark to this day.

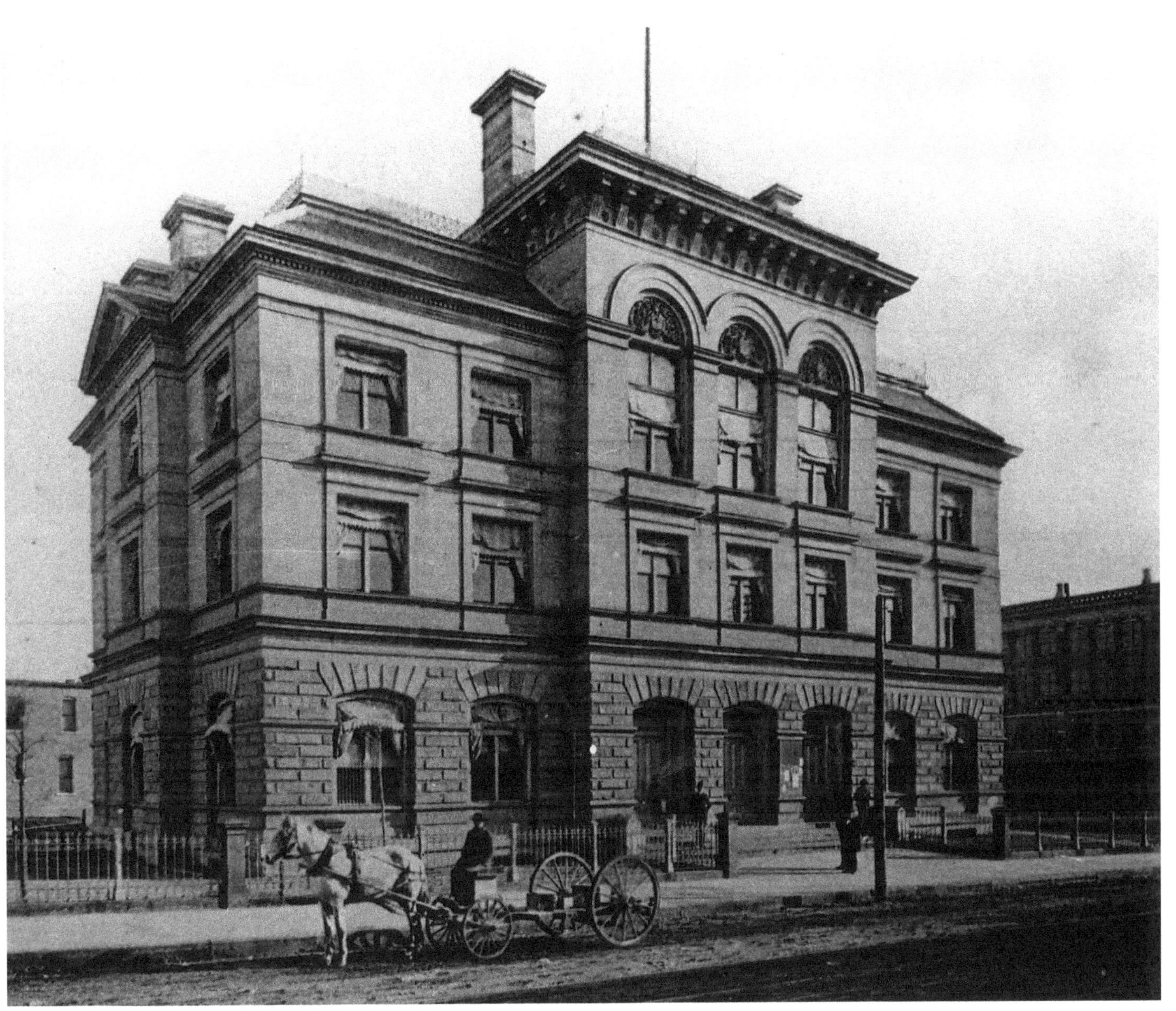

When completed in 1881, the Post Office and Courthouse became noteworthy as a fine example of Victorian-era Italian Renaissance Revival architecture. Located on West 2nd Street, the building has been carefully restored.

The Little Rock Junction Railroad Bridge

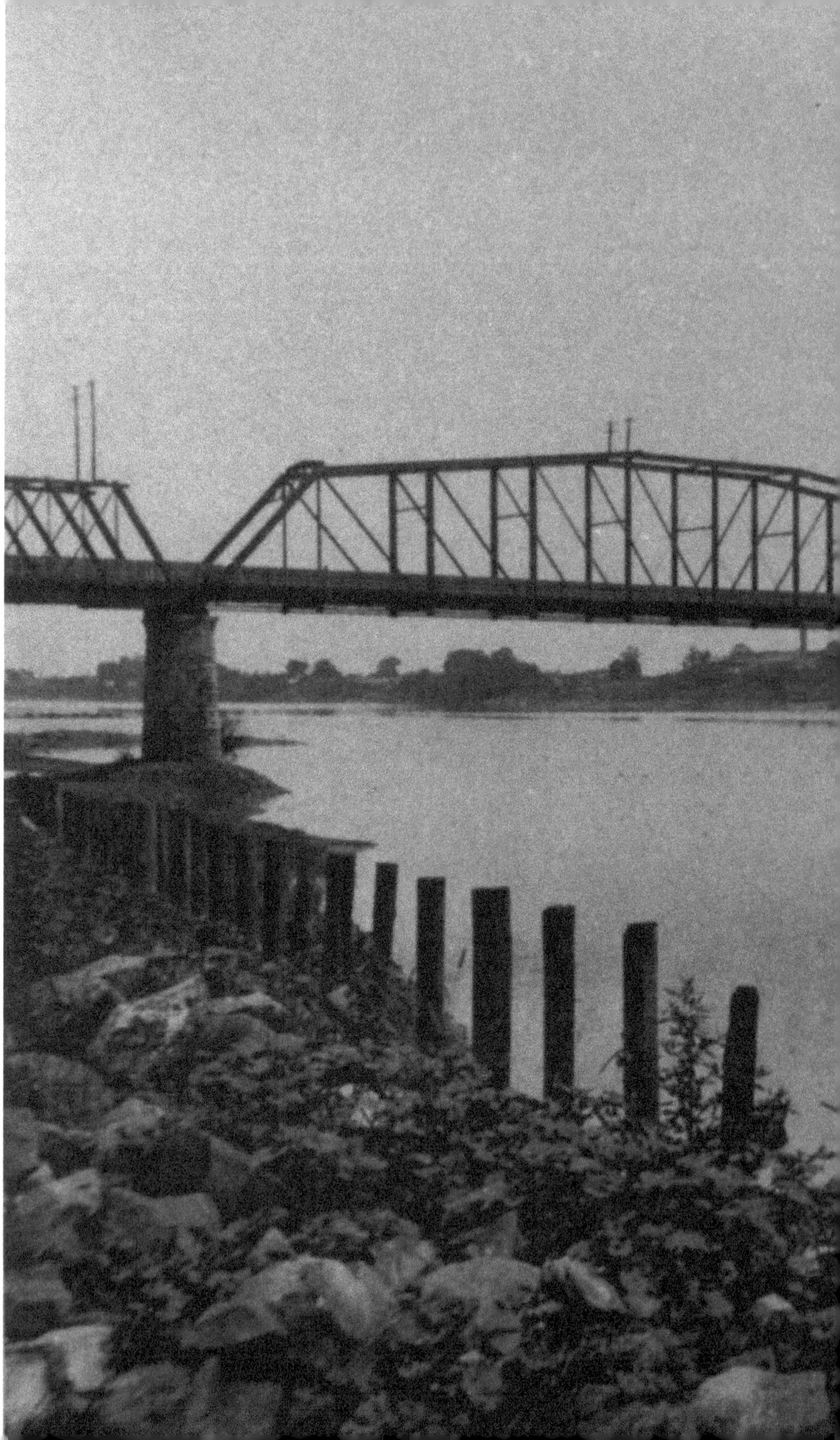

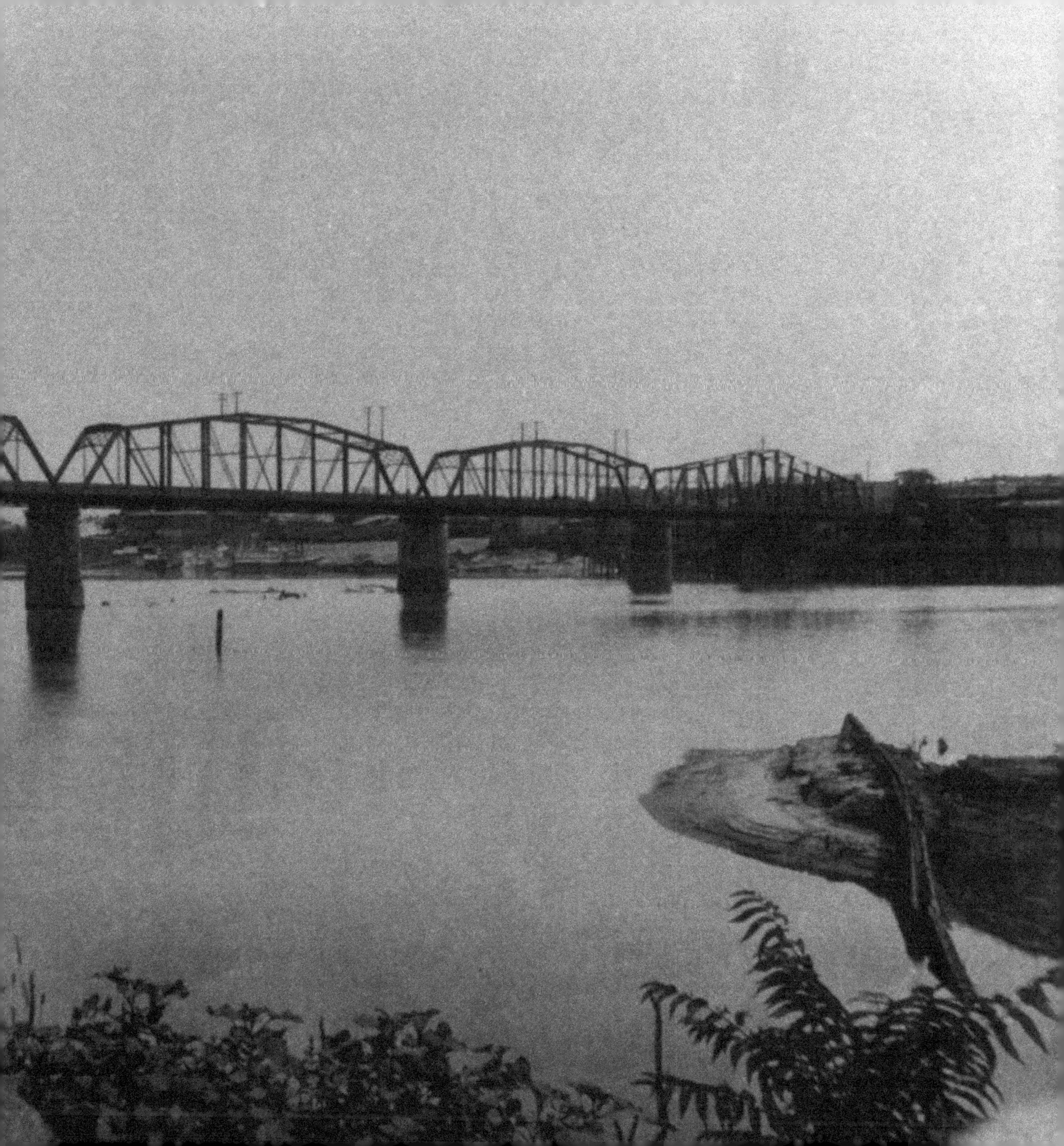

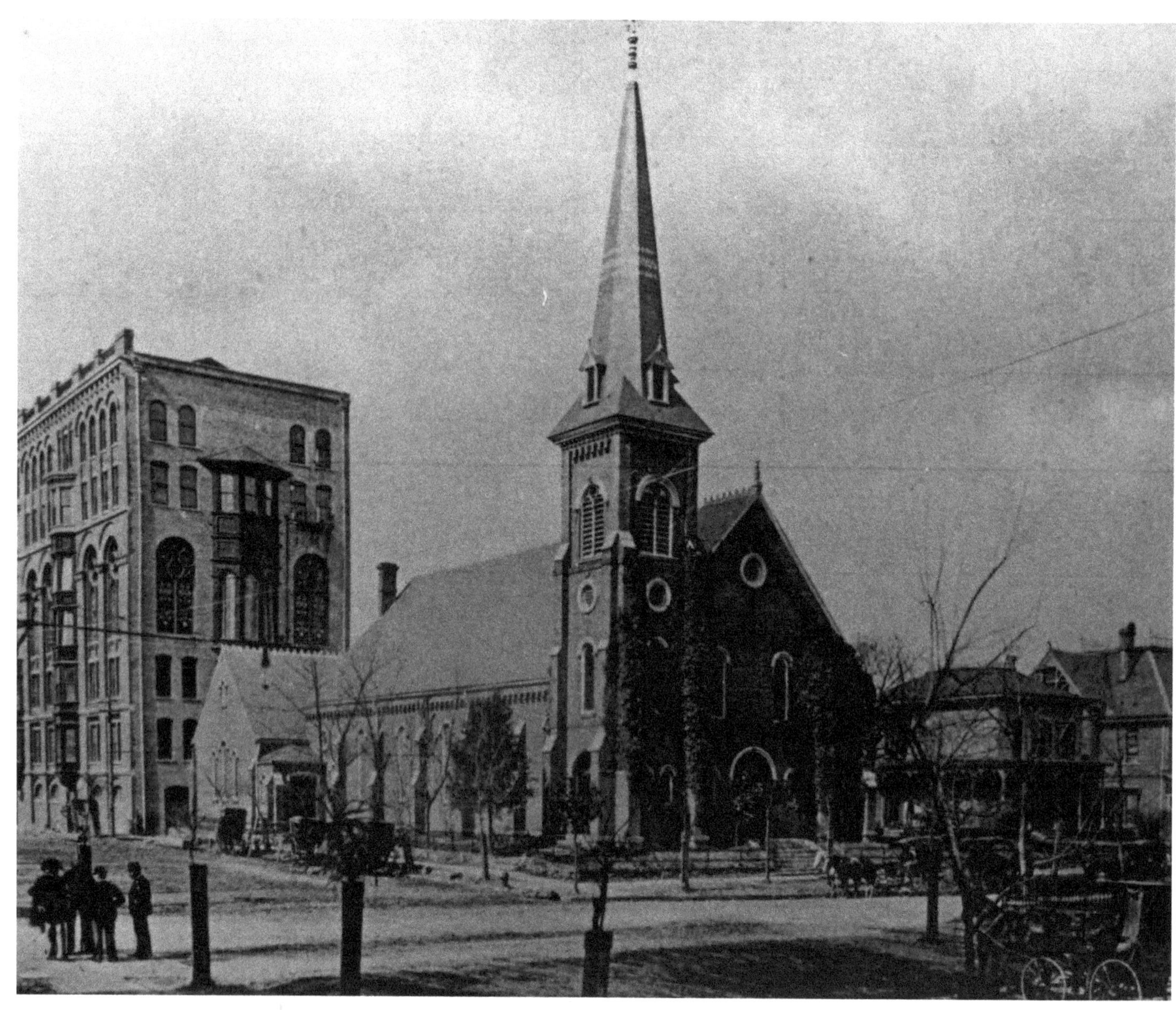

The Masonic Temple Building, located at Fifth and Main streets, in 1892. The building was completed in 1891 to become the largest commercial building in the city. It was destroyed by fire in 1919.

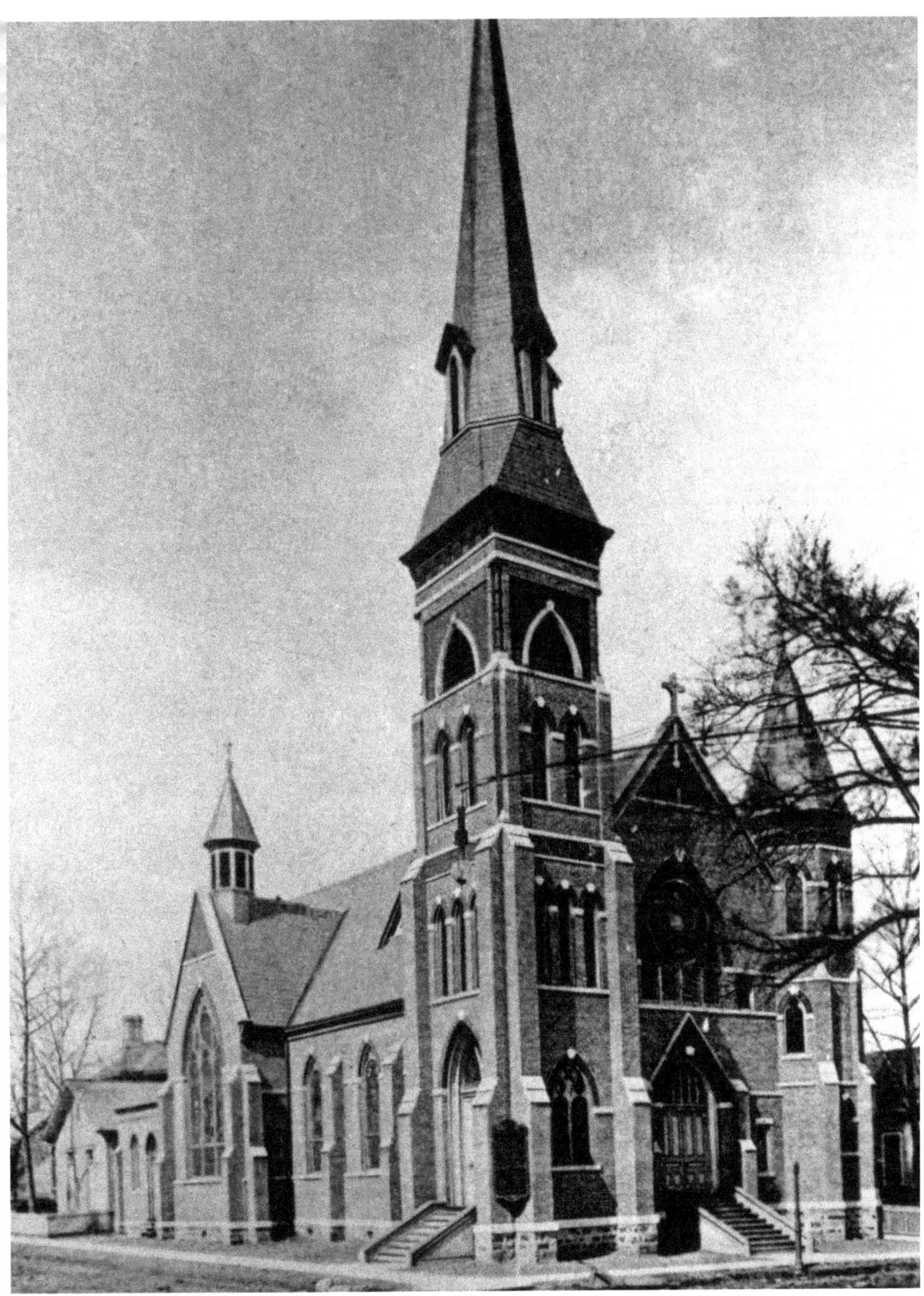

The First German Evangelical Lutheran Church, located at Eighth and Rock streets. Home today to the First Lutheran Church, the building remains standing.

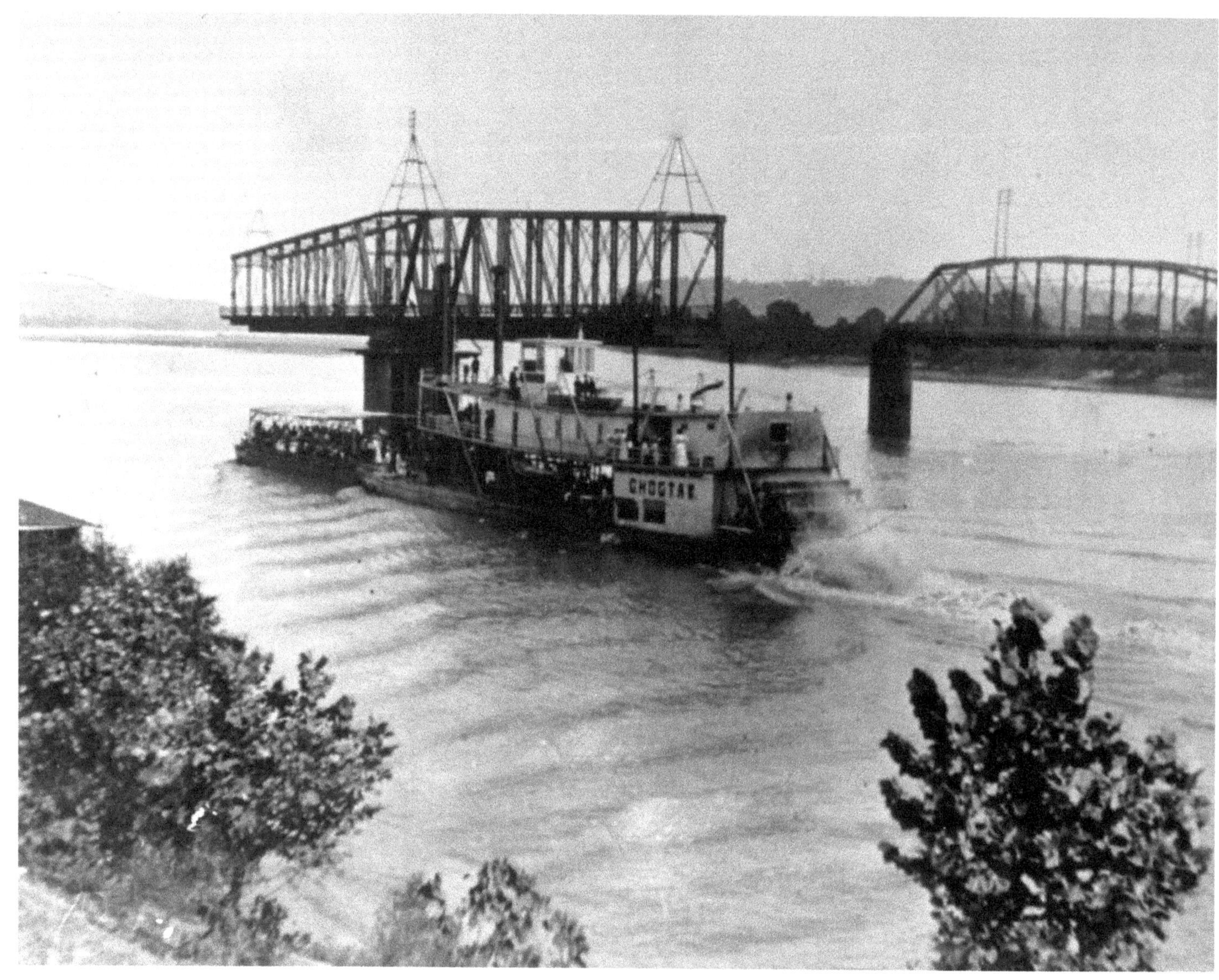

The steamboat *Choctaw* plies the Arkansas River in 1894, passing the first Baring Cross Bridge. Built in 1873, the Baring Cross was the first bridge to span the river at Little Rock. The bridge washed away in the floods of April 1927, but was soon rebuilt by the Missouri Pacific Railroad, reopening in 1929.

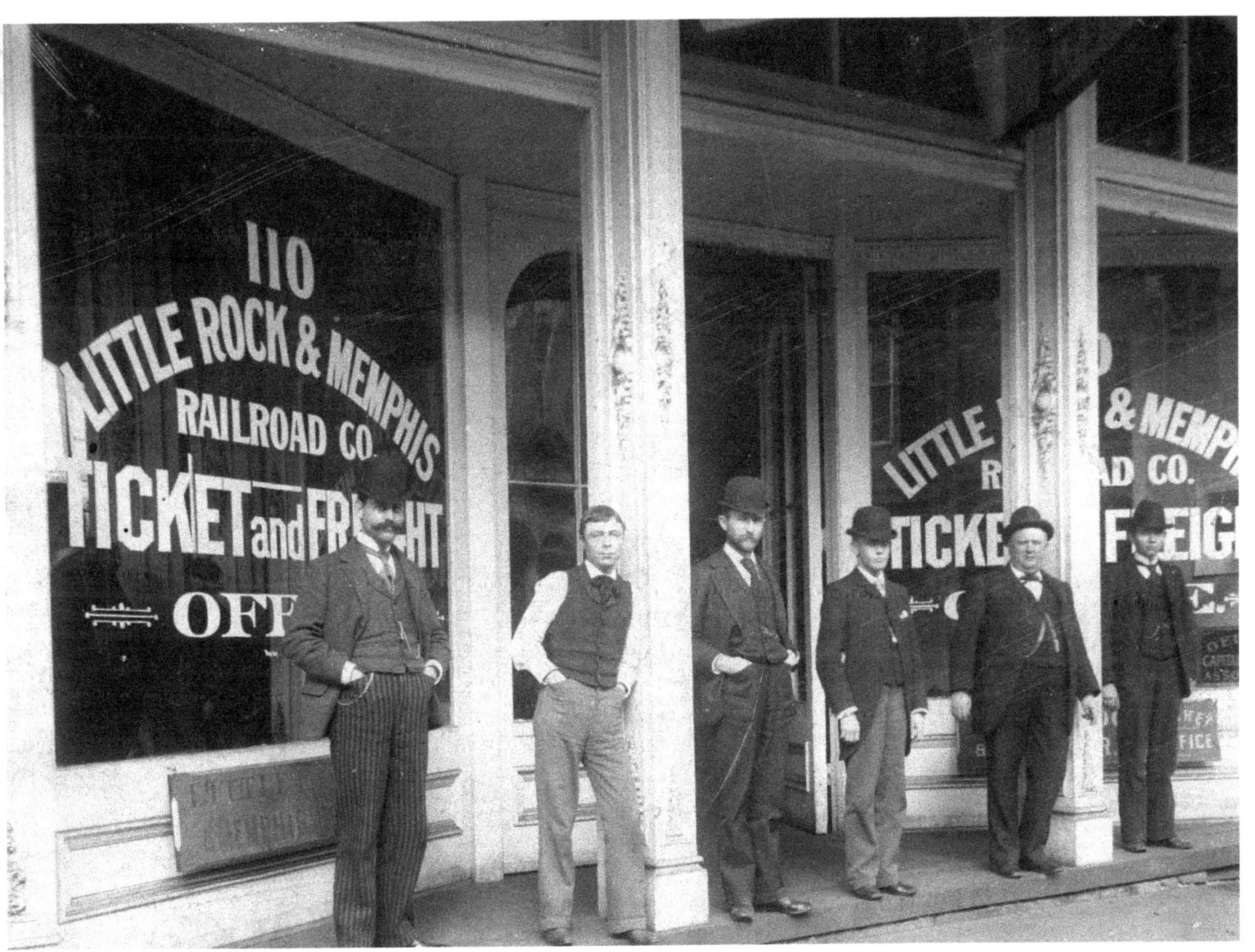

The Little Rock and Memphis Railroad Company Ticket Office, located at 110 East Markham, around 1895.

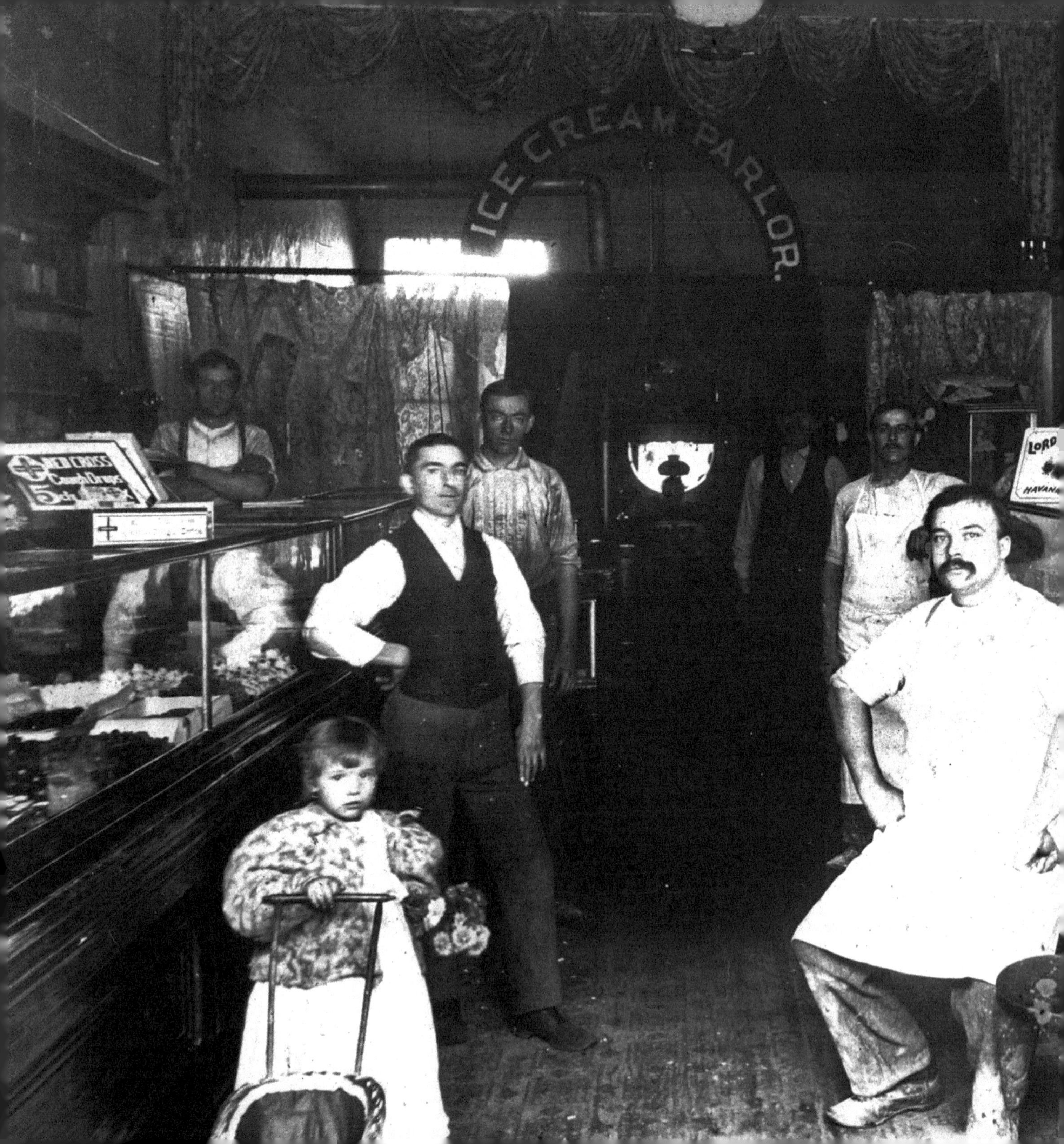
ICE CREAM PARLOR.
Cough Drops

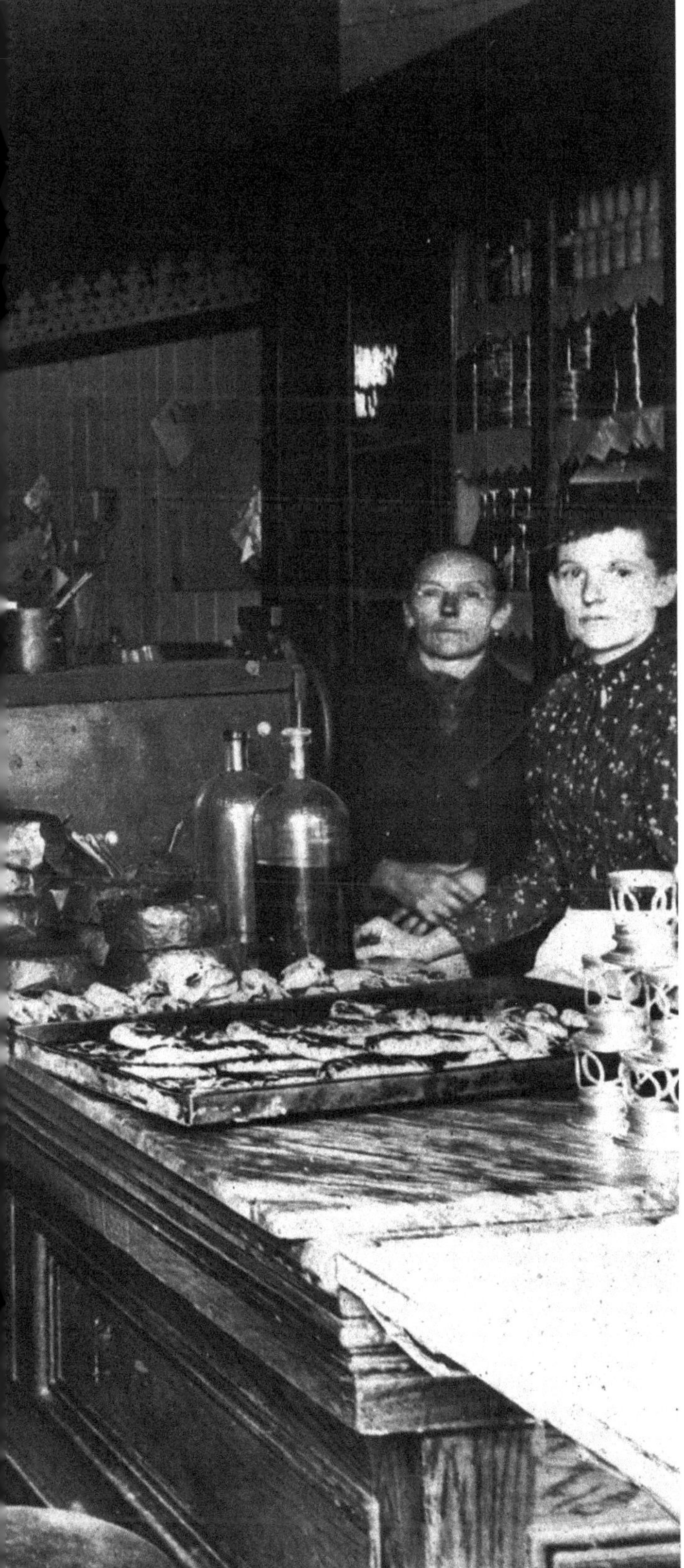

Shoppers and shopkeepers pose for a photograph around 1895 inside B. Heine Confectionery, at 718 Main Street.

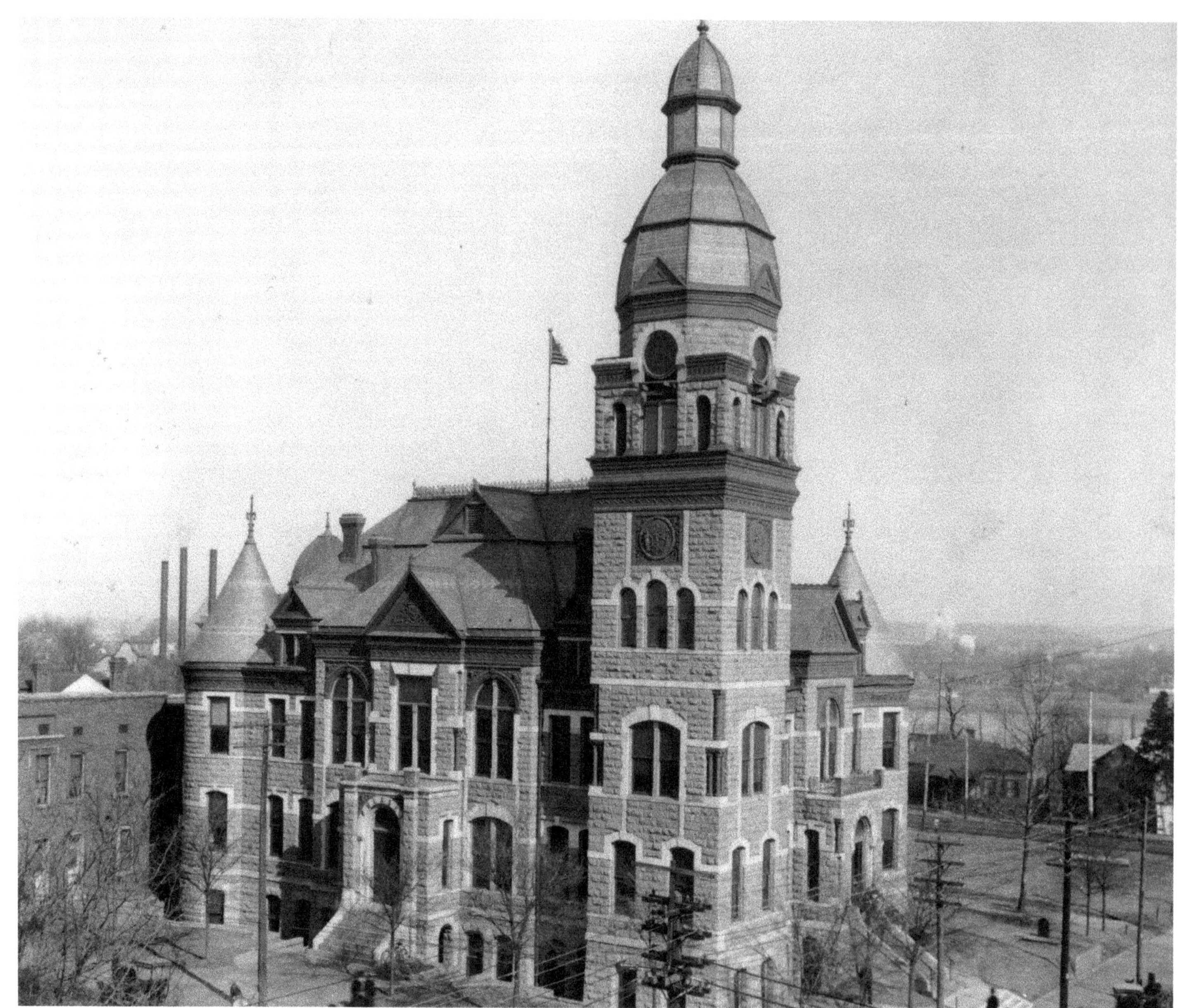

The 1889 Pulaski County Courthouse, located at Second and Spring streets, was built at a cost of $100,000. The courthouse rotunda features a Louis Comfort Tiffany stained-glass ceiling and beneath it a statue of Casimir Pulaski, the Polish officer who helped train American cavalry during the Revolutionary War and for whom the county is named.

Strictly Modern

(1900–1919)

The twentieth century instilled a spirit of optimism in the citizens of the United States and the people of Arkansas. Americans sensed that a new era was beginning. For some, including many Arkansans, these feelings materialized in efforts to transform and reform society, which became known as the Progressive Movement, spearheaded by one of the nation's favorite presidents, Theodore Roosevelt, and other leaders.

The new century also brought many changes to the cityscape of Little Rock, including a new capitol building. The first capitol, the State House, had been completed in 1842, but the government decided it had outgrown the accommodations this building afforded. Construction of a new state capitol began in 1899 but soon succumbed to the plague of controversy and scandal. The governor, Jeff Davis, opposed the project, stating that it was illegal to build a new capitol anywhere but the grounds occupied by the old State House. As construction dragged on, complaints of malfeasance on the part of the contractors, the highly regarded architect George Mann, and lawmakers mounted. These complaints seemed justified when, in 1905, four state senators and two representatives were indicted for accepting bribes in connection with construction appropriations. The next year, the construction company was accused of using substandard building materials, and construction stalled in 1907. In 1909 work resumed, and in 1911 government officials moved into their new offices, albeit while construction continued. The Arkansas State Capitol was finally completed in 1915.

A new capitol was not the only new structure in Little Rock. The city's first skyscraper, the ten-story Southern Trust Building, opened in 1907. It was the first of several skyscrapers built during the period. In 1910, the eleven-story State Bank Building became the tallest building in the city. And in 1908 a new City Hall was built.

The veterans of the Confederacy held a widely attended reunion in 1911, which culminated in a parade so long one could not witness all of it in less than two hours. At the turn of the century, 40,000 Americans called the 80-year-old city home, up from just 3,700 when the city had turned 40. Pulaski Heights had become the city's first suburb, and a public library offered 3,200 books to the reading public. Seventy-five churches and 60 social clubs welcomed citizens to their ranks, and six rail lines connected Little Rock to the rest of the nation.

Detail of the 1881 U.S. Post Office and Courthouse. The edifice would endure through time and stands today at 300 West Second Street.

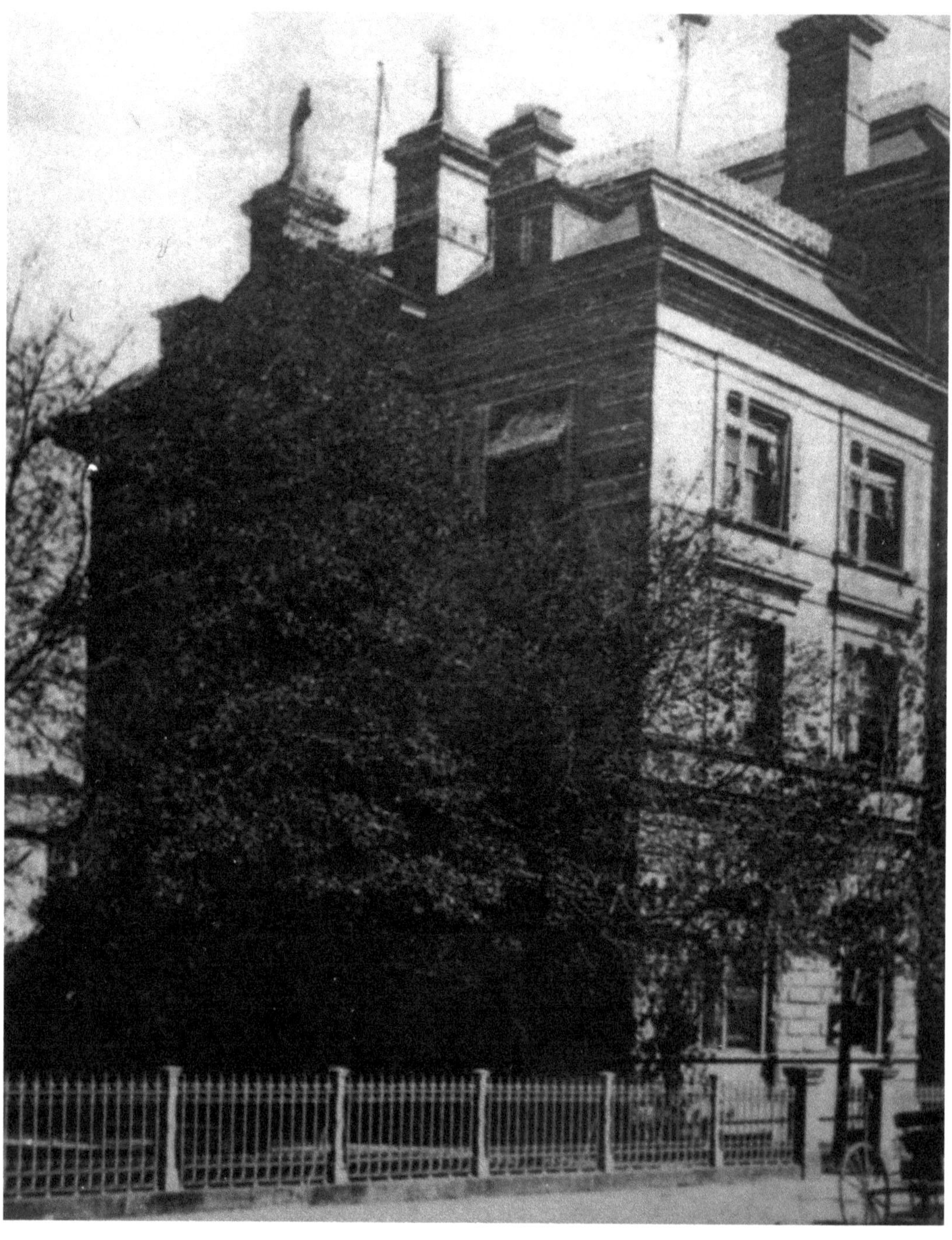

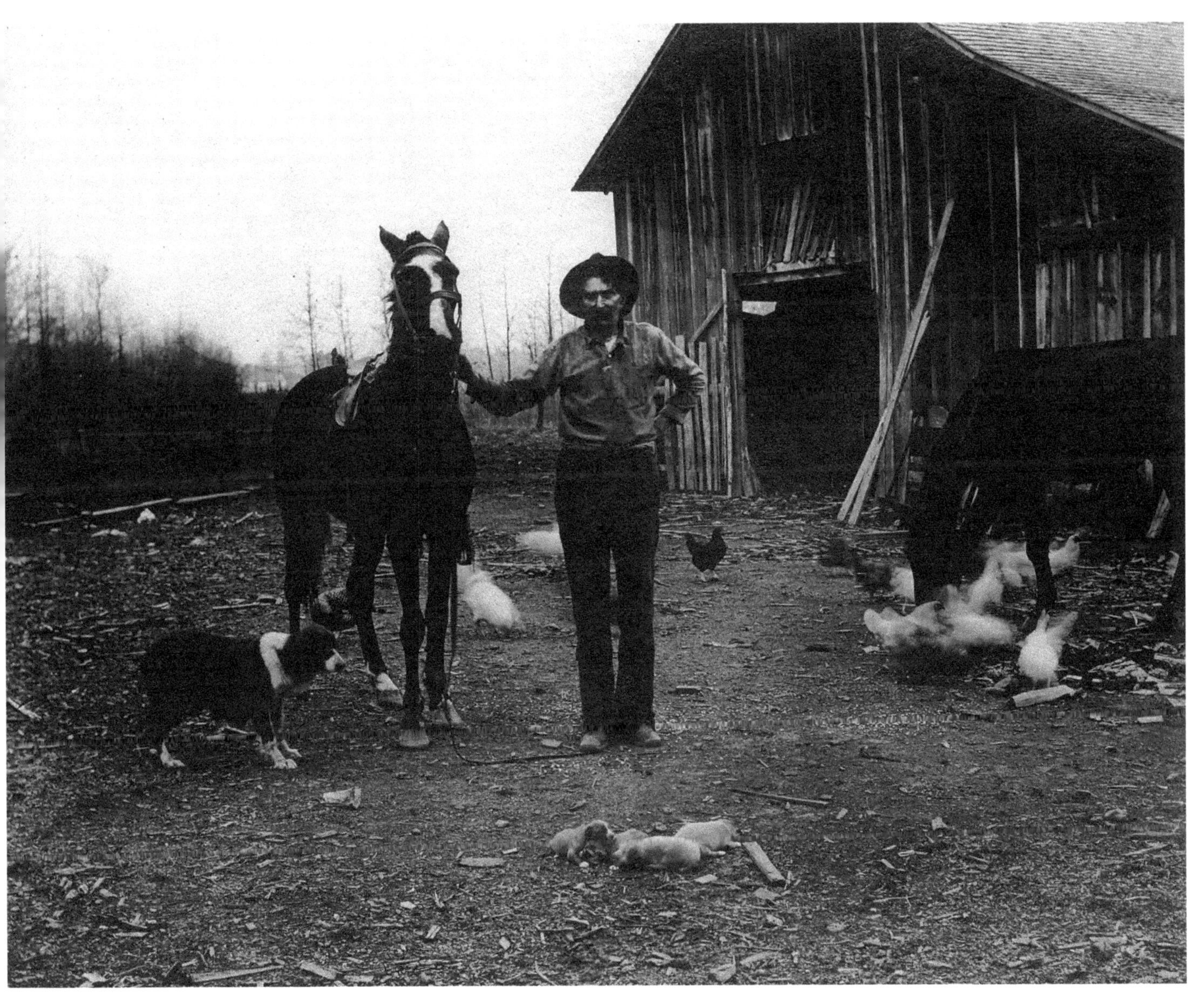

John Jacobs stands surrounded by barnyard animals on a farm near Kanis Road.

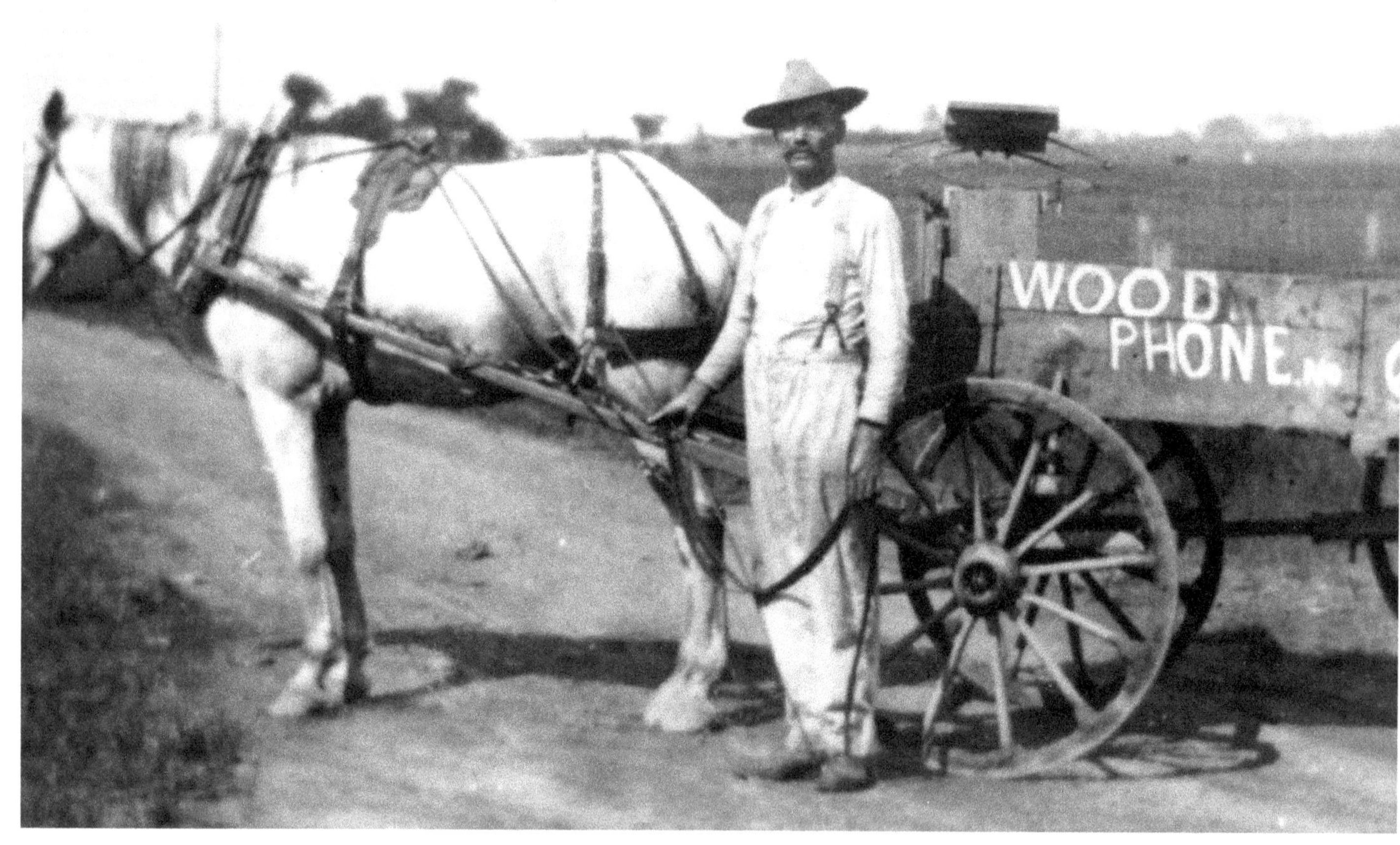

W. Siders, standing with horse and buckboard near Seventeenth and Main streets, seems to be having a sale on wood. Interested parties could reach him at phone 64. Horse-and-buggy transportation would not give way to the automobile until the new century was well under way.

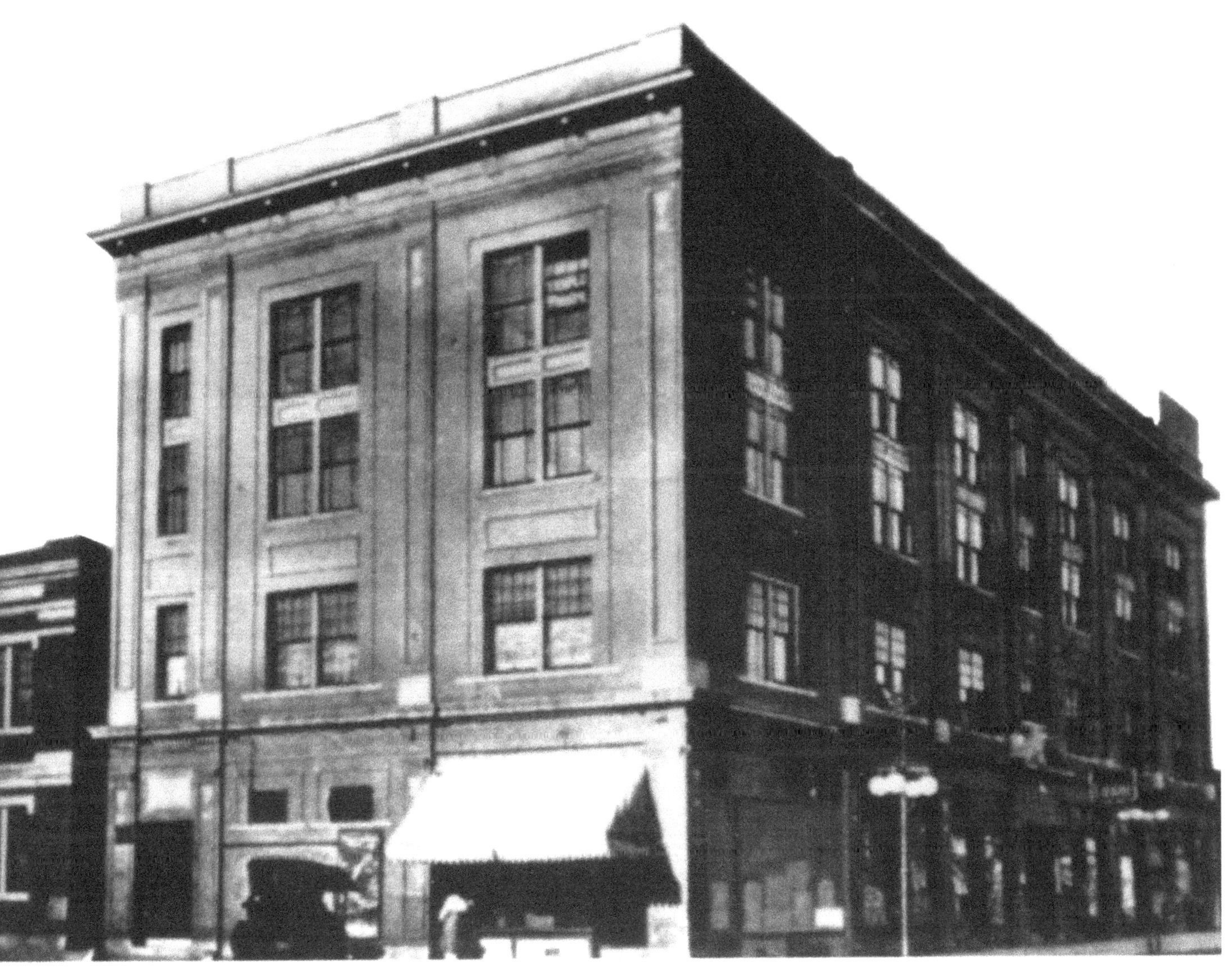

The headquarters of the Mosaic Templars stood at Ninth and Broadway around 1900. The Mosaic Templars were an insurar and fraternal organization whose original purpose was to provide burial insurance. Today the building is the home of an Africa American history museum, the Mosaic Templars Cultural Cent

The Gus Blass Company department store, located at Fourth and Main streets, was one of the first in the South to install an escalator. The company was sold to Dillard's in 1964, and today the building houses offices.

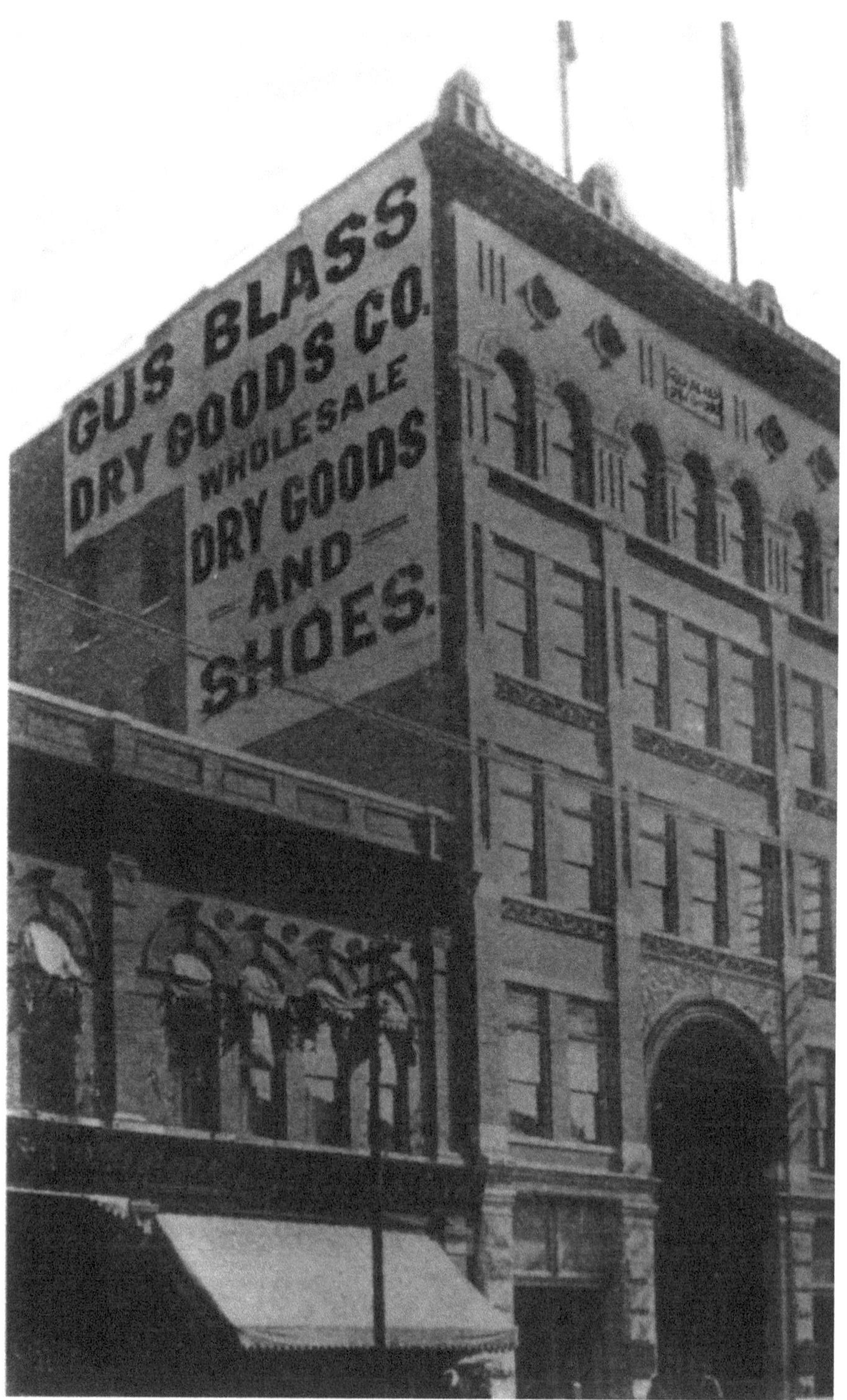

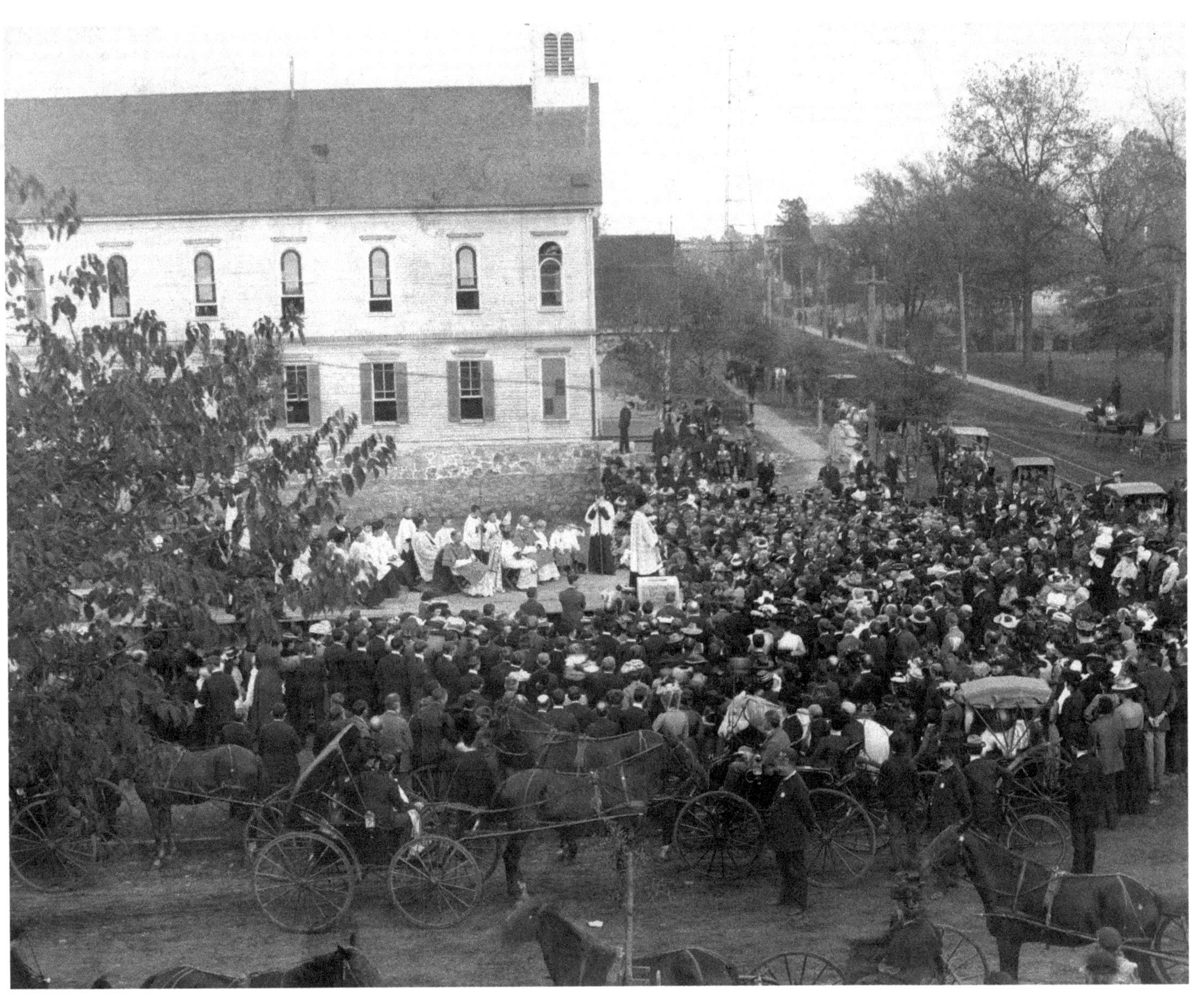

Parishioners gather for a ceremony to celebrate the laying of the cornerstone at St. Edward's Catholic Church on November 10, 1901.

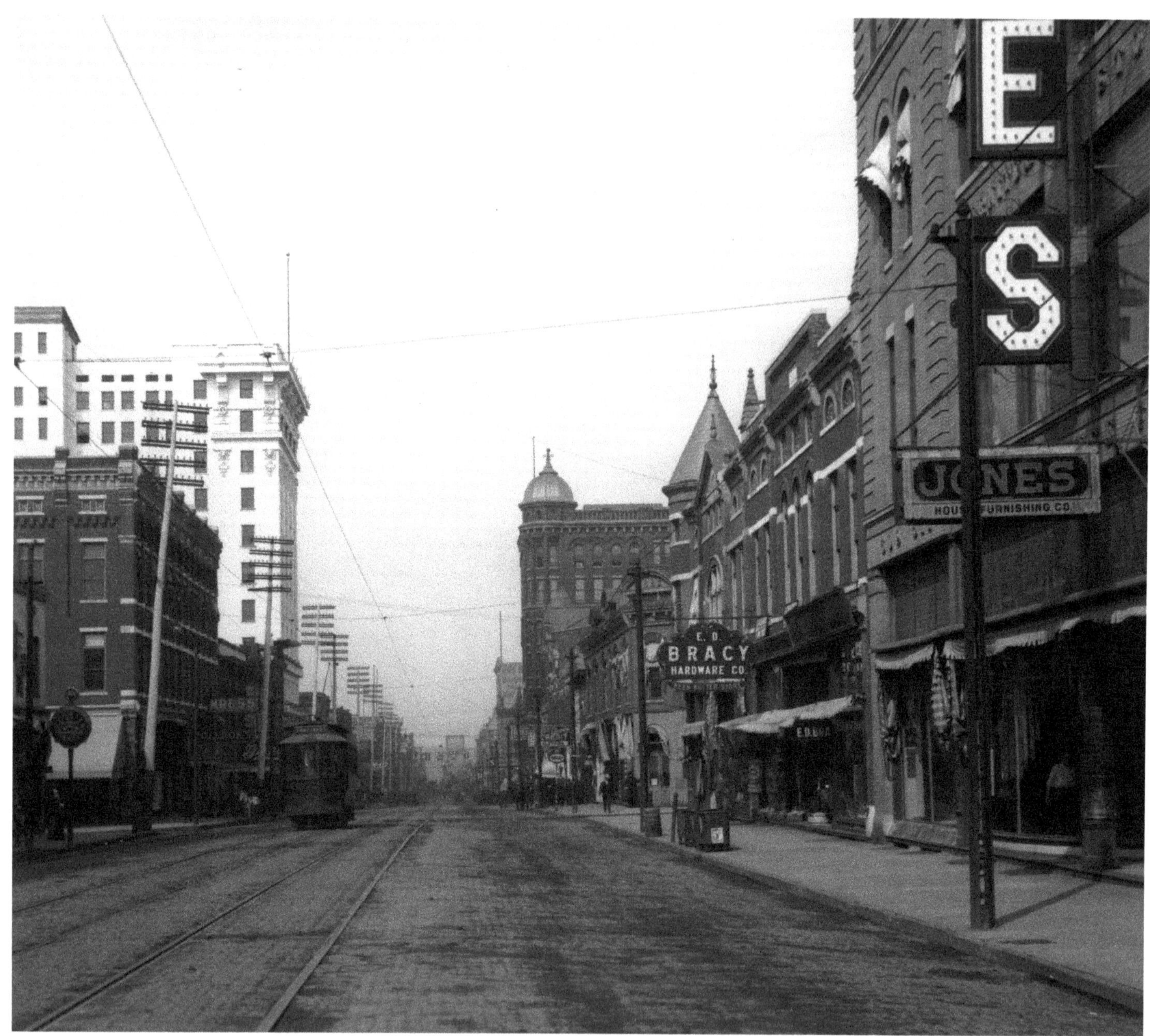

This view of Main Street faces north from Sixth Street toward the river bridge, just visible in the distance, which carried citizens into Argenta, separately incorporated as North Little Rock in 1901. Downtown thoroughfares by this time had been paved, and the streetcar lines had long since been converted to electric power.

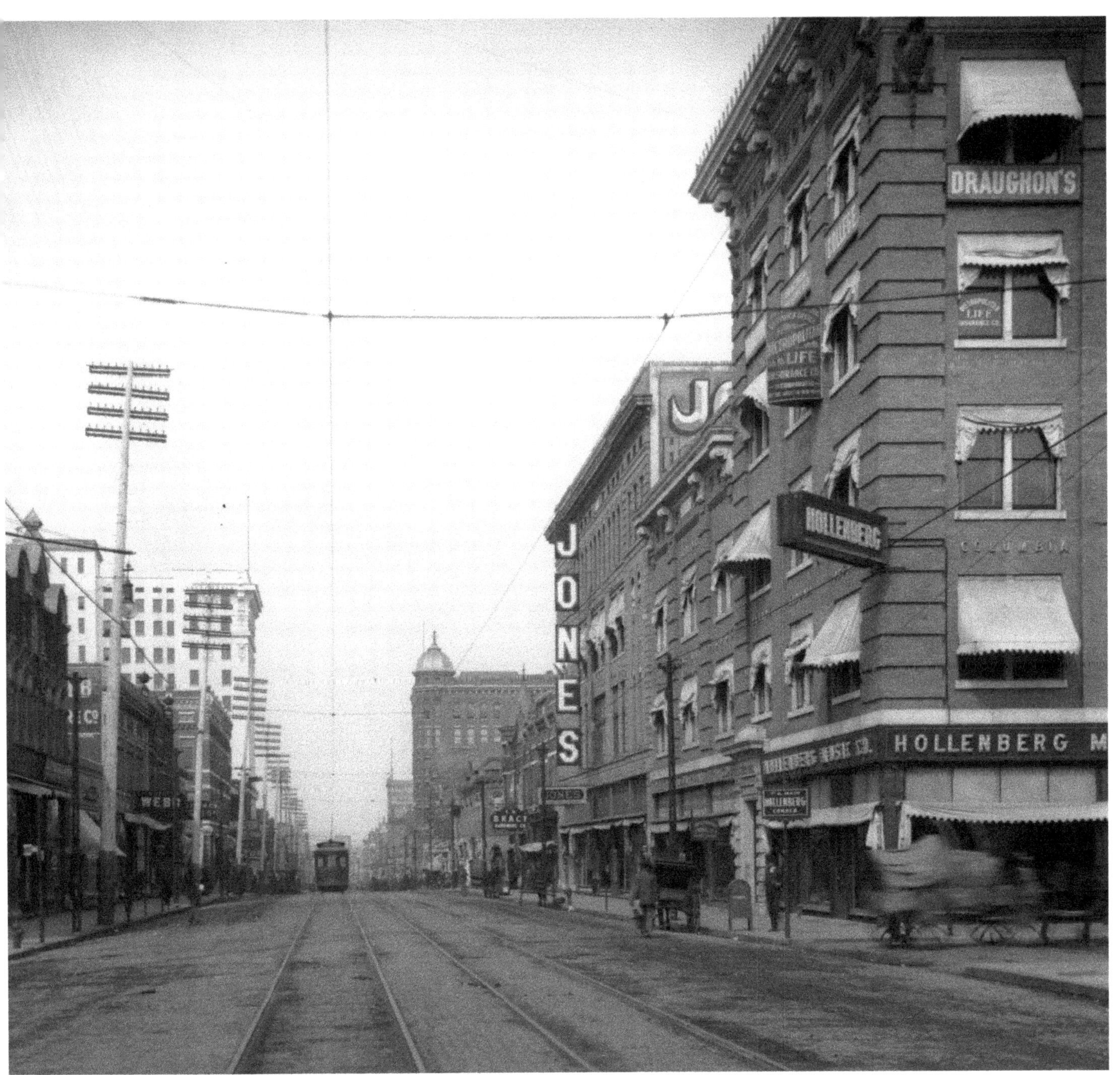

Another view of Main Street, facing north from Sixth Street. Open for business at the corner are Hollenberg Music Company and Metropolitan Life.

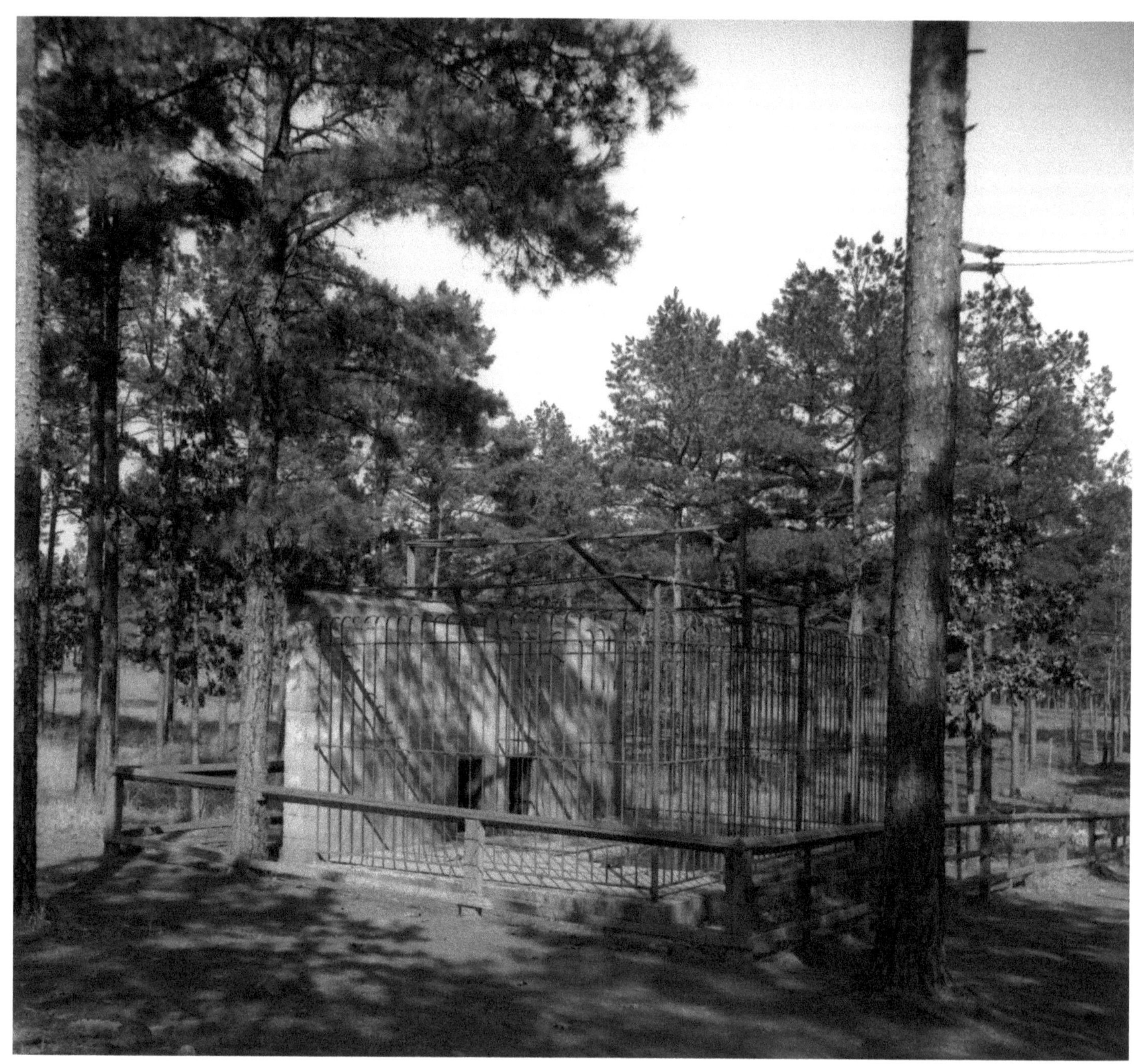

The bear pits in Forest Park, as they appeared in the early 1900s. Located on Kavanaugh Boulevard, Forest Park is occupied today by homes and businesses.

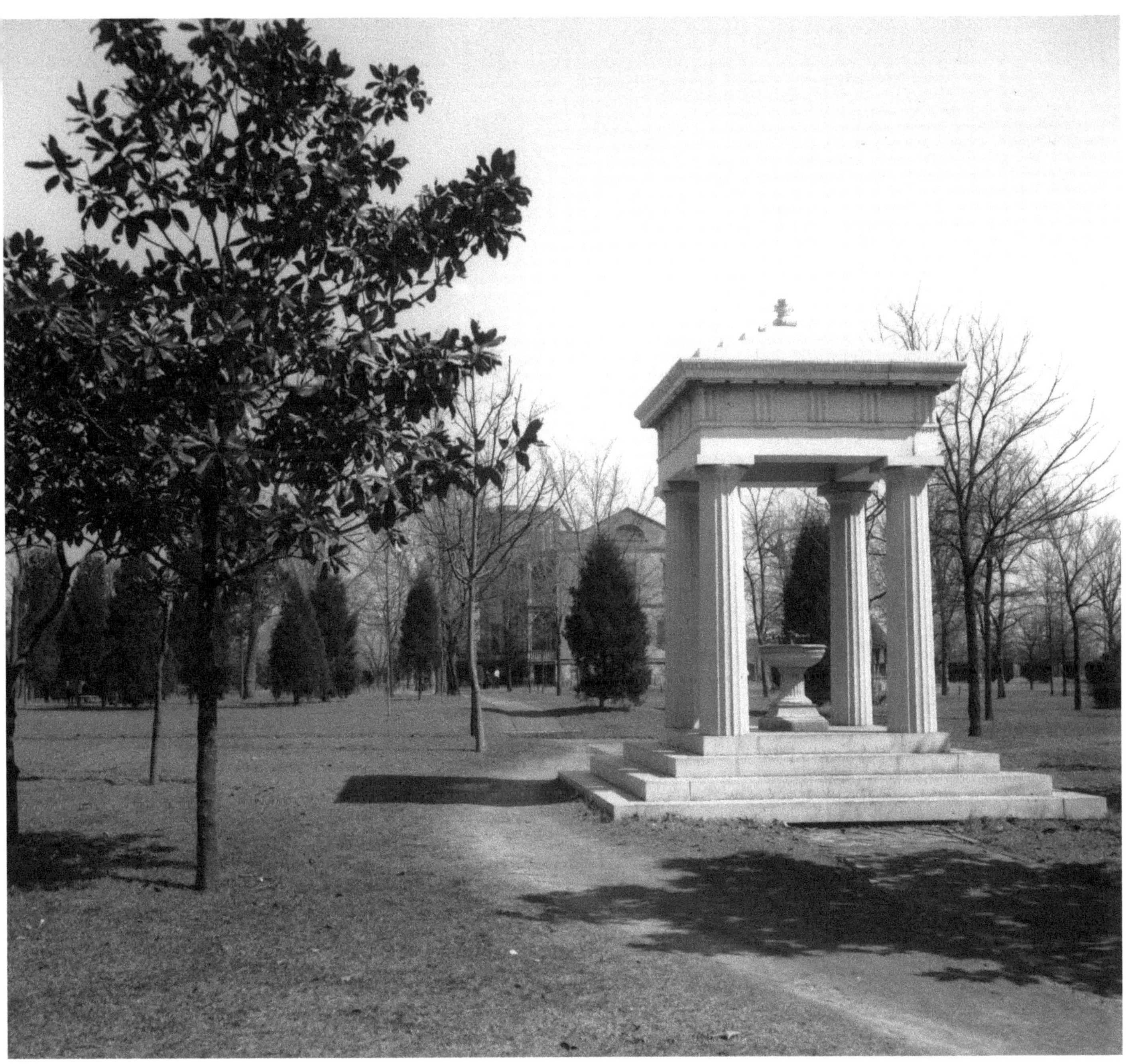

A memorial fountain in City Park, inscribed with the name "Gilbert Knapp." Knapp had owned land near the Toltec Mounds in Scott, Arkansas. Park flora included a lone magnolia tree putting down roots (at left), and a grove of cedars wintering over in the background.

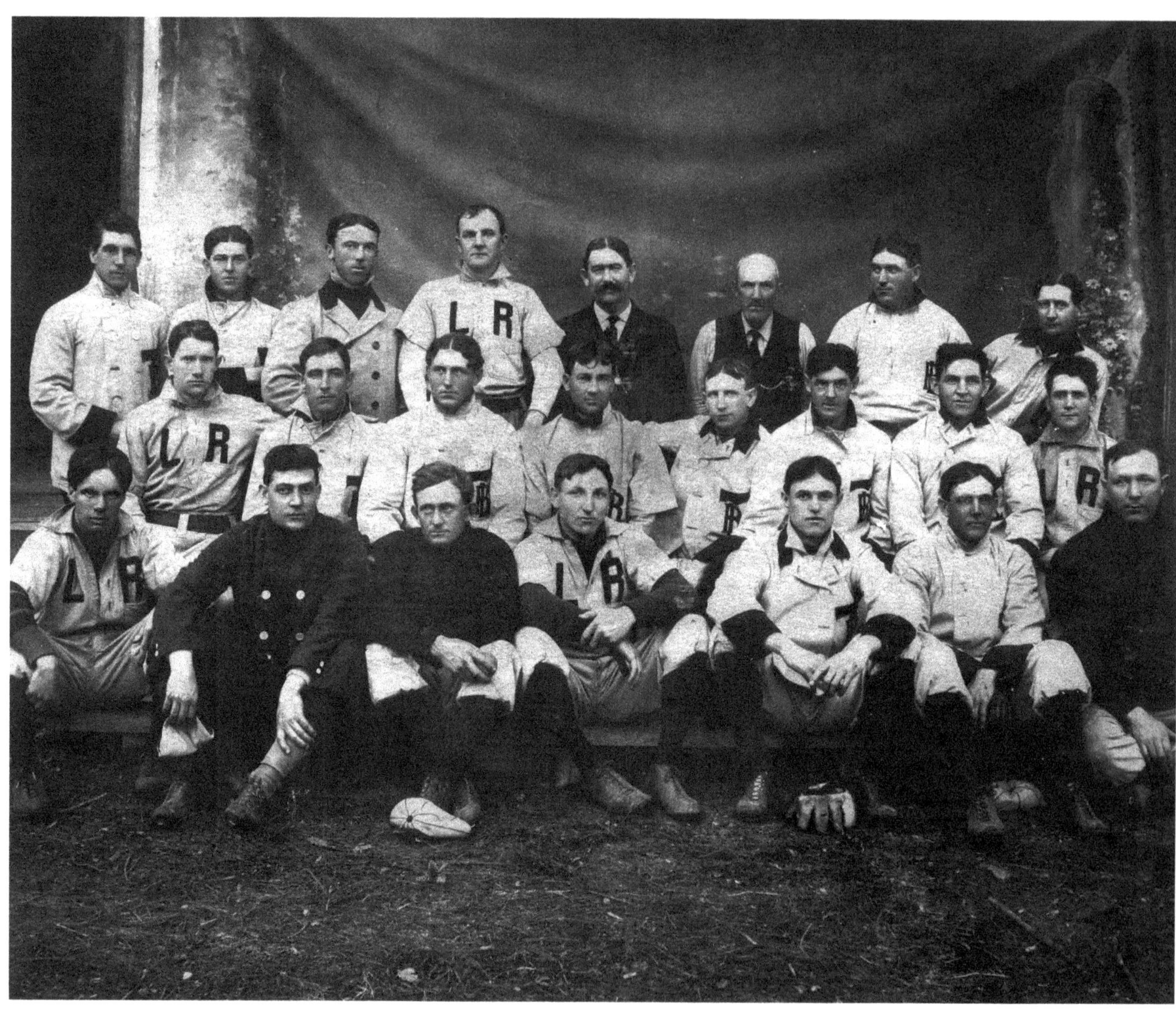

A 1902 group photograph of the Little Rock Travelers baseball team. The team was first organized in 1901. In 1957, they changed their name to the Arkansas Travelers, becoming the first professional team to name themselves after a state. The team also became one of the few franchises to be owned by the fans. Today the Travelers play at Dickie Stephens Park in North Little Rock and are affiliated with the Anaheim Angels.

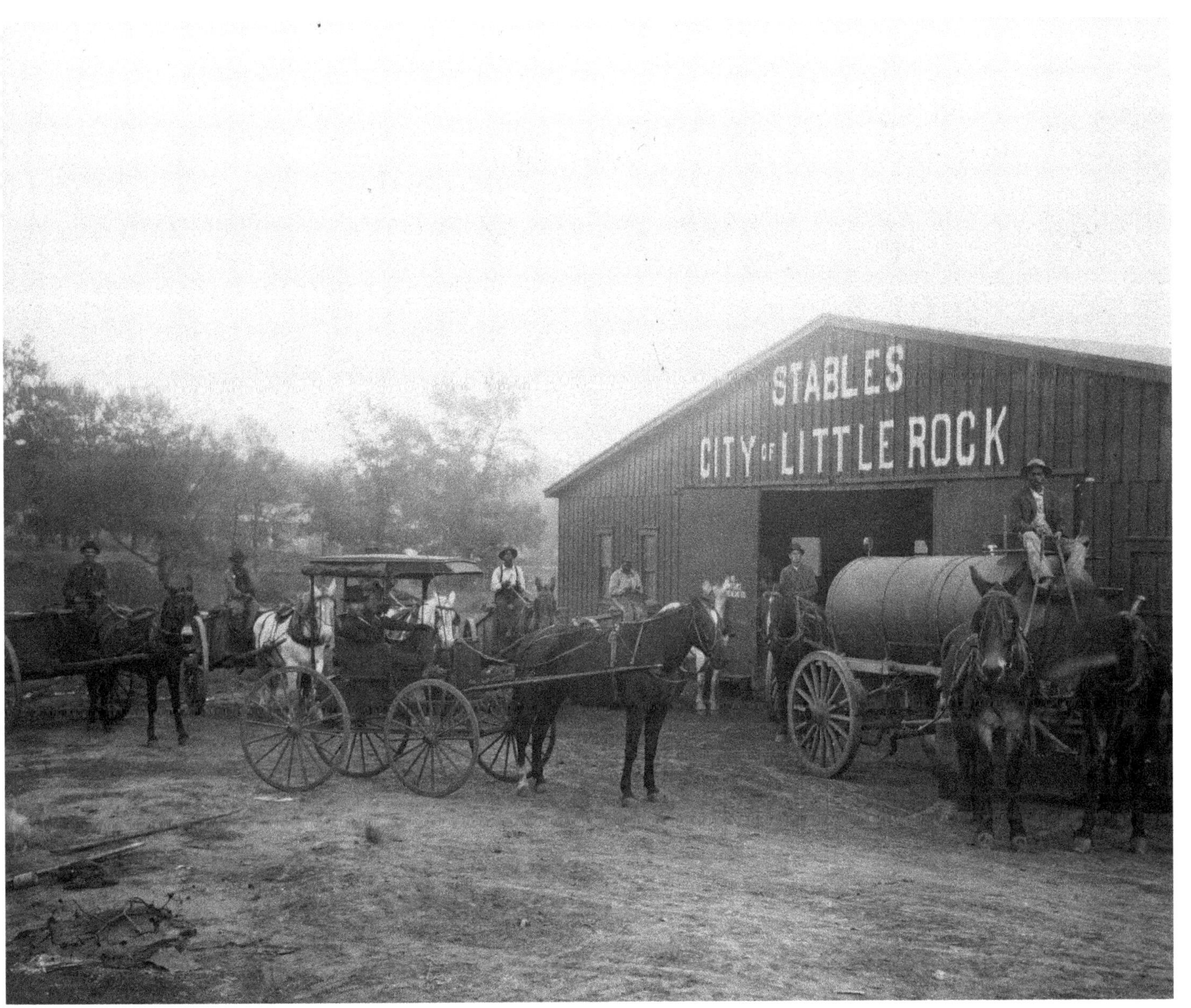

Stables for the city of Little Rock.

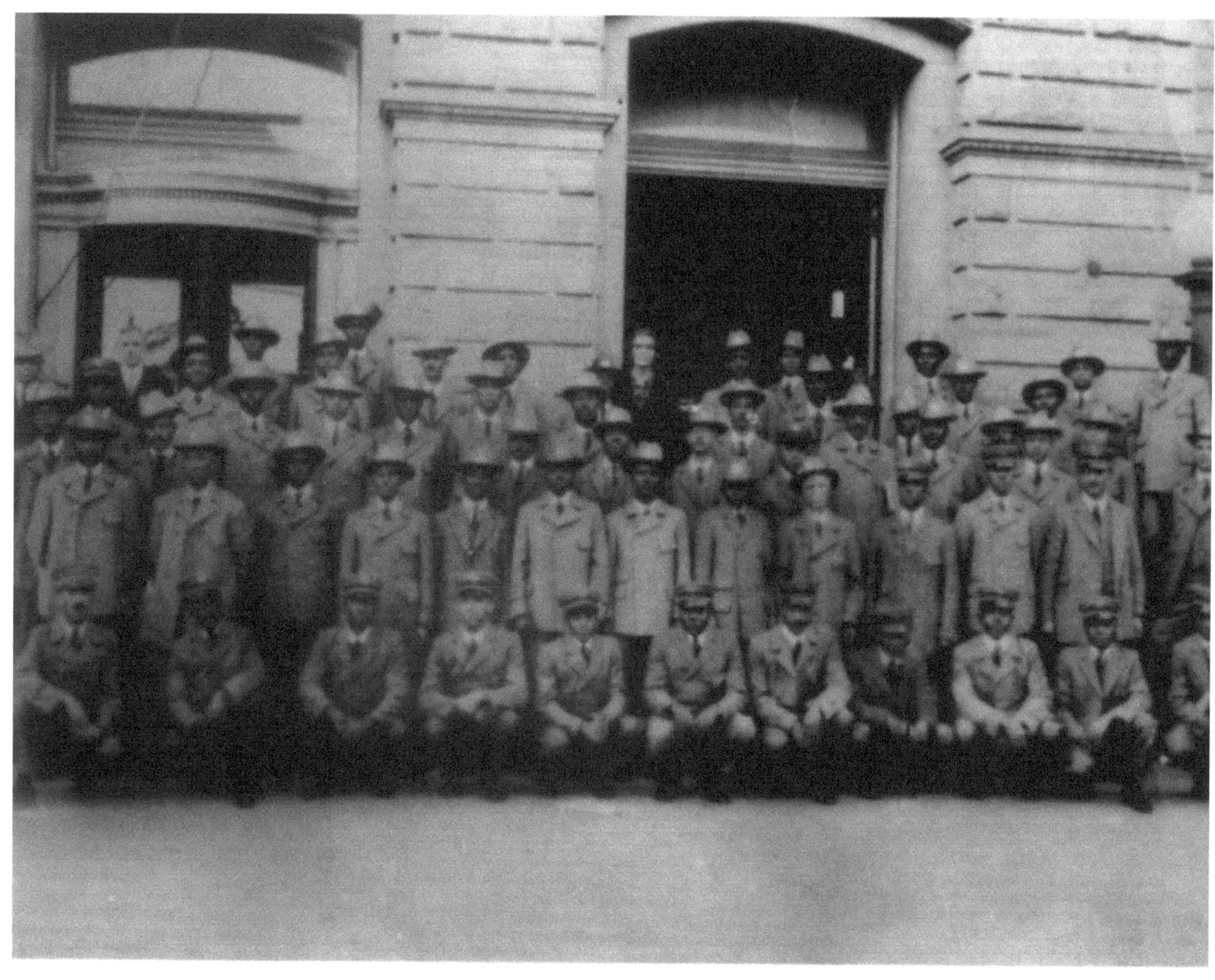

Little Rock post office workers in uniform in front of the Post Office on Capital Street. This group shot was probably recorded sometime before the building was expanded. Construction of two additional wings began in 1908.

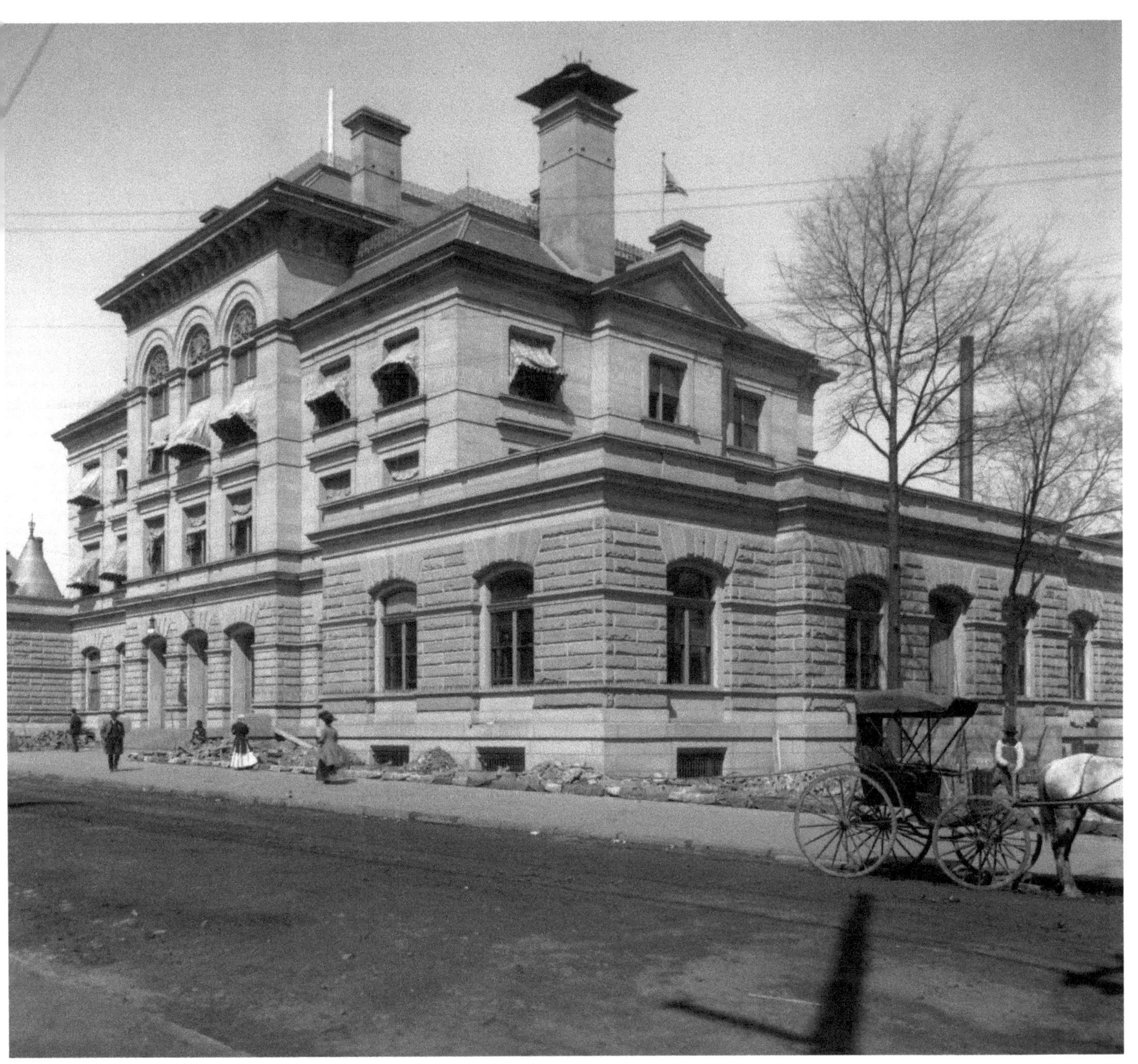

The Little Rock Post Office, this view probably recorded around 1910, following the addition of two wraparound wings to the Italian Renaissance revival structure.

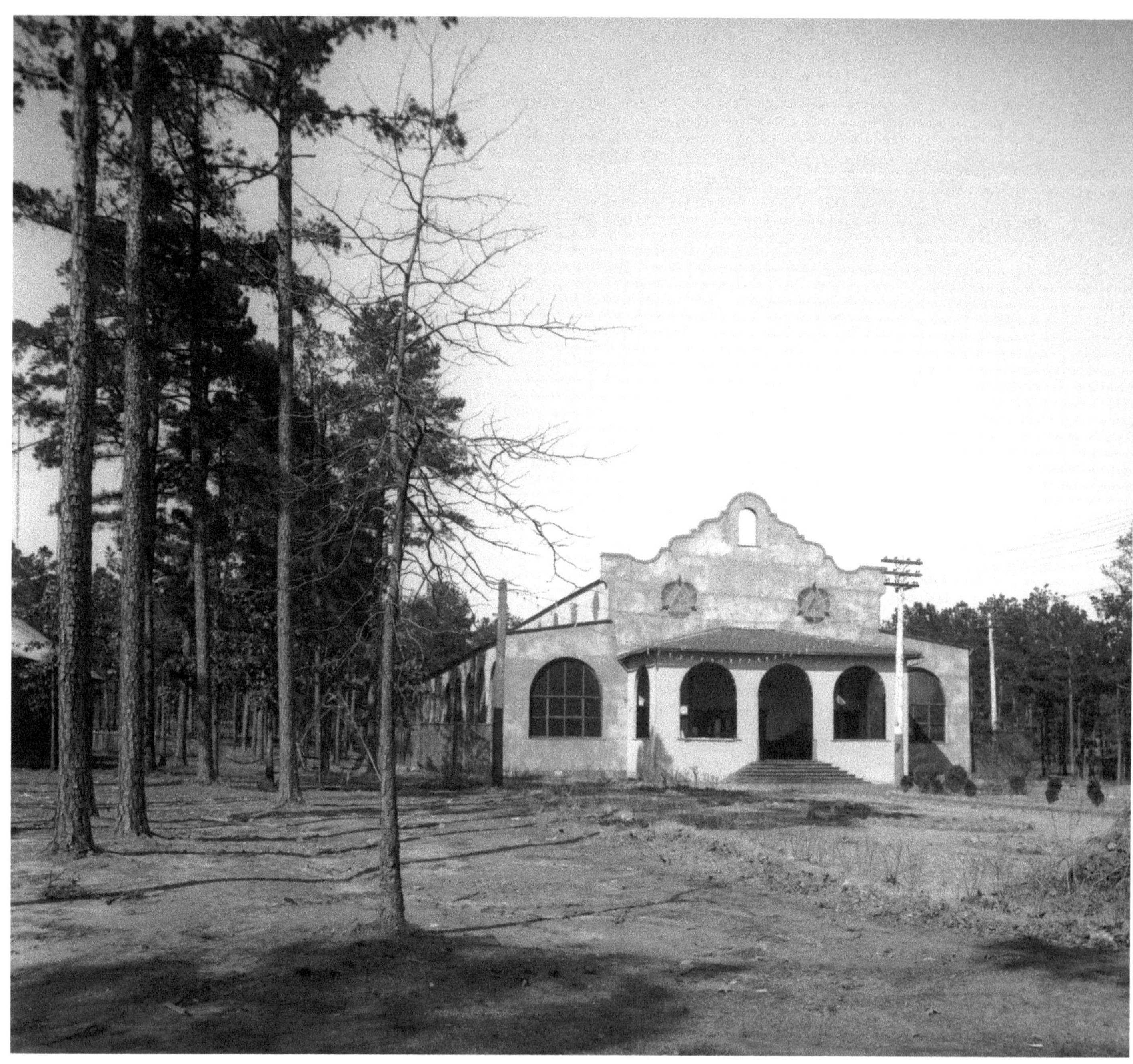

Forest Park Theater, located in Forest Park, hosted minstrel shows, concerts, plays, and silent films. The celebrated actress Sarah Bernhardt reportedly once appeared in *Camille* at the theater.

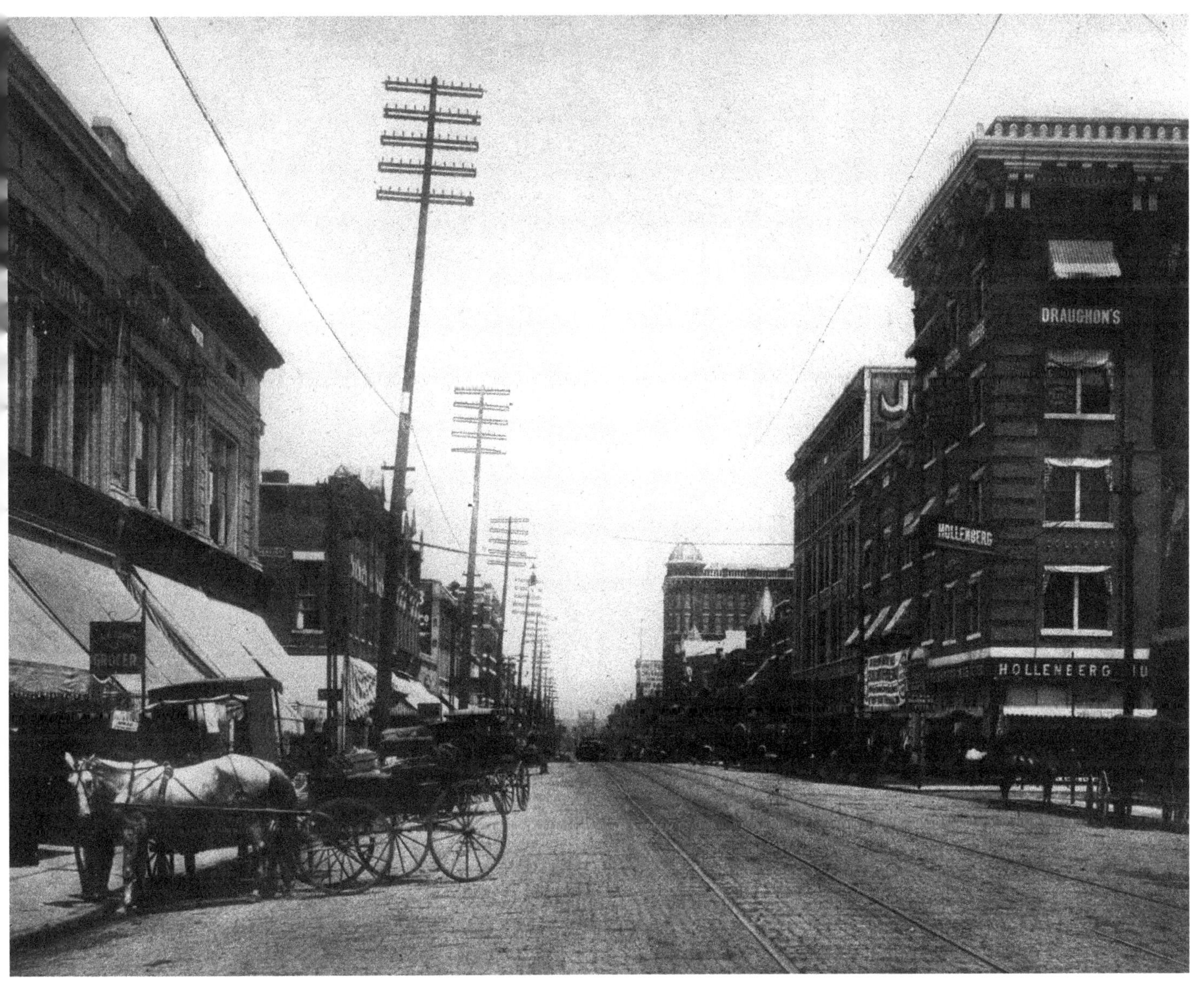

This is horse-and-buggy-days Main Street, facing north toward the river, from Seventh Street.

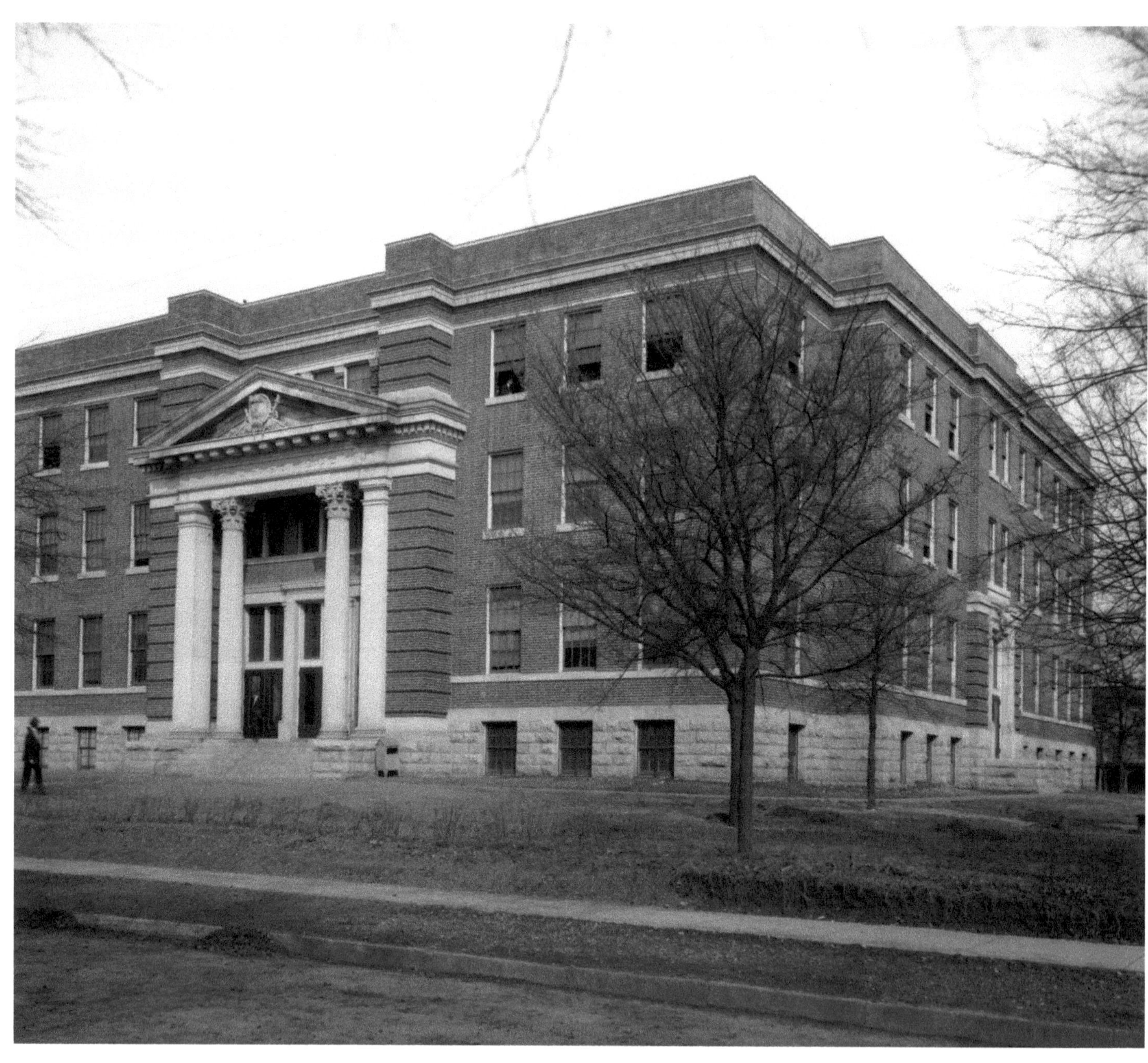

Little Rock High School, around the early 1900s, was the city's high school for white students until the opening of Central High School in 1927. The building served many purposes until it was closed in 1997.

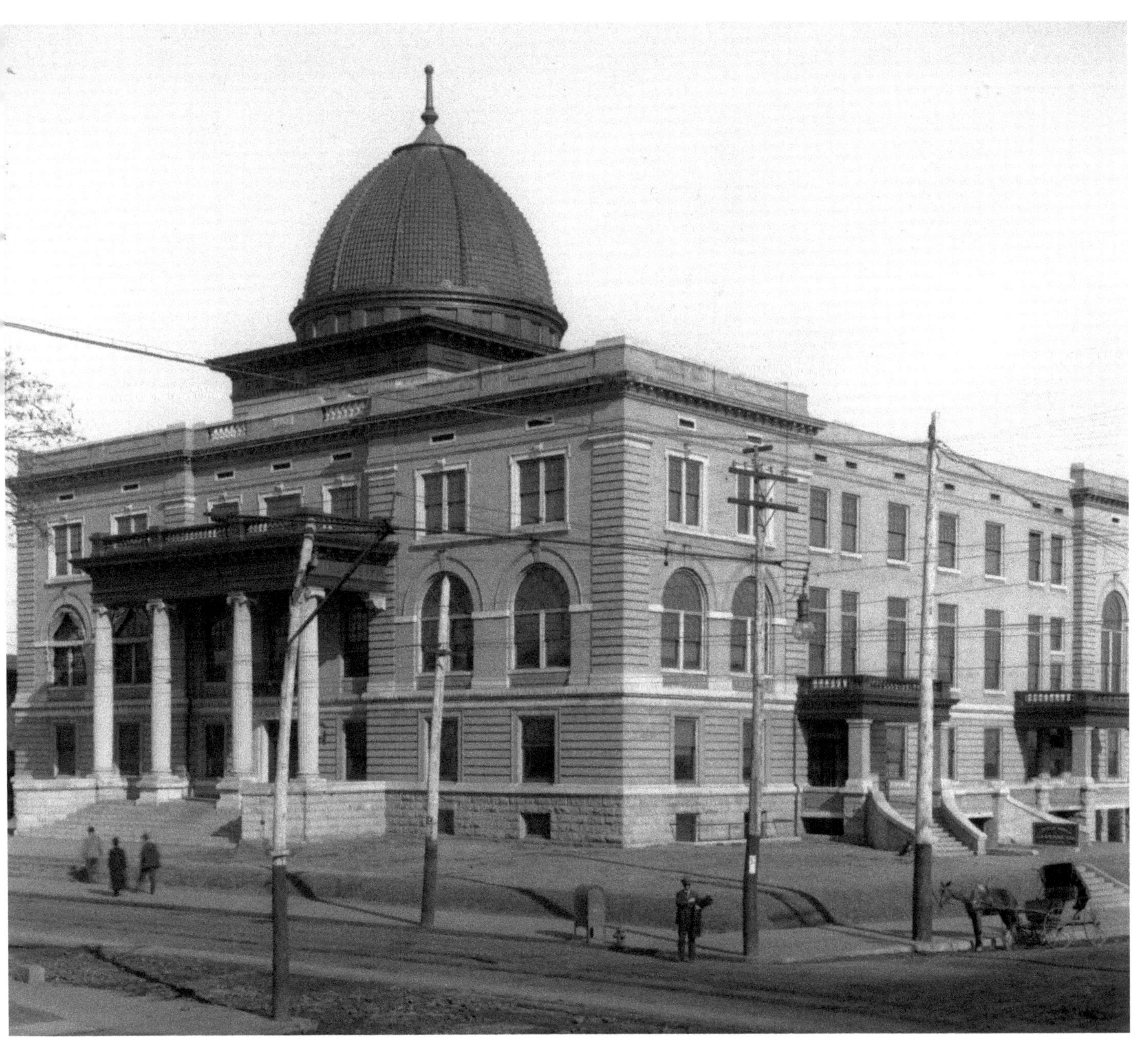

City Hall was designed by Charles Thompson and built in 1908. The dome was removed in 1956.

The Fred Kramer School, located on Sherman Street, around 1905. The school was built in 1895 and is the oldest surviving school building in Little Rock. In 1997, the structure became a resident artists' gallery.

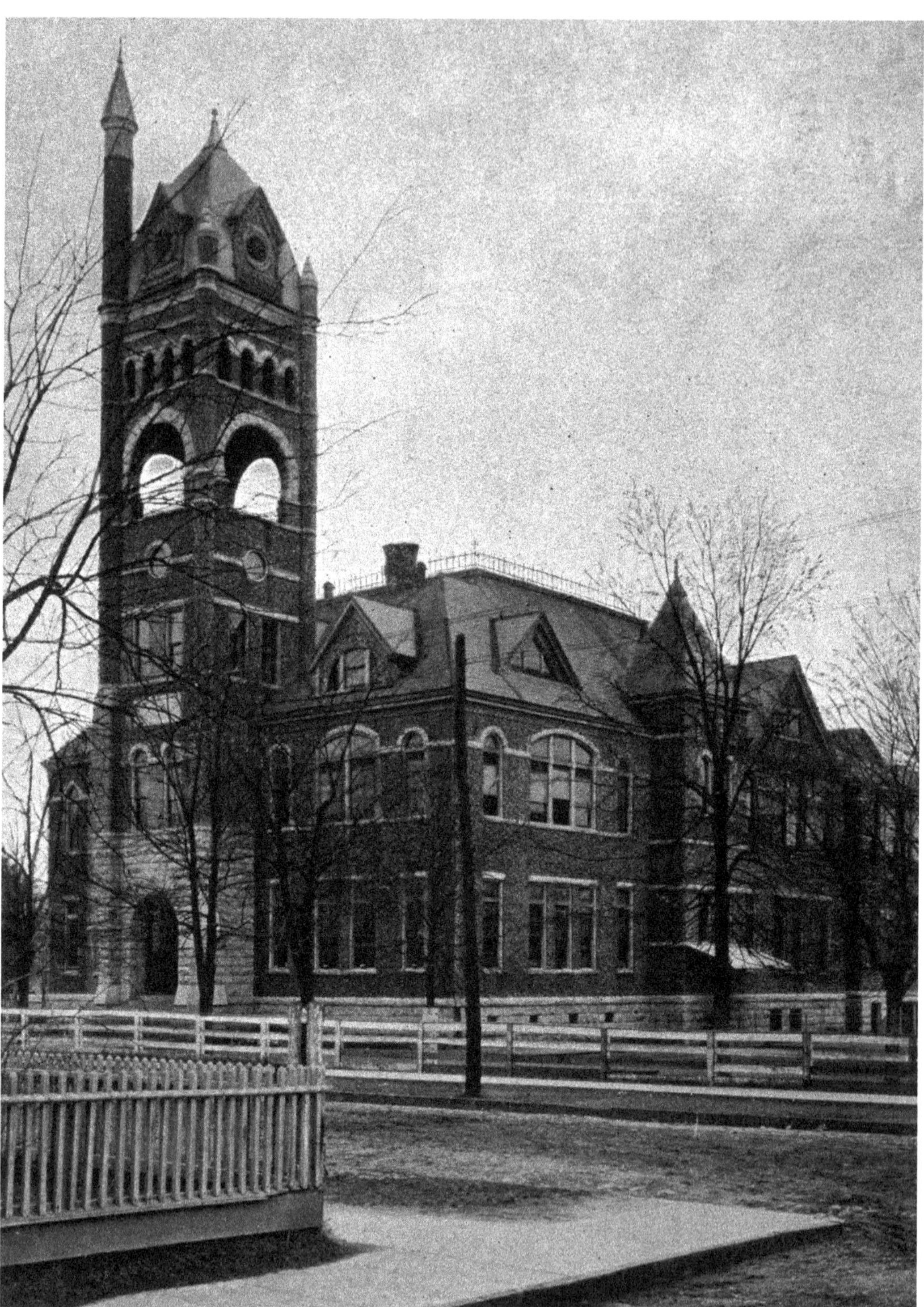

The Arkansas School for the Blind, around the early 1900s. The school was founded in 1859 in Arkadelphia, as the Institute for the Education of the Blind, by Reverend Haucke, a blind Baptist minister. In 1868, the school moved to Little Rock and in 1877 was renamed the Arkansas School for the Blind. In October 1939, the school relocated to 2600 West Markham Street, where it remains today.

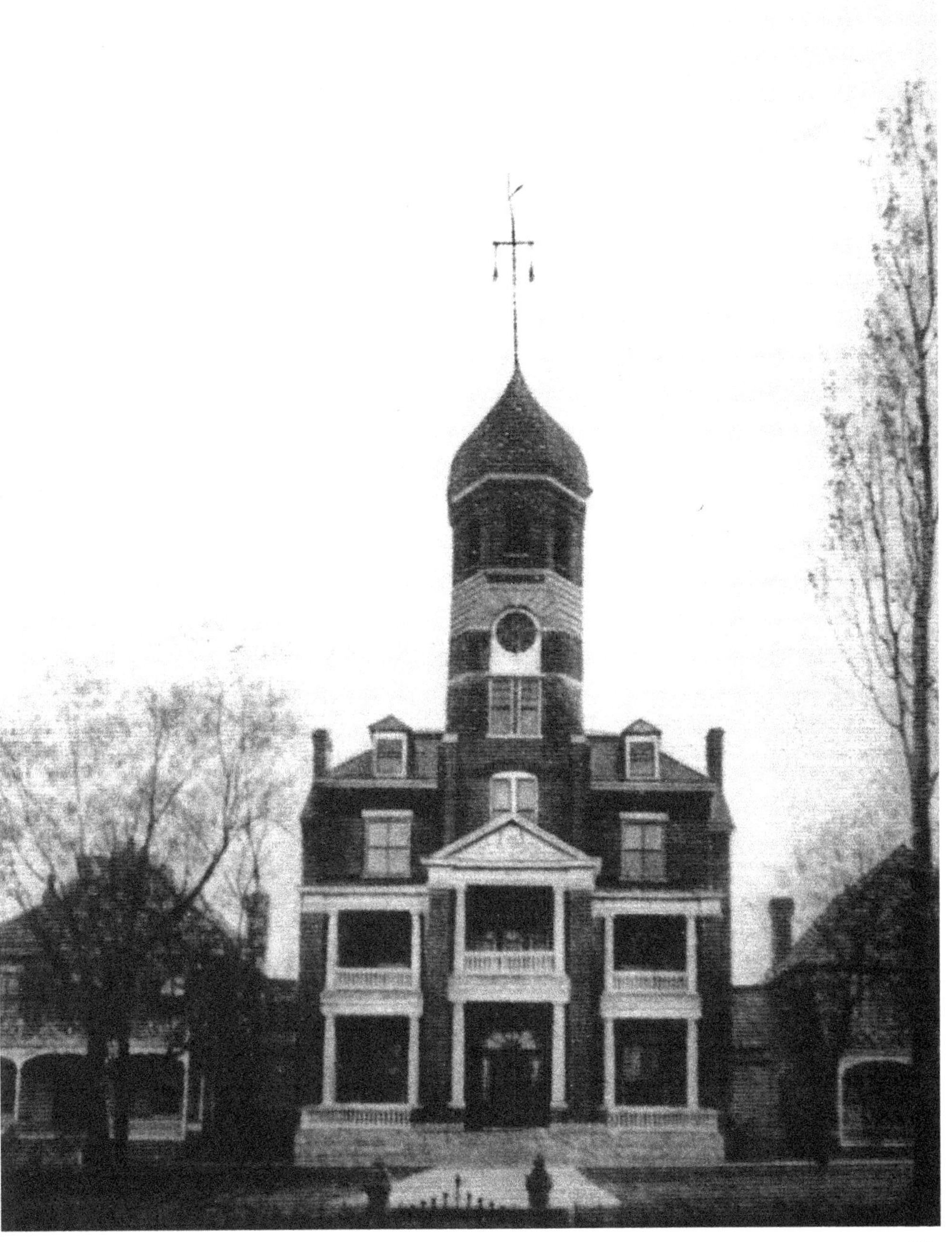

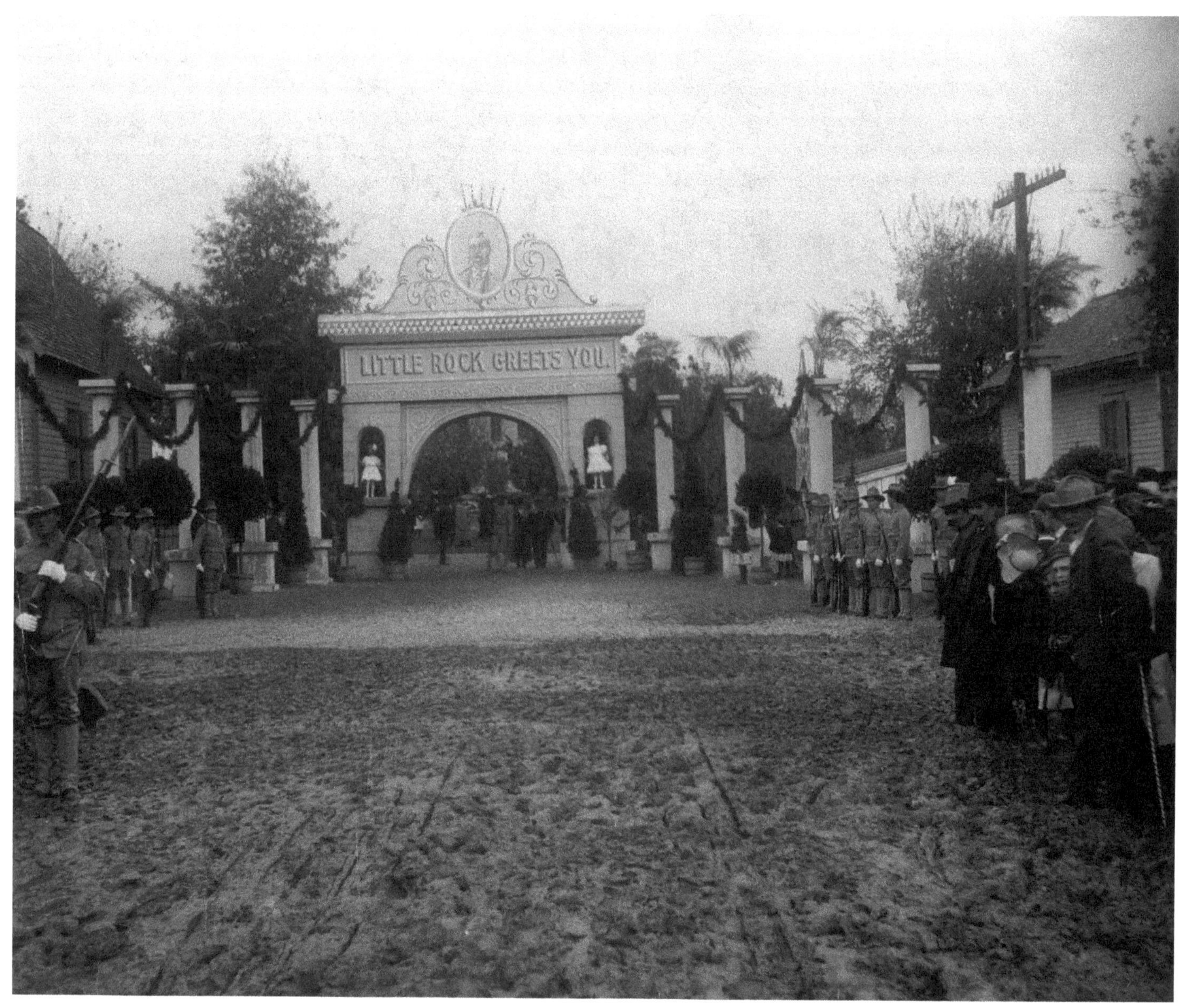

A welcoming gate for President Theodore Roosevelt, champion of the Progressive era, on his visit to Little Rock on October 25, 1905. Little Rock was a stop on the president's trip through the southern states. He made several speeches in the city, including one at City Park.

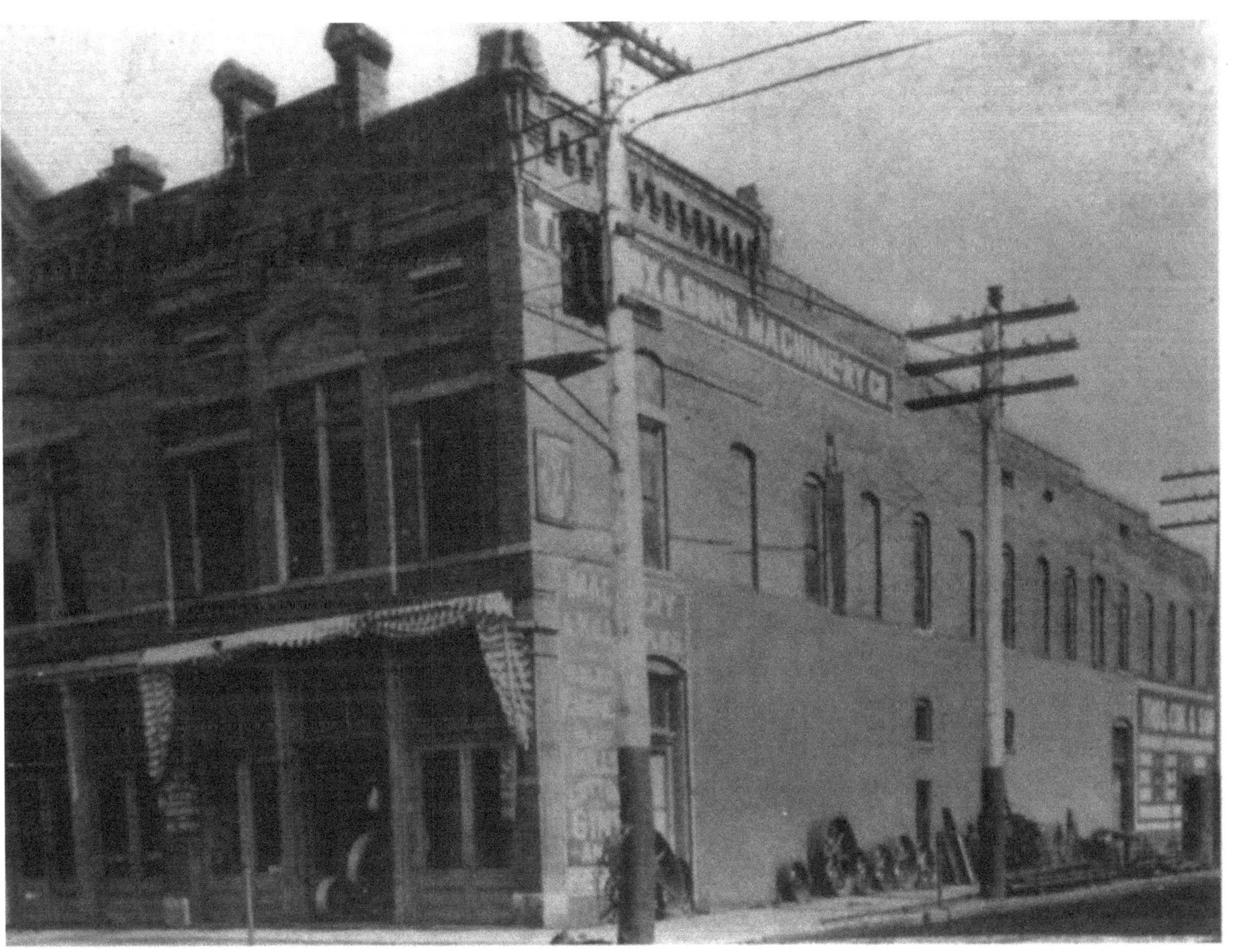

The offices of Thomas Cox and Sons Machinery Company, located on East Markham Street, in 1907, with signage advertising sawmills, cotton gins, and other equipment. The iron wheels leaning against the building are probably inventory for steam-powered farm implements used in the production of cotton and other regional crops.

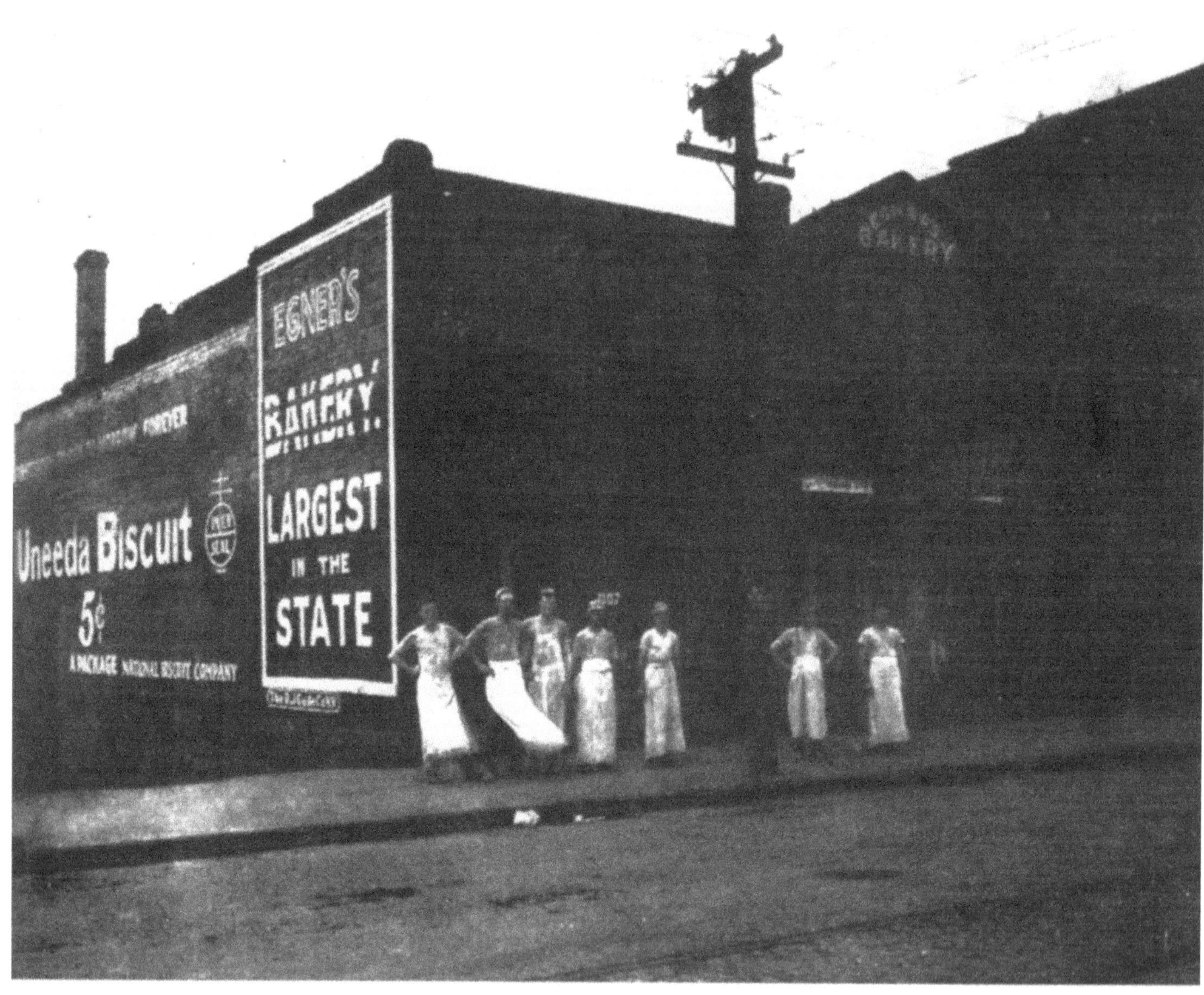

These bakers are standing in front of Egner's Bakery for a photograph in 1907. The bakery was located at 1109 West Markham Street.

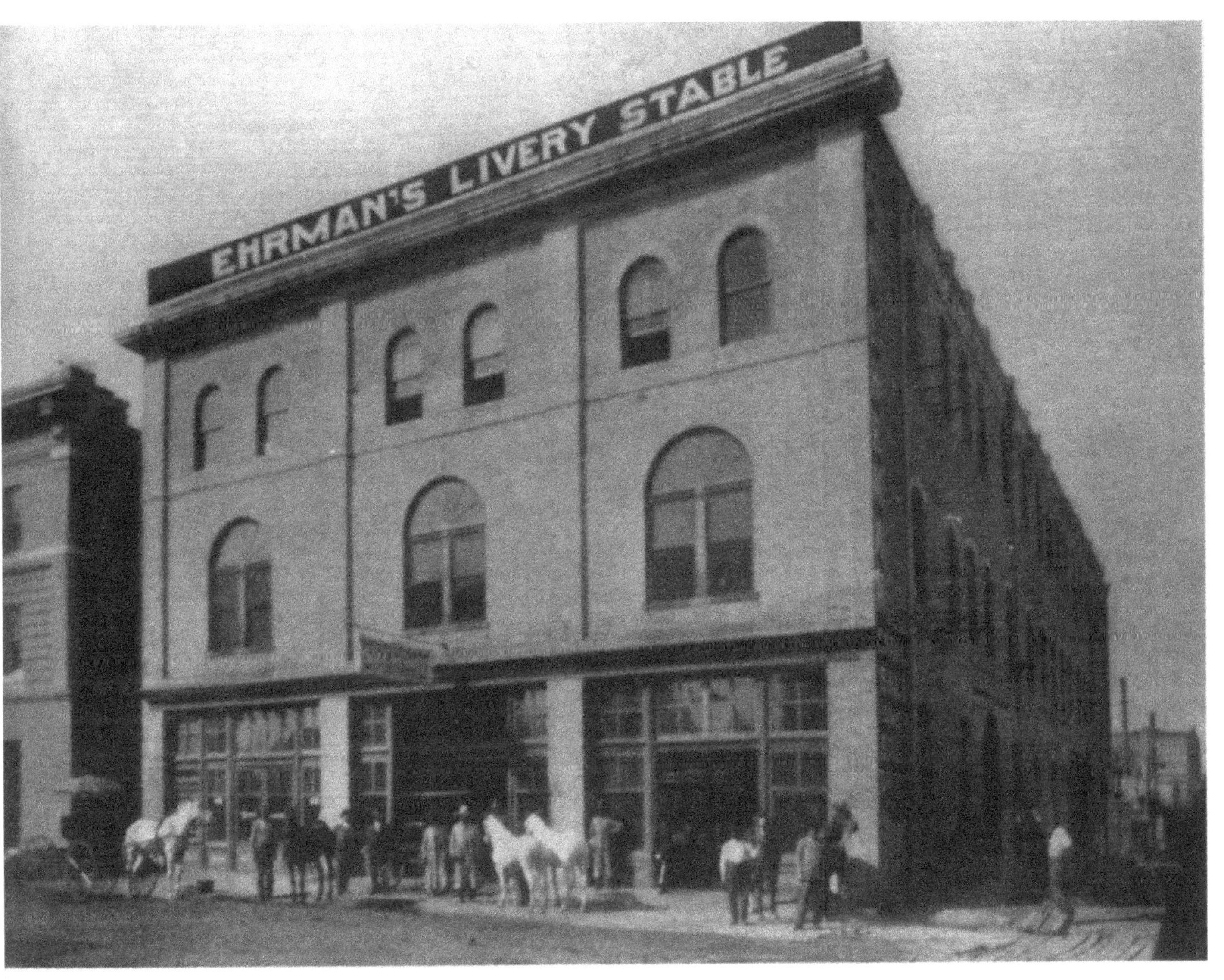

Ehrman's Livery Stable was located on West Fourth Street. The automobile had arrived, but in small numbers. In 1902, Little Rock counted 3 horseless carriages skulking around the city. By 1914, half a dozen years after this image was recorded, there were nearly 5,000.

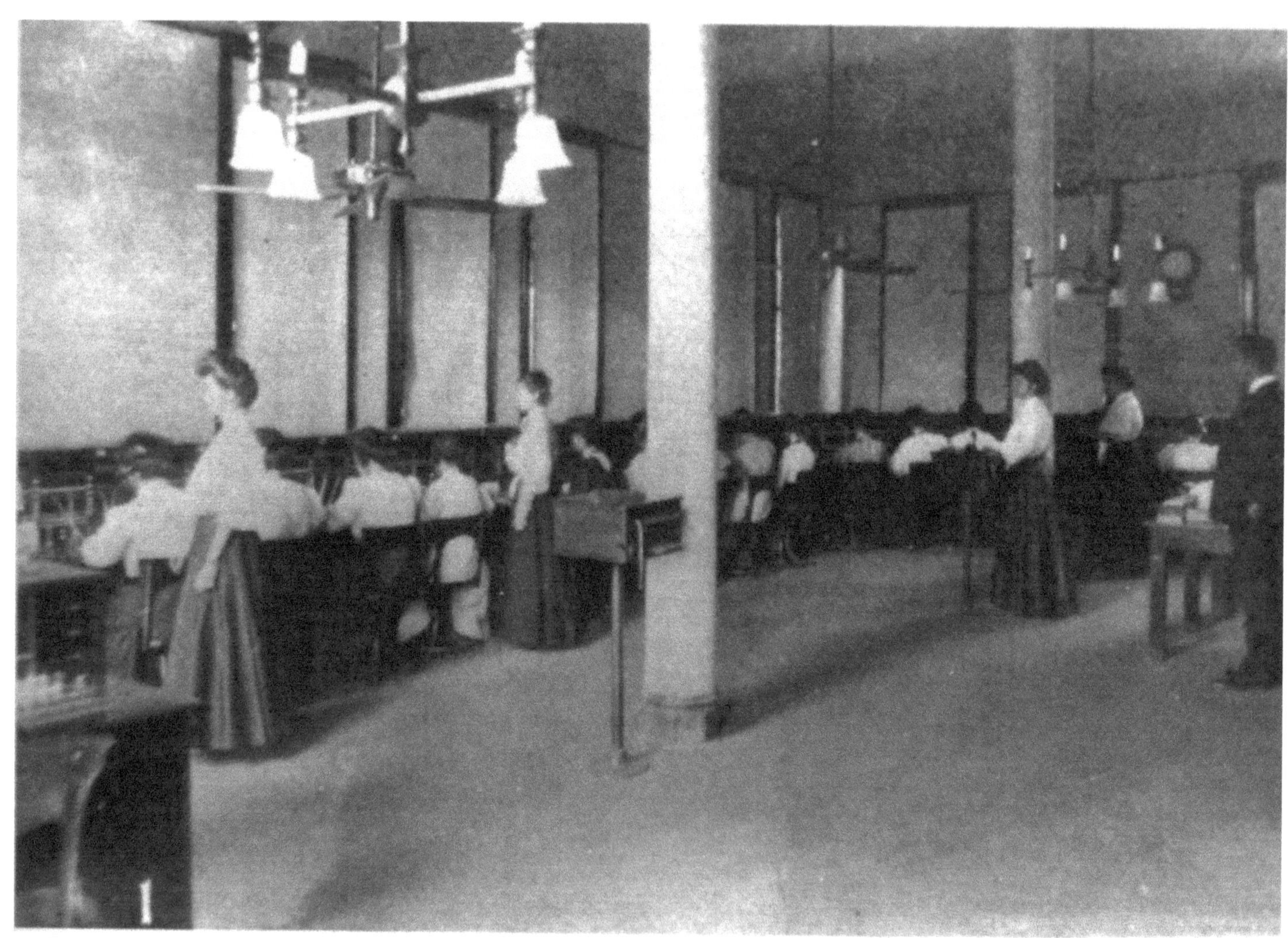

These operators are working the long-distance lines at Southwestern Telegraph and Telephone Company in 1907.

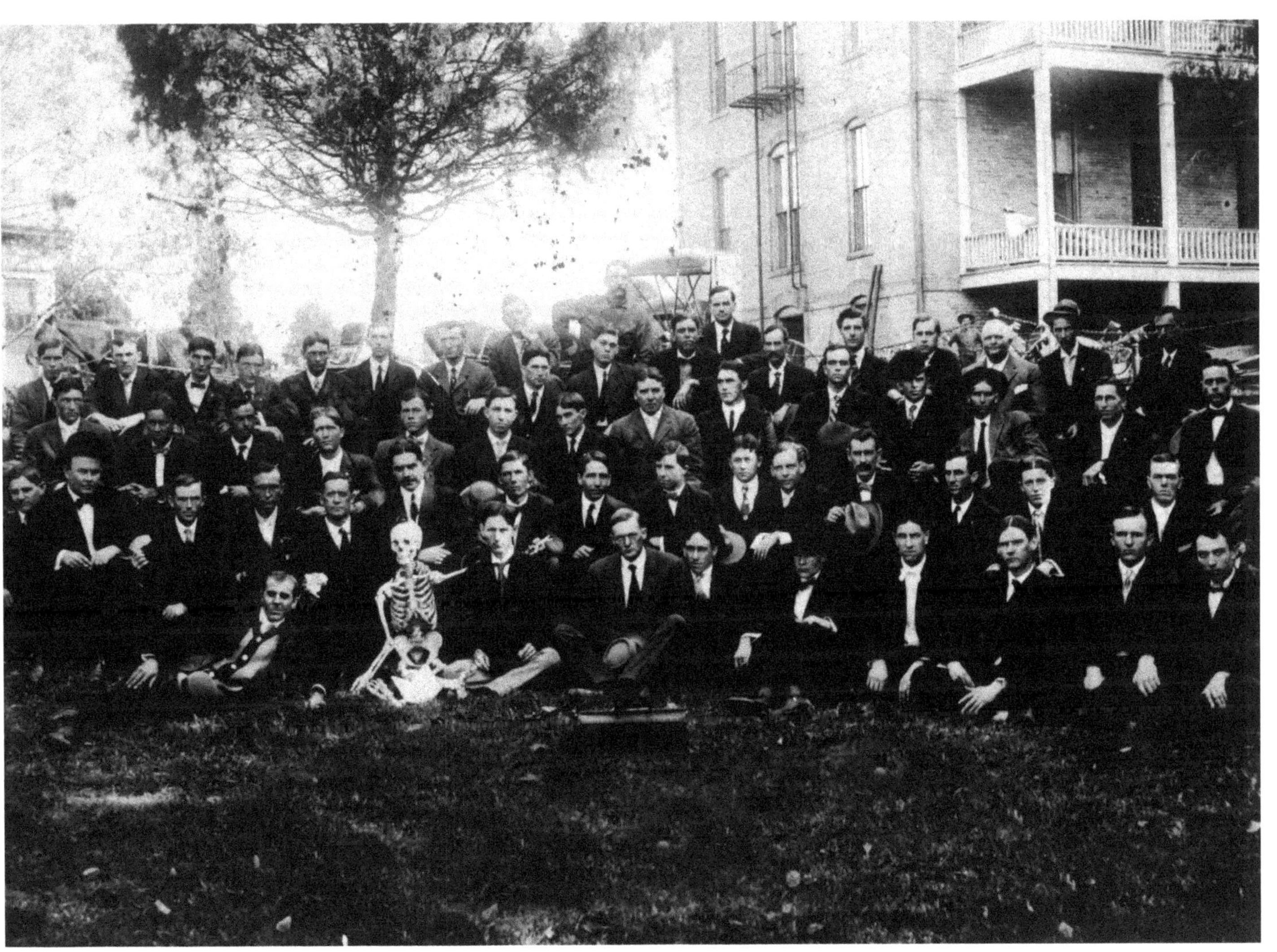

A 1908 group shot of medical students at the University of Arkansas for Medical Sciences. UAMS was founded in 1879 and today is the state's premier medical facility. It appears that the mascot for anatomy class campaigned for a spot in this class portrait.

A physical geography class takes a field trip to Pulaski Heights in 1908. Pulaski Heights, dating to the early 1890s, was one of Little Rock's first suburbs. It was incorporated by the city in 1916.

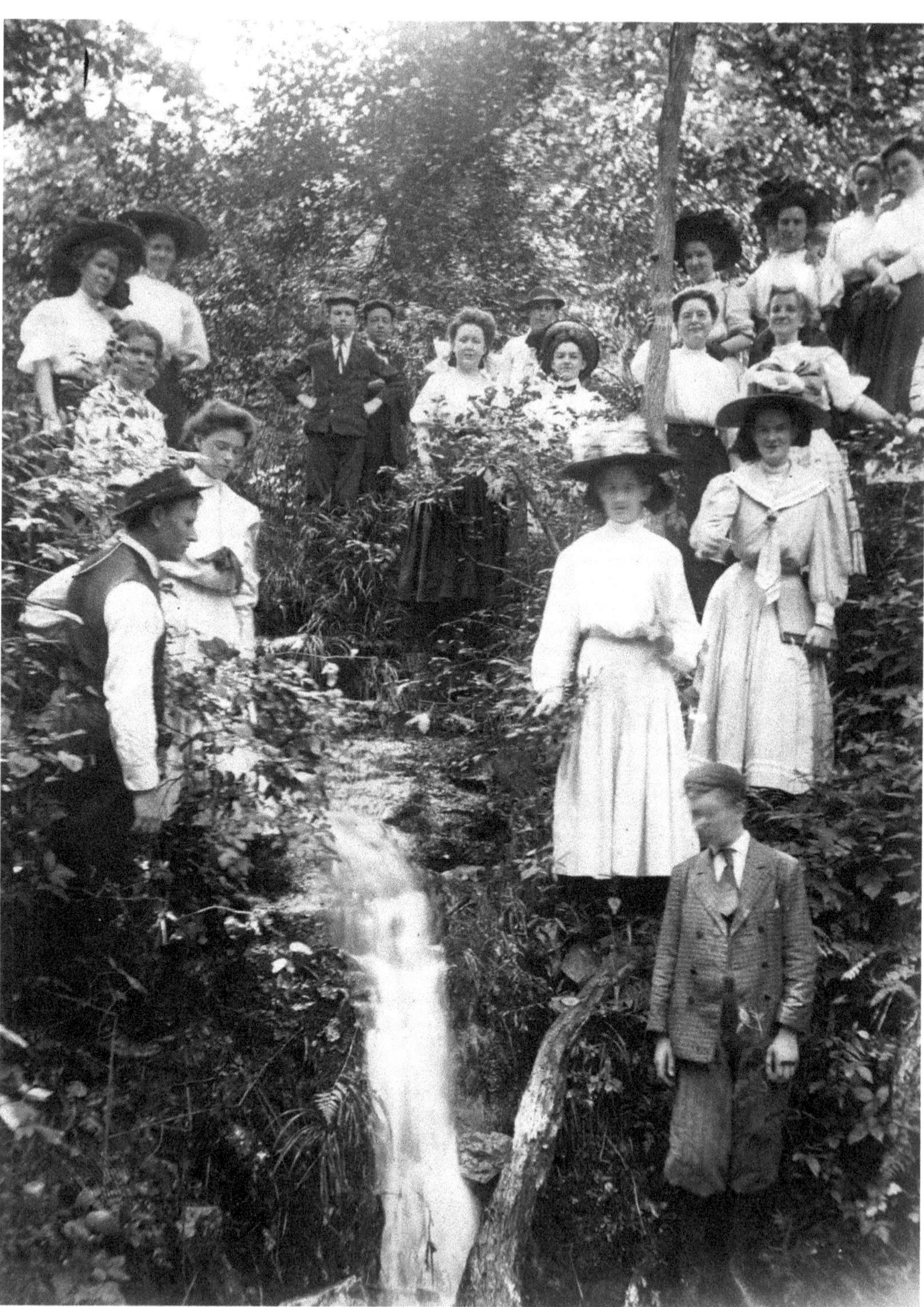

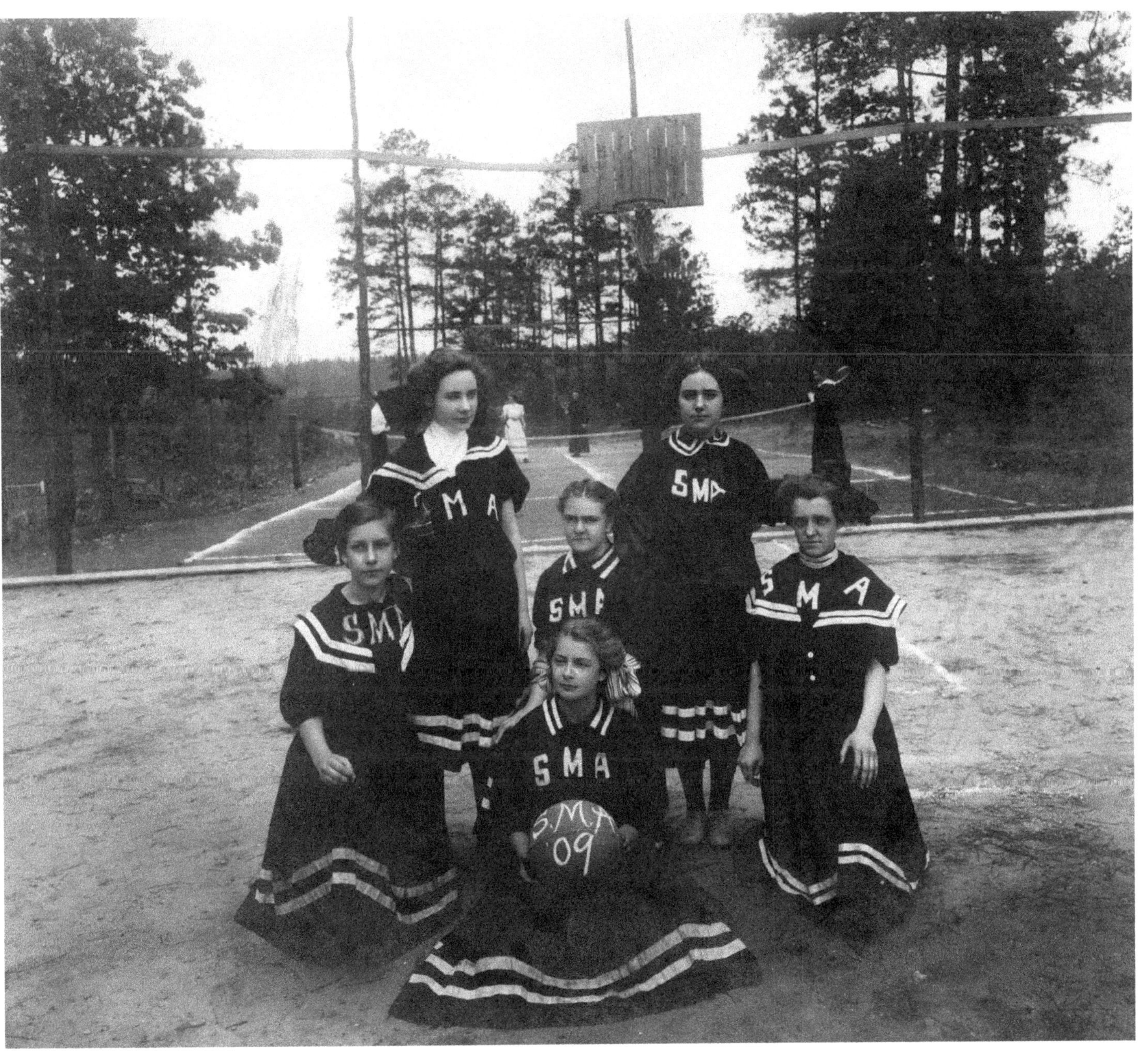

The Mount St. Mary's Academy 1909 basketball team. Behind these players, four women pose with racquets on a tennis court in what is evidently a doubles match in progress. Sports facilities have not always been well-endowed. This basketball court features a bare-earth surface and a backboard made of what appear to be boards from old shipping crates.

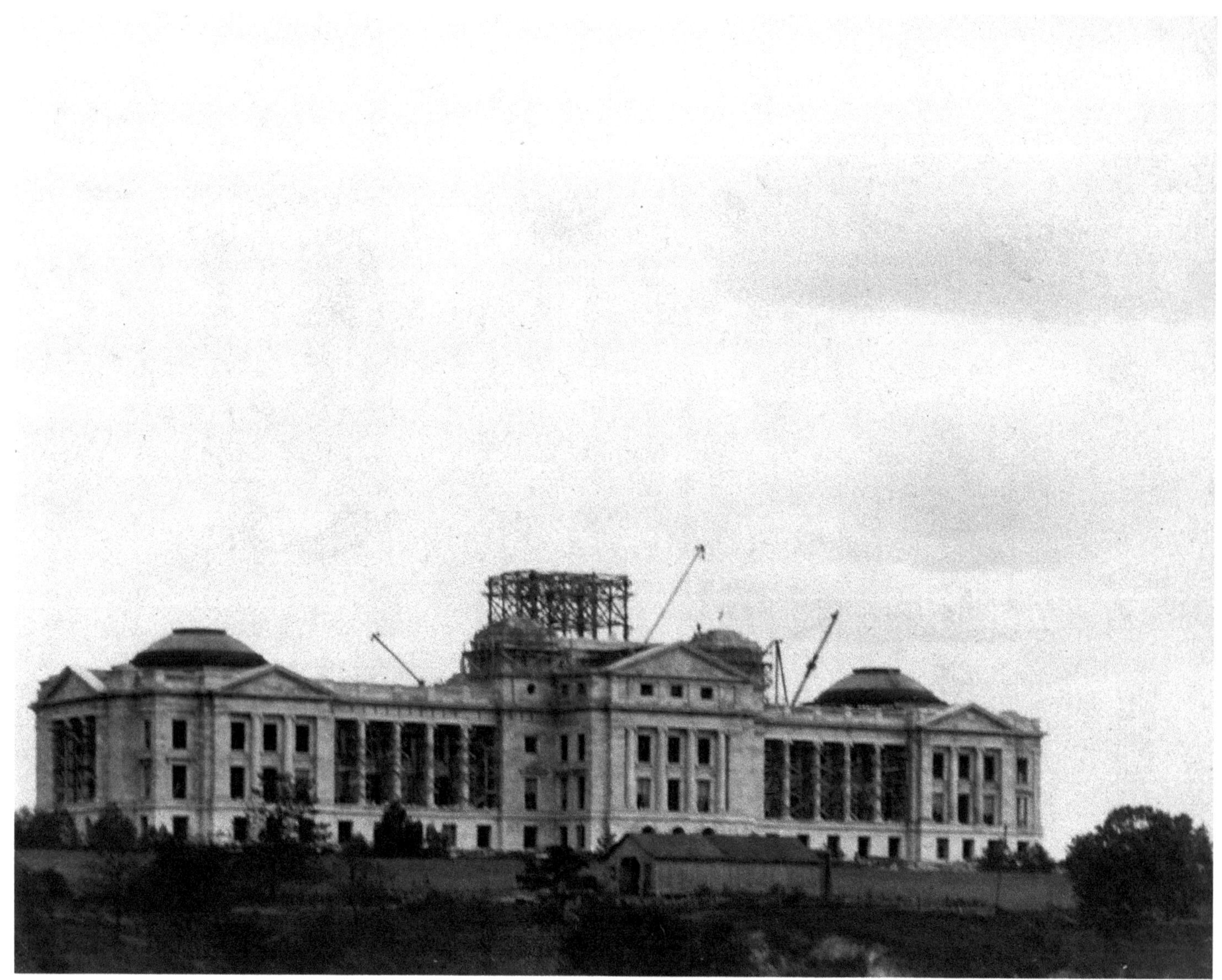

Construction of the Arkansas State Capitol as it appeared around 1910. The work had begun in 1899 but the Capitol was not completed until 1915, delayed by inefficiency and a bribery scandal. The edifice is a smaller-scale replica of the nation's Capitol in Washington, D.C.

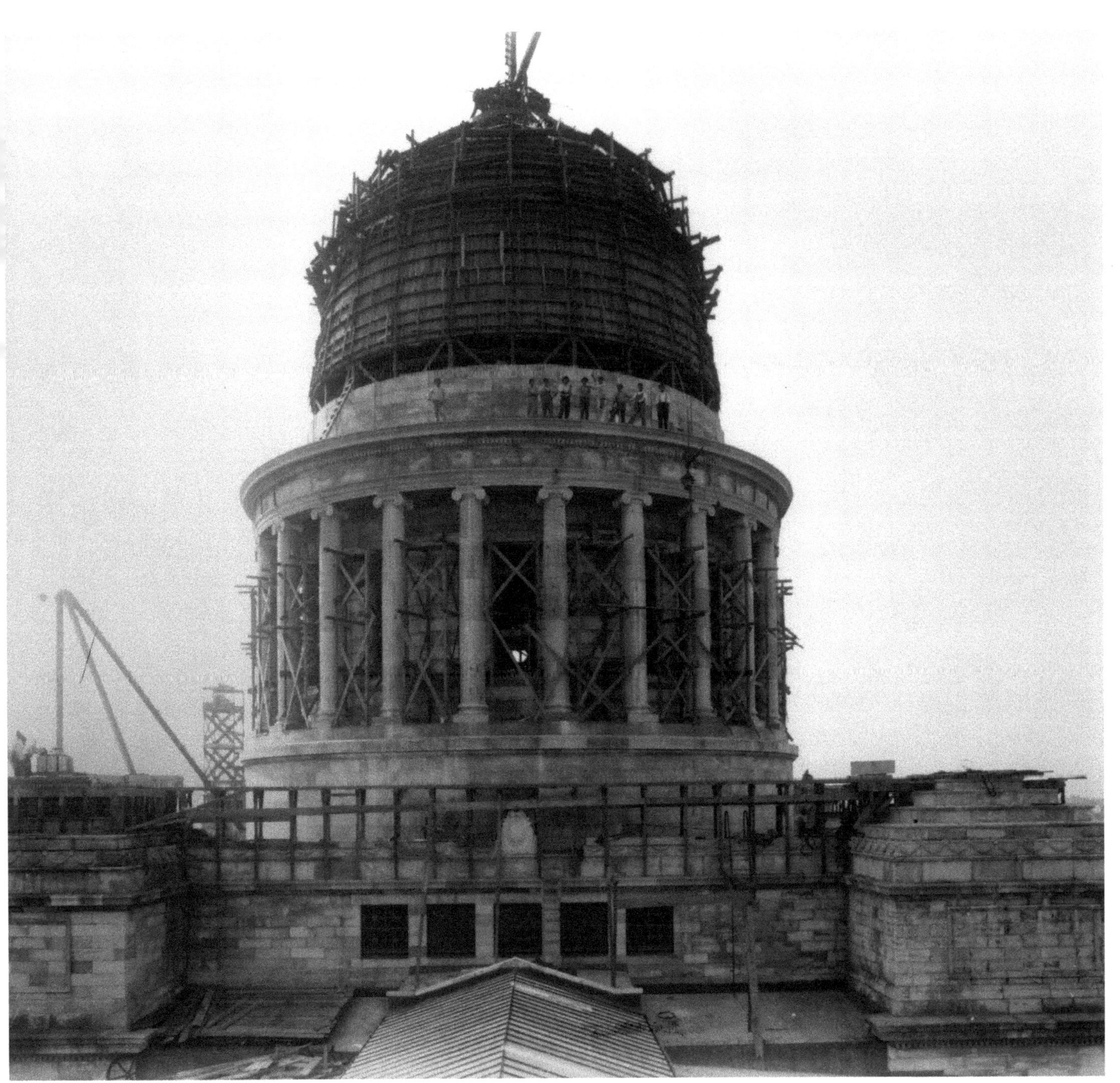

Construction of the Arkansas State Capitol, showing work in progress on the dome.

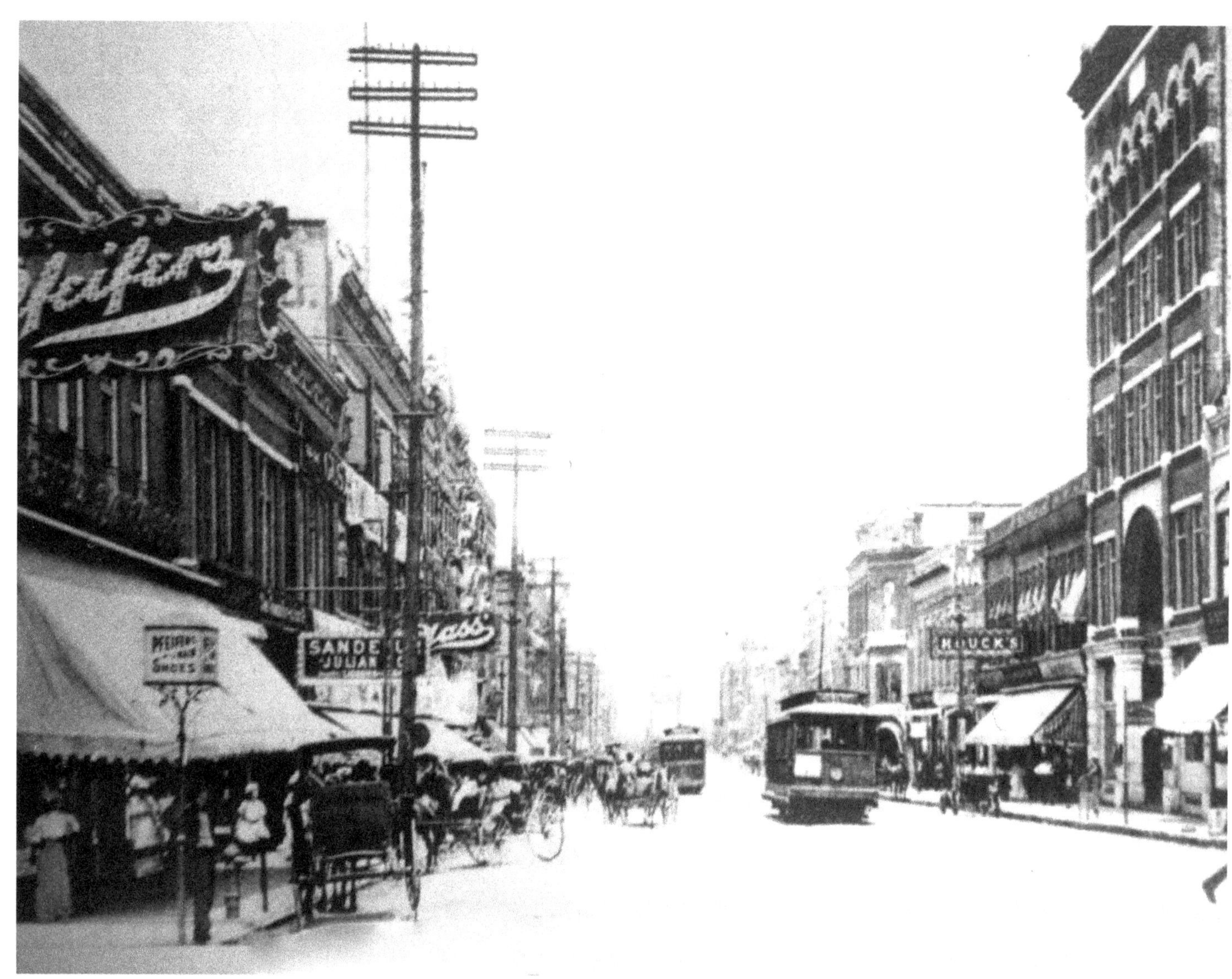

A single automobile is visible in this early 1900s view of downtown Little Rock.

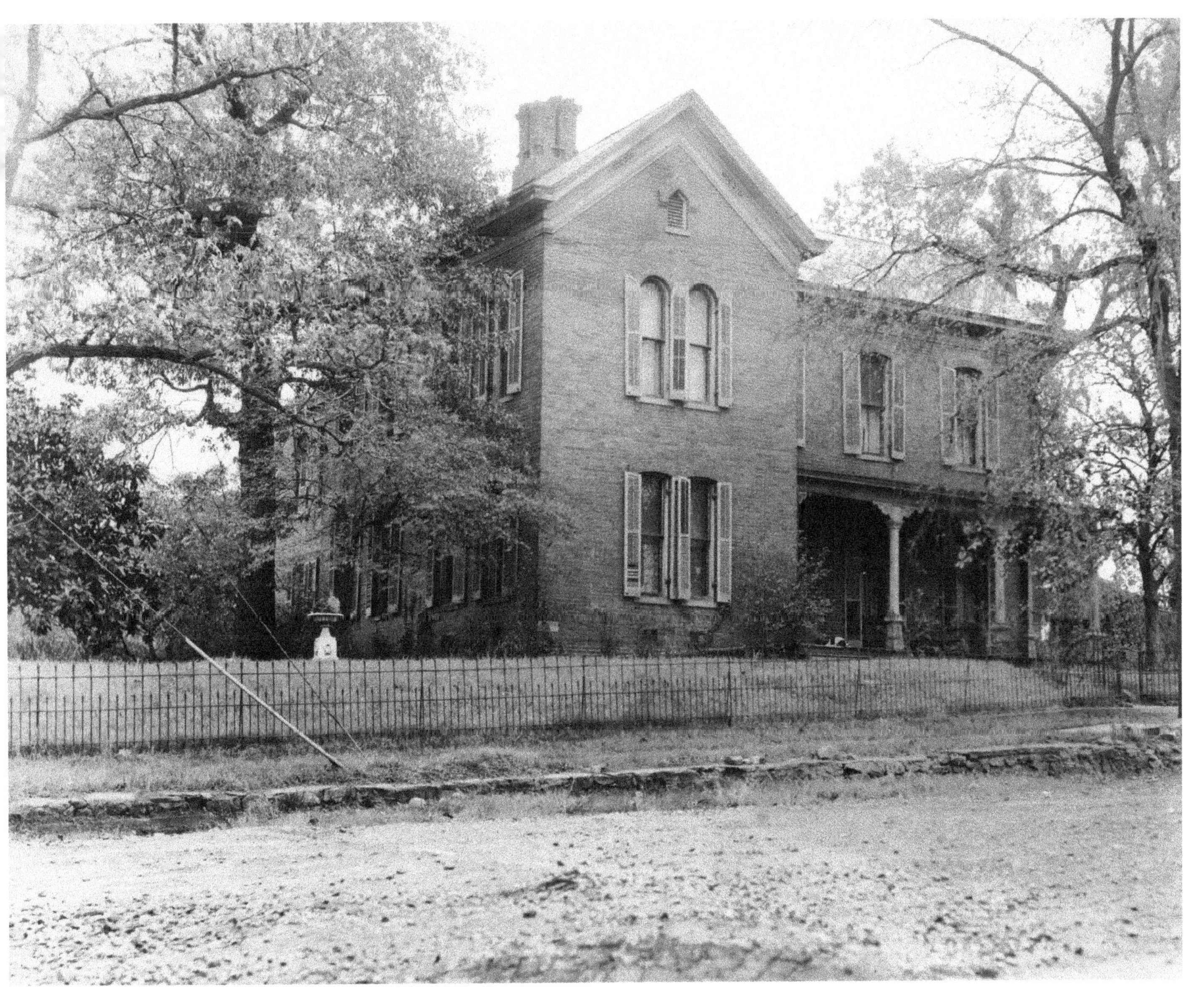

The George Reichardt House, located at 505 Rector Avenue, around 1910.

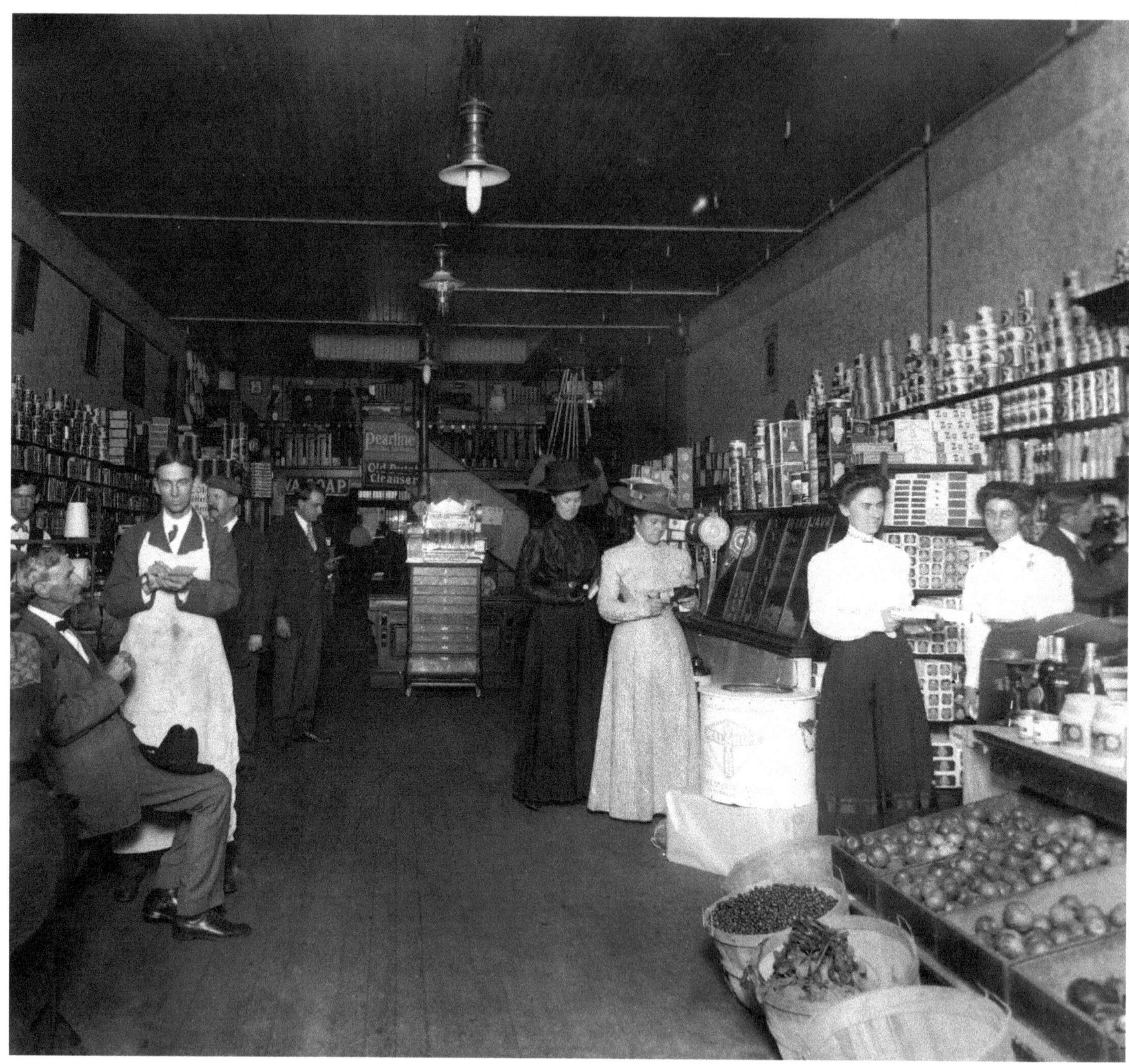

Indoors at C. J. Kramer and Company, around 1910. This general store offered a wide variety of products. On the shelf at right are boxes of Zu Zu gingersnaps, an early product of the National Biscuit Company, familiar today as Nabisco.

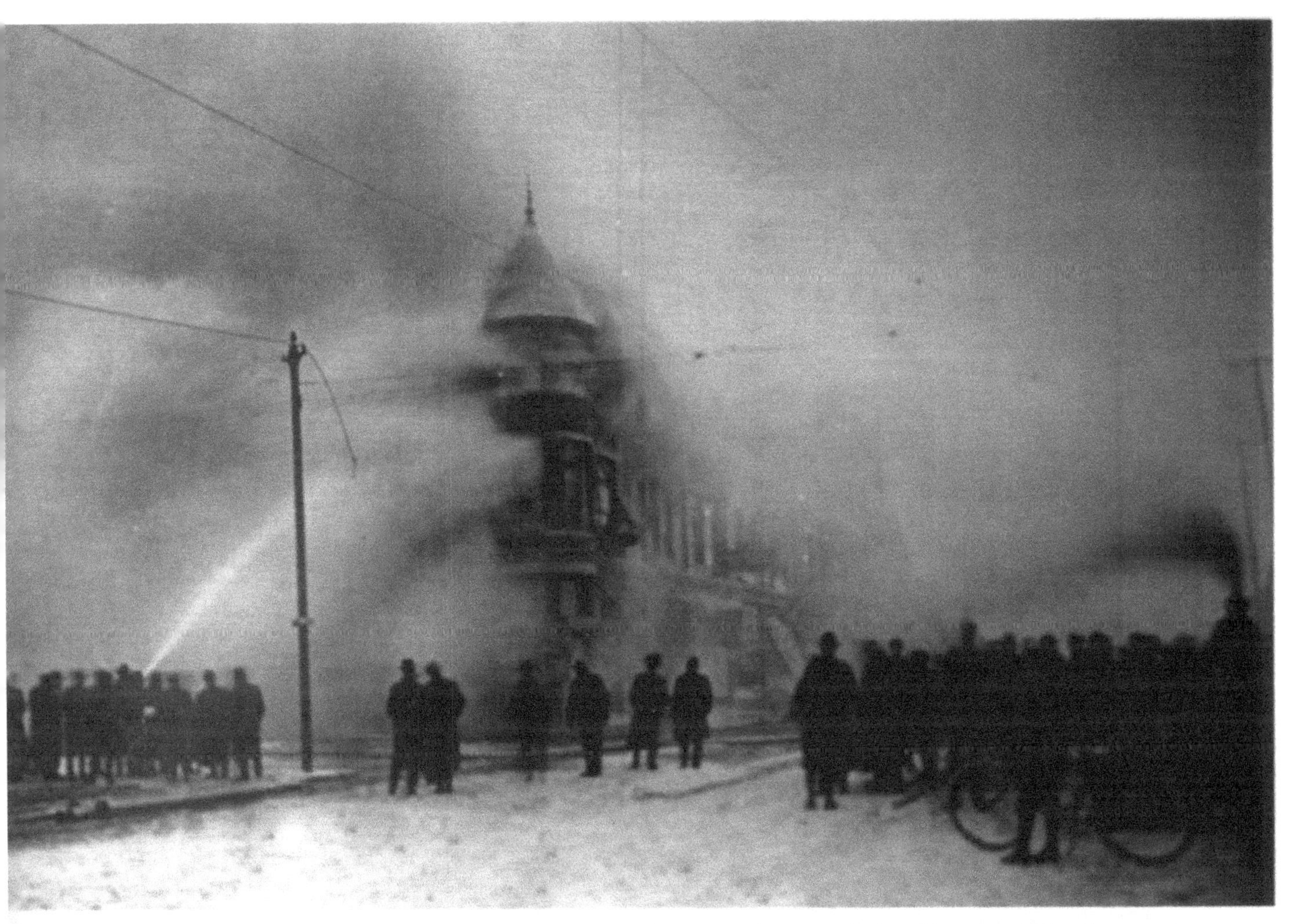

The worst fire in Little Rock's history was started by two boys working late at the Hollenberg Music Store on January 3, 1911. One boy threw a cigarette into a box of oily rags. Five hours later flames burst through the upper windows of the building. Inadequate water pressure and equipment were blamed after fire fighters failed to extinguish the blaze. Almost an entire block of Main Street was lost in what became known as the million-dollar fire.

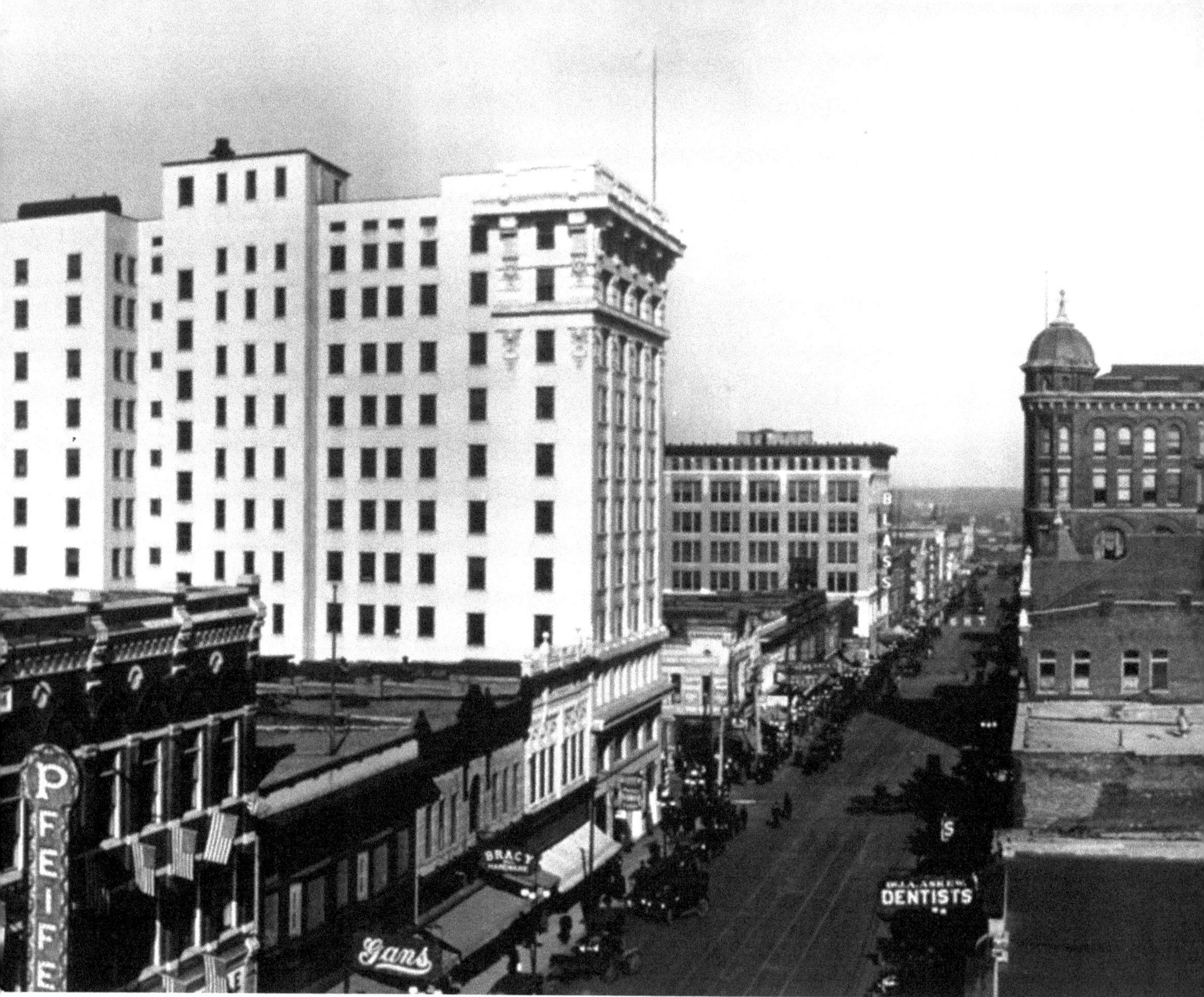

Bird's-eye panorama of Little Rock.

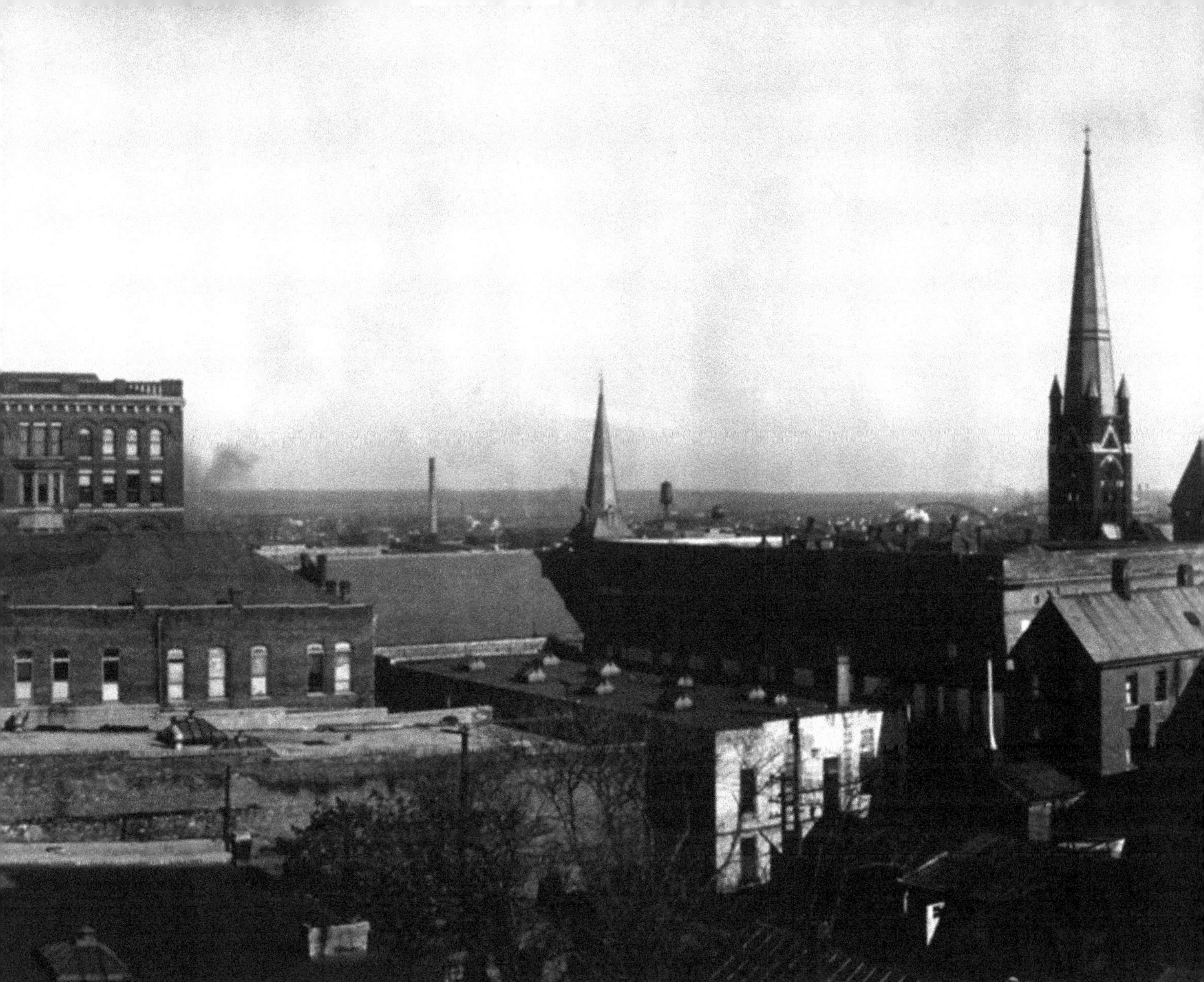

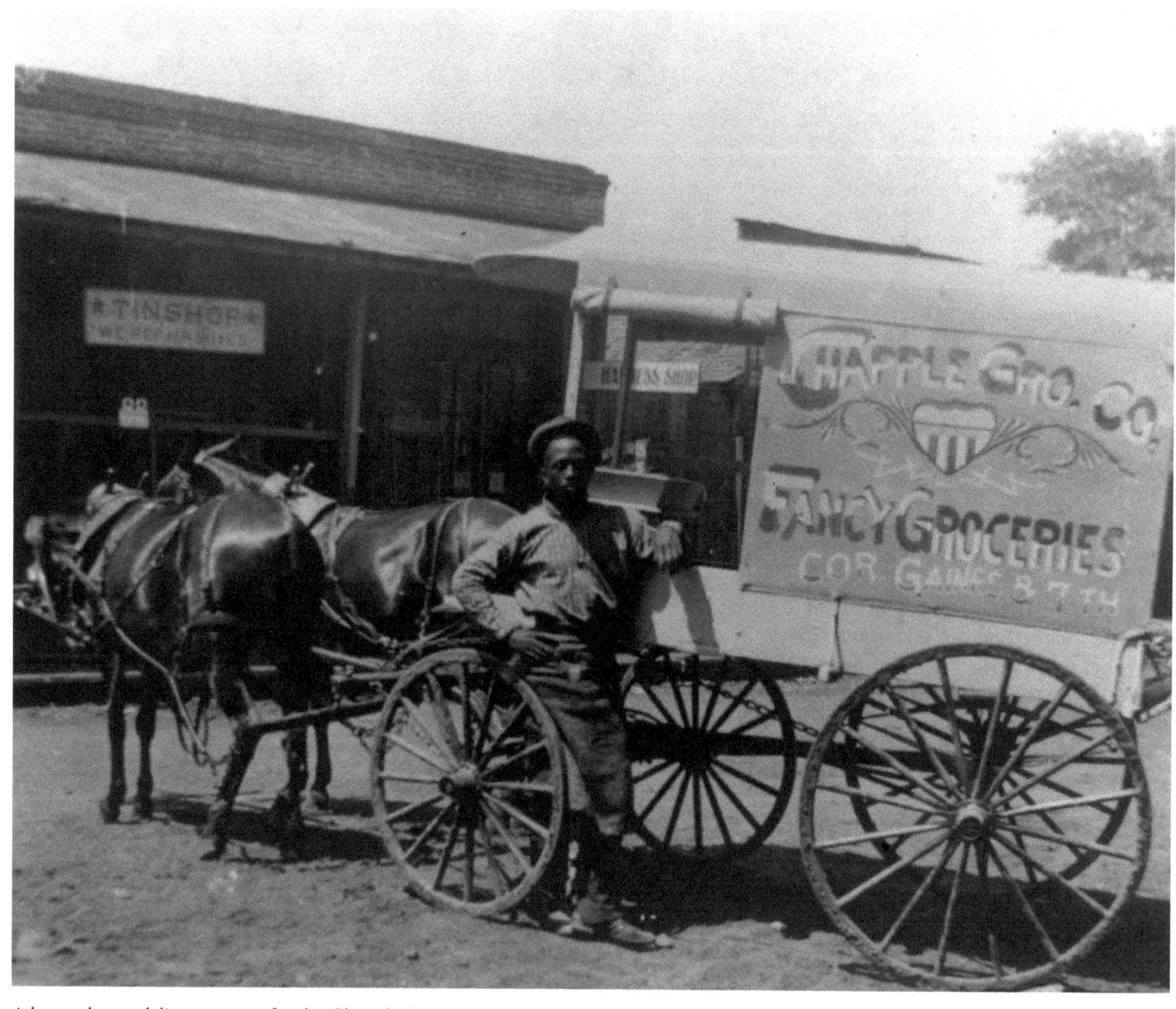

A horse-drawn delivery wagon for the Chapple Grocery Company, which was located at Seventh and Gaines.

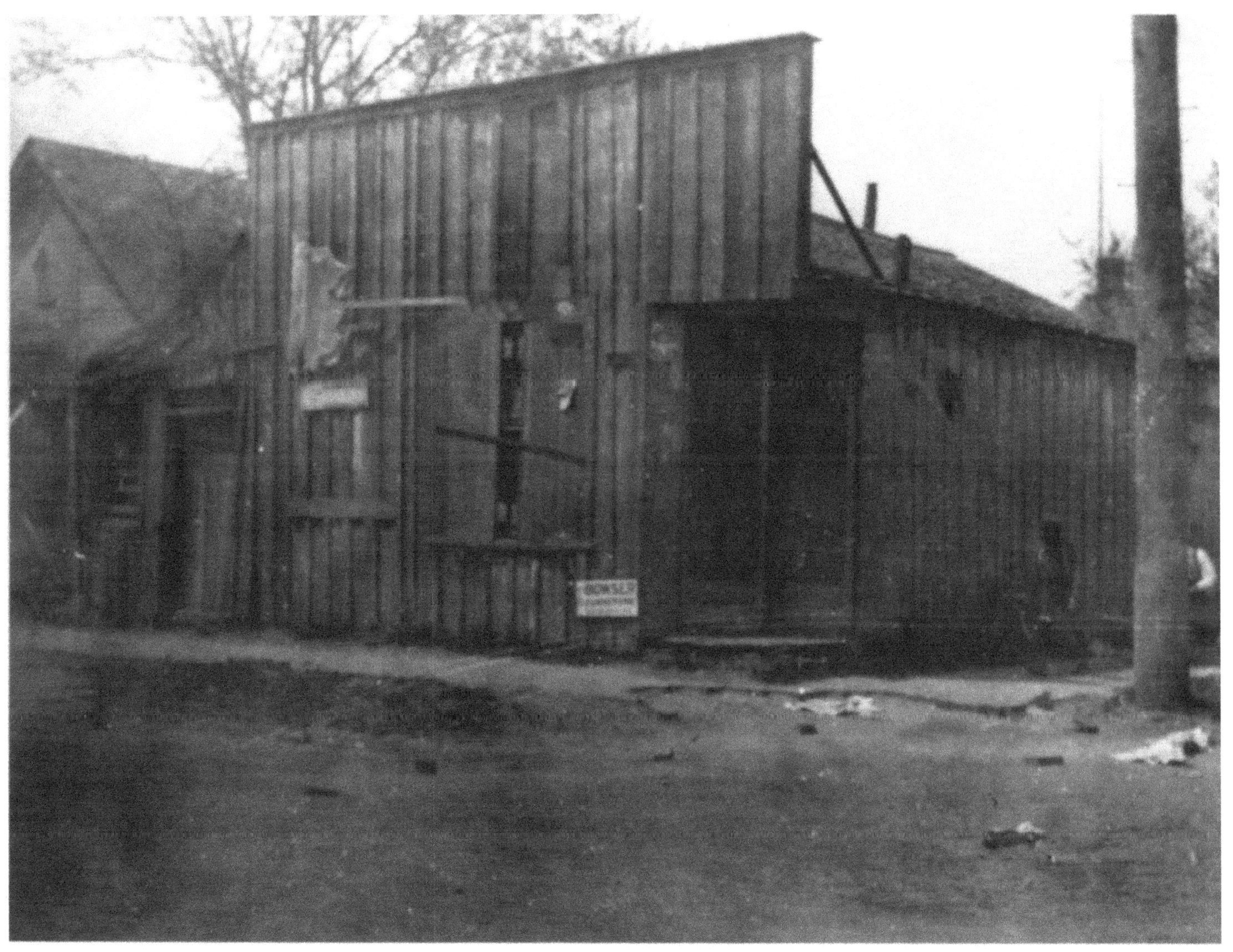

On the outside of this unidentified wooden building is an advertisement for Bowser Furniture, which was located at 210 Main Street in downtown Little Rock.

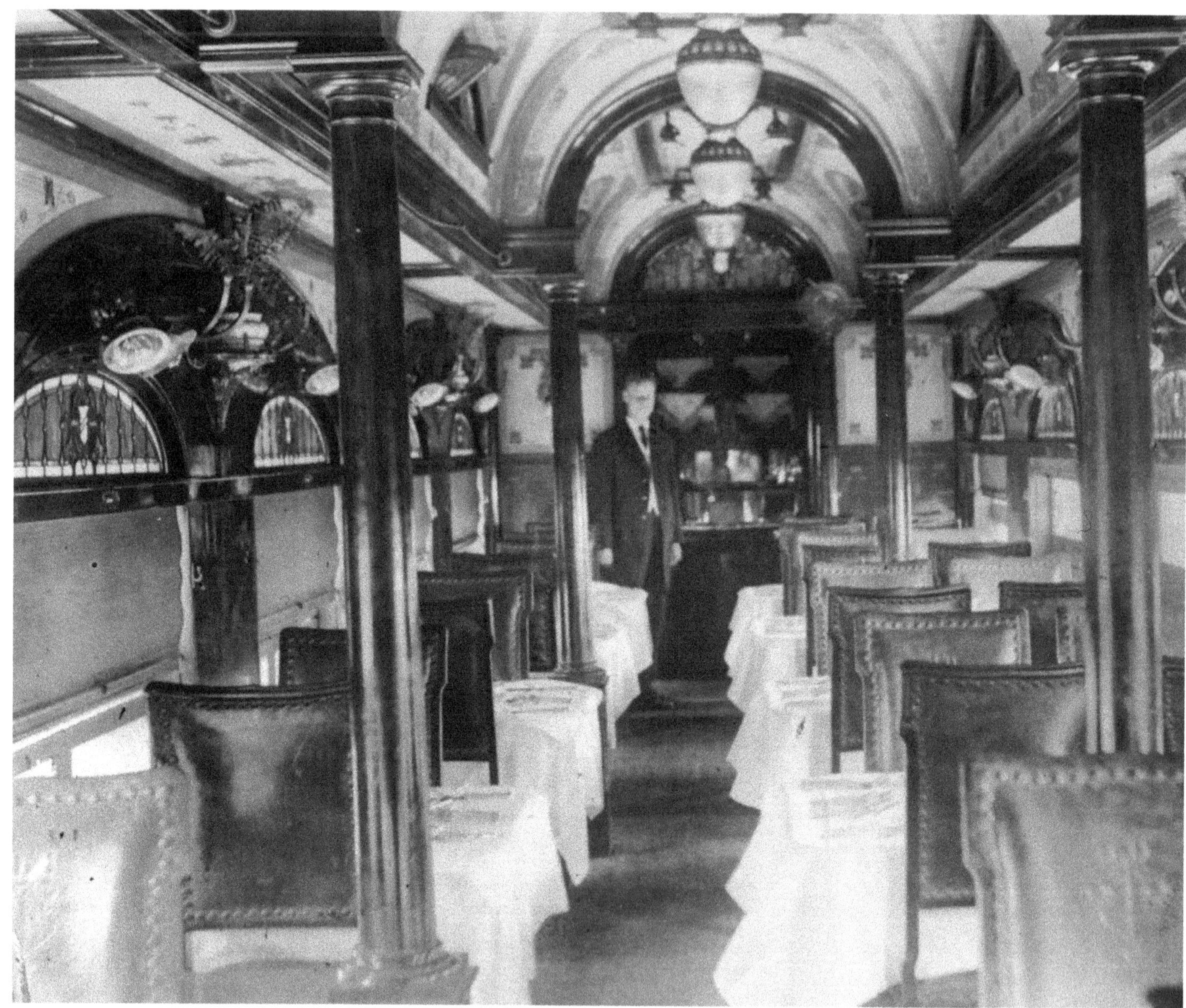

The dining car of the Donaghey and Bryan special train, with its plush interior and stained-glass transoms, is illustrative of the finest in railroad accommodations during the golden era of the railroads. From September 6 to 10, 1910, Governor George W. Donaghey and William Jennings Bryan toured Arkansas stumping for the adoption of the proposed Initiative and Referendum amendment to the state constitution. The tour covered 1,750 miles and included 55 speeches. The amendment passed, becoming the seventh amendment of article five in the constitution.

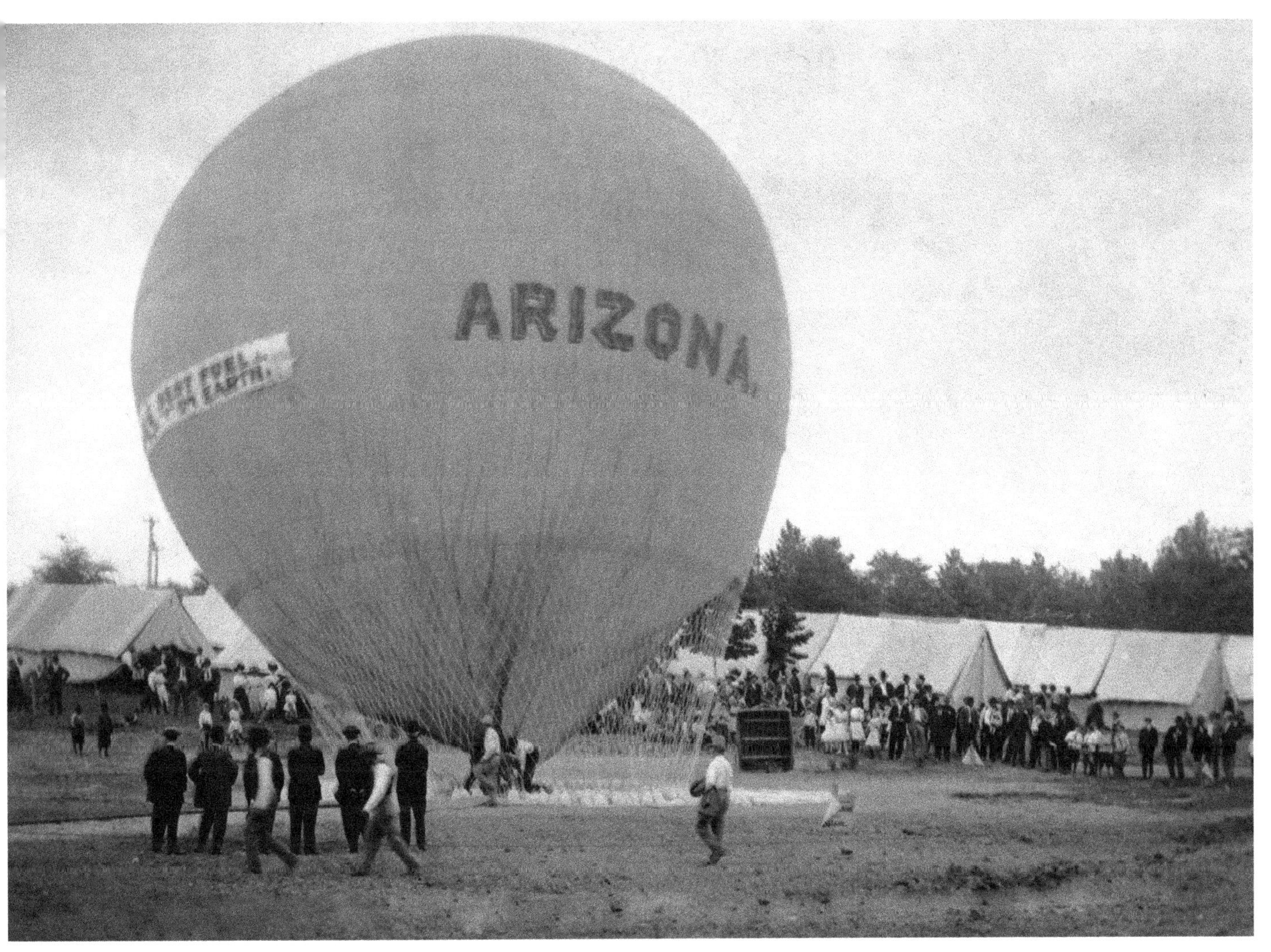

The hot-air balloon *Arizona* is grounded at Camp Shaver at City Park (now MacArthur Park) during the United Confederate Veterans Reunion held May 16-18, 1911. Camp Shaver provided free temporary housing for veterans during the reunion and consisted of approximately 1,330 tents. It was named for Colonel Robert G. Shaver, who commanded the Seventh Arkansas Regiment for the Confederate Army during the Civil War. This image and several to follow all depict various activities at the reunion.

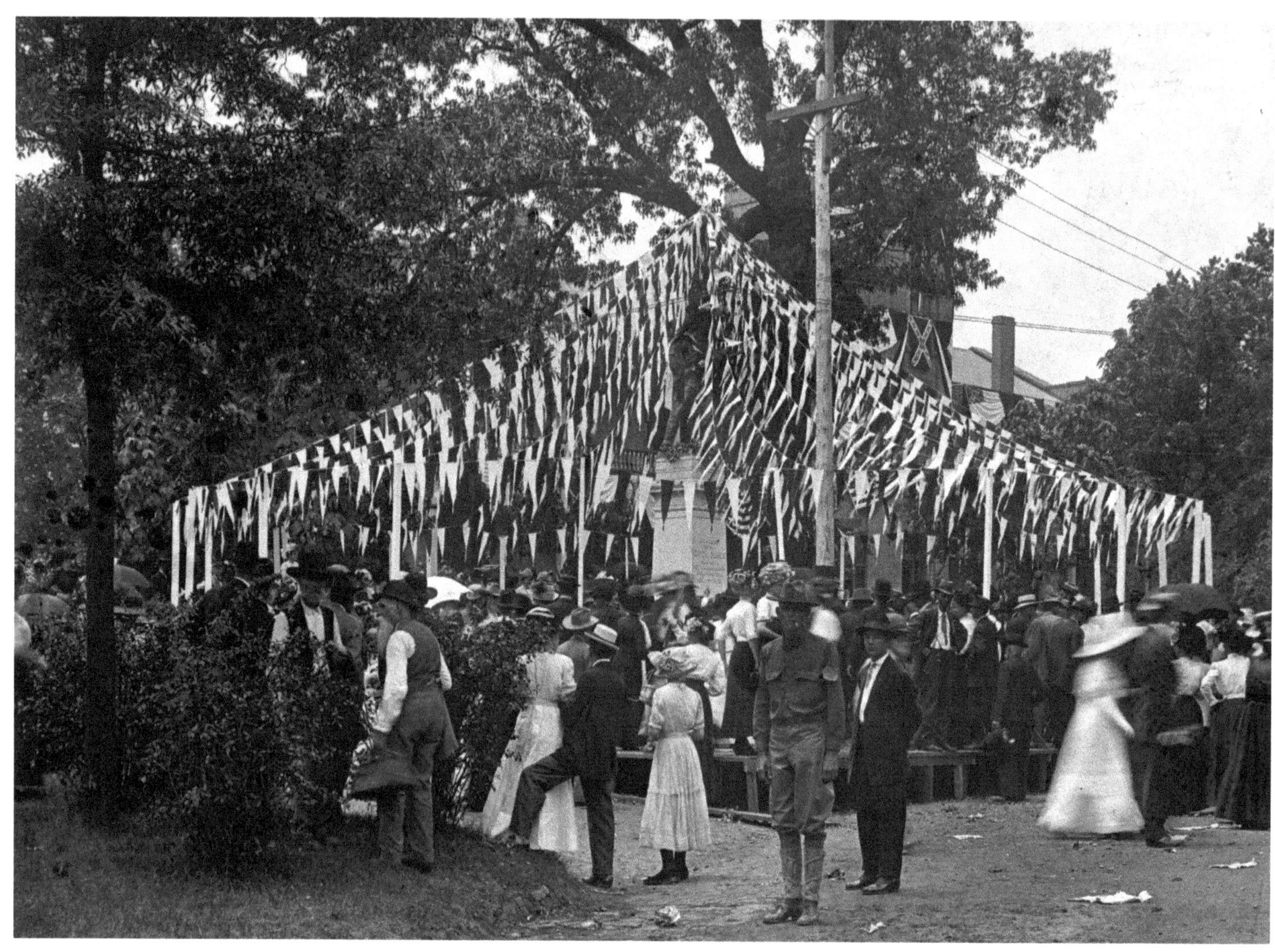

Spectators gather to watch the unveiling of a monument to the Capital Guard at City Park sometime during the May reunion. The monument was erected in memory of the members of Company A, Sixth Arkansas Infantry, Cleburne's Division, who fought during the Civil War.

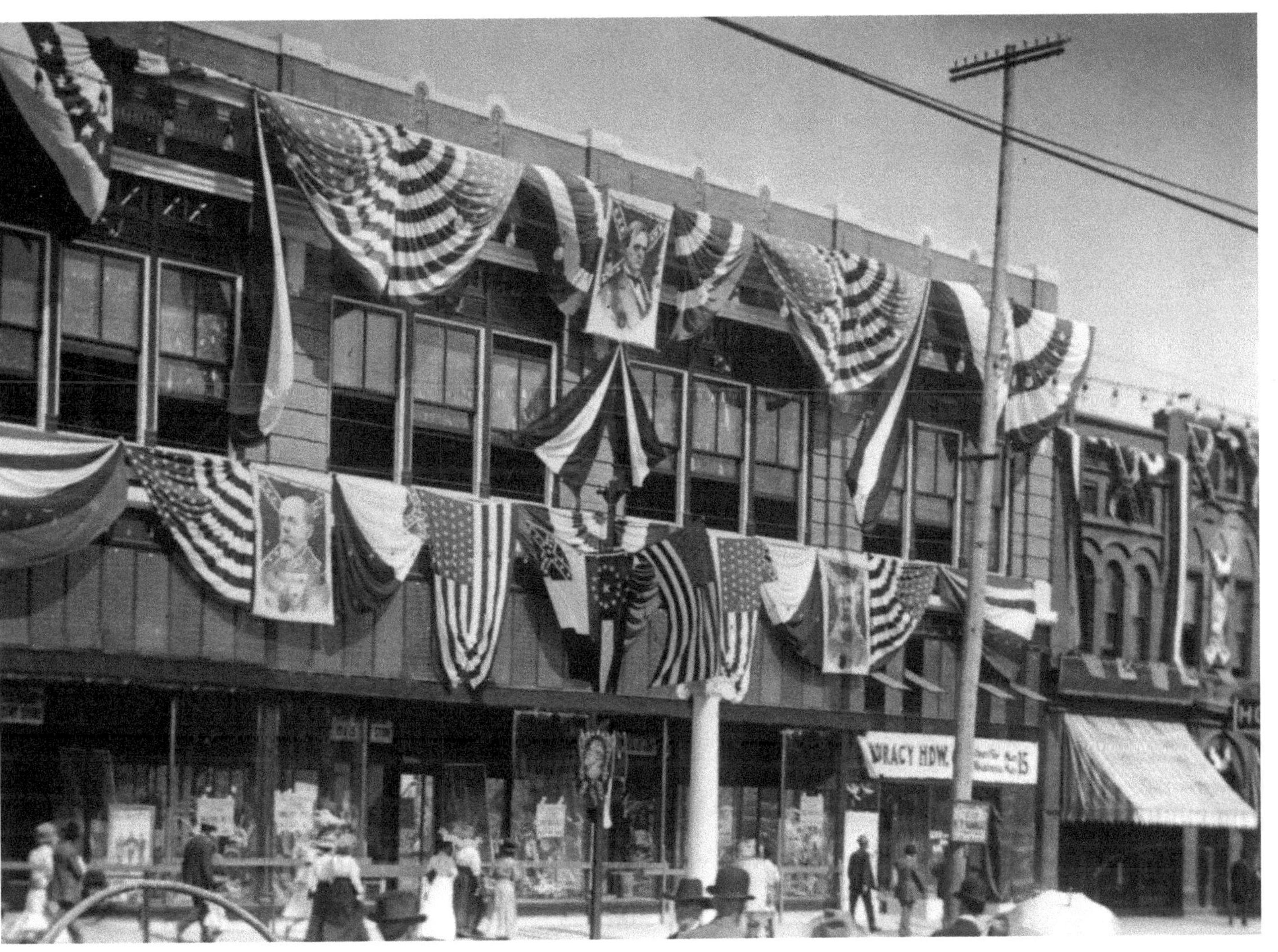

The S. H. Kress and Company's 5-10-15 Cent Store, located on the 600 block of Main Street, is decorated with banners and flags for the United Confederate Veterans Reunion on May 16.

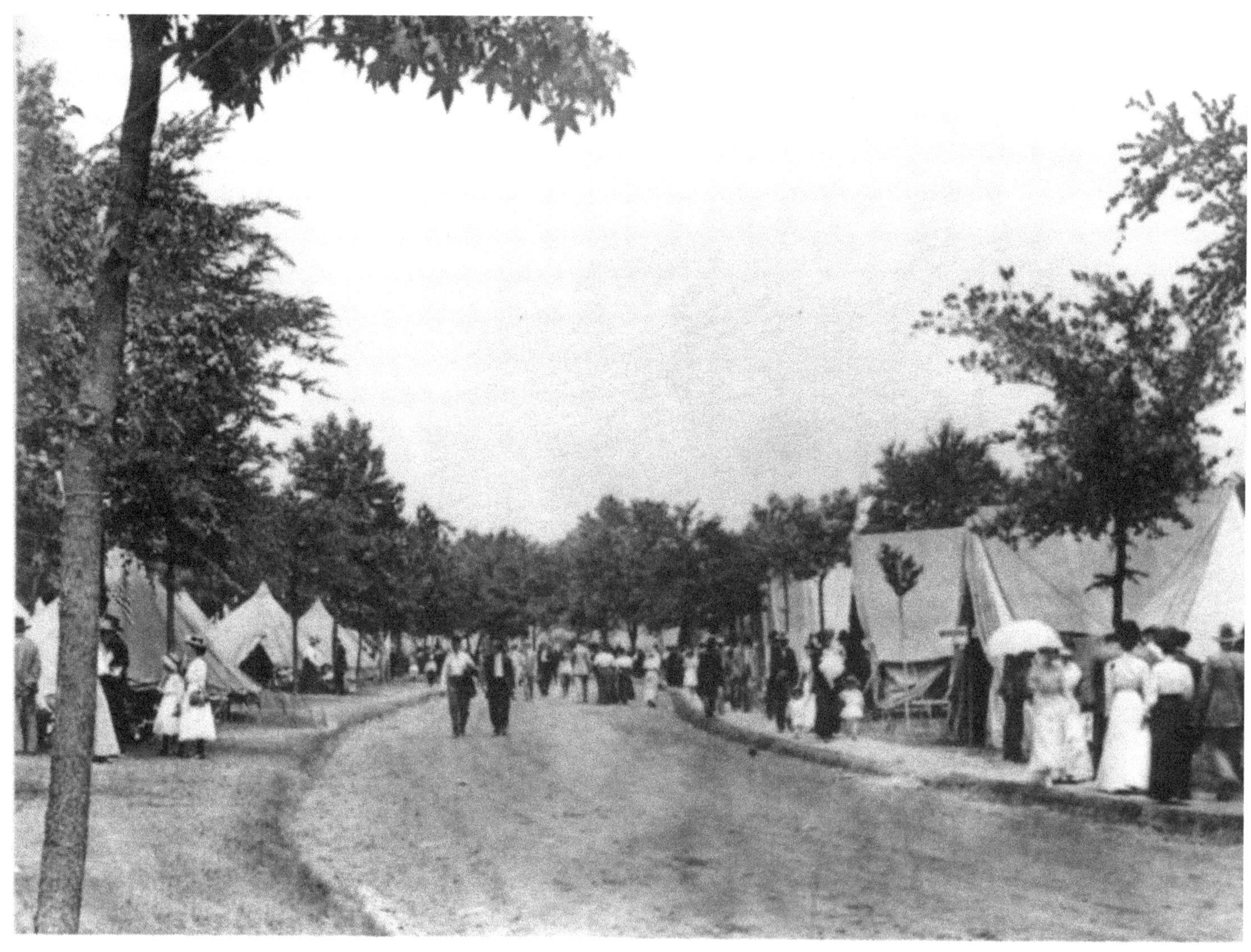

Attendees stroll through Camp Shaver, visiting Civil War veterans. The reunion drew more than 140,000 people, among them 12,000 veterans, and was on record as the largest event in Little Rock history throughout most of the twentieth century.

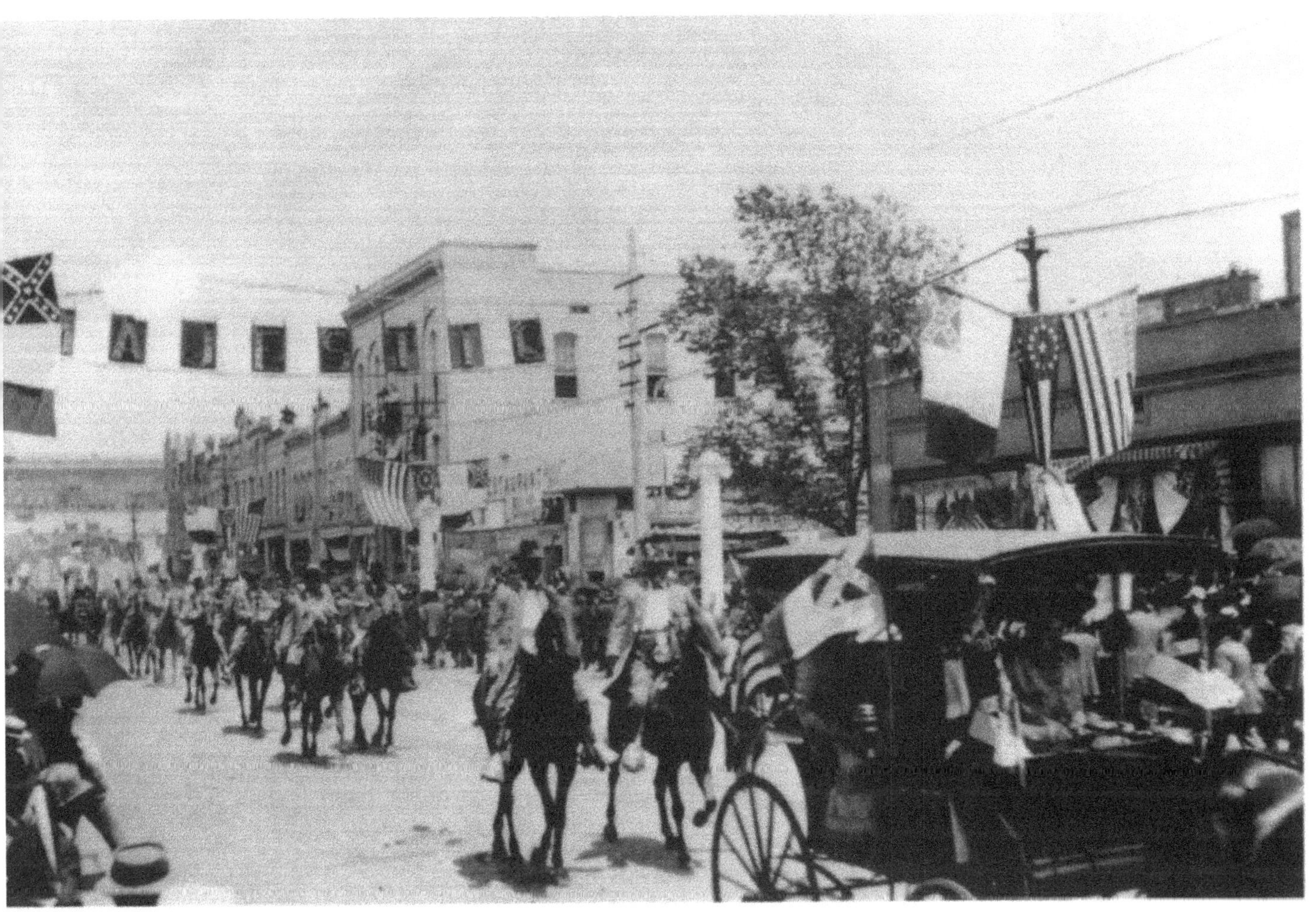

Men on horseback follow a carriage past the 800 block of Main Street in a parade on May 18. The parade, which ran from the Old State House to City Park and back again, was the highlight of the reunion. So many people participated that the parade needed two hours to pass any given observation point.

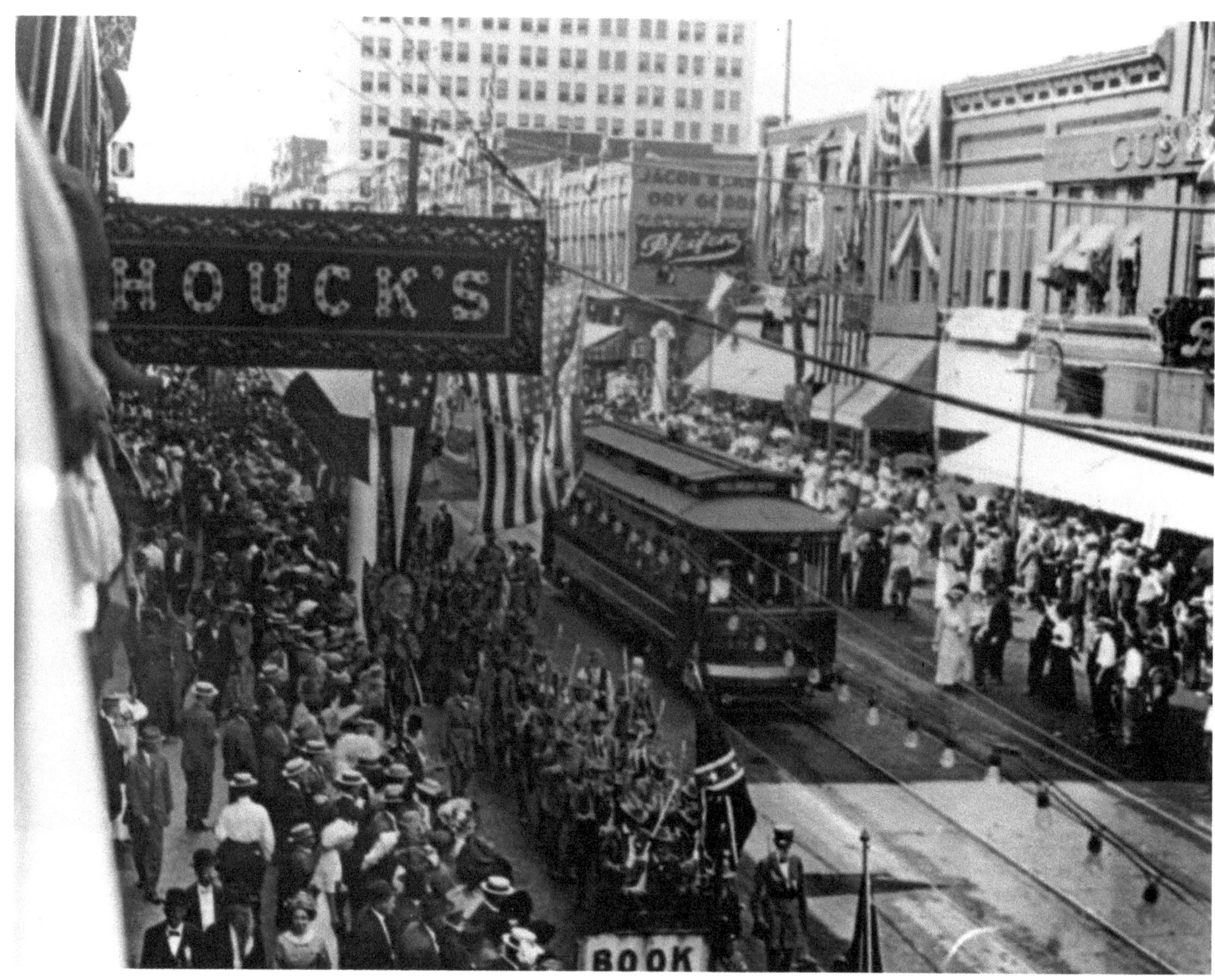

A view of the 300 block of Main Street during the Confederate Veterans' reunion parade.

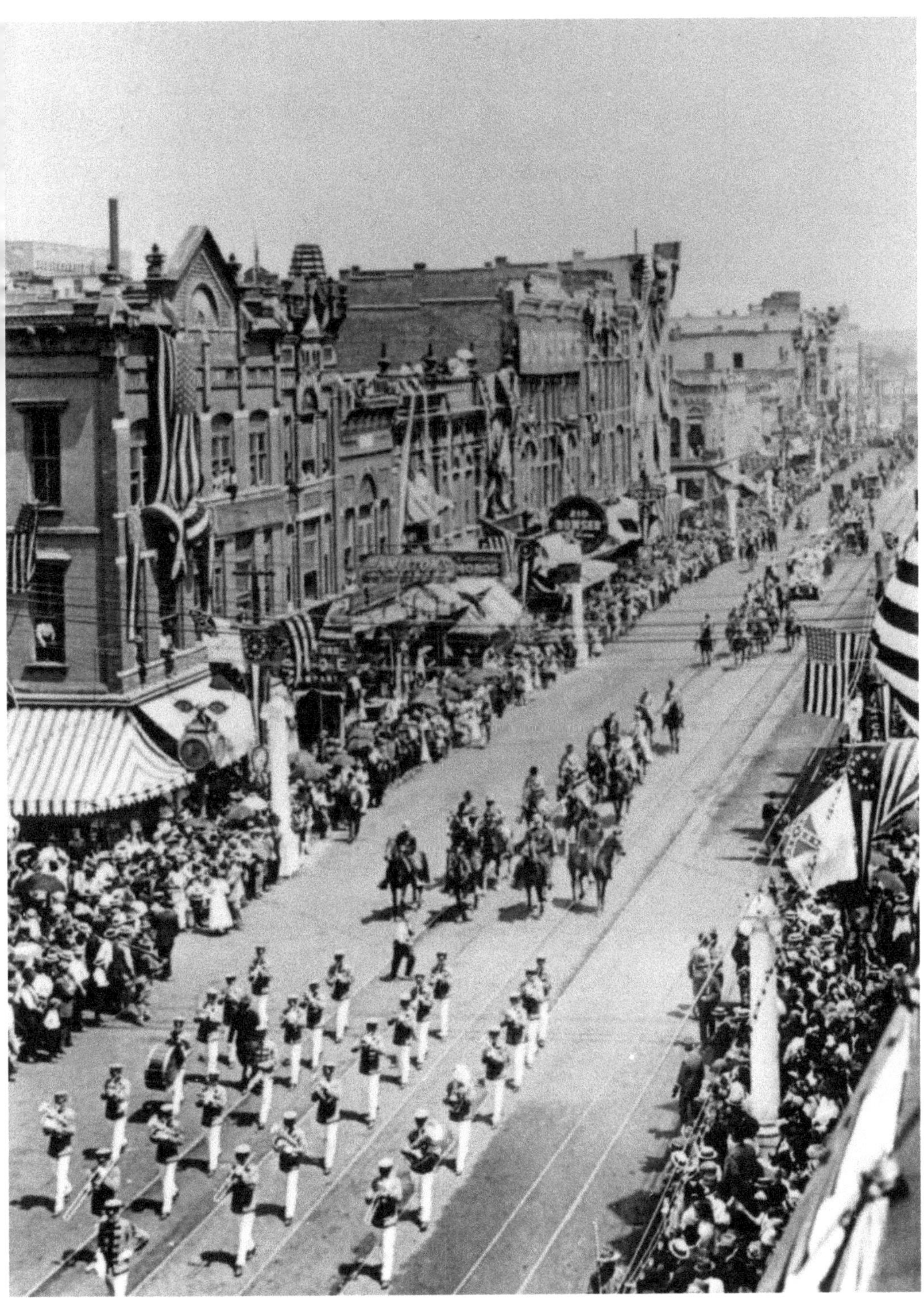

A rooftop view of the reunion parade in progress, facing north toward the 200 block of Main Street.

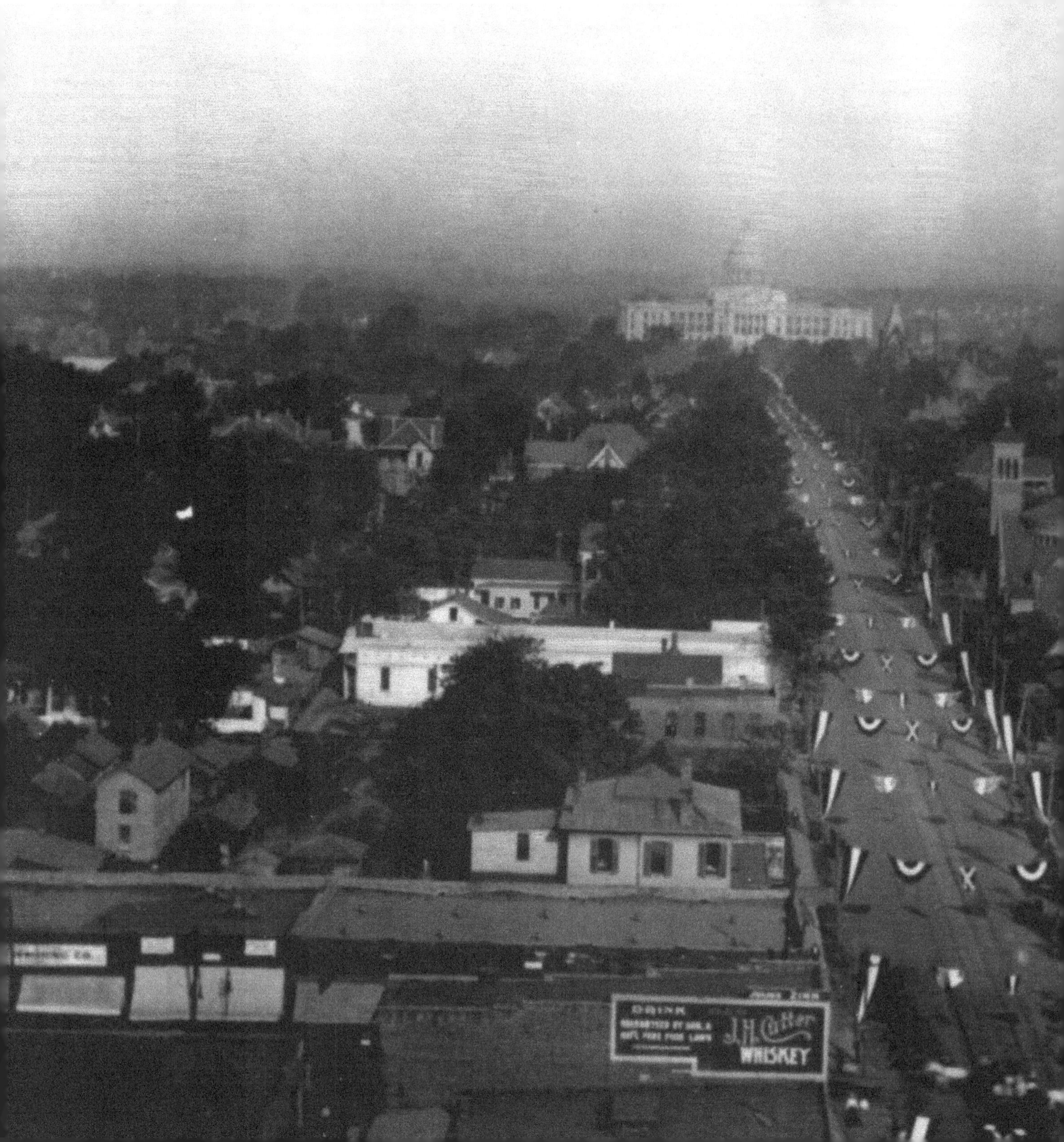
DRINK
J.H. Cutter
WHISKEY

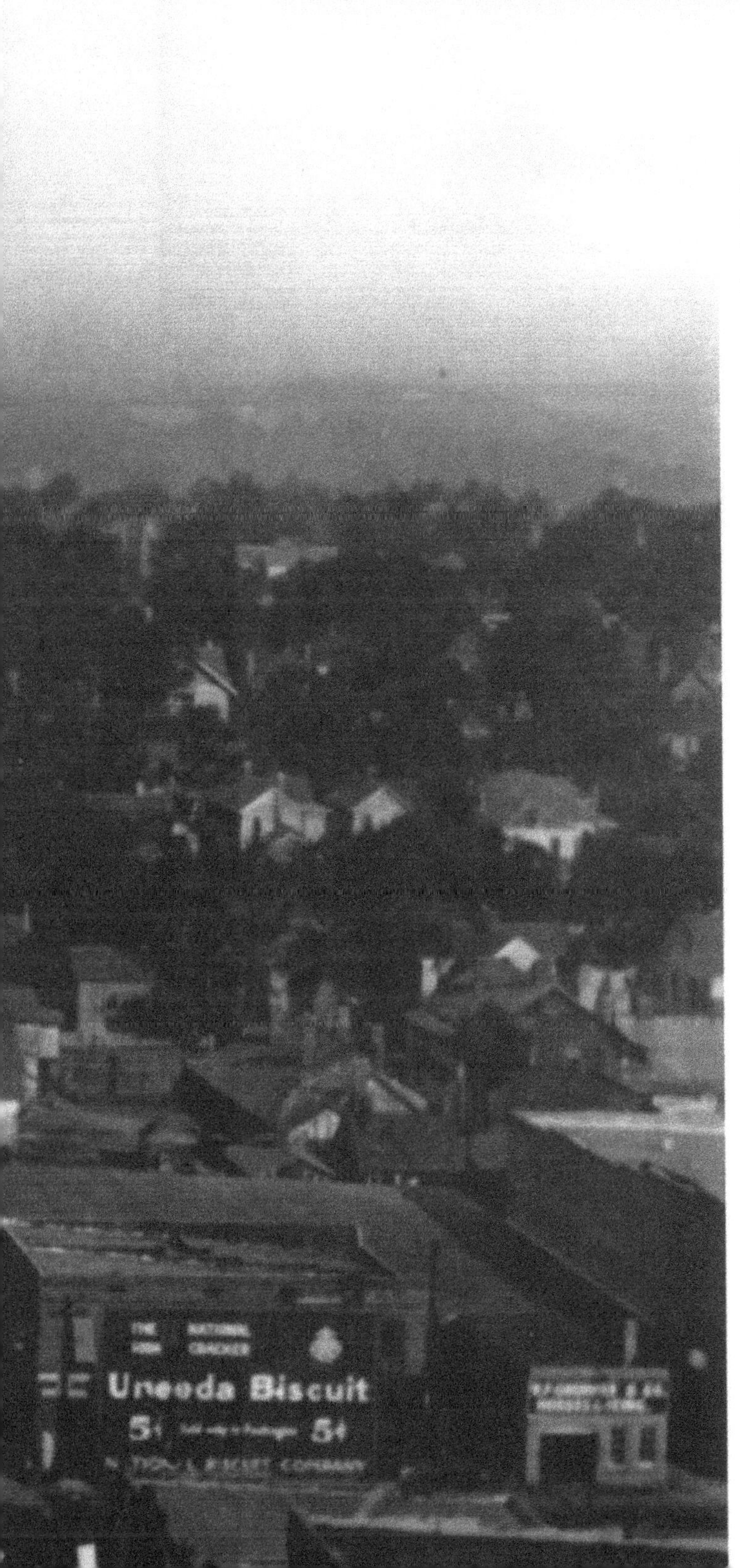

Facing west down Fifth Street (now Capitol Avenue) toward the State Capitol from the top of the State National Bank Building (today's Boyle Building) during the United Confederate Veterans Reunion. The reunion concluded the evening of May 18 with a veterans' ball attended by 5,800 guests.

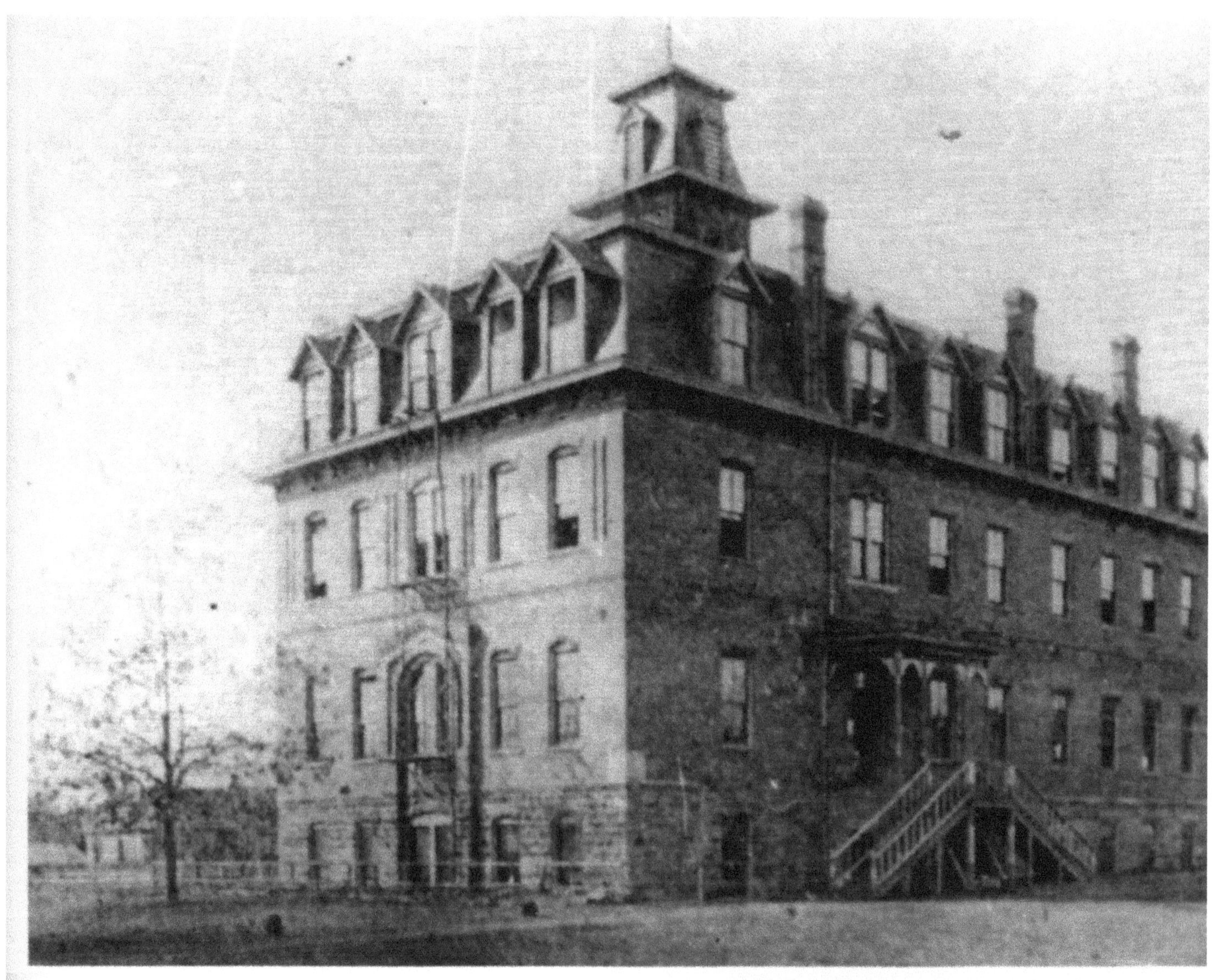

The main building of Arkansas Baptist College, located on High Street, in 1911. Arkansas Baptist College was founded in 1884 as the Ministers' Institute by the Colored Baptists of the State of Arkansas. In 1885 the campus relocated to Sixteenth and High Street, where it remains today.

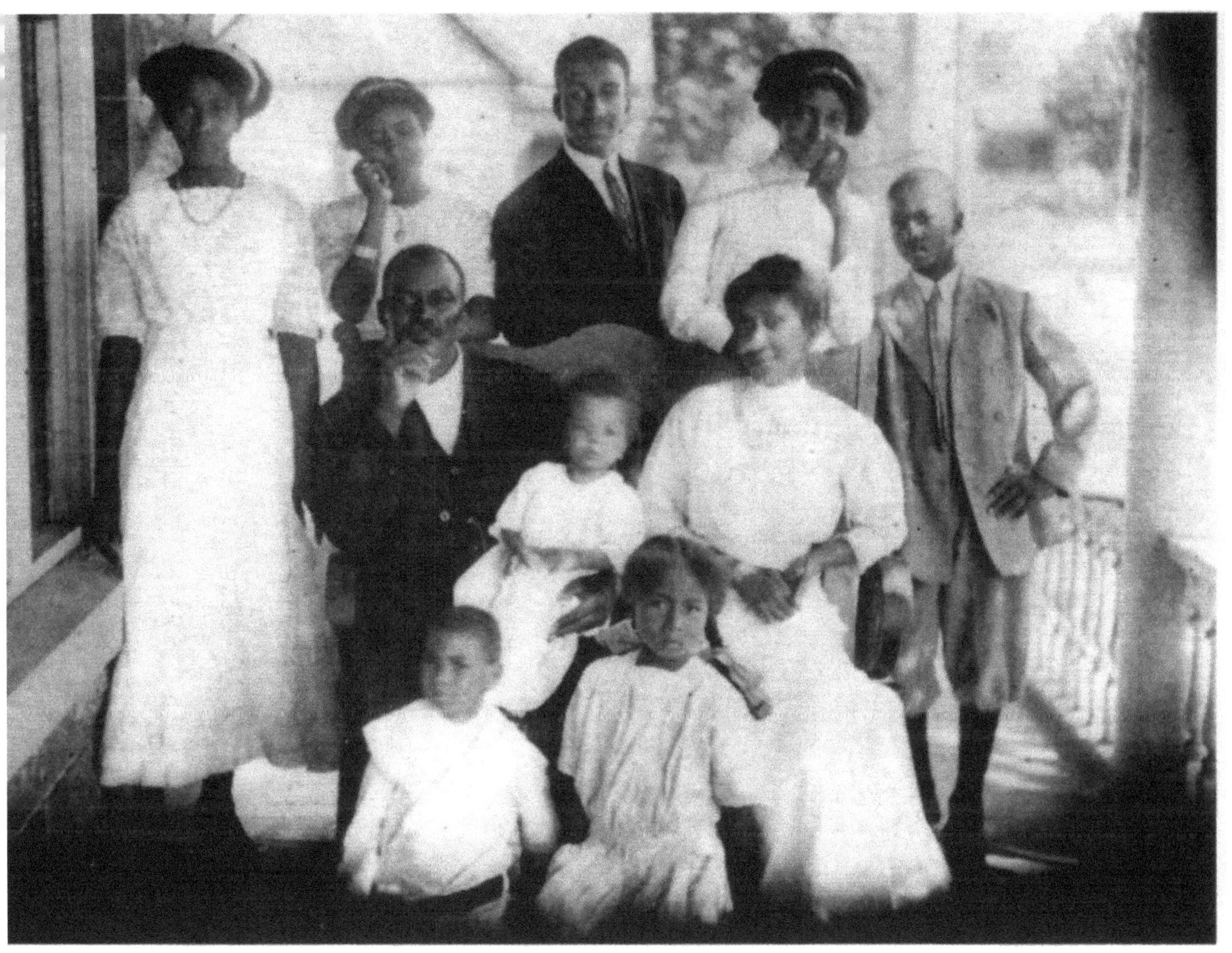

The Joseph Booker family in 1911. Booker was an ordained minister and the president of Arkansas Baptist College for 39 years (1887–1926). Pictured are, back row (left to right): Helen M., Carrie J., Joseph Robert, Mattie A., and William A.; and front row: Joseph A., Baby James H., Mrs. Mary C., Walter M., and Sarah A.

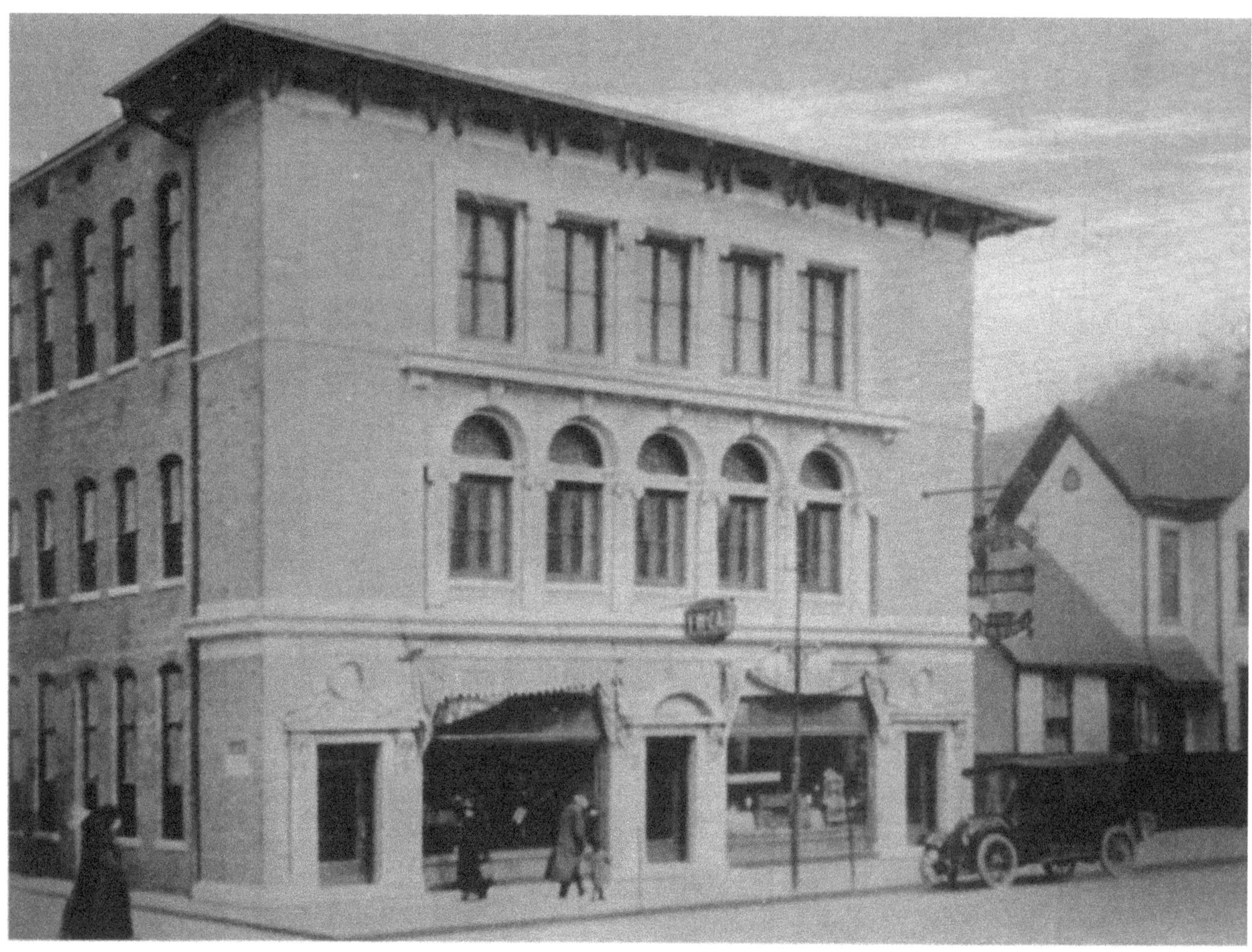

The Y.W.C.A. was located at 114 East Seventh Street in downtown Little Rock in the early 1900s. A home that provided lodging for young women was available in an adjacent house. The building was destroyed in the million-dollar fire of 1911 and today the site is occupied by a parking deck.

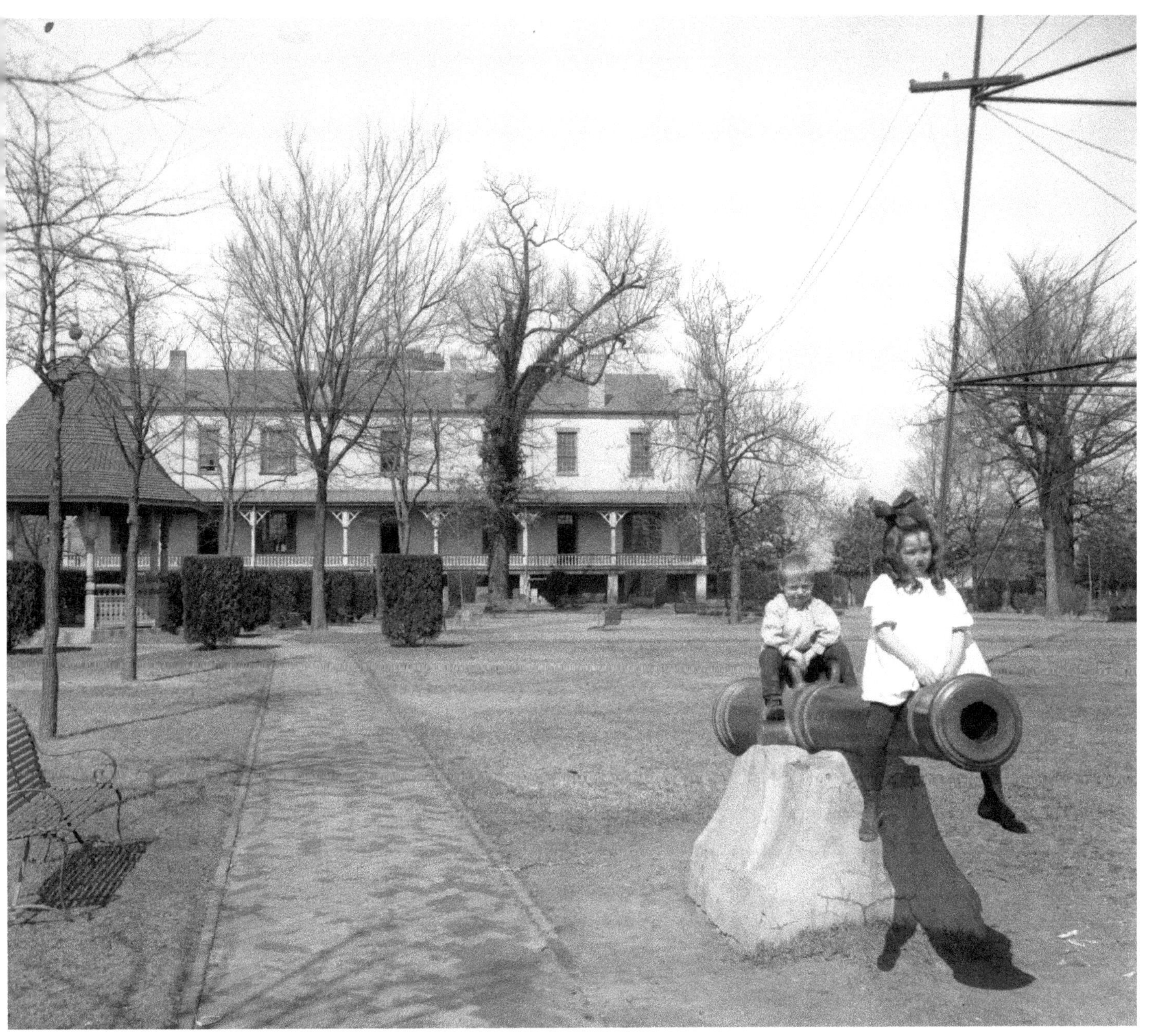

Two children play on a cannon in front of the Little Rock Barracks in City Park around 1905. The 12-foot brass cannon was forged in Spain in 1796 and captured in Cuba during the Spanish-American War. The city of Little Rock would donate the cannon to the war effort as scrap metal during World War II.

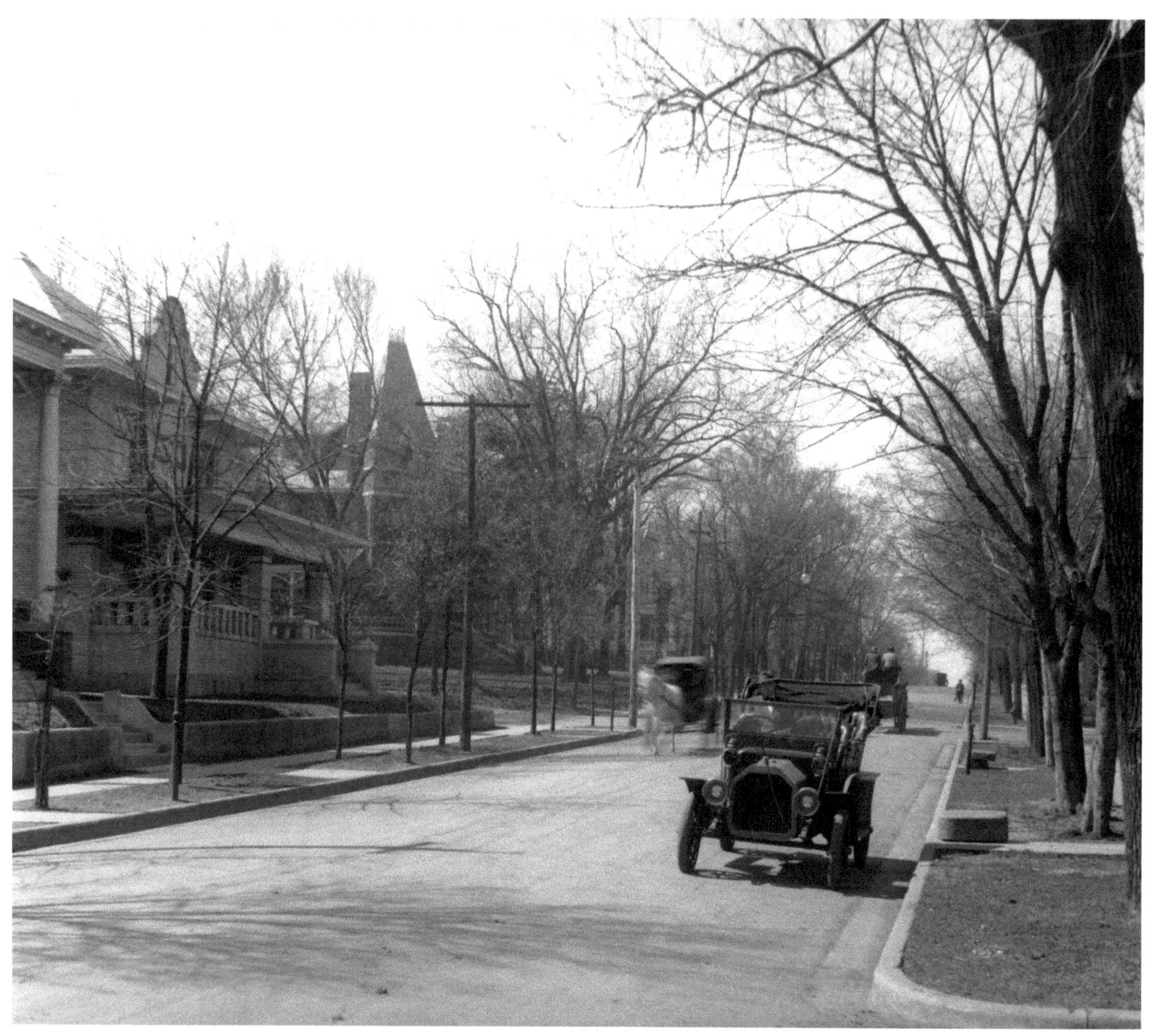

An automobile travels down West Second Street in the early 1900s.

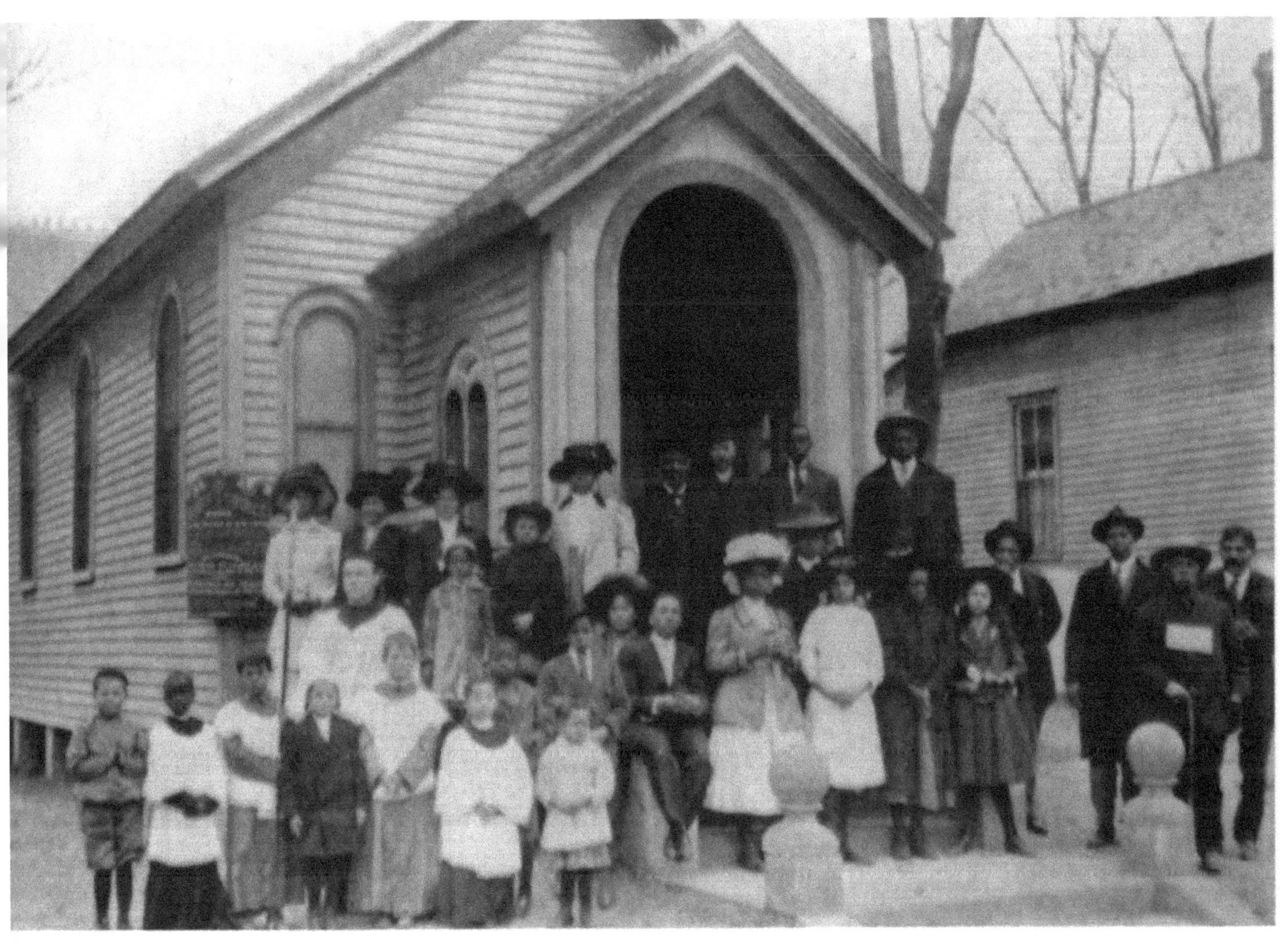

Members stand in front of Saint Bartholomew's Church, located at 1624 Marshall Street. The church was founded for African-Americans by Bishop John B. Morris in 1910. The next year the church moved to its current location at 1622 Marshall Street.

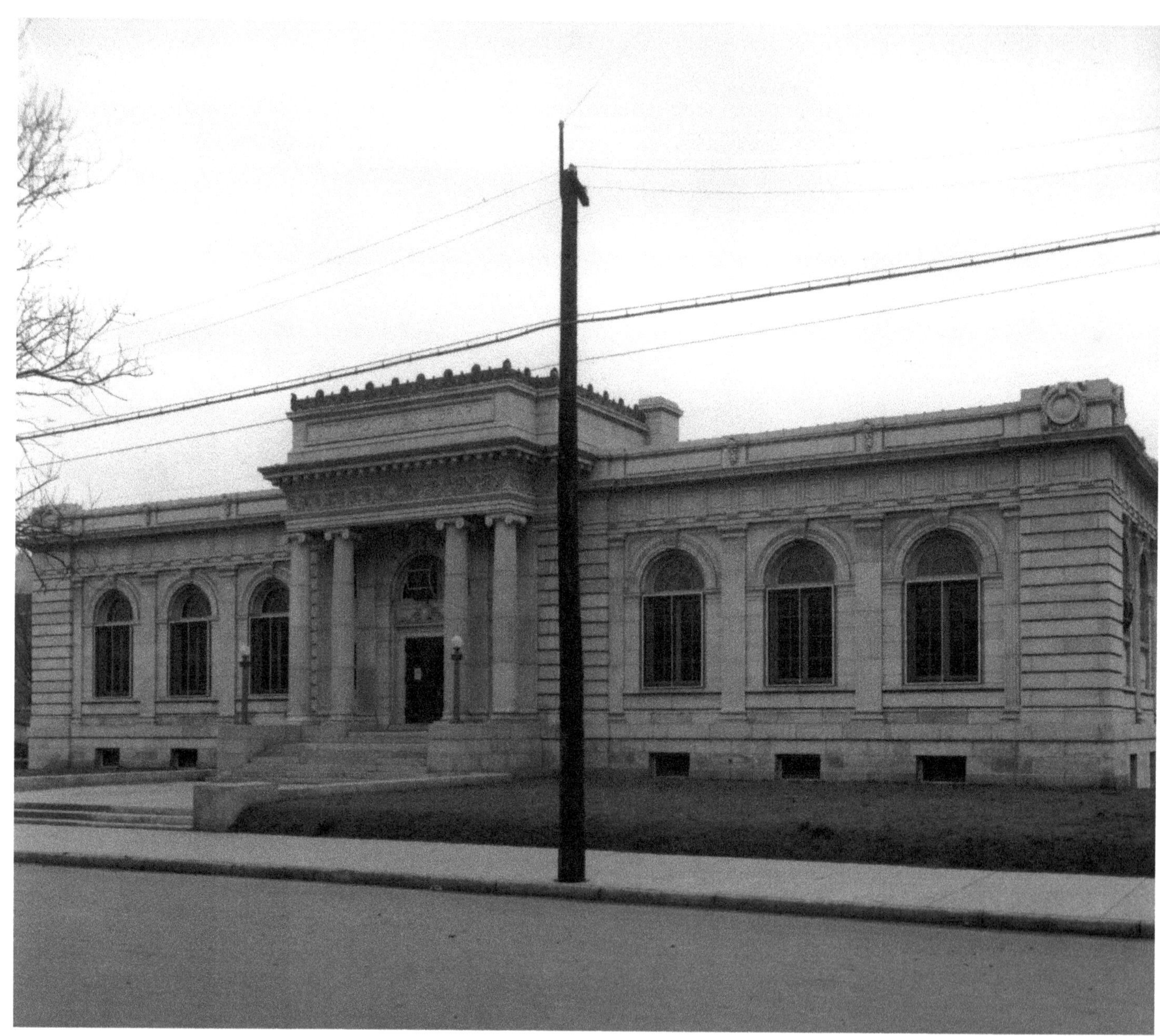

Little Rock's first public library opened in 1910 at the corner of Seventh and Louisiana streets. It was designed by local architect Charles L. Thompson and, like so many libraries across the nation of the day, was made possible through funds given by steel magnate and philanthropist Andrew Carnegie. Some of the libraries Carnegie funded thrive today. This one was leveled in 1963.

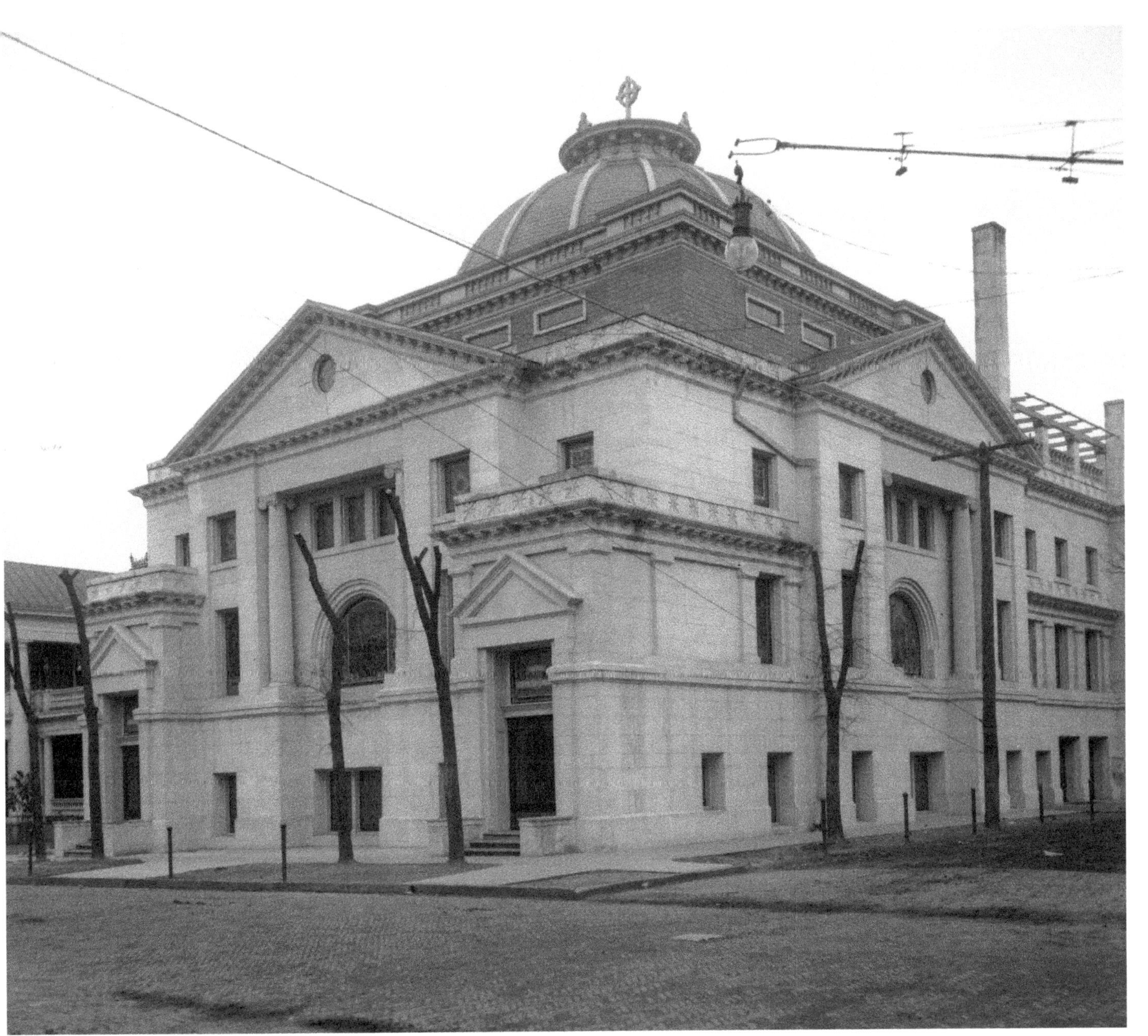

Little Rock's Second Baptist Church.

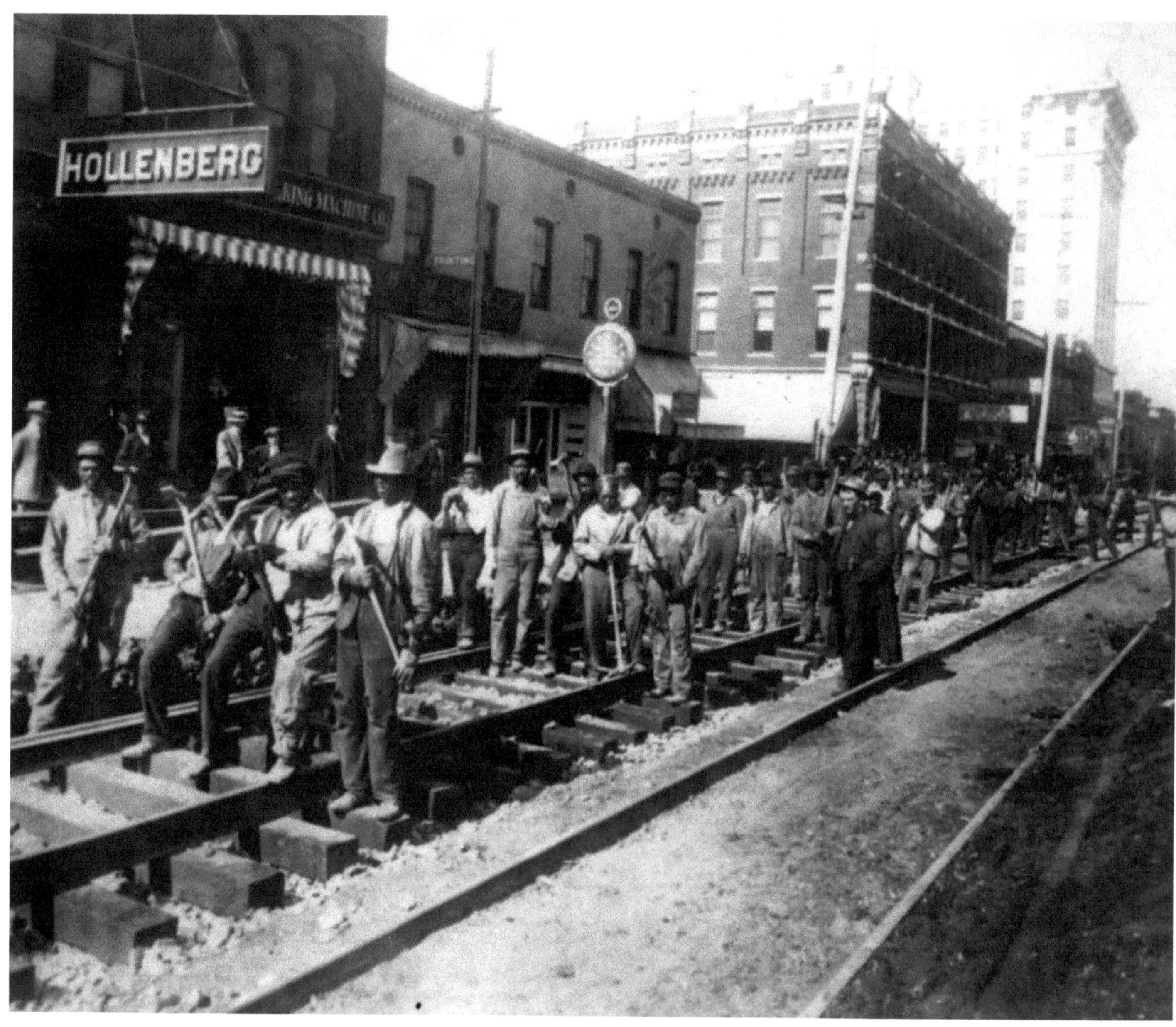

Trackmen, sometimes informally known as gandy dancers, lay streetcar tracks in the 600 block of Main Street in the early 1900s.

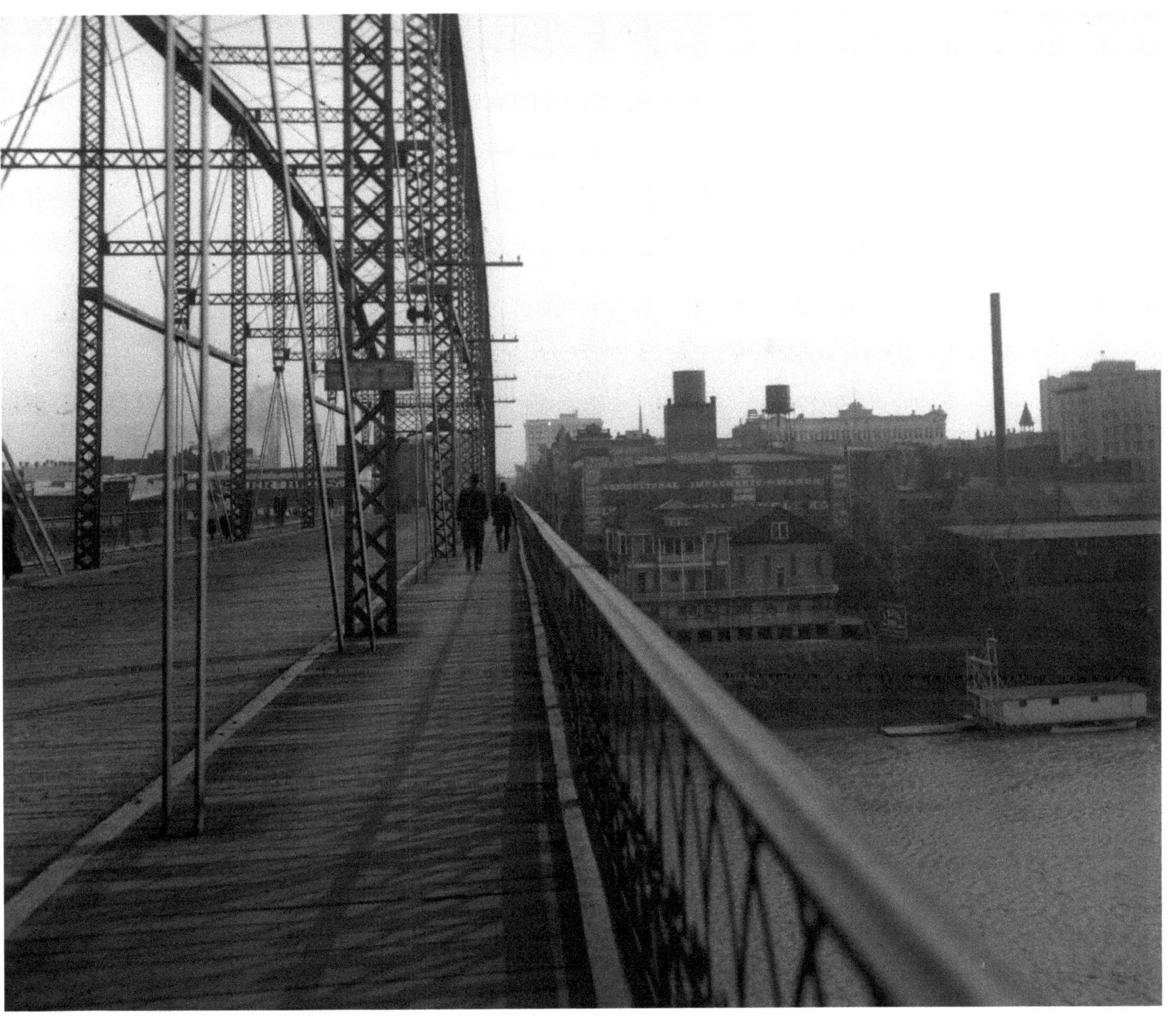

A view of Little Rock from the Free Bridge. The Free Bridge, built in 1897, was the first bridge in the city to span the Arkansas River designed not for use by a railroad, but for pedestrian and wagon traffic. No toll was collected on the road, hence the name "Free" Bridge.

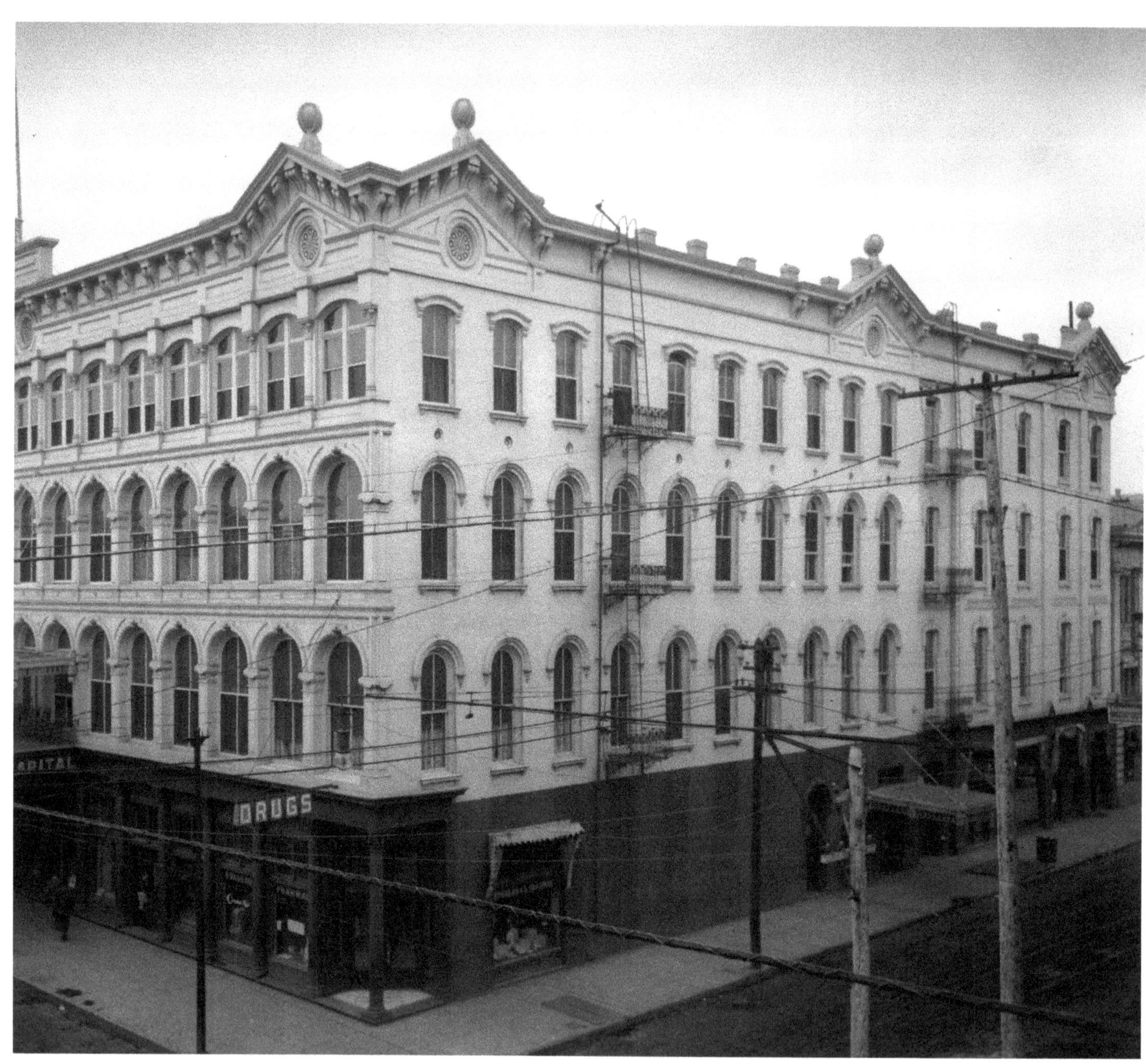

The Capital Hotel, originally the Denckla Block, was built in 1872 to house offices, shops, and gentlemen's apartments. It reopened as a hotel in January 1877 after the Metropolitan Hotel burned. More than a century later, in 1983, it reopened again, restored to its original opulence.

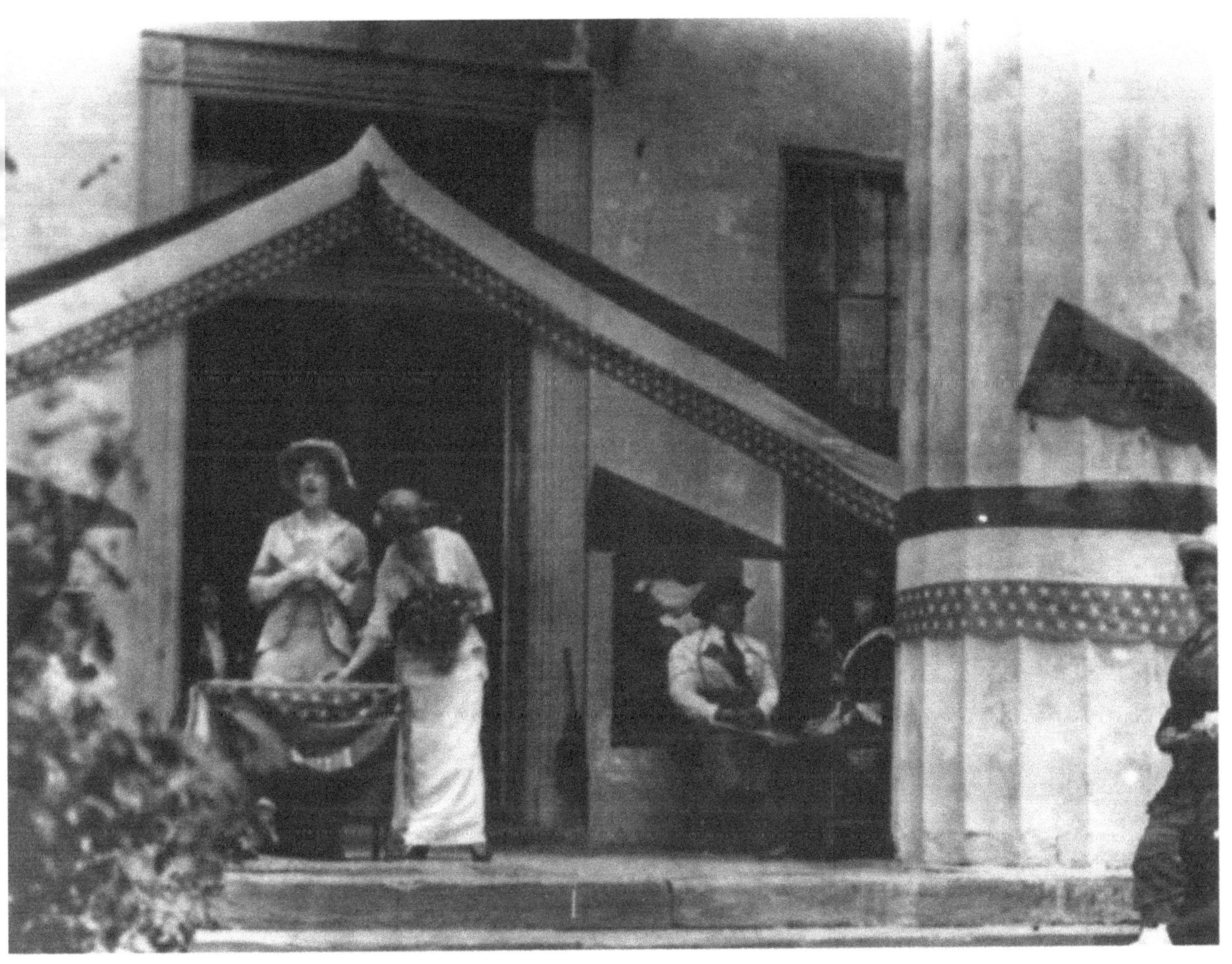

Women participate in a Suffrage Day rally at the Old State House in 1914. The 19th Amendment to the U.S. Constitution granted women the right to vote six years later.

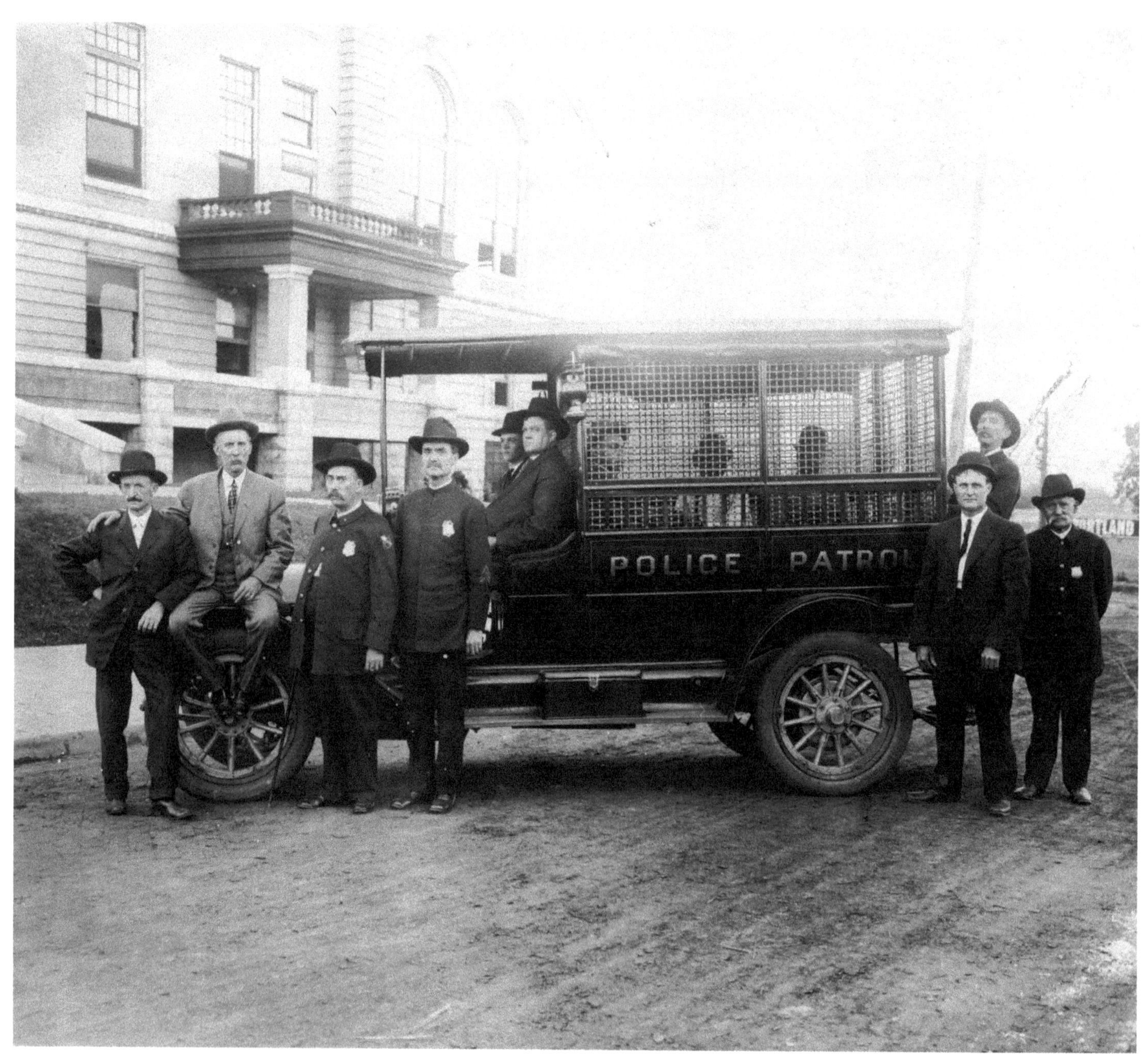

Members of the Little Rock Police Patrol pose for a group shot in front of City Hall around 1915.

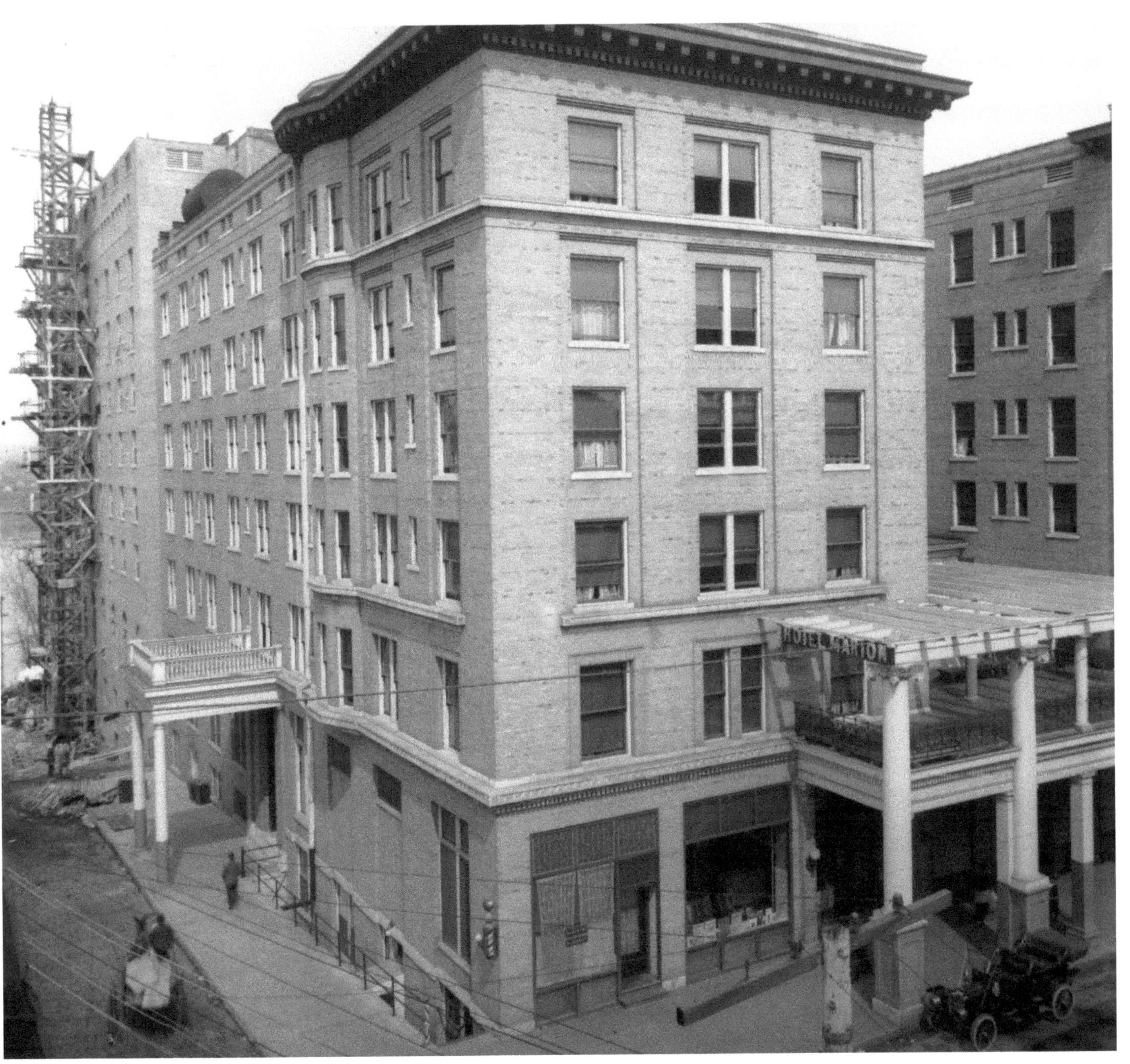

Herman Kahn built the Hotel Marion (named for his wife) in 1905. The hotel soon became known as "the meeting place of Arkansas." It closed in the 1970s and was demolished in 1980 to make way for the Excelsior Hotel (now the Peabody Hotel) and a convention center.

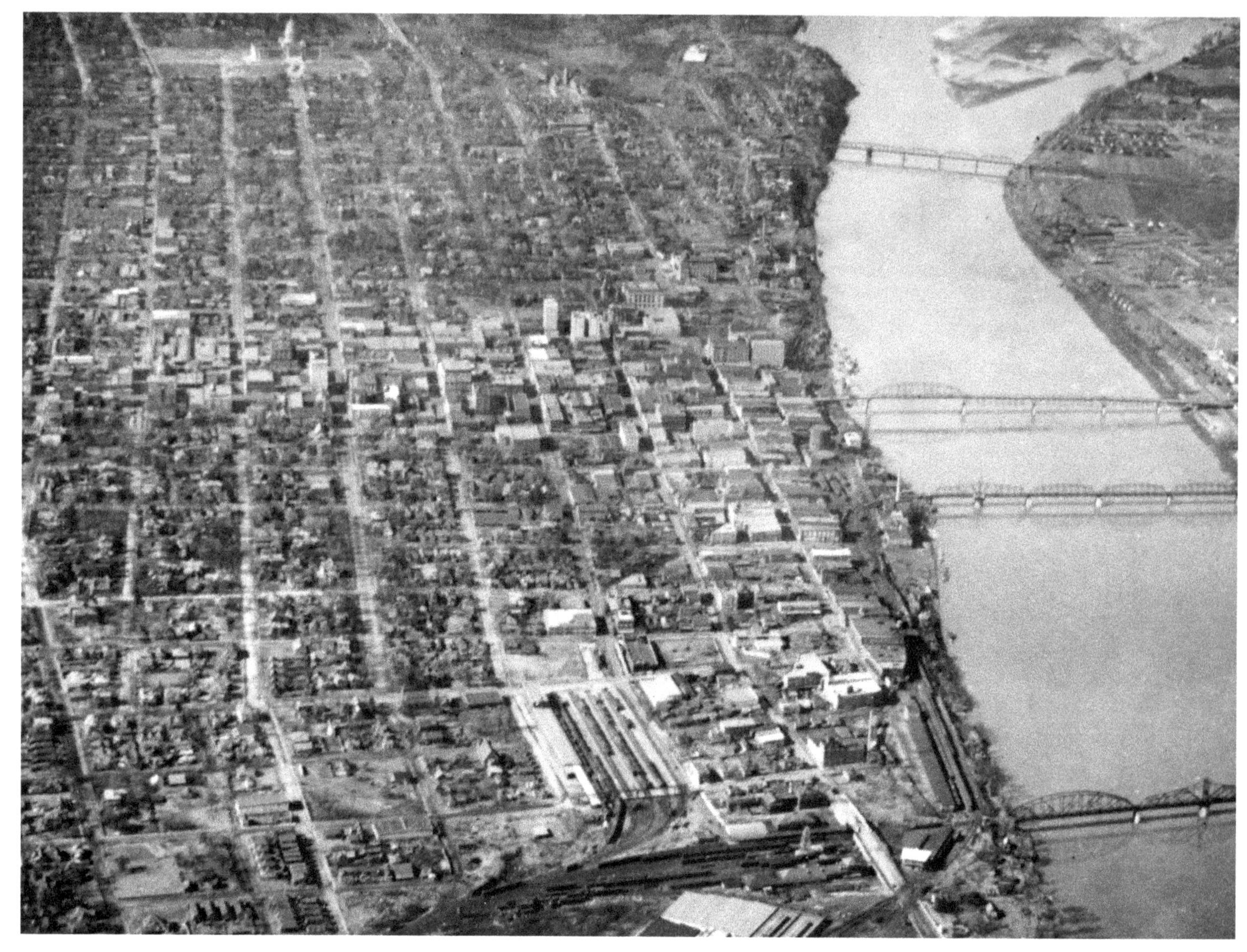

An aerial view of the riverside area of Little Rock as it appeared in 1918.

Collisions

(1920–1939)

Unlike much of the nation, Little Rock did not experience the 1920s as a period of prosperity. In 1927, the most destructive flood in Arkansas history hit the city. Record amounts of rain fell in April, and more than seven inches fell in Little Rock alone in only a few hours. Hitting ground already saturated by rainfall, the water had nowhere to go. The floods devastated eight states, but Arkansas bore the worst of the destruction and could get little help from relief agencies or the federal government. Secretary of Commerce Herbert Hoover called the flood "America's greatest peacetime disaster," but federal dollars for every national ill great or small were not then the mainstay of a nation born of self-reliance and bred on hometown answers.

Little Rock was still recovering from the flood when the Great Depression hit, affecting Little Rock as much as every other place in America. Population growth slowed and improvements to the physical appearance of Little Rock trailed off. When it rains, it pours—or stops raining altogether. In 1930 Arkansas experienced its worst drought of the twentieth century. The drought affected 23 states. In June and July of 1930, rainfall was the lowest on record and by July temperatures had surpassed 100 degrees Fahrenheit. By early August, Little Rock had experienced 71 consecutive days without rain and many days when temperatures surpassed 110 degrees. As shortages of food and other basic necessities rose, sharecroppers in the area and around the state resorted to hunting, fishing, and drought-tolerant turnips to feed their families. The drought began to ease in mid-1931, but Arkansans continued to struggle.

The period between the world wars was not without a bright side for the city. In April 1922, Little Rock's first radio station, WSV, began broadcasting. The Little Rock Zoo opened, founded by chance. After the 1926 state fair closed, a number of abandoned animals were found at Fair Park (now War Memorial Park), and pens were built for them. During the 1930s, the Works Progress Administration, a federal program that appropriated tax dollars to creating jobs for out-of-work Americans, employed citizens to expand and improve the zoo's facilities. These buildings are still part of the zoo today. In 1927, the Little Rock Junior College was founded, its descendant known today as the University of Arkansas at Little Rock. And in 1937, legendary baseball player Brooks Robinson was born in the city.

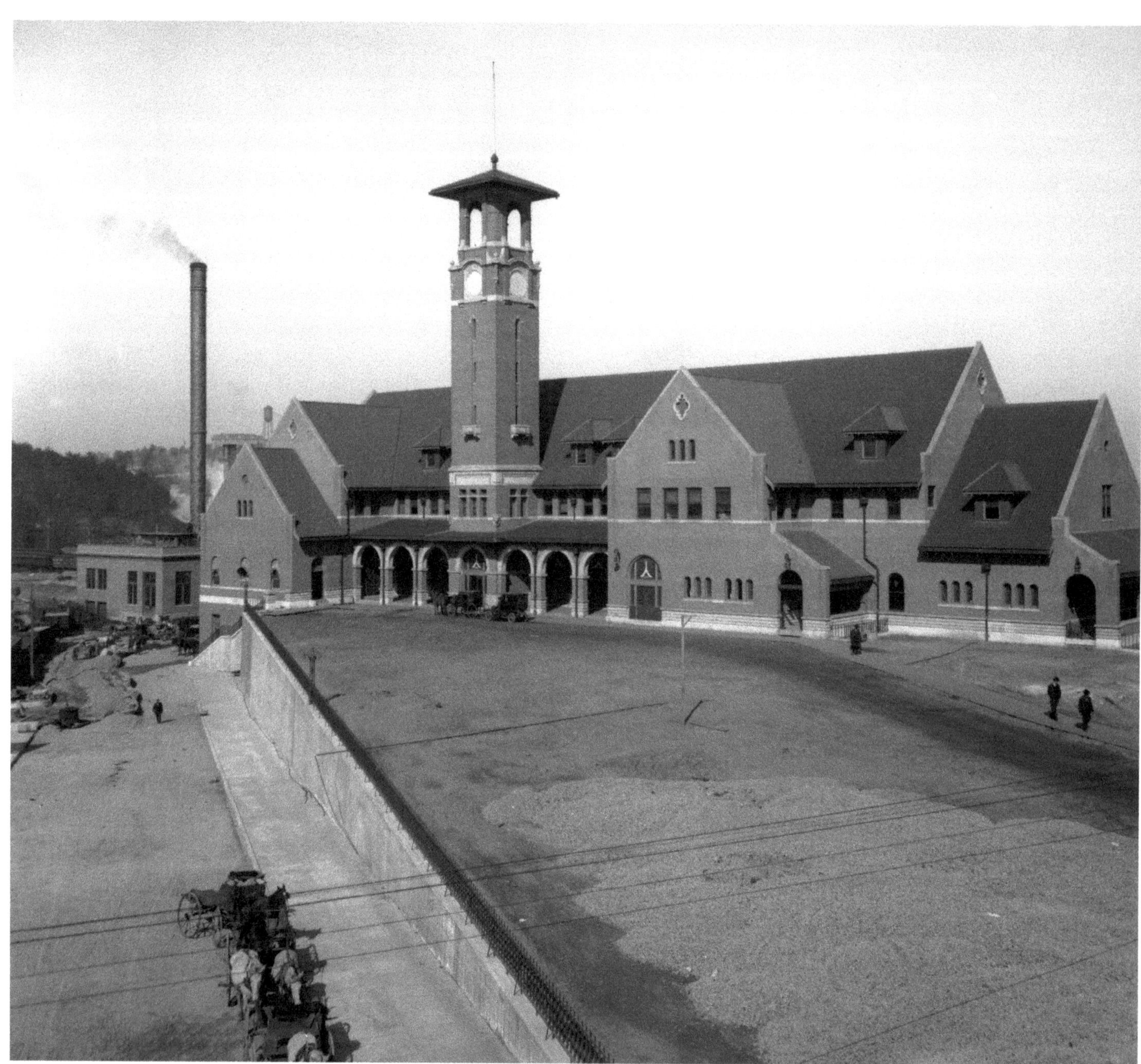

Little Rock's Union Station at 1400 West Markham was built in 1921 after a fire destroyed the older terminal. Today the handsome structure is home to other commercial interests, but Amtrak also uses part of the building.

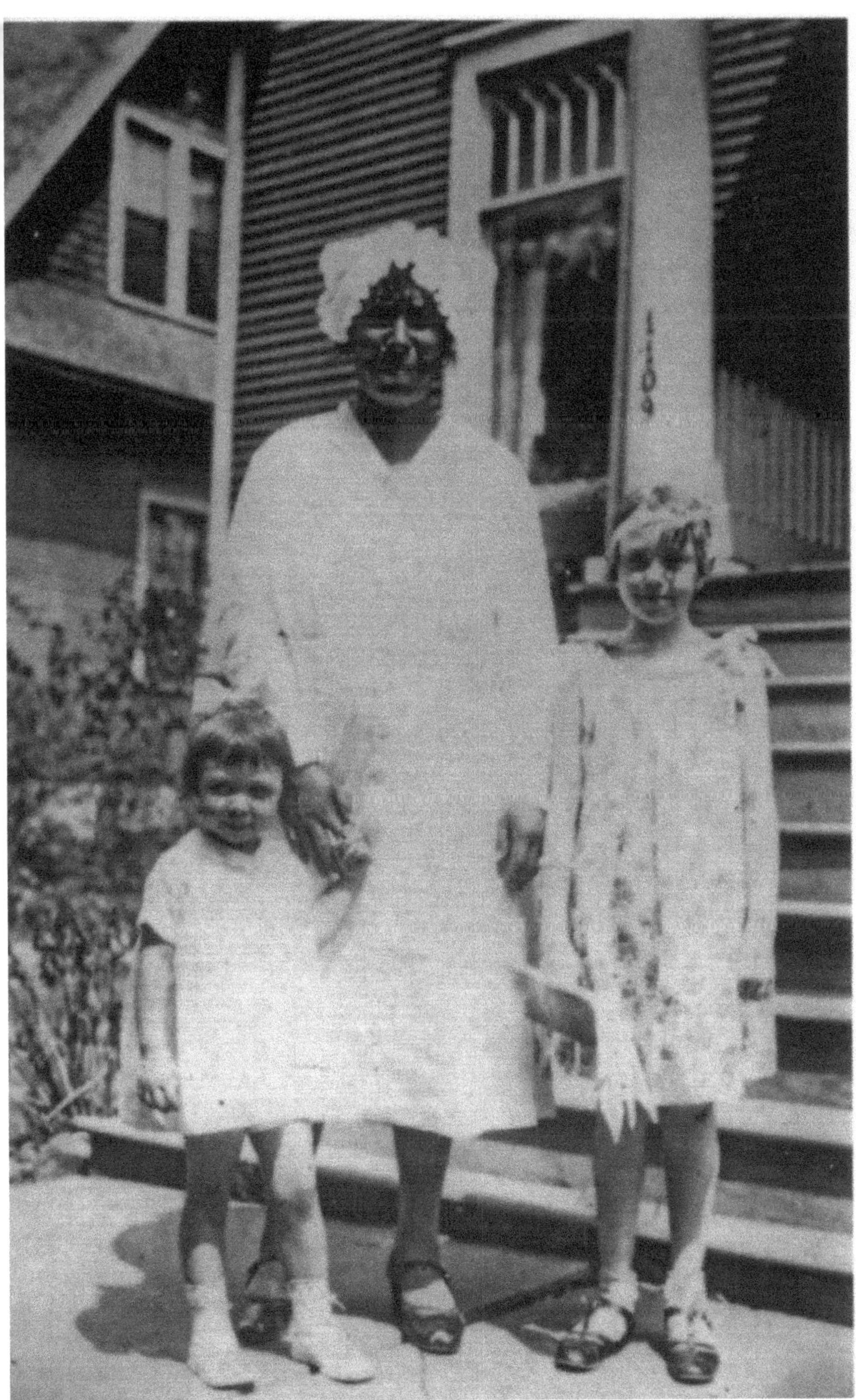

Kay Radcliffe Peterson, her nursemaid Myrtle, anc cousin, Betty Ortmeyer, stand for a photograph in of Kay's grandmother's house at 1109 Rice Street a the 1920s. Kay was the daughter of the artist Kath Wood Radcliffe and Jay V. Radcliffe, president of I Engraving Company in Little Rock. Her grandmo was Rhea W. Ortmeyer, wife of Oliver V. Ortmeye traveling salesman.

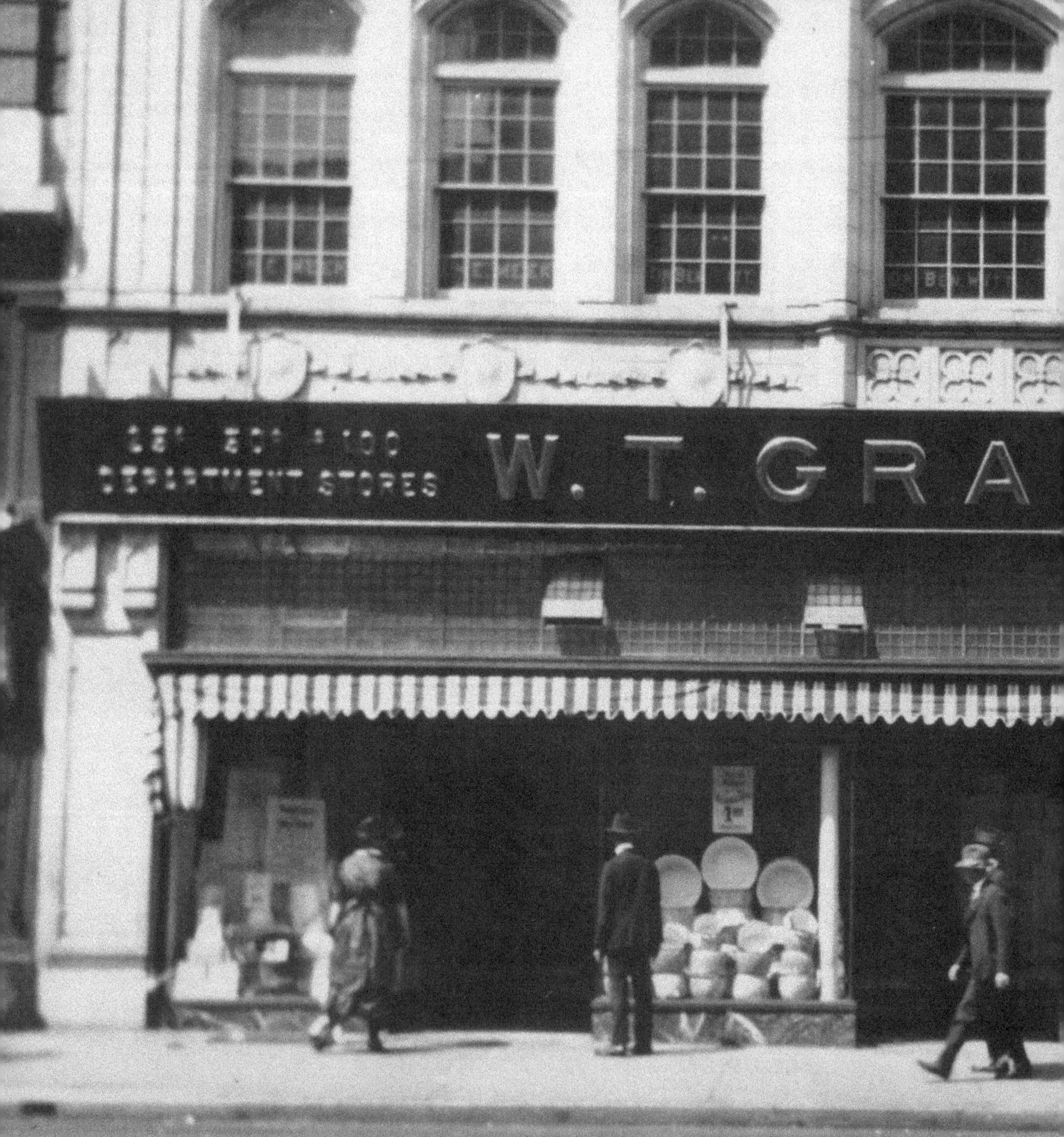
DEPARTMENT STORES
W. T. GRA

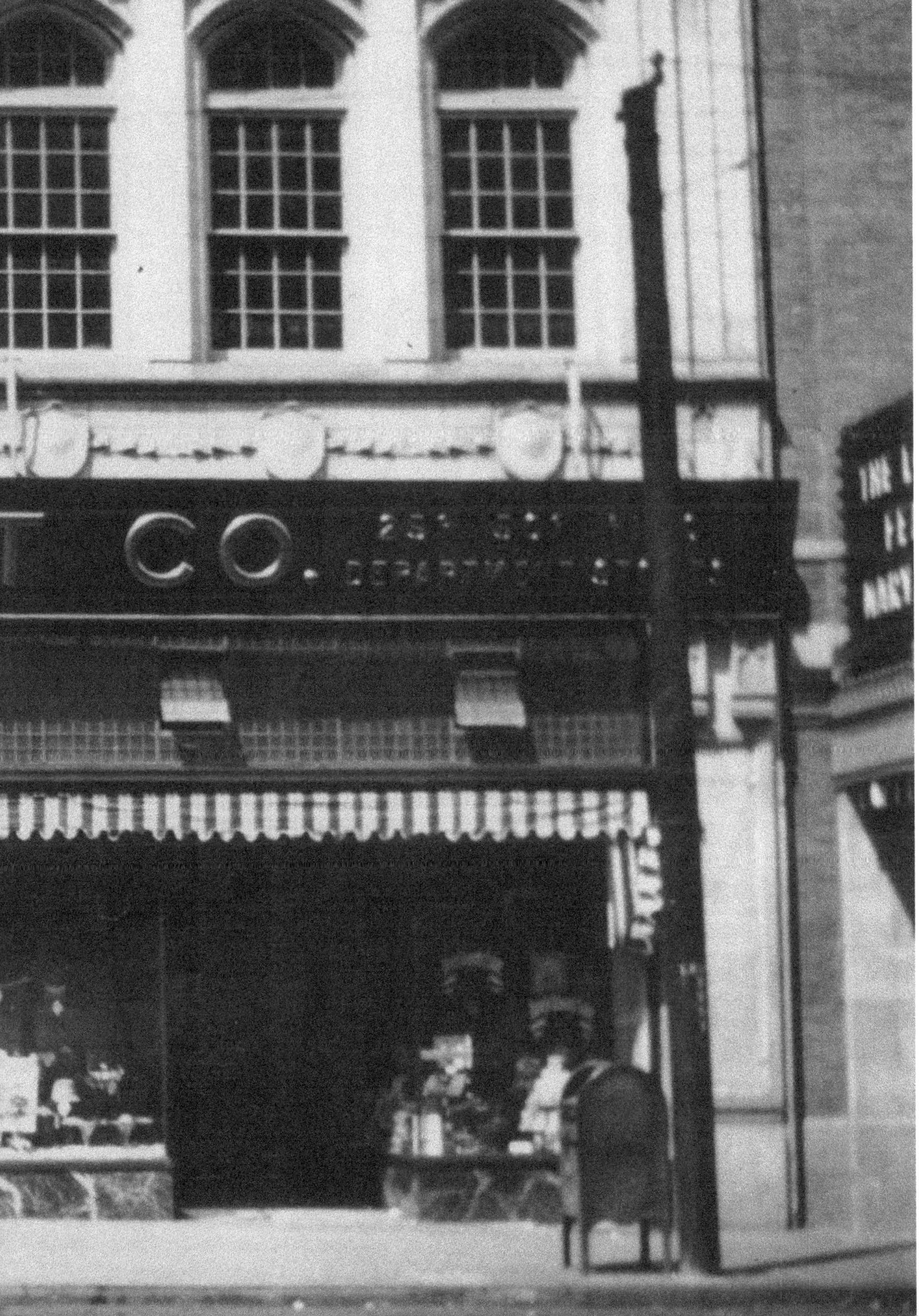

The W. T. Grant Company 25¢-50¢-$1 department store is open for business in 1922

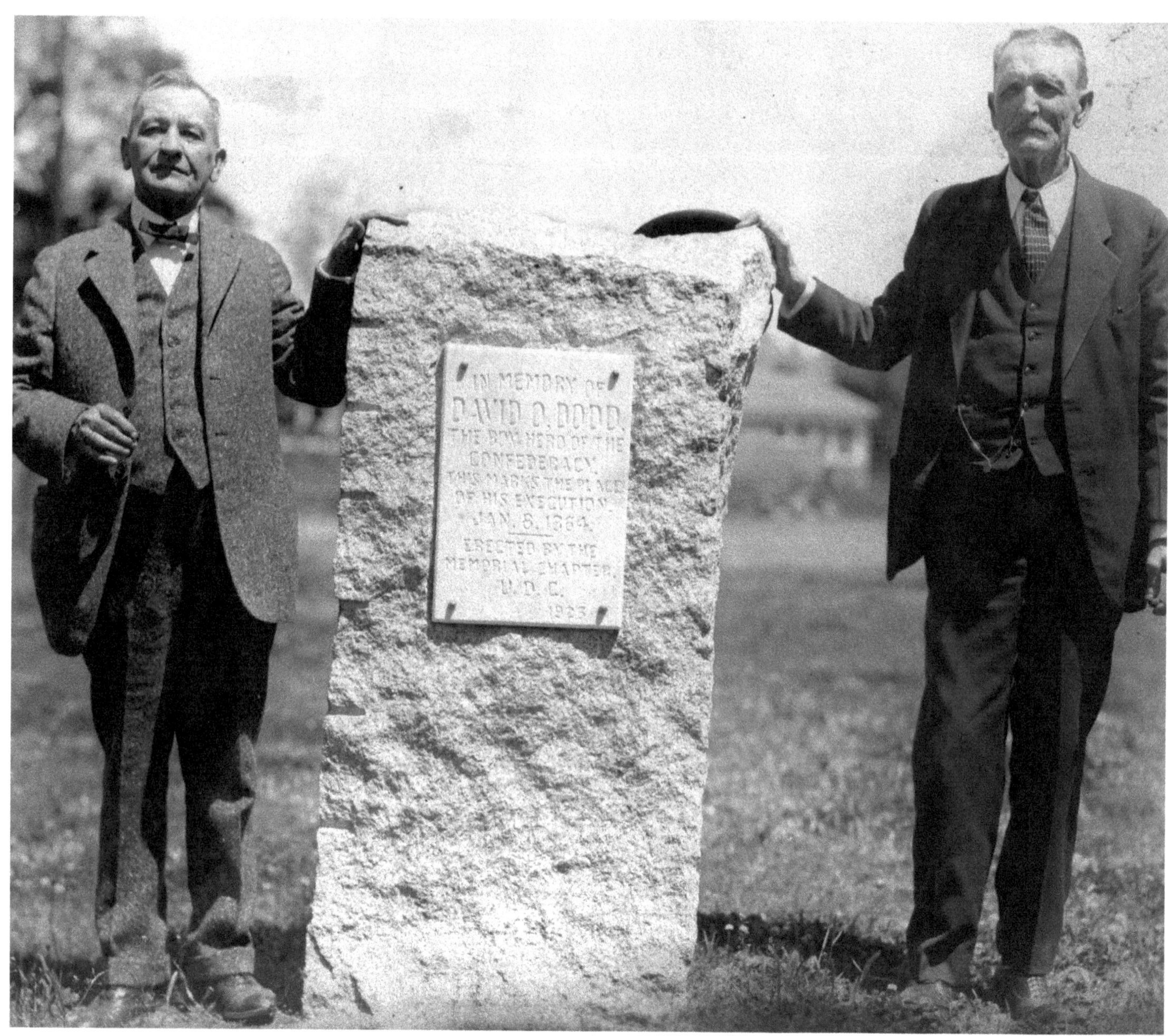

Two men stand beside the David O. Dodd Memorial in 1925. Dodd was a young man visiting his family during the Christmas holidays after the Union occupation of Little Rock began in 1863. Dodd was arrested behind enemy lines and accused of being a Confederate spy after coded papers were found in his boot. He was tried and hanged on January 8, 1864, and is buried at Mount Holly Cemetery.

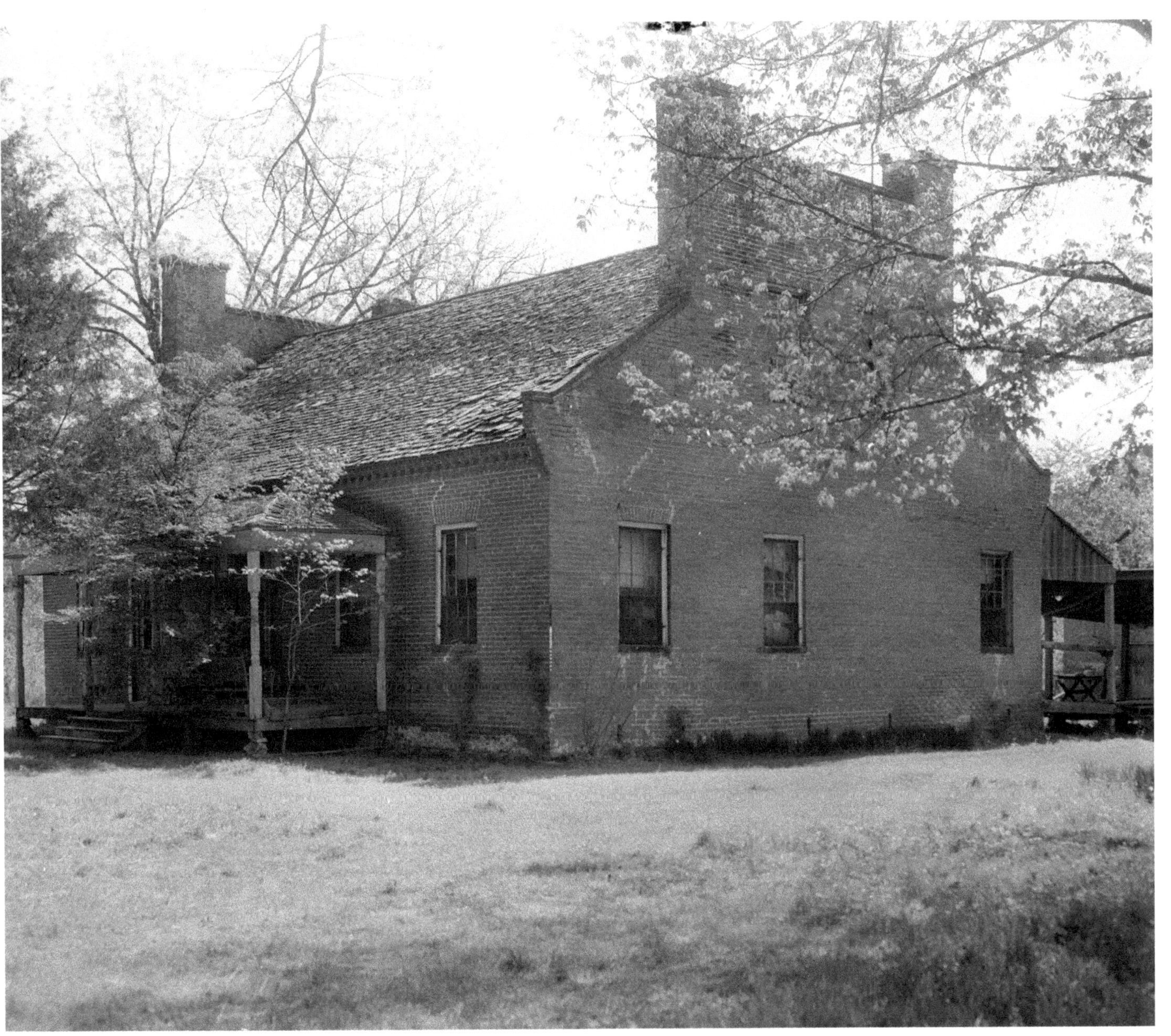

The McHenry House, also known as the Ten Mile House or the Stagecoach House, is located on Highway Five and is shown here as it appeared in 1933. It was built by Archibald McHenry sometime between 1825 and 1836 and was a stopping point on the Southwest Trail stagecoach line. Union Troops commandeered the house during the Civil War. Its smokehouse served as a prison for David O. Dodd before his trial.

The Wallace Building, one of the many projects of prolific architect George Richard Mann, was built on the southeast corner of Main and Markham streets. Mann was the man behind many of Little Rock's better known buildings constructed in the early twentieth century.

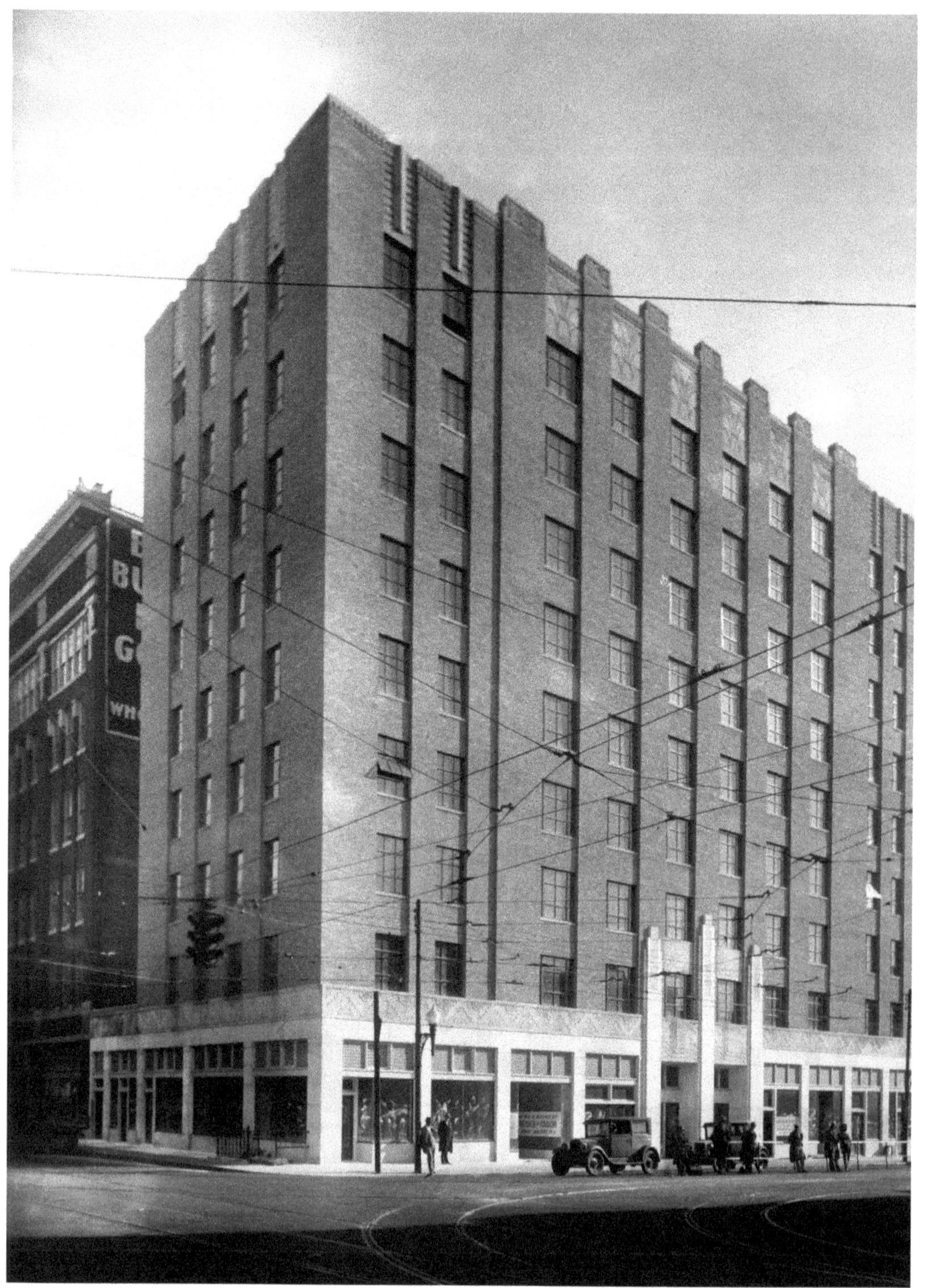

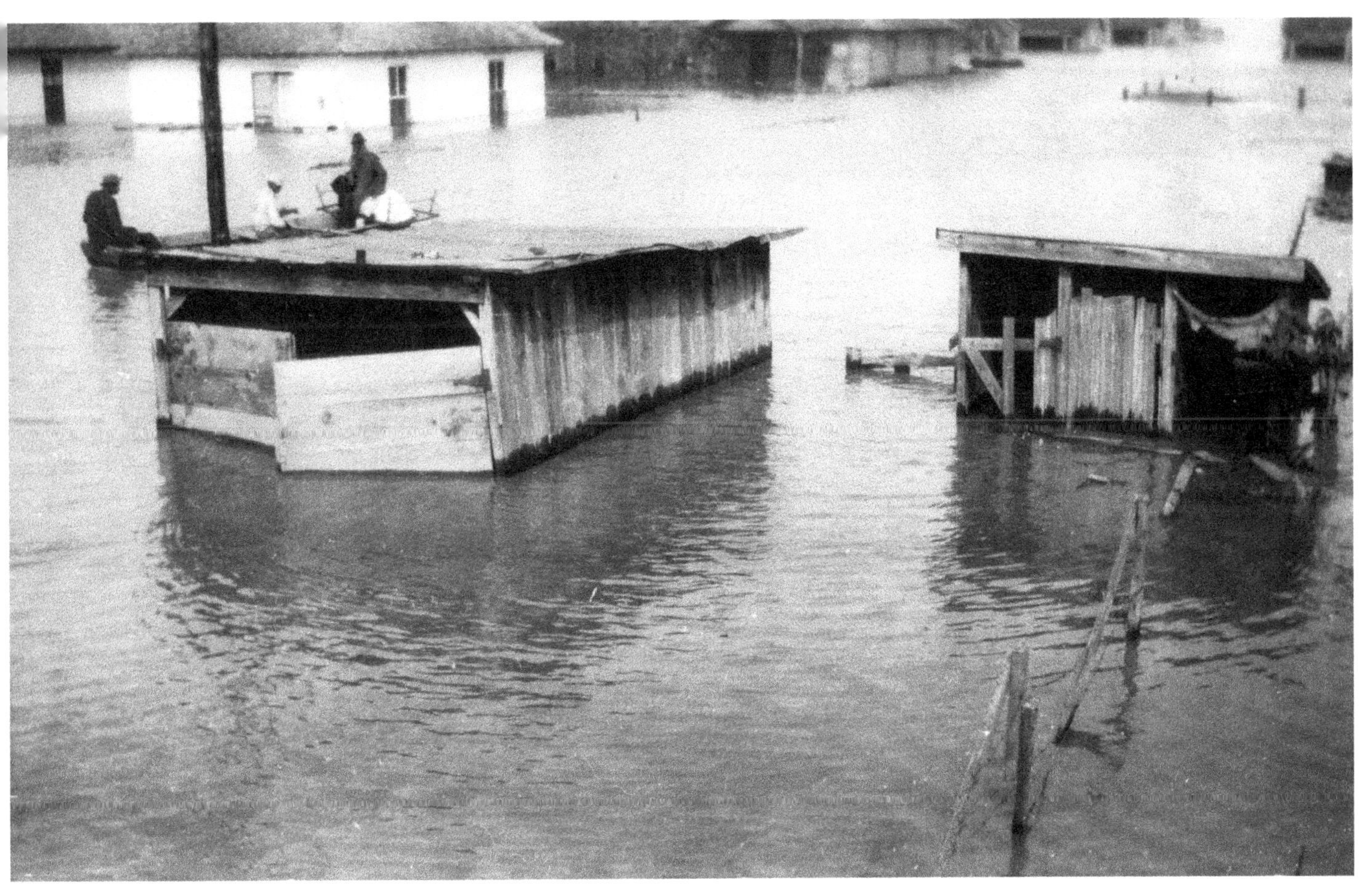

This view faces north from the corner of East Ninth and Foster streets during the flood of 1927.

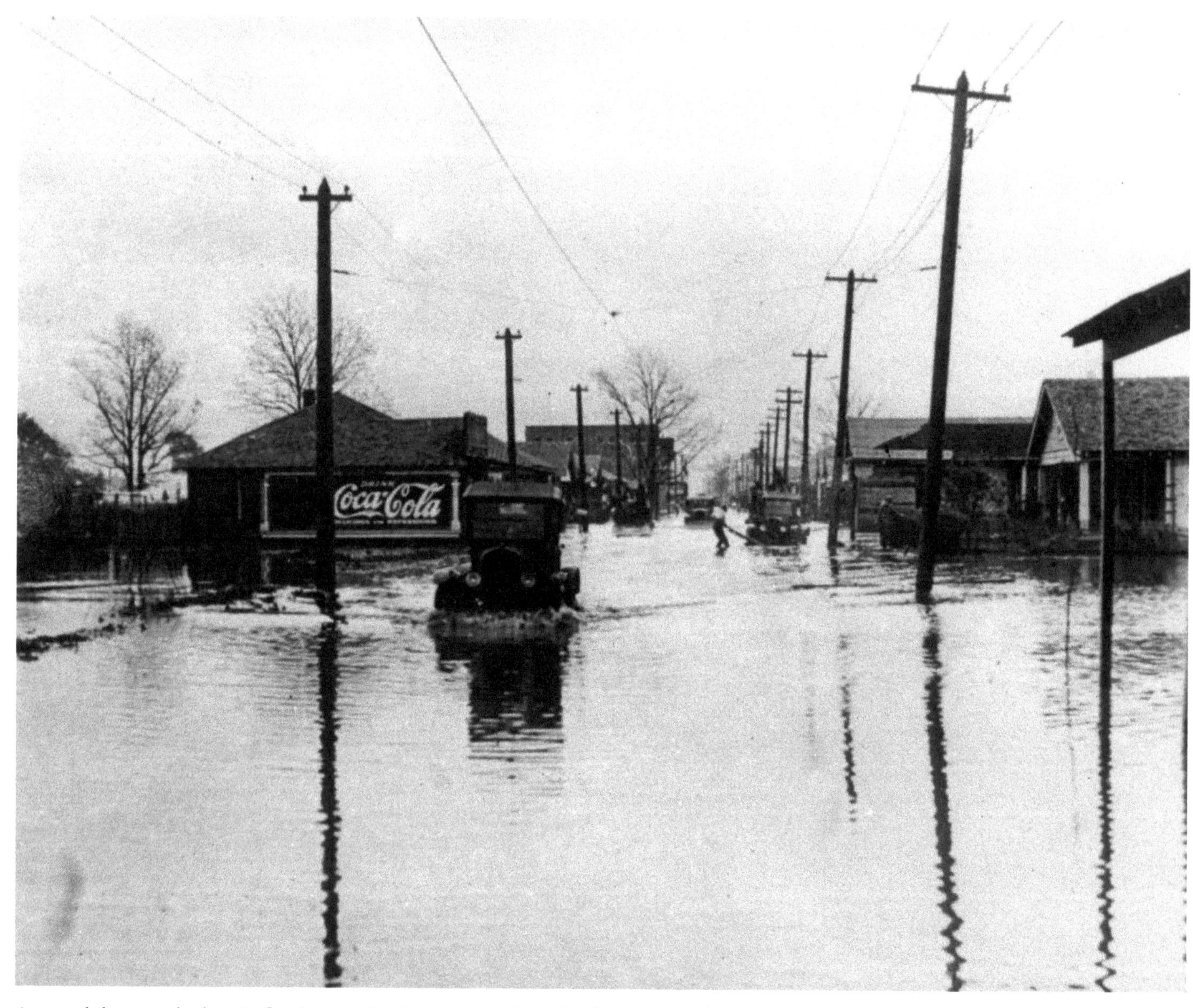

Automobiles are axle-deep in floodwaters that have hit East Little Rock, shown in this view from the 1920s.

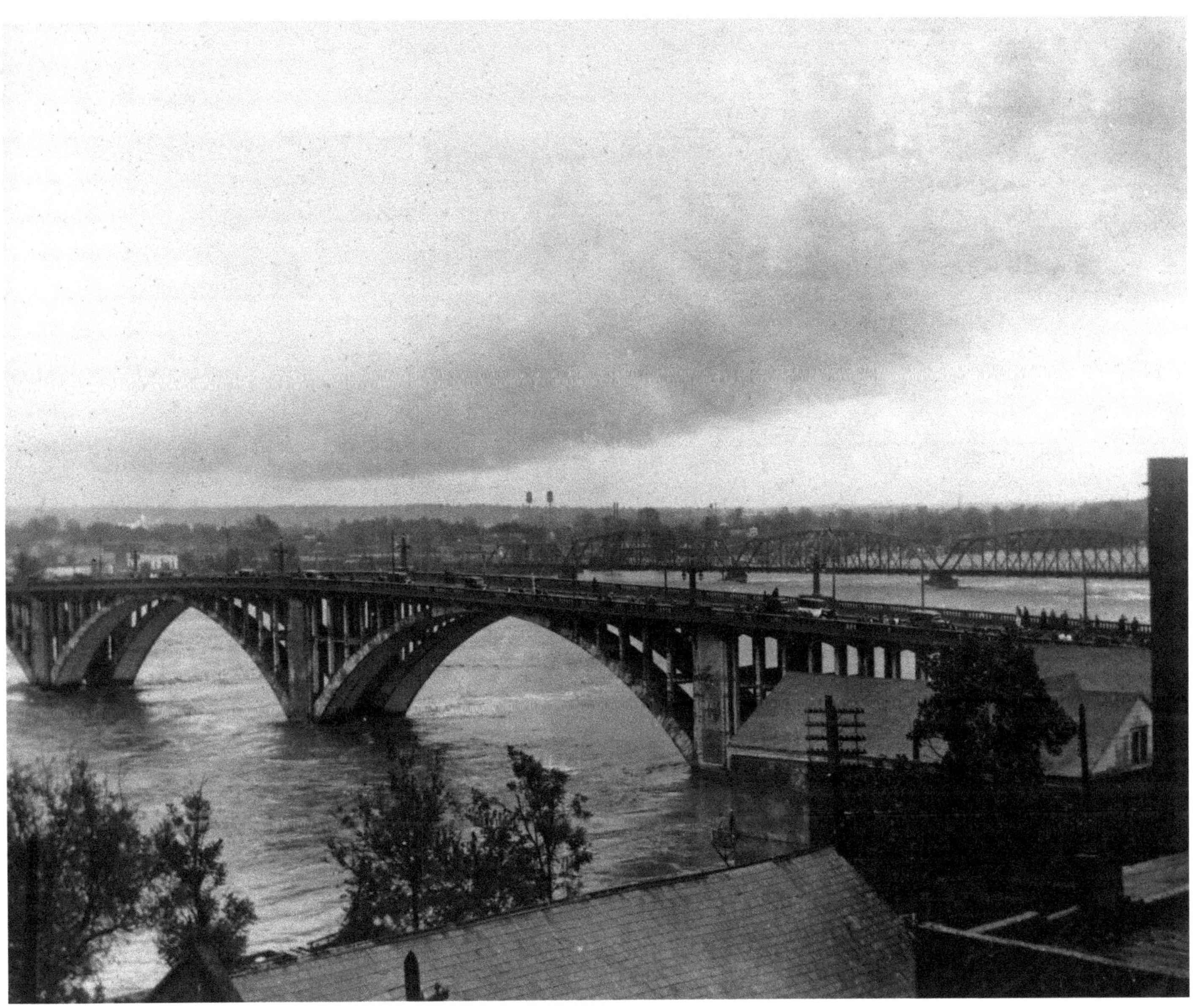

Spectators watch the raging floodwaters of the Arkansas River from the Main Street Bridge during the Great Flood of 1927. The flood was the most destructive in Arkansas history, and similar inundations swept many towns and communities across the United States, especially in the South, presaging the nationwide hardships to follow with the coming of the Great Depression. Thirty-six of the 75 counties in Arkansas were flooded, and 100 Arkansans died.

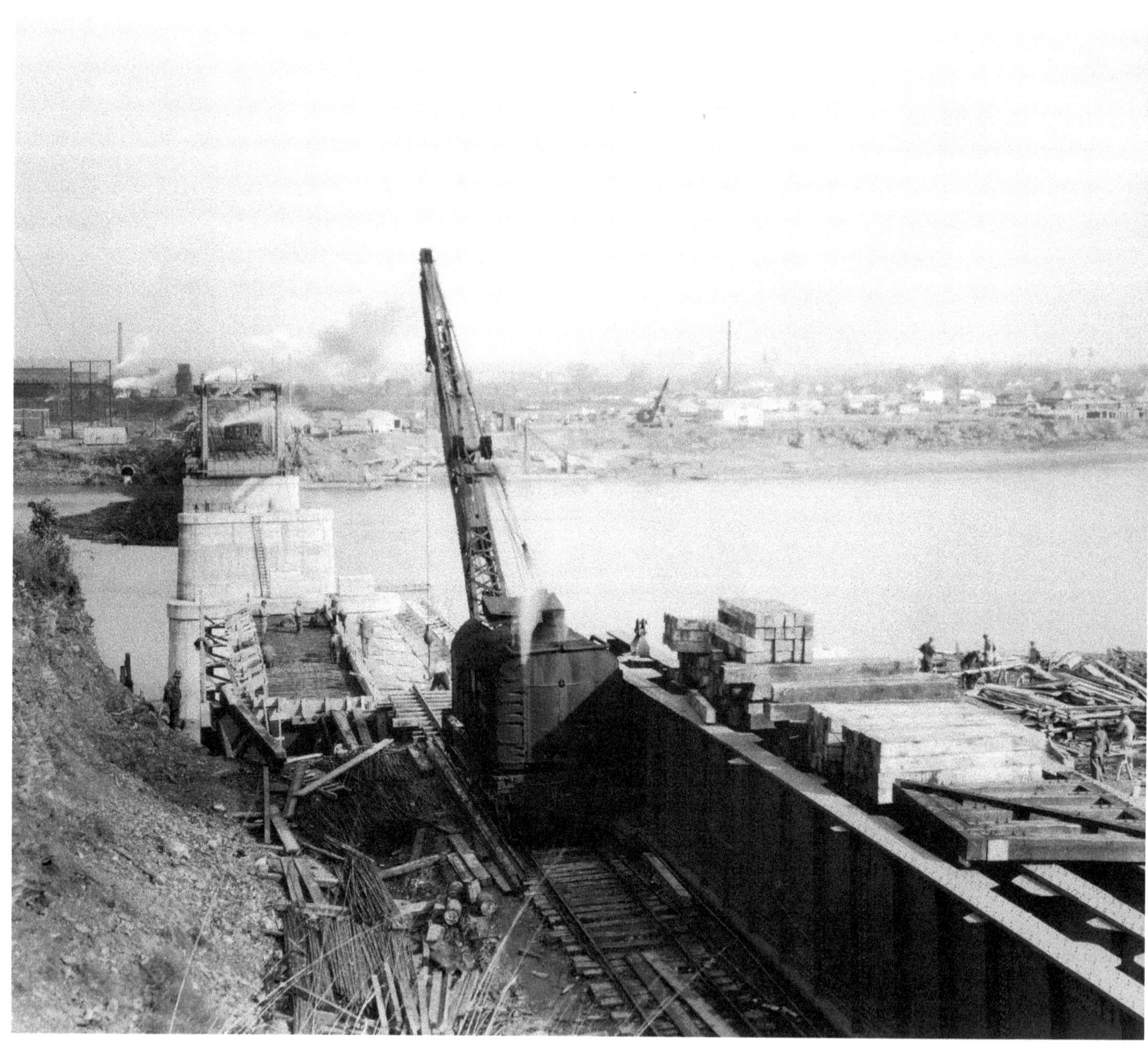

Construction of the new Baring Cross bridge is under way in the late 1920s. The original bridge was named for Baring and Company, the London bank that financed the project. The president of the Cairo and Fulton Railroad Company added the word "cross." When the original bridge washed away in the deluge of 1927, the Missouri Pacific Railroad pledged to rebuild it. The new bridge opened in 1929.

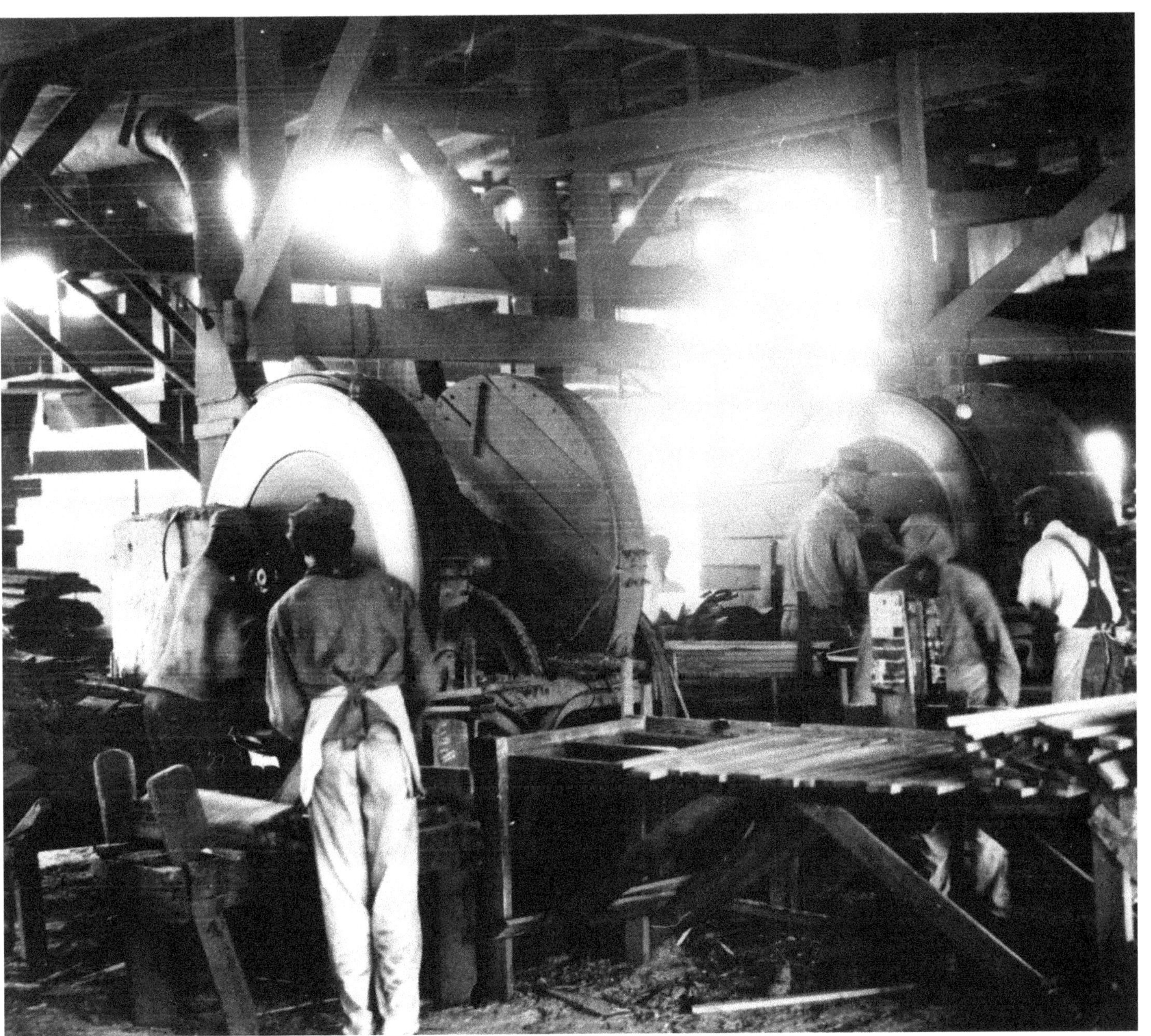

These men are shown working at the Jamlin Stave Company on August 21, 1928. Staves were narrow strips of wood used in the manufacture of barrels.

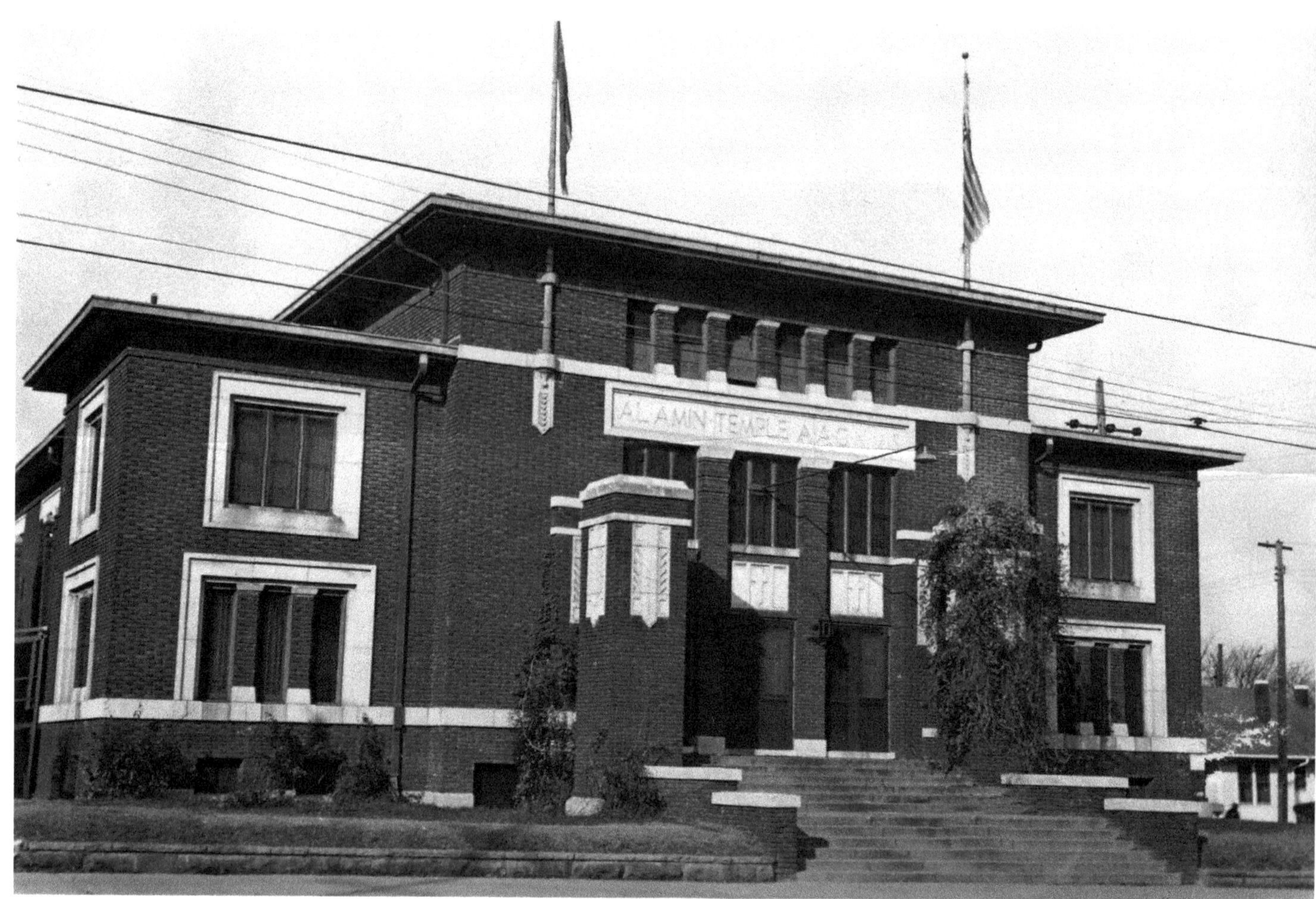

The Al Amin Shrine Temple in 1933.

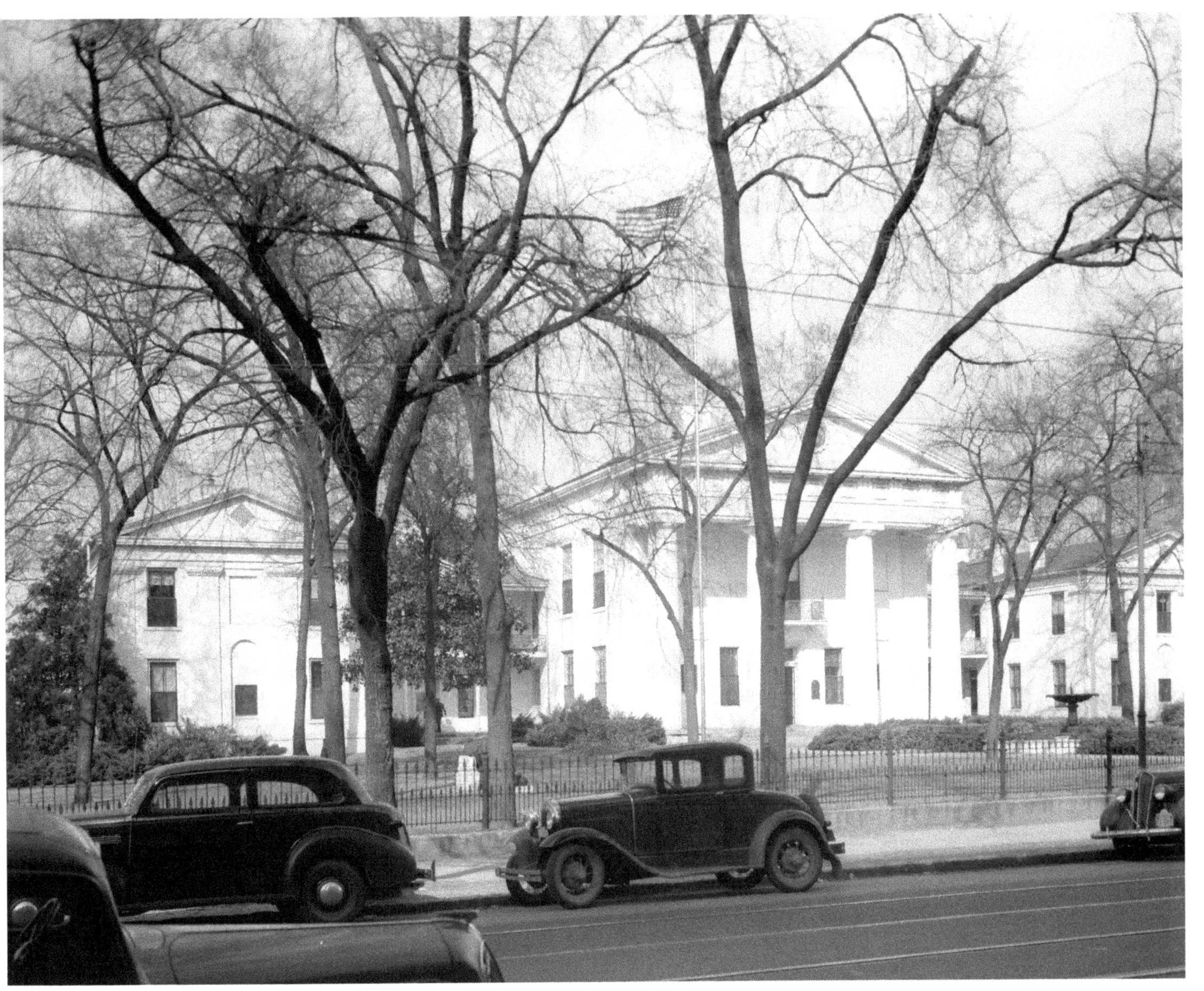

The Stars and Stripes flies over the Old State House on April 12, 1934.

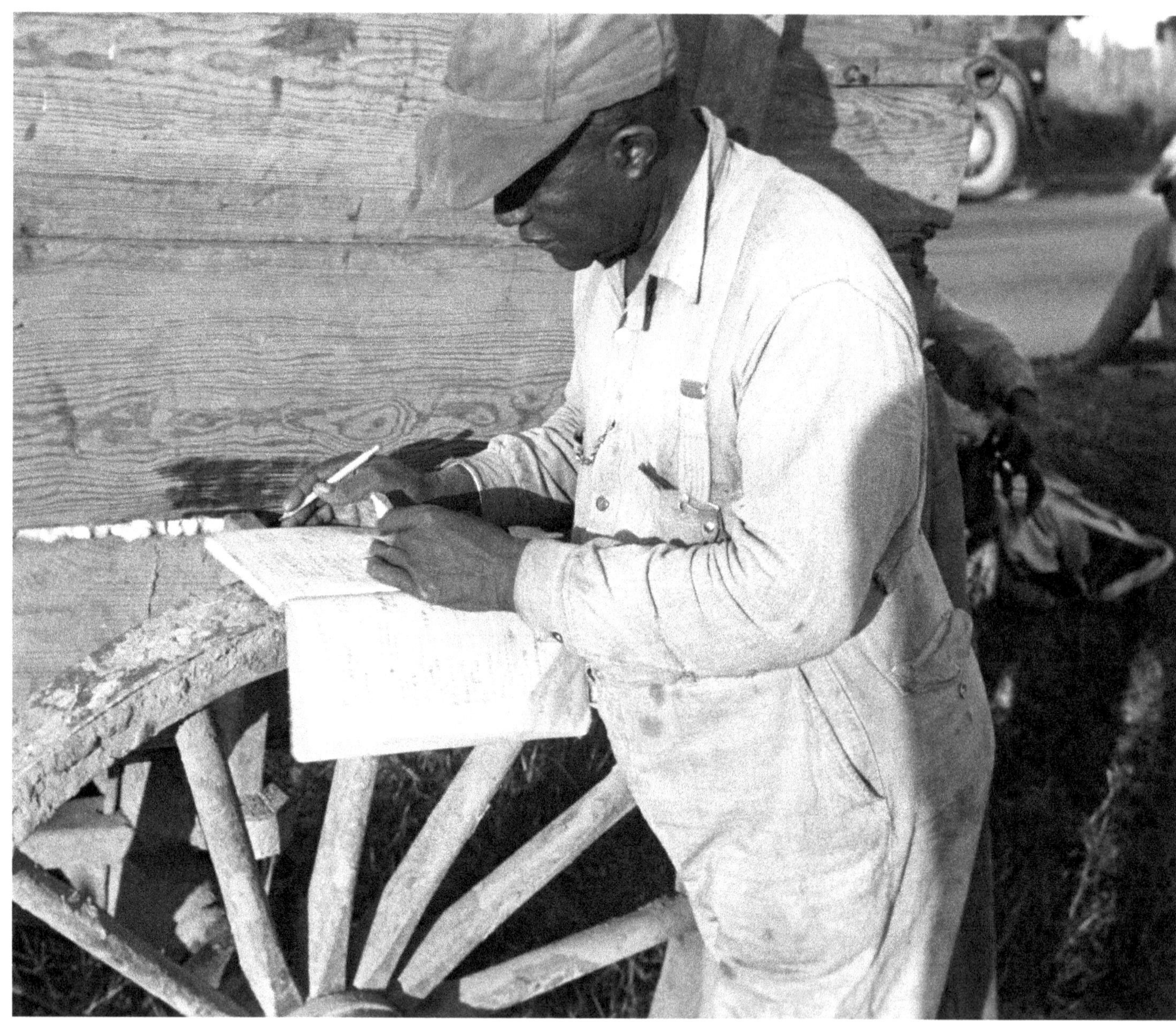

A Little Rock worker checks in cotton in 1935. Cotton remained the leading commercial crop throughout most of Arkansas in the 1930s. When the worst drought of the twentieth century struck the area in 1930 and 1931, farmers were hard hit, relying on hunting, fishing, and turnips for sustenance.

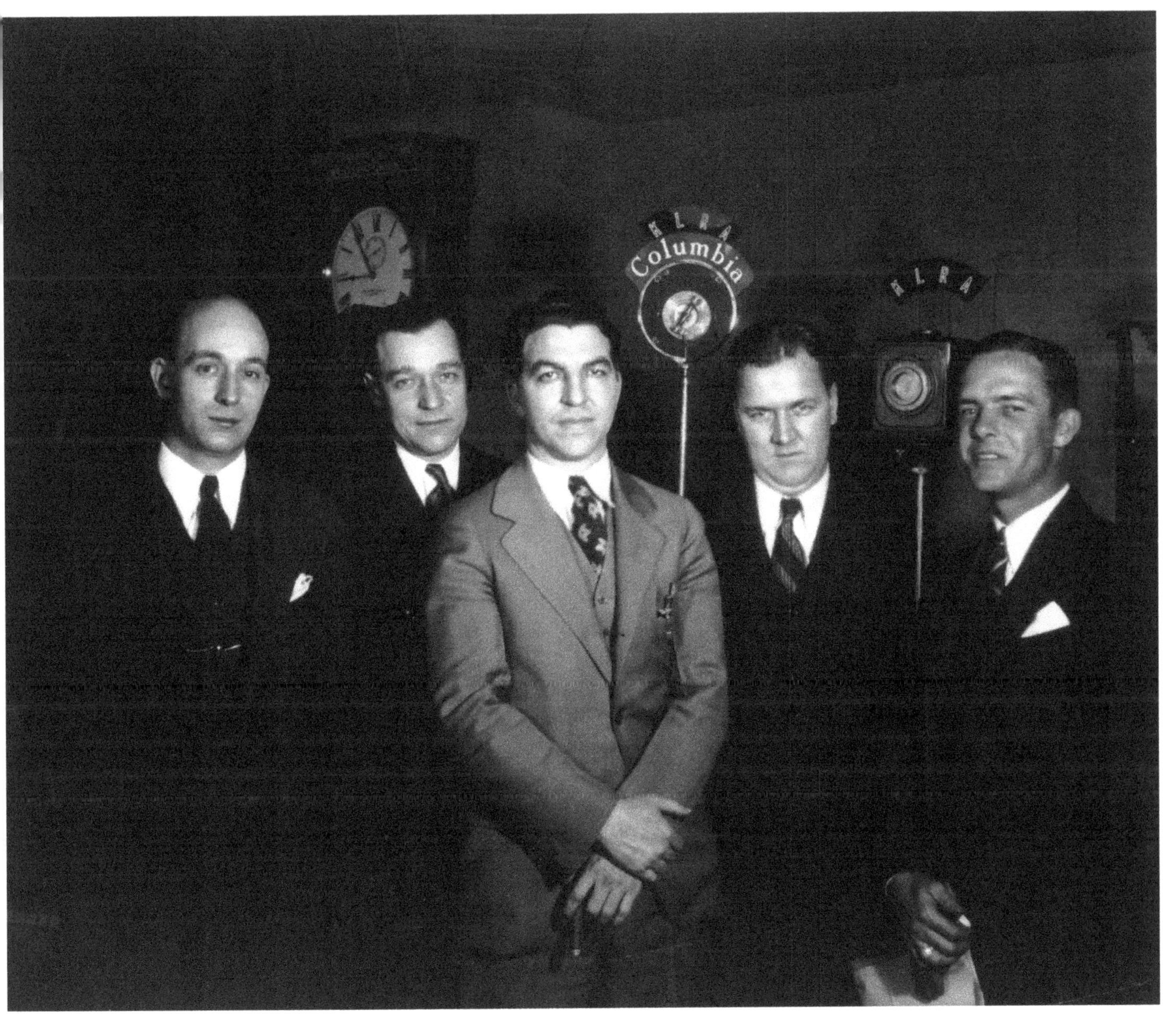

Members of the Columbia System and Red Cross staff met at the KLRA radio station on Janury 31, 1931, to discuss plans for a drought relief program. In January 1931, the Red Cross initiated the program, helping alleviate the shortage of basic necessities by mid-1931.

A family of sharecroppers gather together in 1935. After the Civil War, farm economies in the South, Arkansas among them, depended on the labor of disadvantaged black and white Americans working the land to eke out a living. Landowners provided the acreage and equipment, sharecroppers provided the labor, and profits were to be shared. Mechanization and other changes would lead to the decline of the much-criticized system.

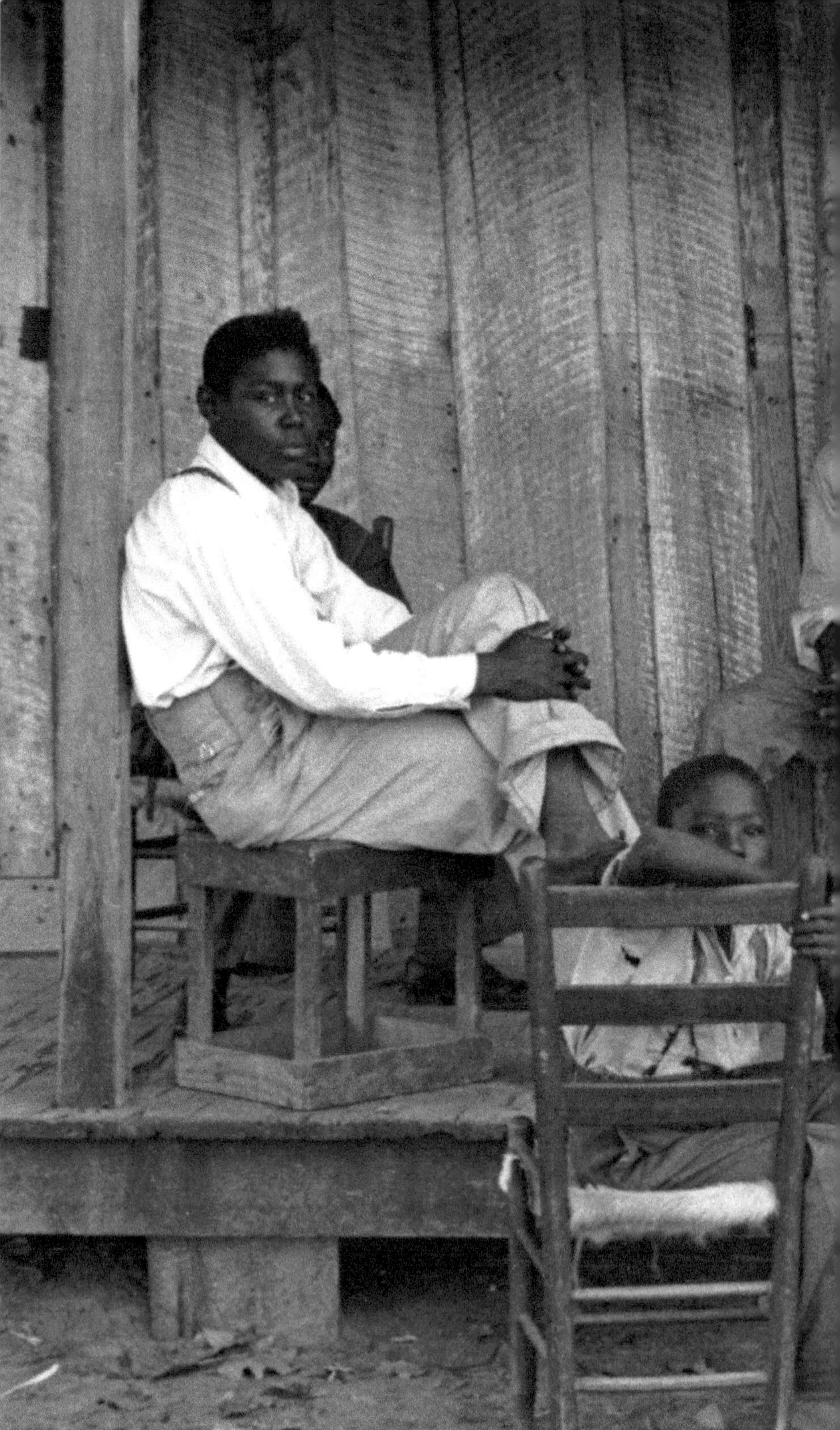

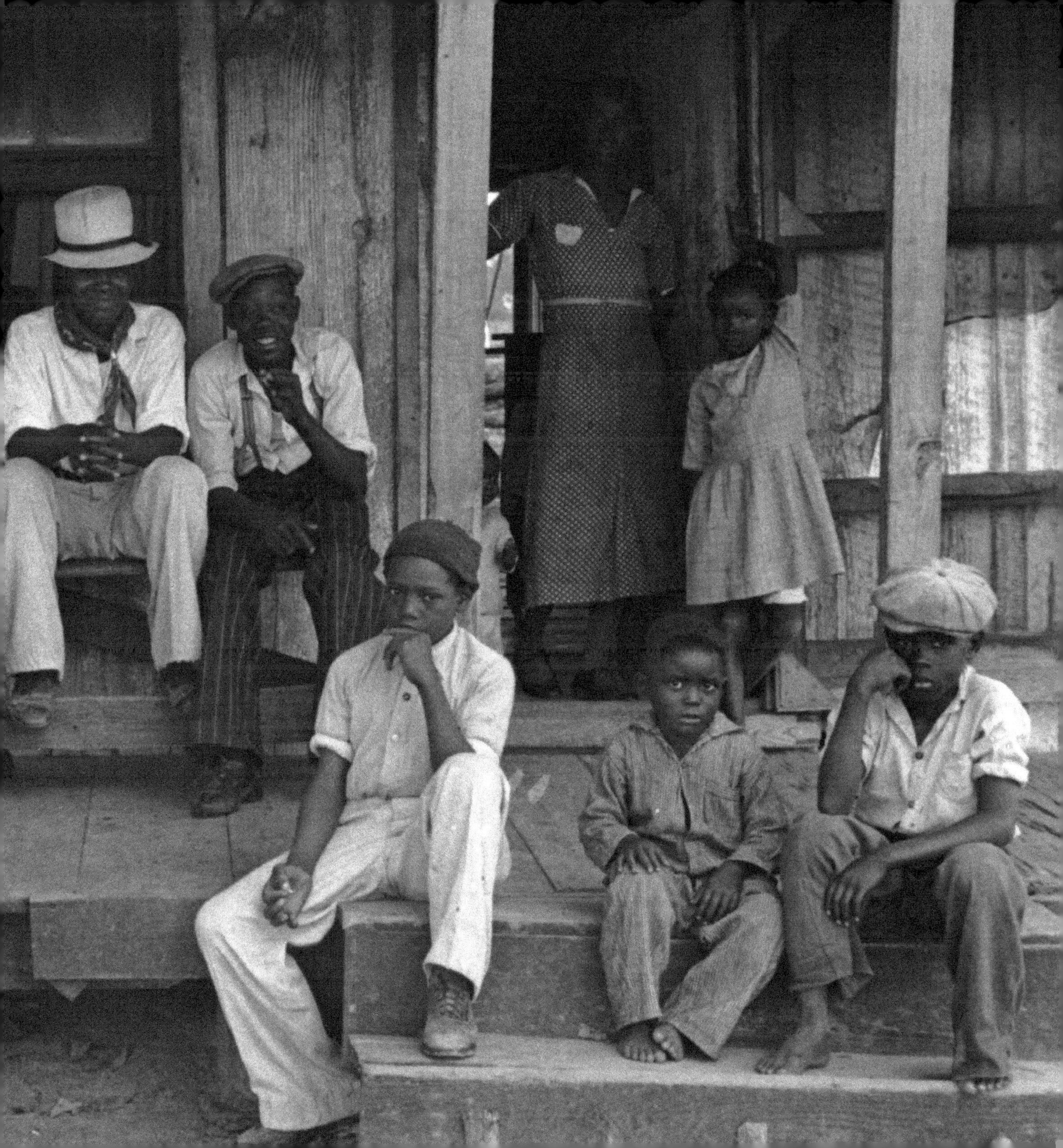

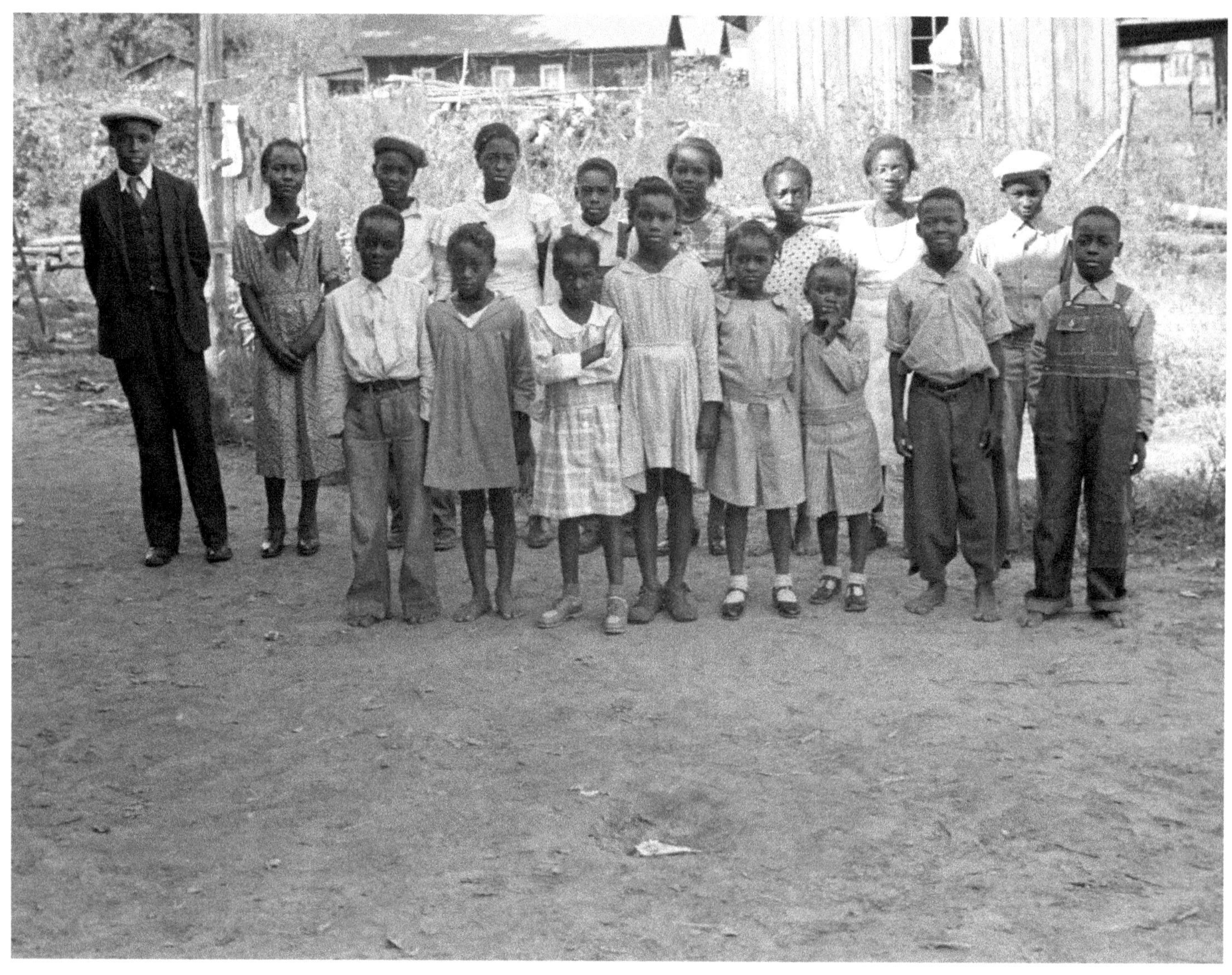

The children of sharecroppers pose for the photographer in October 1935. Americans everywhere were struggling through the worst of the Great Depression.

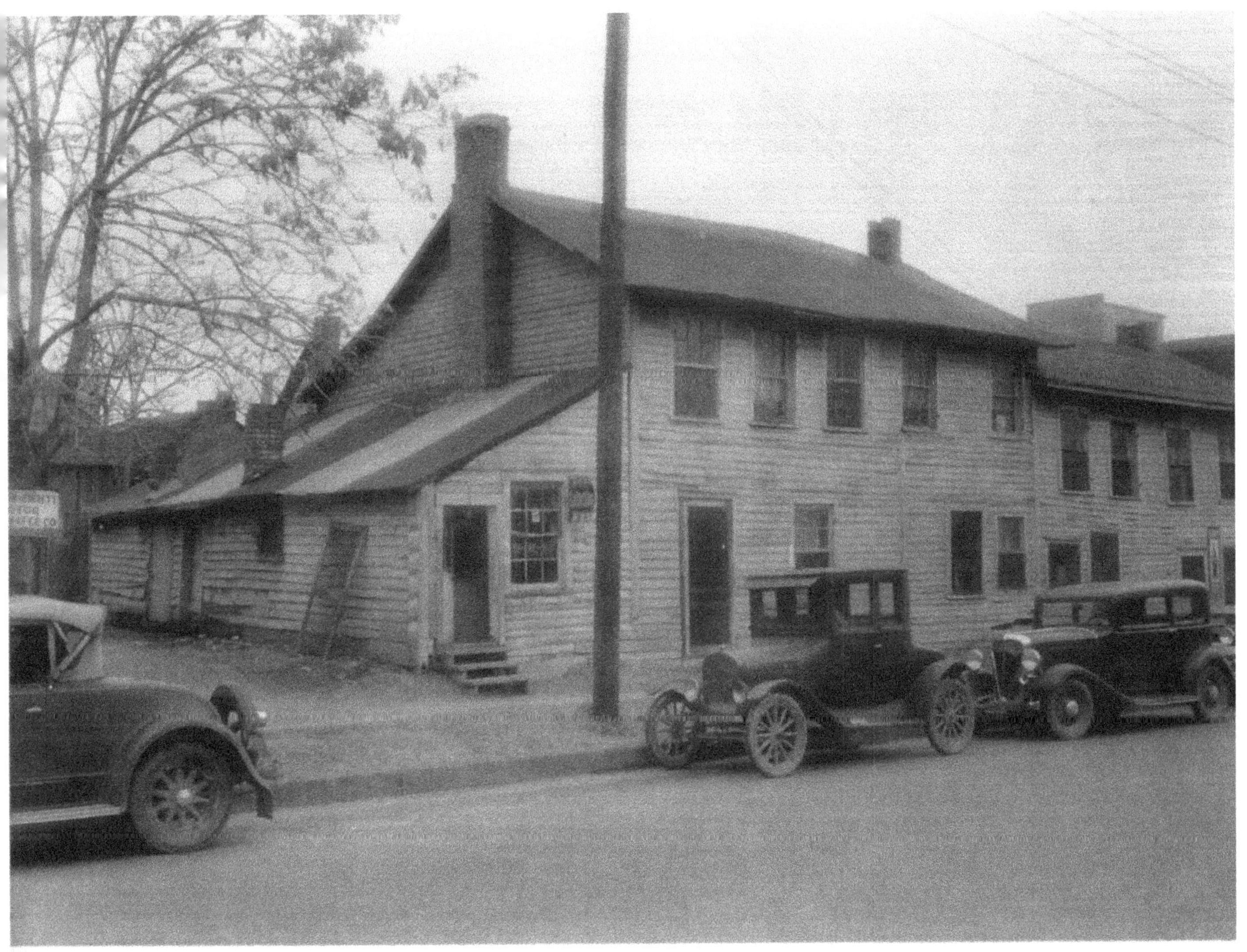

A ramshackle Henderliter Place at Second and Cumberland streets in February 1934. The sign in the barbershop window at center says "U-R-Next." At far-right, signage advertises soft drinks, barbecue, and beer. The two-seater Model T Ford coupe, parked beside the telephone pole, marks automotive designs of an era gone by—the last Model T had come off Henry Ford's assembly line in 1927.

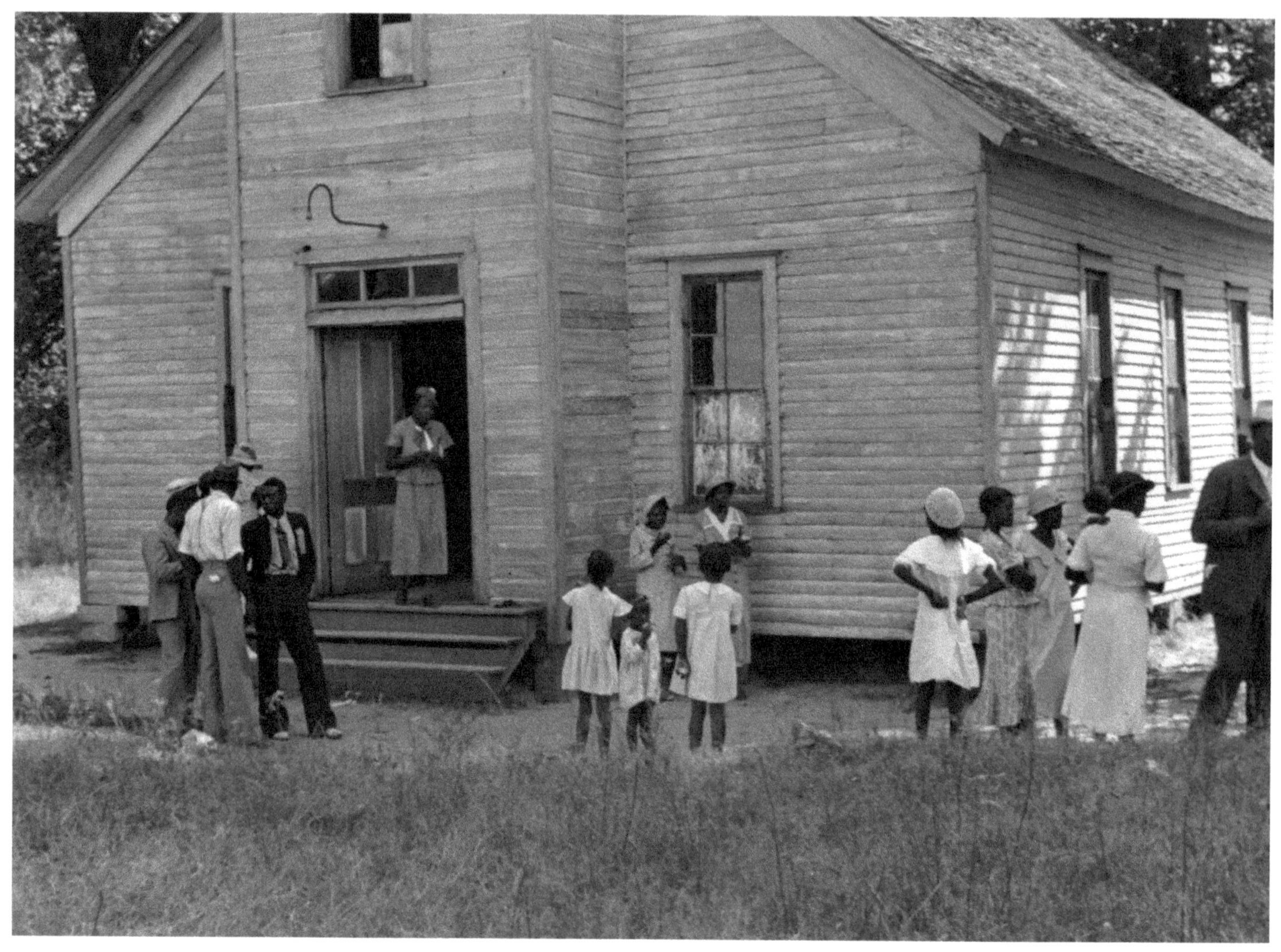

A typical October Sunday in Little Rock in 1935.

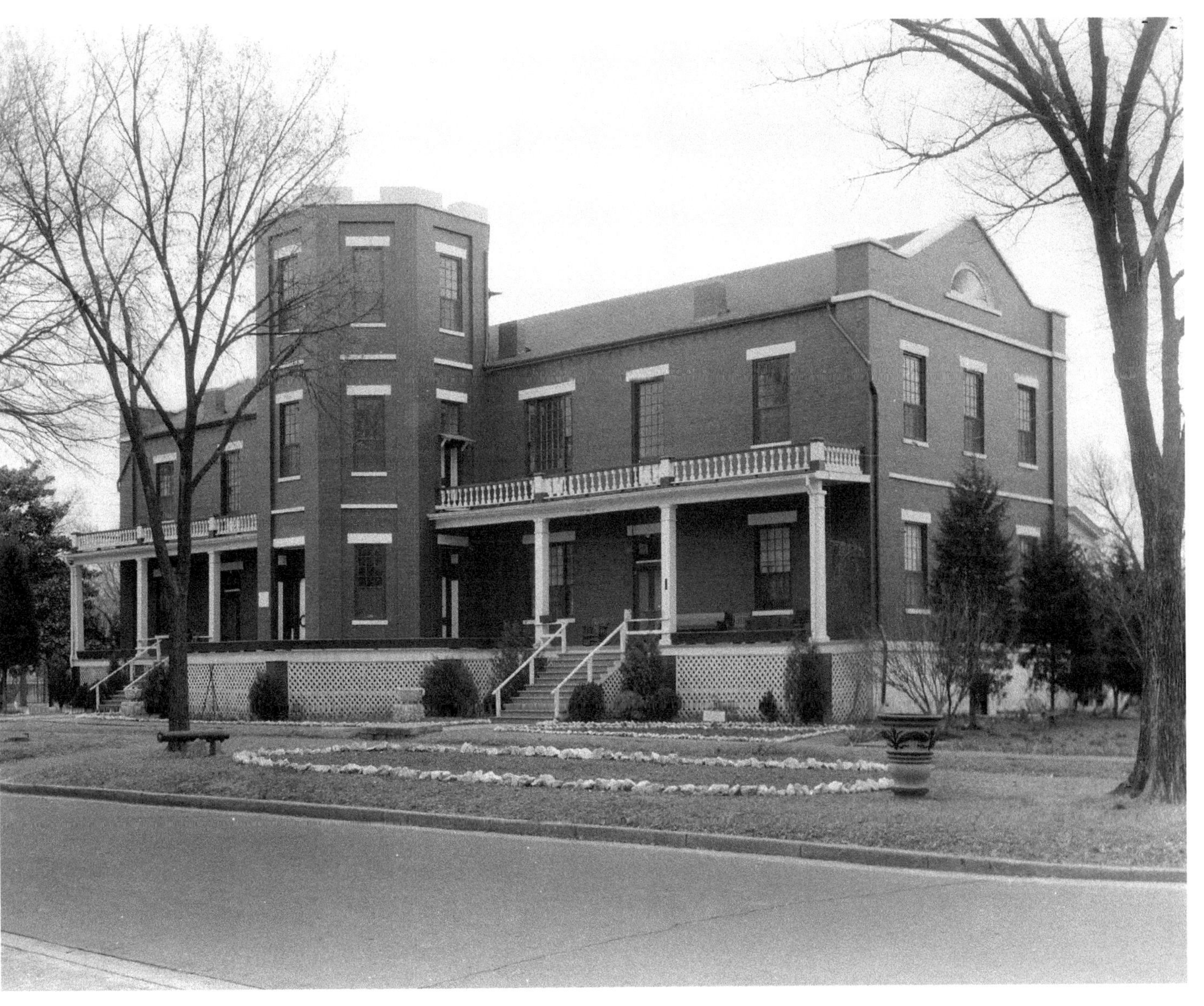

The United States Arsenal Building in City Park as it appeared on April 12, 1934. The arsenal was built in 1840, and General Douglas MacArthur was born here in 1880. Today the park is known as MacArthur Park and the building houses the MacArthur Museum of Arkansas Military History, in tribute to the illustrious general of World War II.

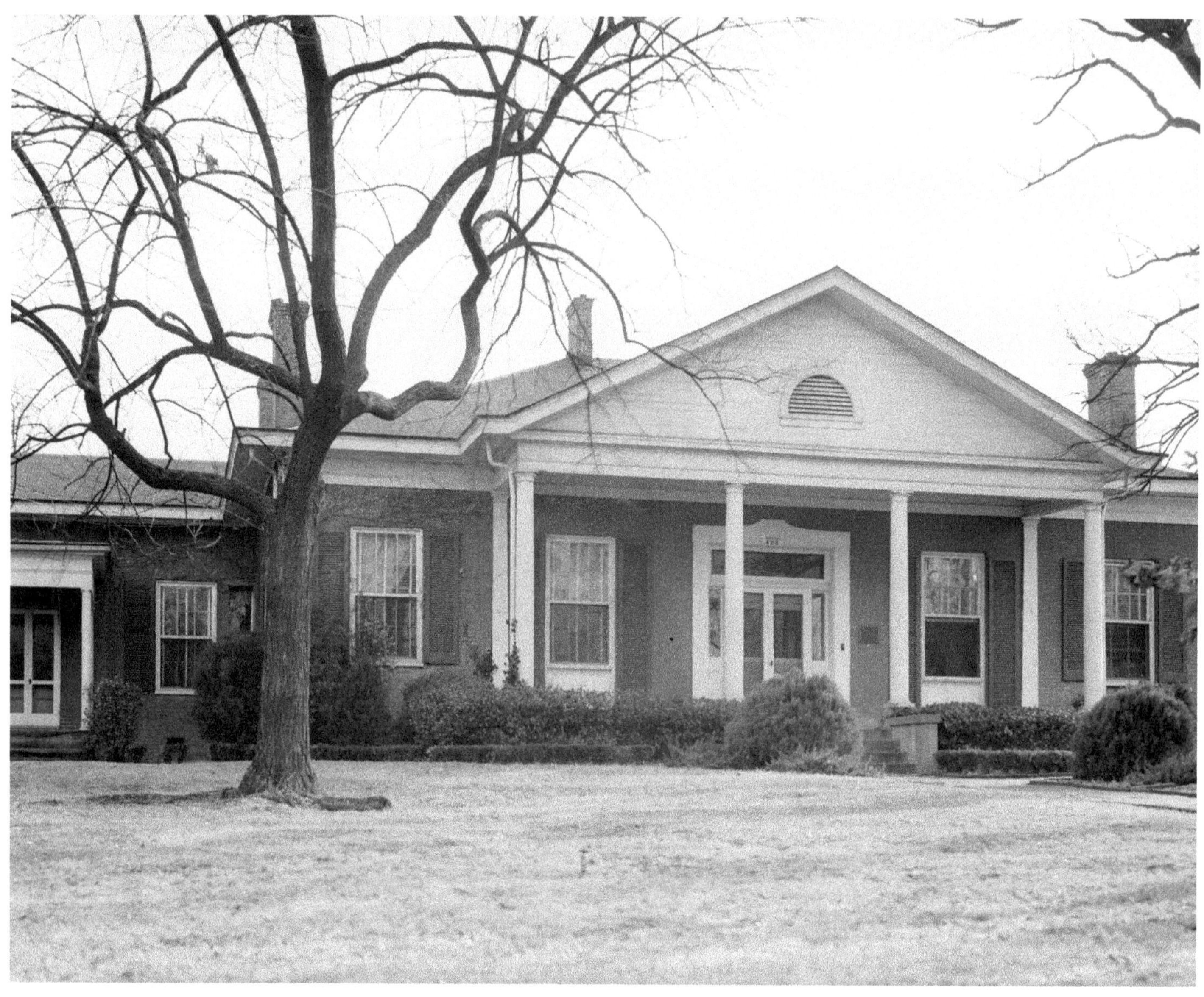

Trapnall Hall, at 423 East Capitol Avenue, around the 1930s. Trapnall Hall was built in 1843 as one of few brick homes in early Little Rock. It was owned by Martha and Frederic Trapnall, a merchant and lawyer who served in the Arkansas state legislature before the Civil War. Today the Greek Revival home has been restored and serves as the official receiving hall for governors of Arkansas.

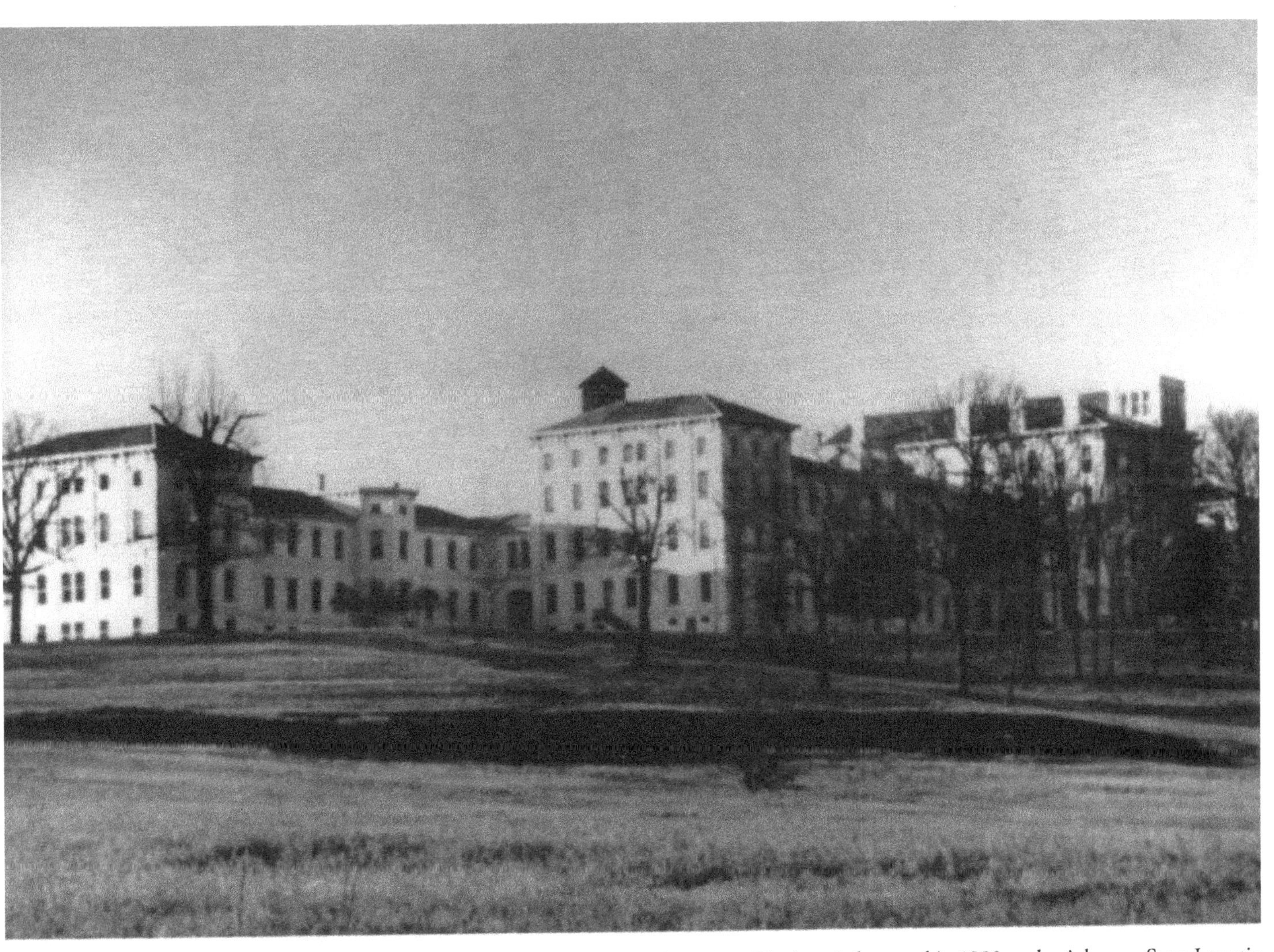

The State Hospital, located on West Markham Street, around the 1930s. The hospital opened in 1883 as the Arkansas State Lunatic Asylum. These buildings would be torn down in the 1960s and replaced with a new state hospital dedicated in 1964.

These young boys reach the summit of a soft-drink stand in June 1938, waving to the photographer in triumphant glee.

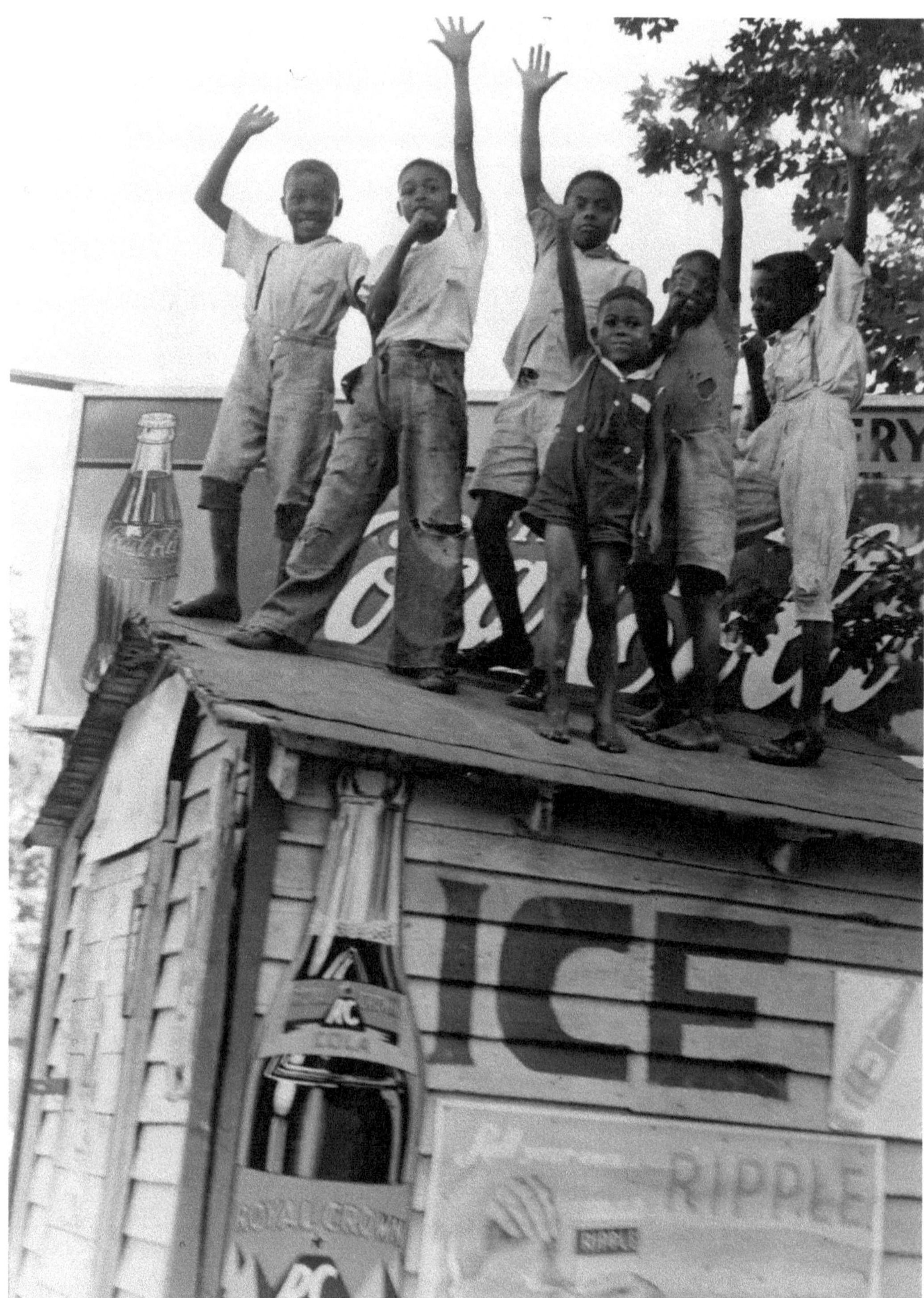

Crisis and Redemption

(1940–1960s)

From the war years forward, Little Rock was transformed into a metropolitan city. The city experienced a population boom as families moved in during World War II to be closer to husbands stationed at Camp Pike (now Camp Robinson) in North Little Rock. The unreliable Arkansas River was finally tamed by the McClellan-Kerr Arkansas River Navigations system, and the river once again became an important mode of transportation. Buses replaced streetcars as the main form of public transportation on city streets, and politicians proposed a series of highways, including Interstate 30, to improve ground transportation generally. In April 1953, Little Rock's first television station, KRTV, began broadcasting. A second station, KARK, joined it a short time later. The first modern shopping center, the Town and Country Center, was built in 1956 at the corner of Asher and University.

In 1957 Little Rock faced a crisis that propelled the city into the national spotlight, ultimately tarnishing the city's reputation. In 1955 the Little Rock School District presented a plan to integrate public schools. Central High School was chosen as the first school to be desegregated. On September 4, 1957, nine black students attempted to enter the school, but the Arkansas National Guard was instructed by Governor Faubus to turn them away. In response, the federal government under President Eisenhower federalized the Guard and sent in the 101st Airborne Division to enforce the new laws. Still protesting, Little Rock citizens voted in fall 1958 to close all the city's high schools for the next school year. Desegregation prevailed, the schools reopened in 1959, and Ernest Green became the first black student to graduate from Central High.

In the 1960s, construction began on Interstate 630, Little Rock's major east-west expressway. The Interstate and Urban Renewal would change the face of the city. Many of the stores on Main Street closed and the street was shut down to vehicular traffic. The Quapaw Quarter Historic District was formed to help save historic houses on the east side of the city and today includes several neighborhoods and historic sites, among them MacArthur Park, Mount Holly Cemetery, the Governor's Mansion, and the South Main residential area. The Quapaw District helped offset losses created by federal highway and urban renewal programs, preserving portions of Little Rock's built history for future generations to experience and enjoy.

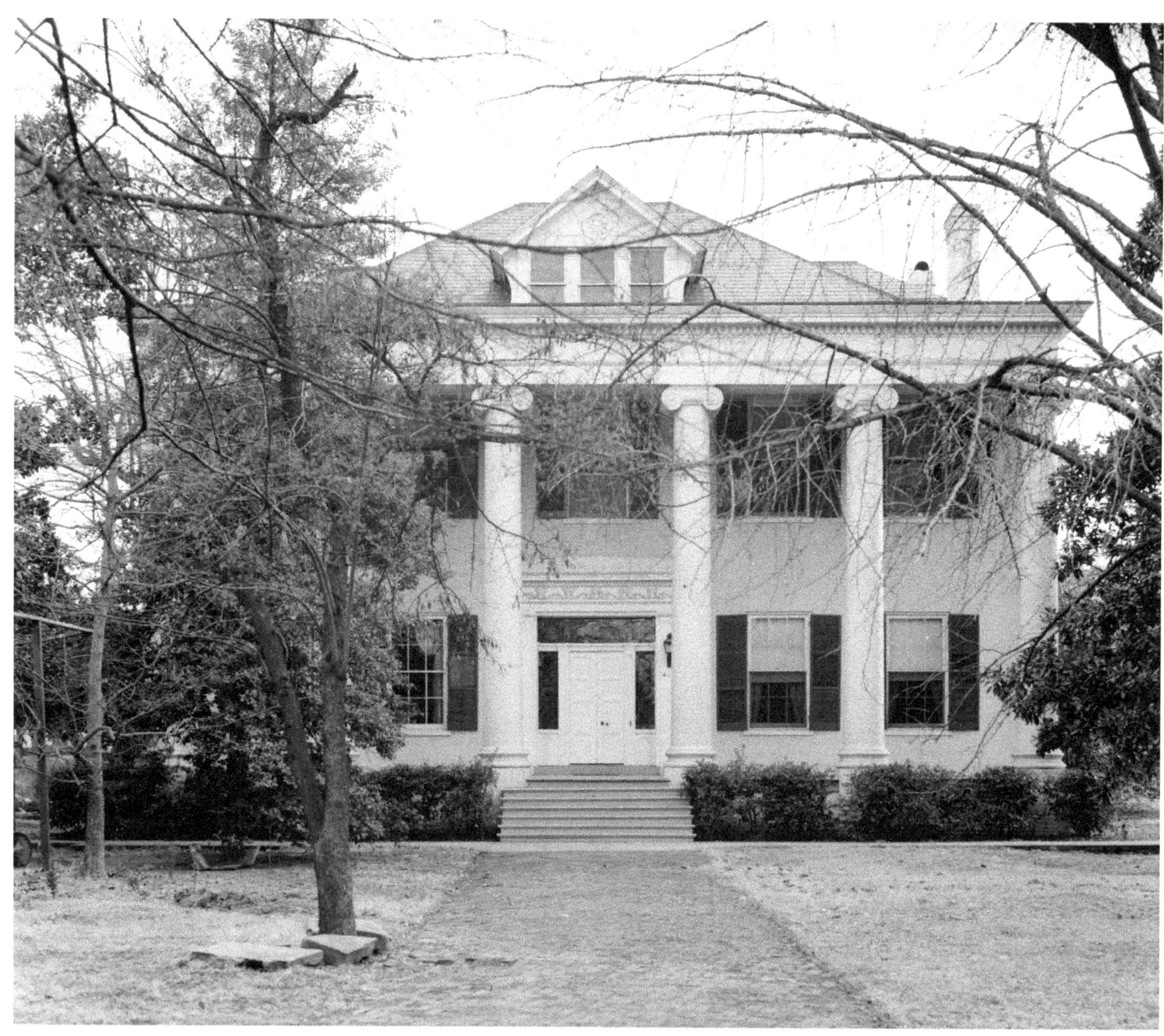

The Albert Pike House (now the Pike-Fletcher-Terry House) at 411 East Seventh Street, on March 1, 1940. Albert Pike, a Confederate general at the Battle of Pea Ridge, built the house in 1840. It was later the home of Pulitzer Prize–winning author John Gould Fletcher. Adolphine Fletcher Terry and her sister, Mary Drennan, left the mansion to the city of Little Rock in 1976. The Decorative Arts Museum opened here in 1985.

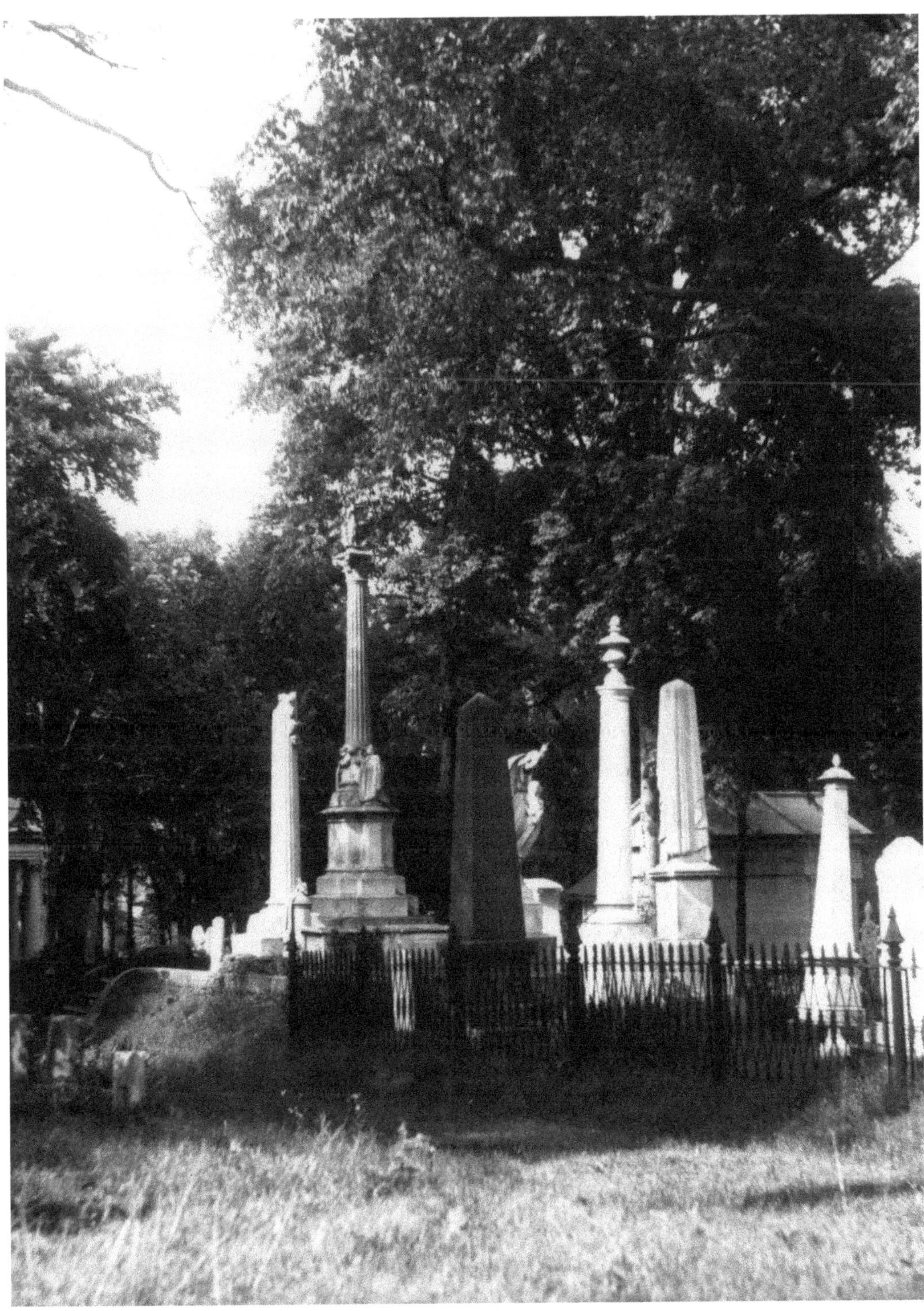

Mount Holly Cemetery is the most historically significant cemetery in Arkansas. It was established in 1843 and is the final resting place of many of Arkansas's early leaders, including 10 former governors, 6 United States senators, 14 Arkansas Supreme Court justices, 21 mayors of Little Rock, and many more historical figures. It is located at Broadway and Twelfth Street.

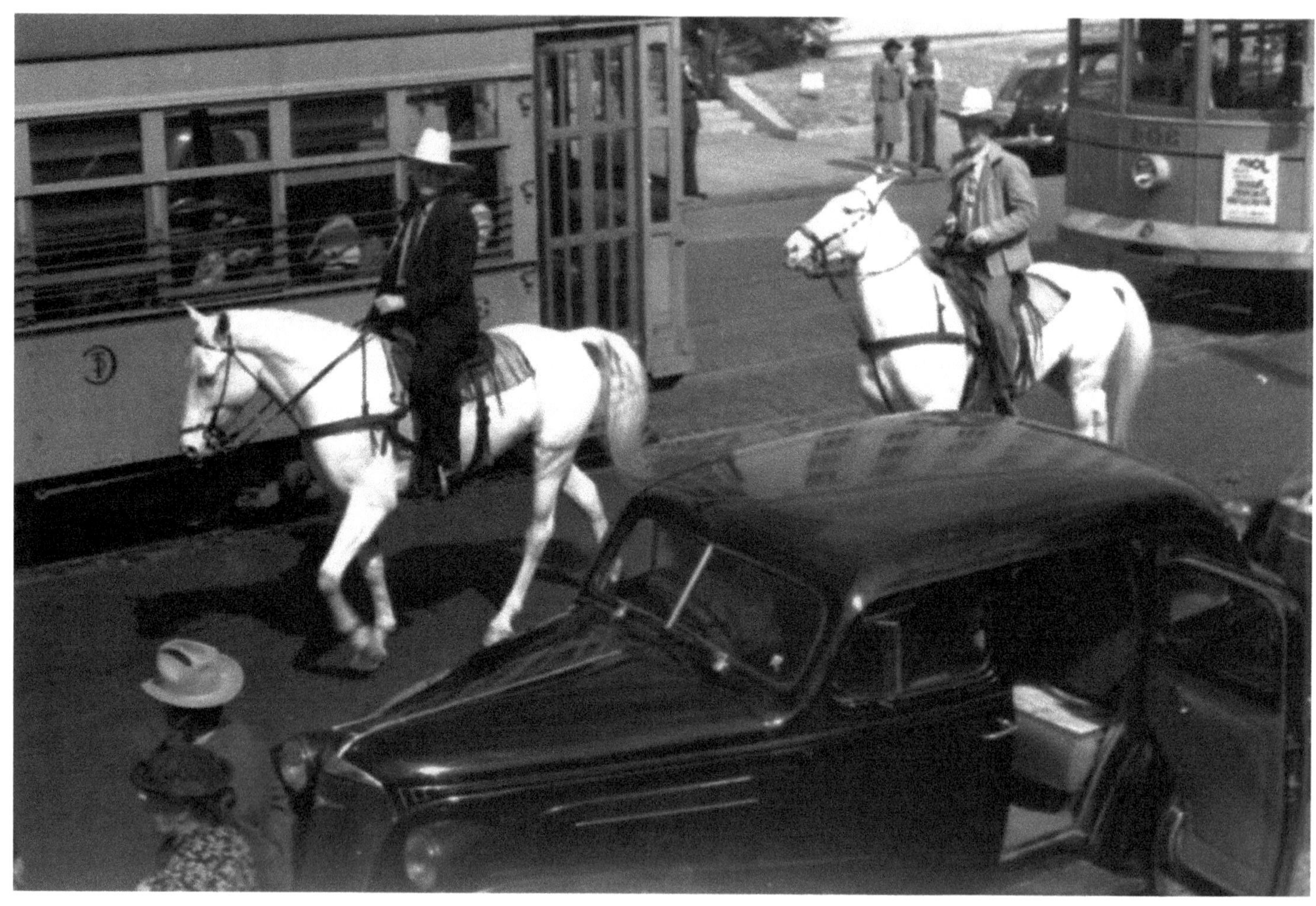

Members of the El Dorado delegation ride through downtown Little Rock in a parade for the Arkansas State Livestock Show in 1940. El Dorado had become Arkansas's boomtown for discoveries of oil there in the 1920s and 1930s.

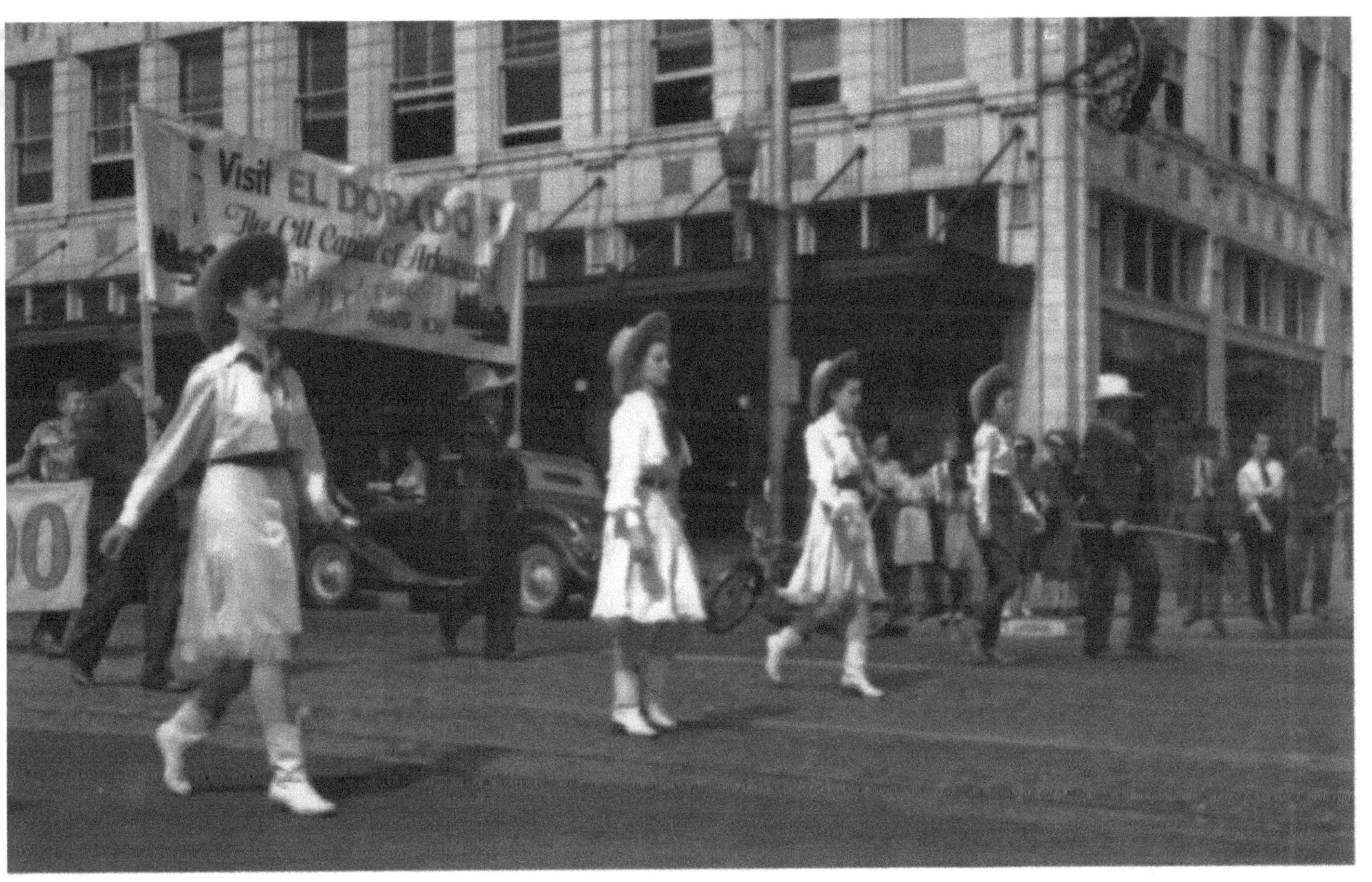

Members of the El Dorado delegation march downtown in the Arkansas State Livestock Show parade.

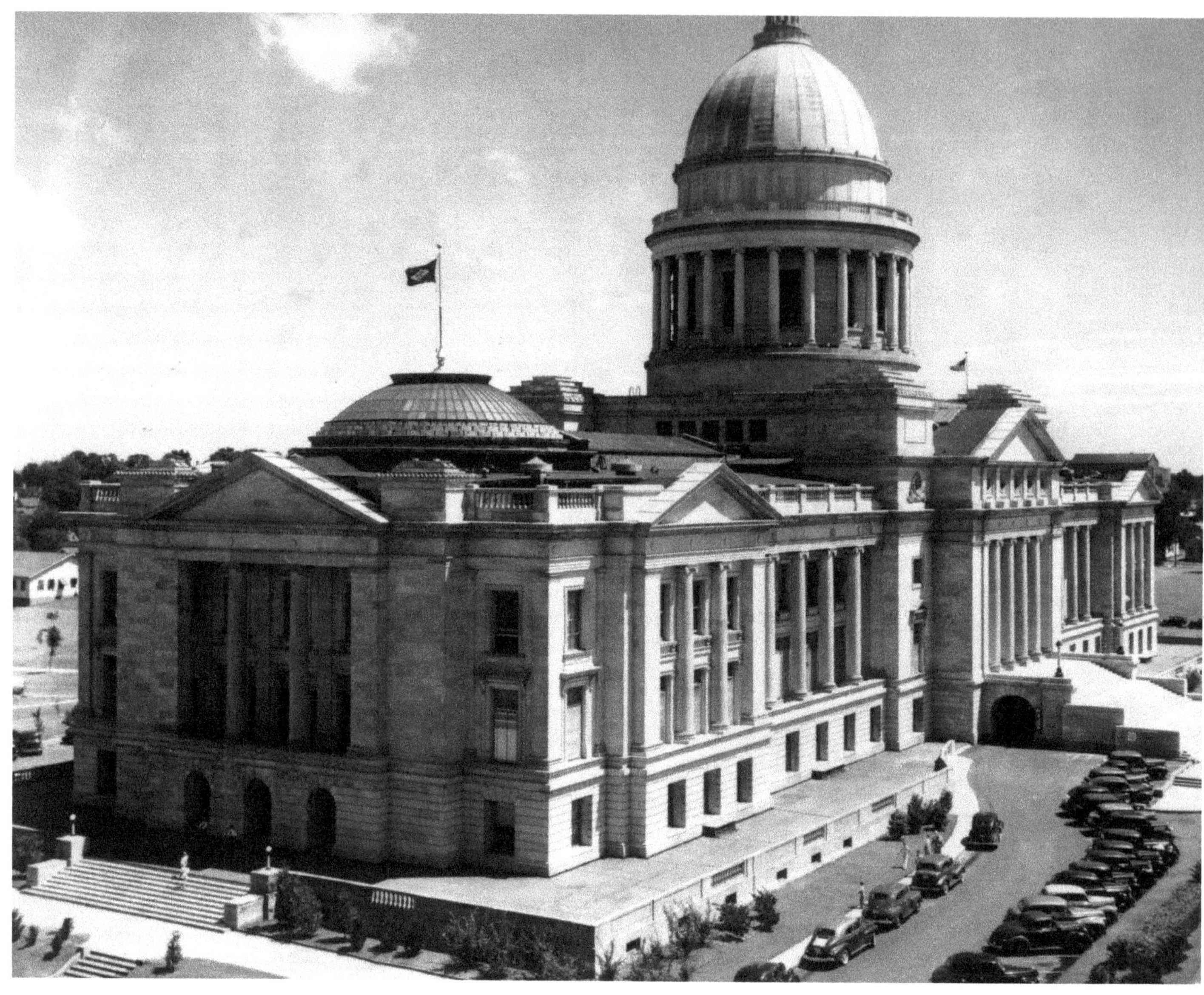

The Arkansas State Capitol around 1941. The building is a replica of the Capitol in Washington, D.C., and has appeared in many movies, including *Stone Cold* and *Under Siege*.

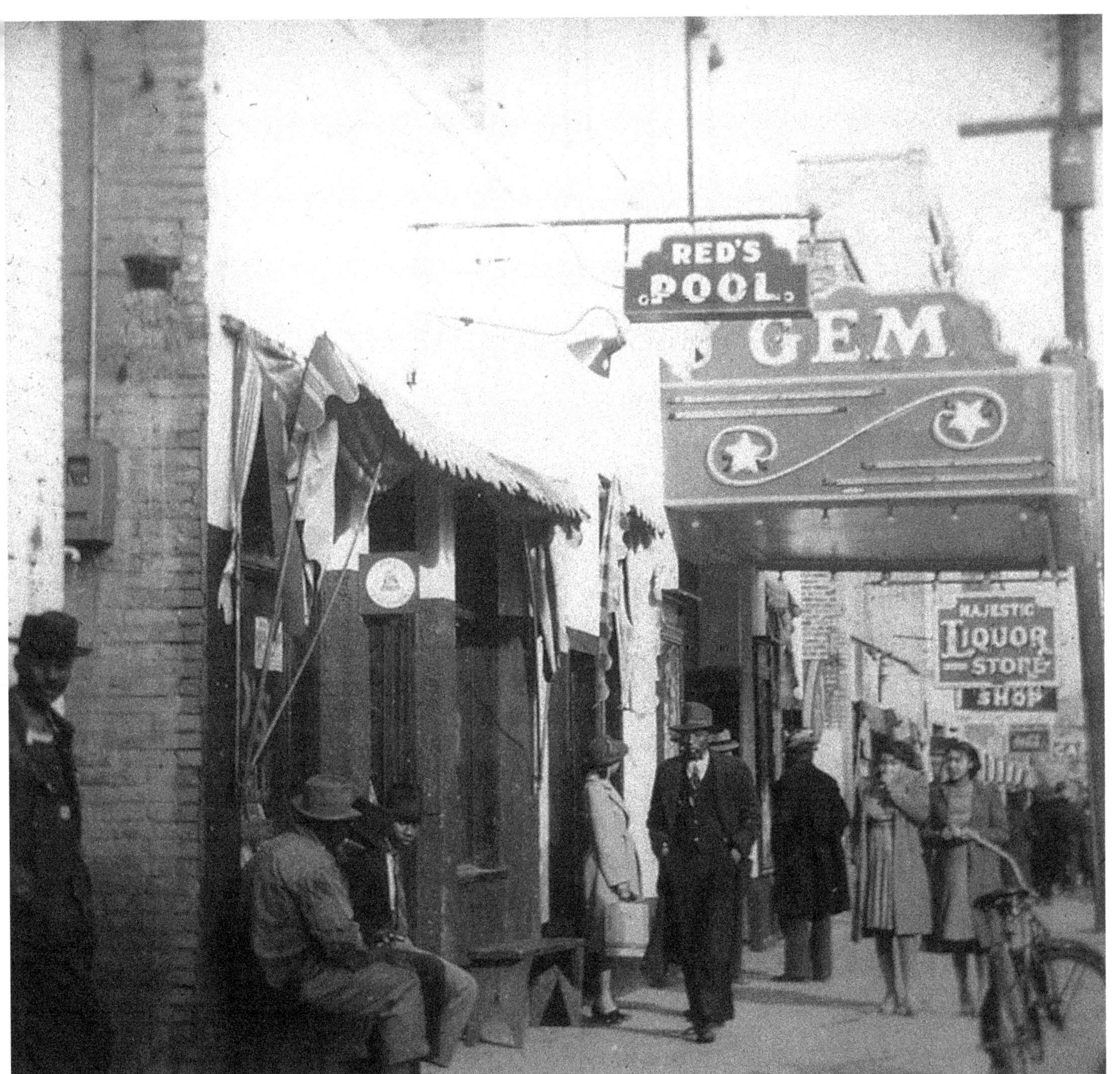

Red's Pool Hall and the Gem Theater were located on Ninth Street.

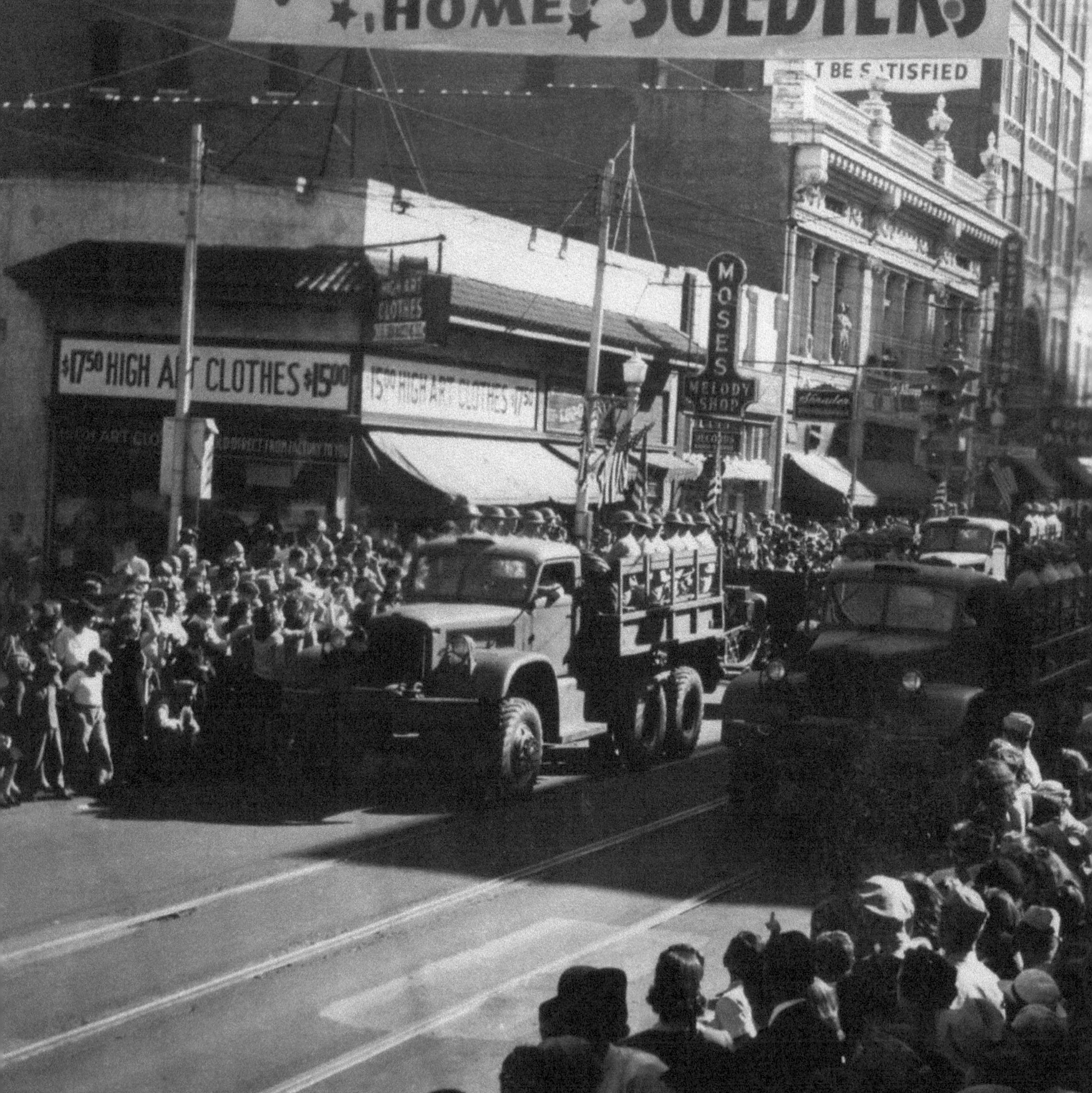
WELCOME HOME! SOLDIERS
T BE SATISFIED
HIGH ART CLOTHES
$17.50 HIGH ART CLOTHES $15.00
15.00 HIGH ART CLOTHES 17.50
MOSES
MELODY SHOP

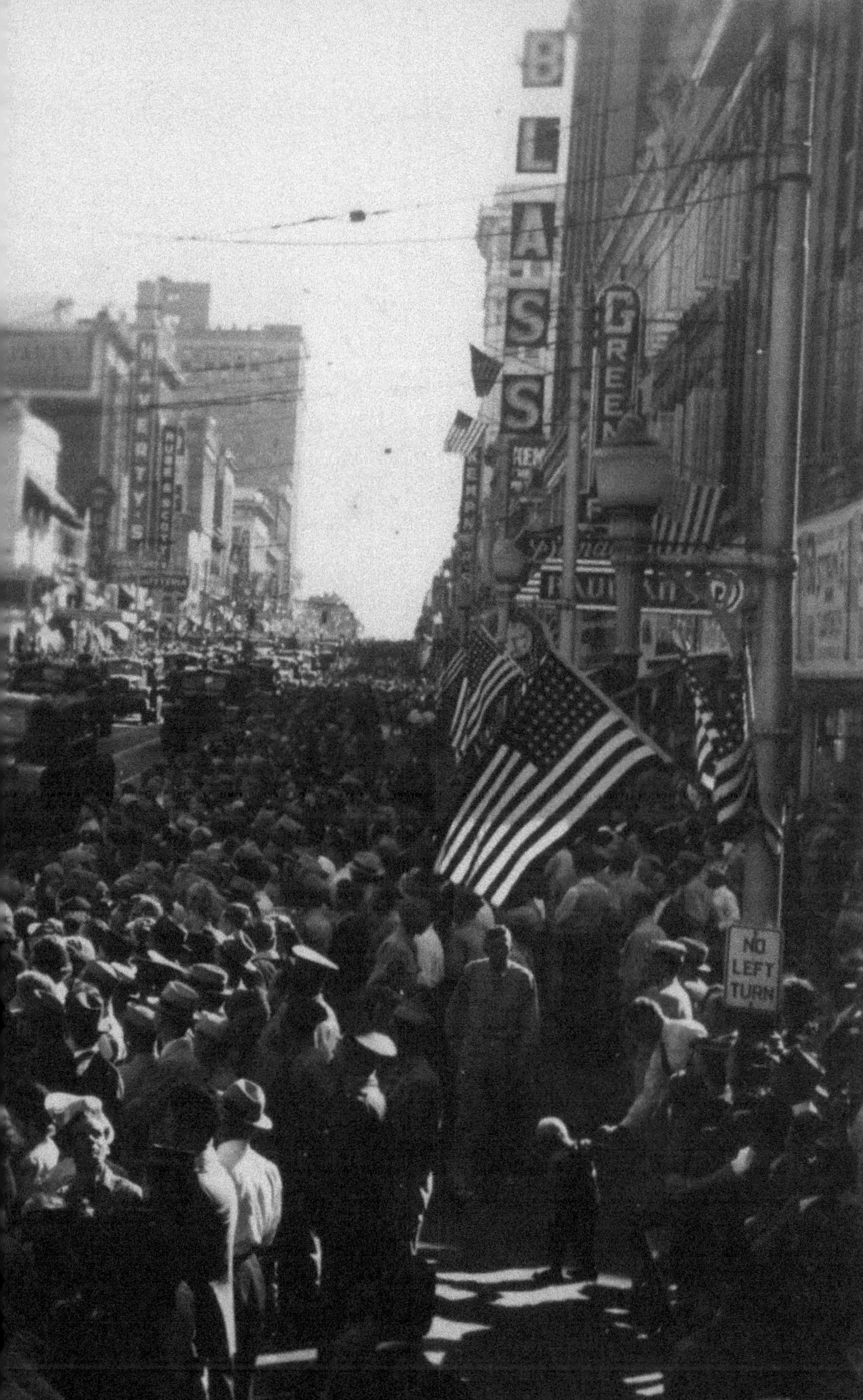

Locals gather for a parade in tribute to soldiers on the homefront, those riding the transport trucks in this image still wearing World War I helmetry. When Hitler and the Axis powers threatened the world with tyranny, the nations's armed forces headed overseas to fight a second world war.

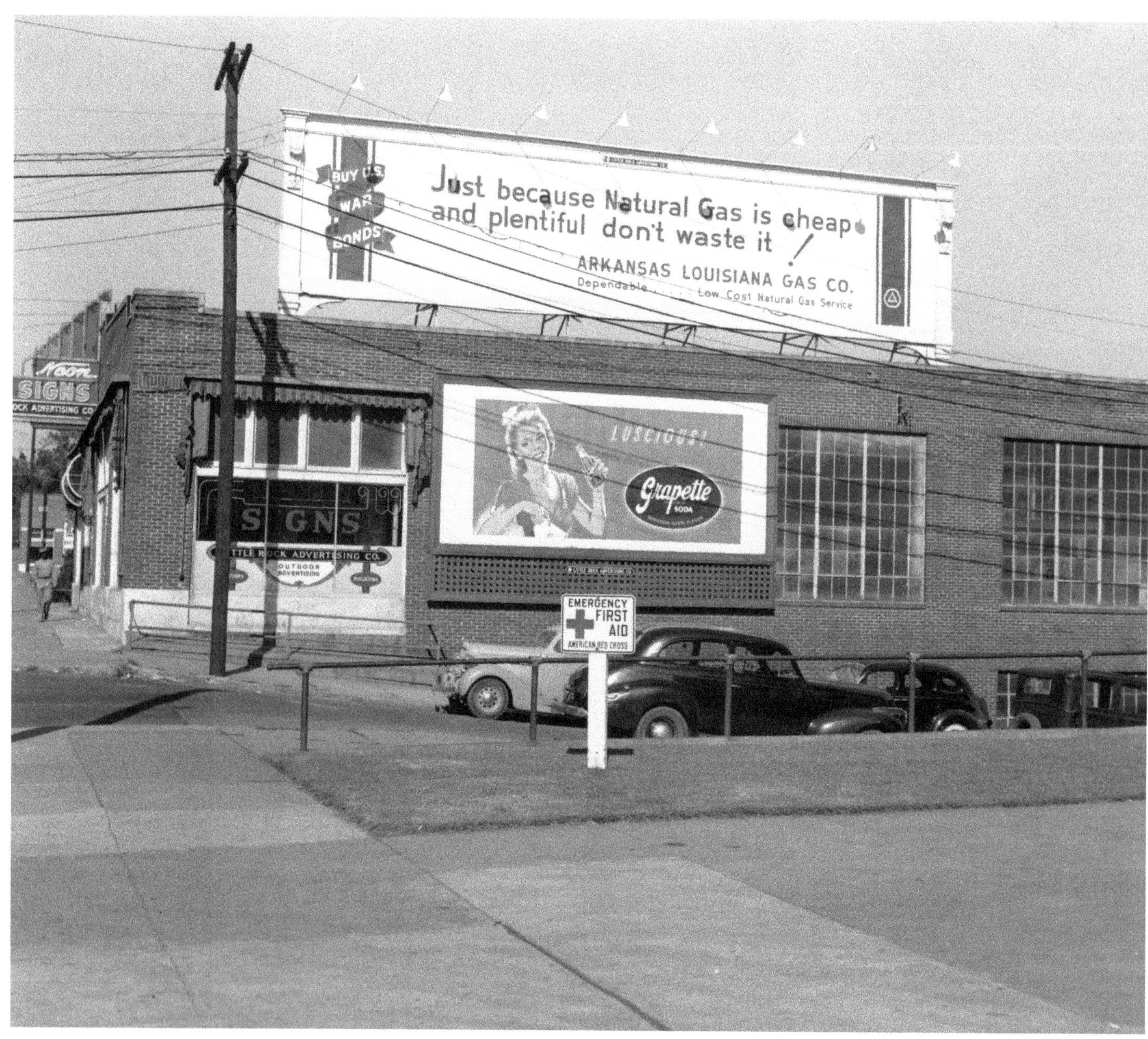

In 1942, this war-era billboard cautions citizens to conserve natural gas. Another gas, neon, had become fashionable for use in signage during the World War II era. Neon signs are being promoted by the Little Rock Advertising Company, in view here.

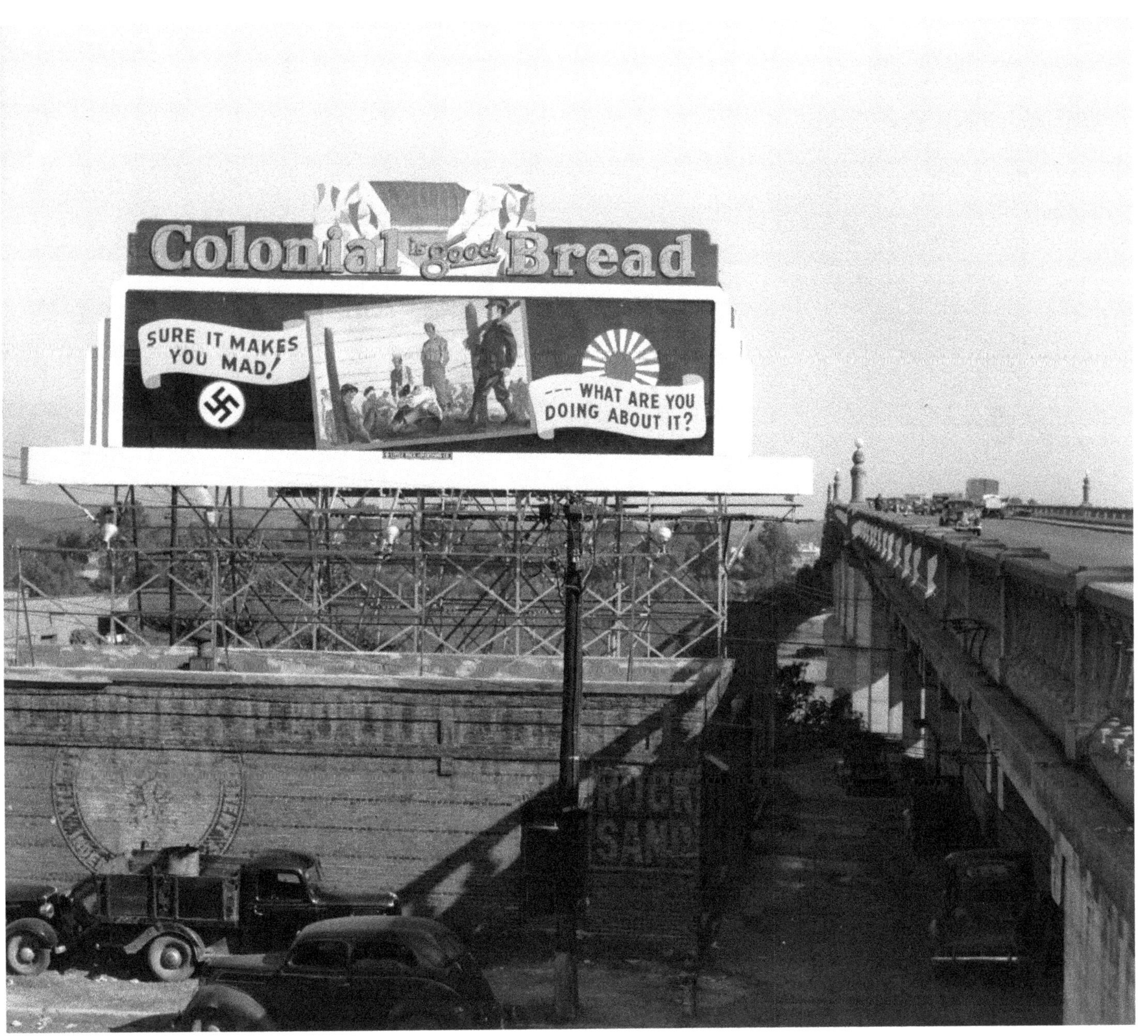

A billboard for Colonial Bread beside a bridge into Little Rock shows support for the Allies during World War II.

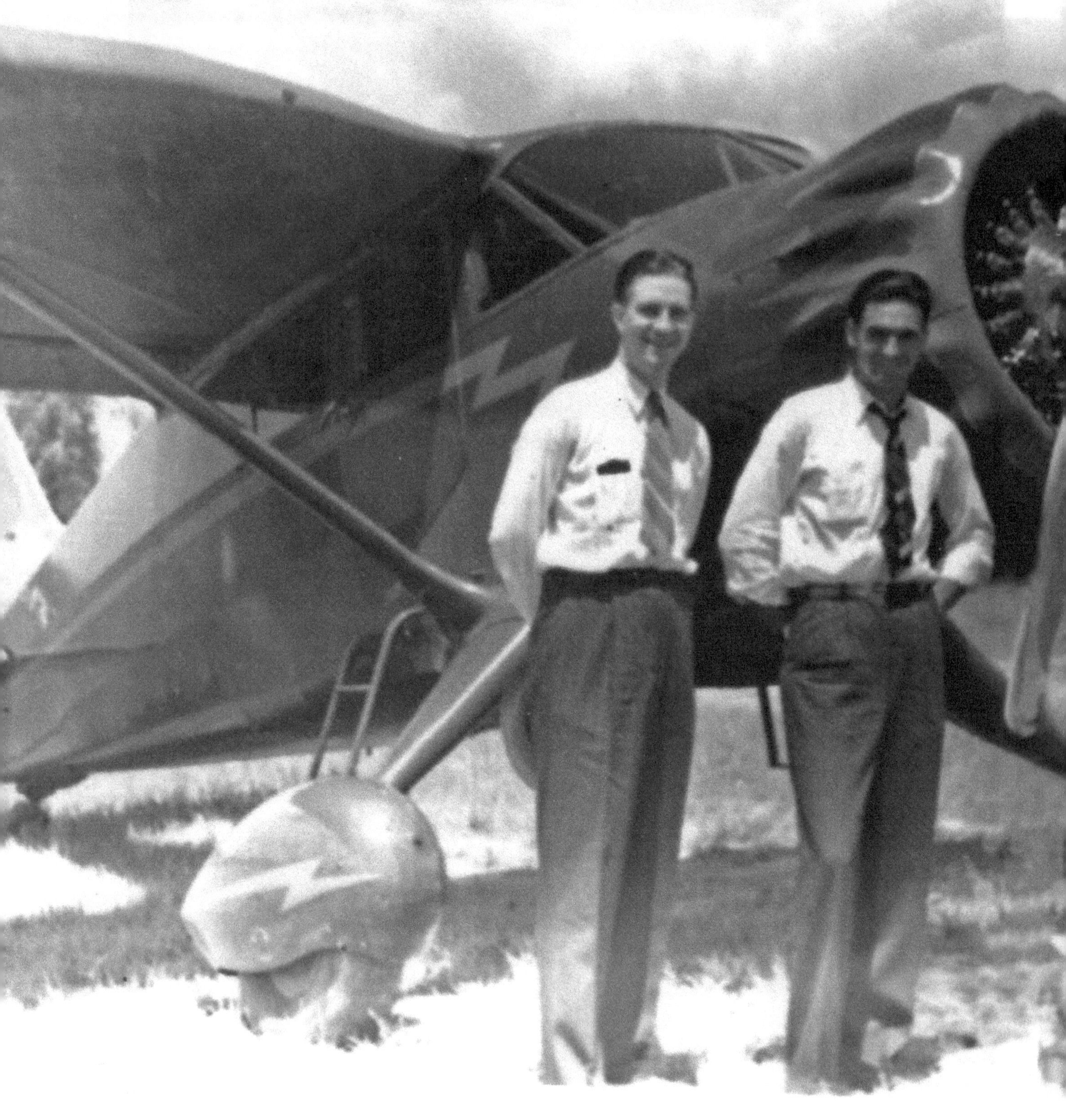

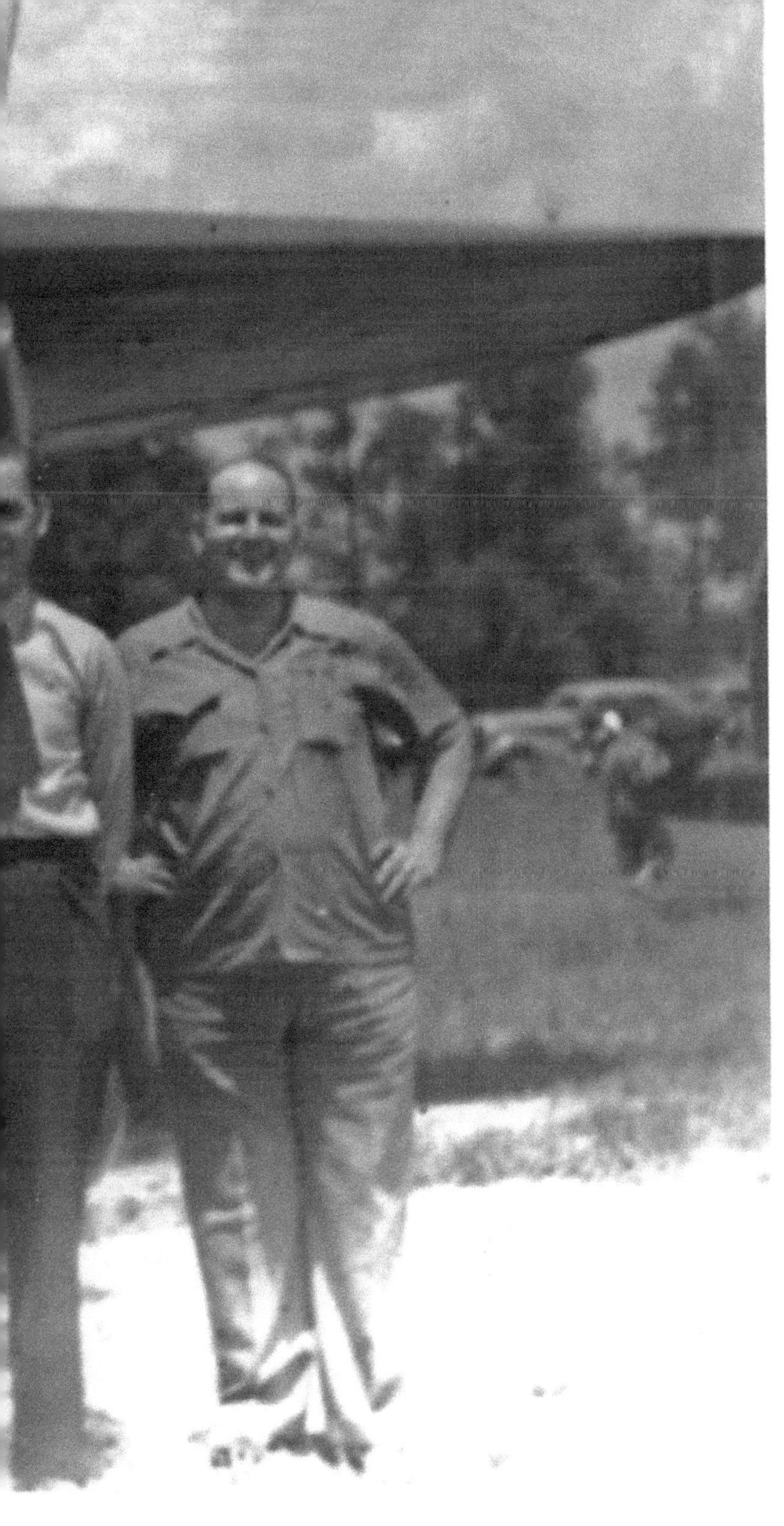

Members of the Arkansas Air Tour pose with a Stinson Reliant propeller airplane in 1941.

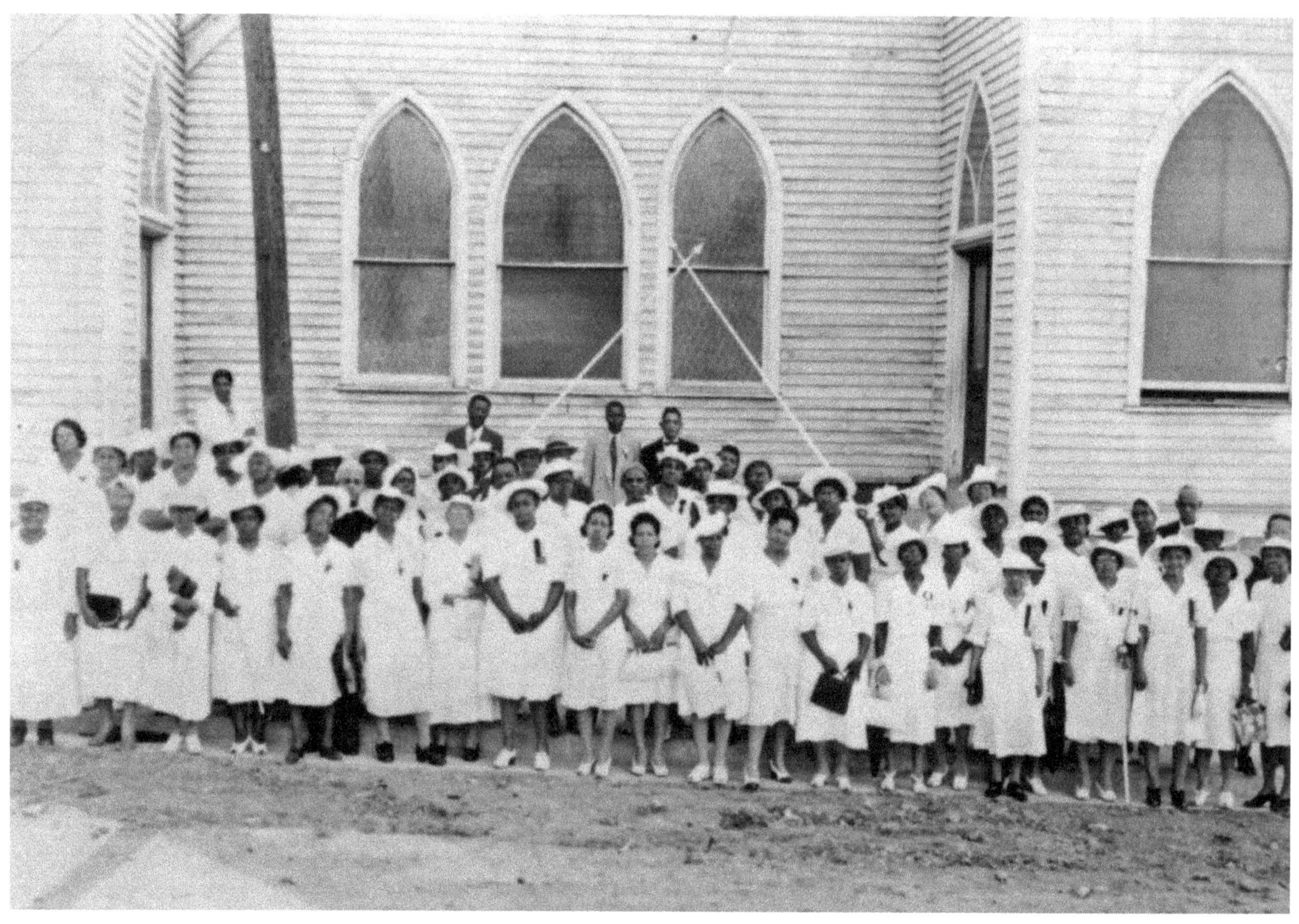

A group portrait outside Shiloh Baptist Church, located at 1200 Hanger Street, around 1942. Shiloh Baptist Church was established in 1888.

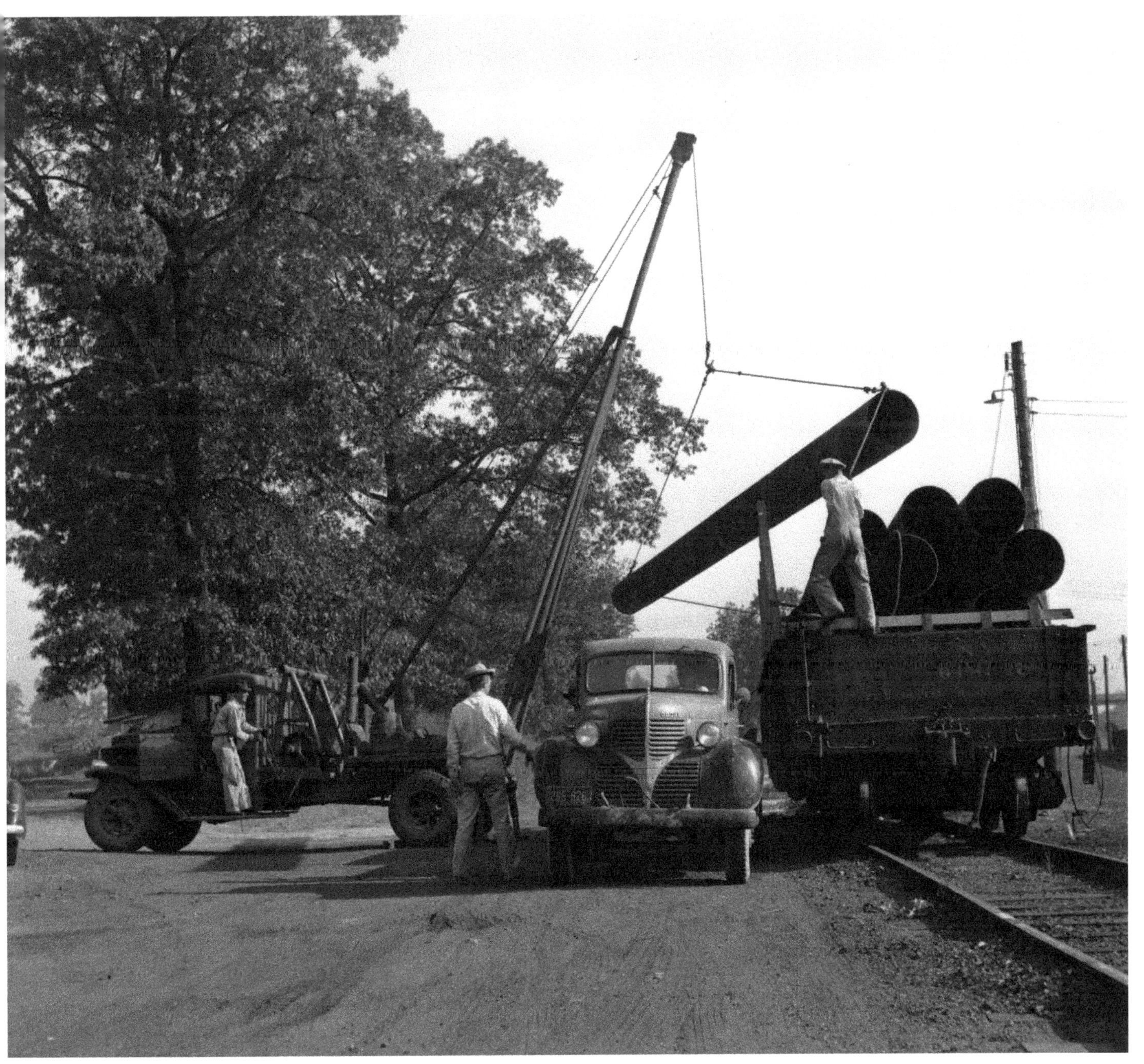

Three men load 40-foot sections of pipe onto stringing trucks in Little Rock in October 1942. The sections of pipe were part of a war emergency pipeline that ran from Longview, Texas, to Norris City, Illinois.

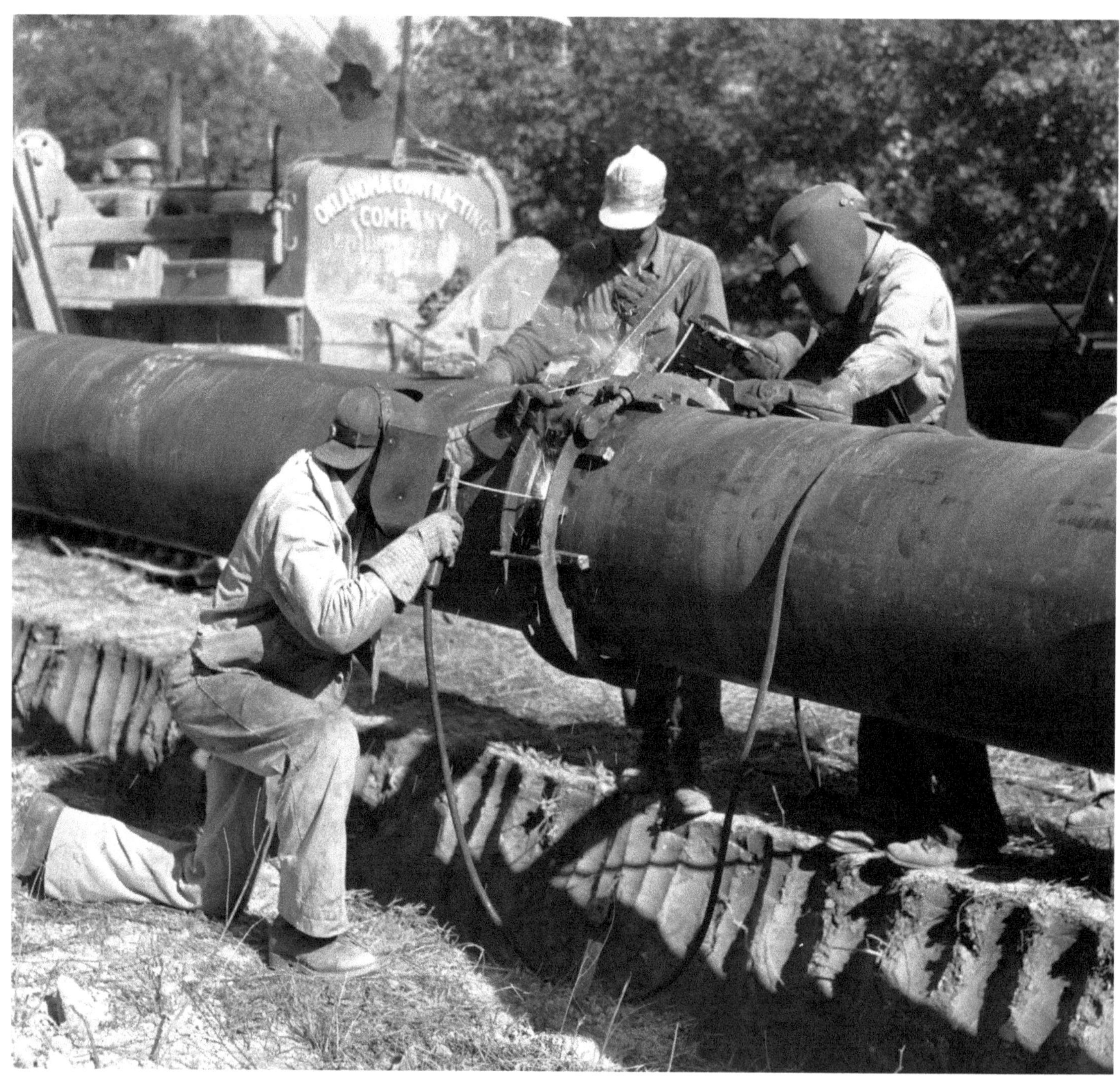

Construction workers weld sections of the gas pipe together.

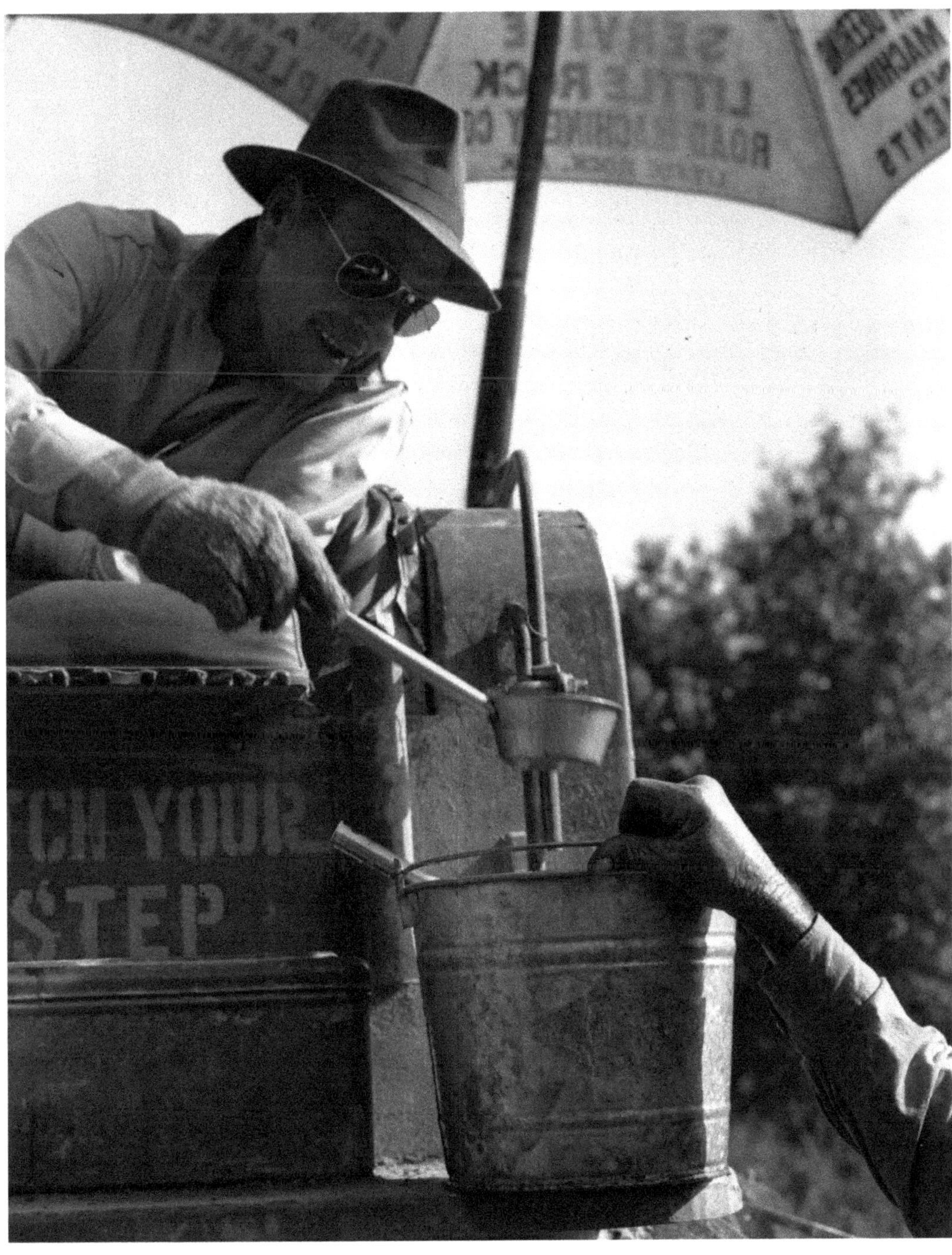

A heavy machinery operator working on the emergency pipeline takes a break and a sip of water.

Signage in front of City Hall in October 1942 promotes war bonds as a means of funding the construction of military aircraft. The United States had been engaged in the conflict overseas for nearly a year.

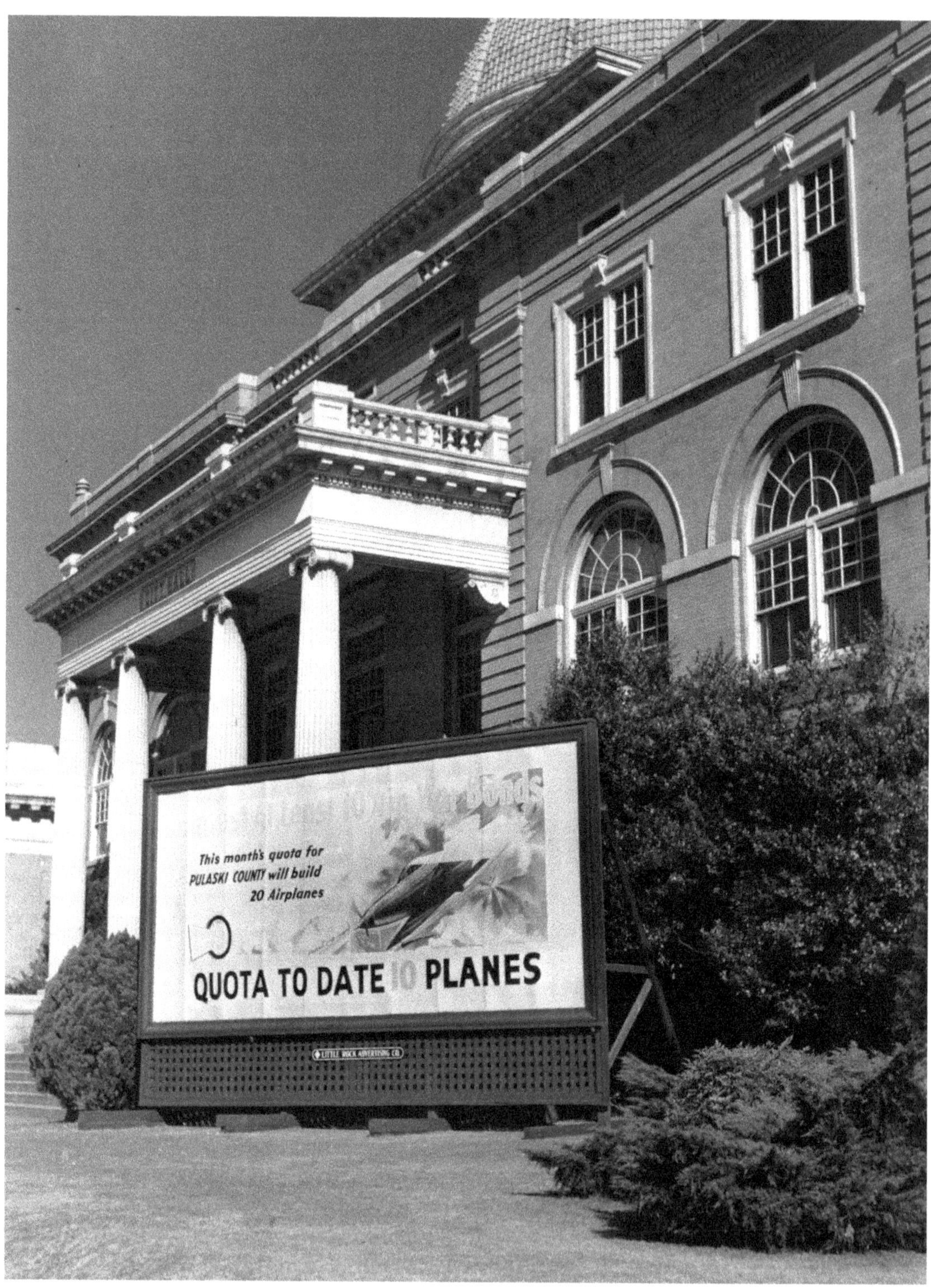

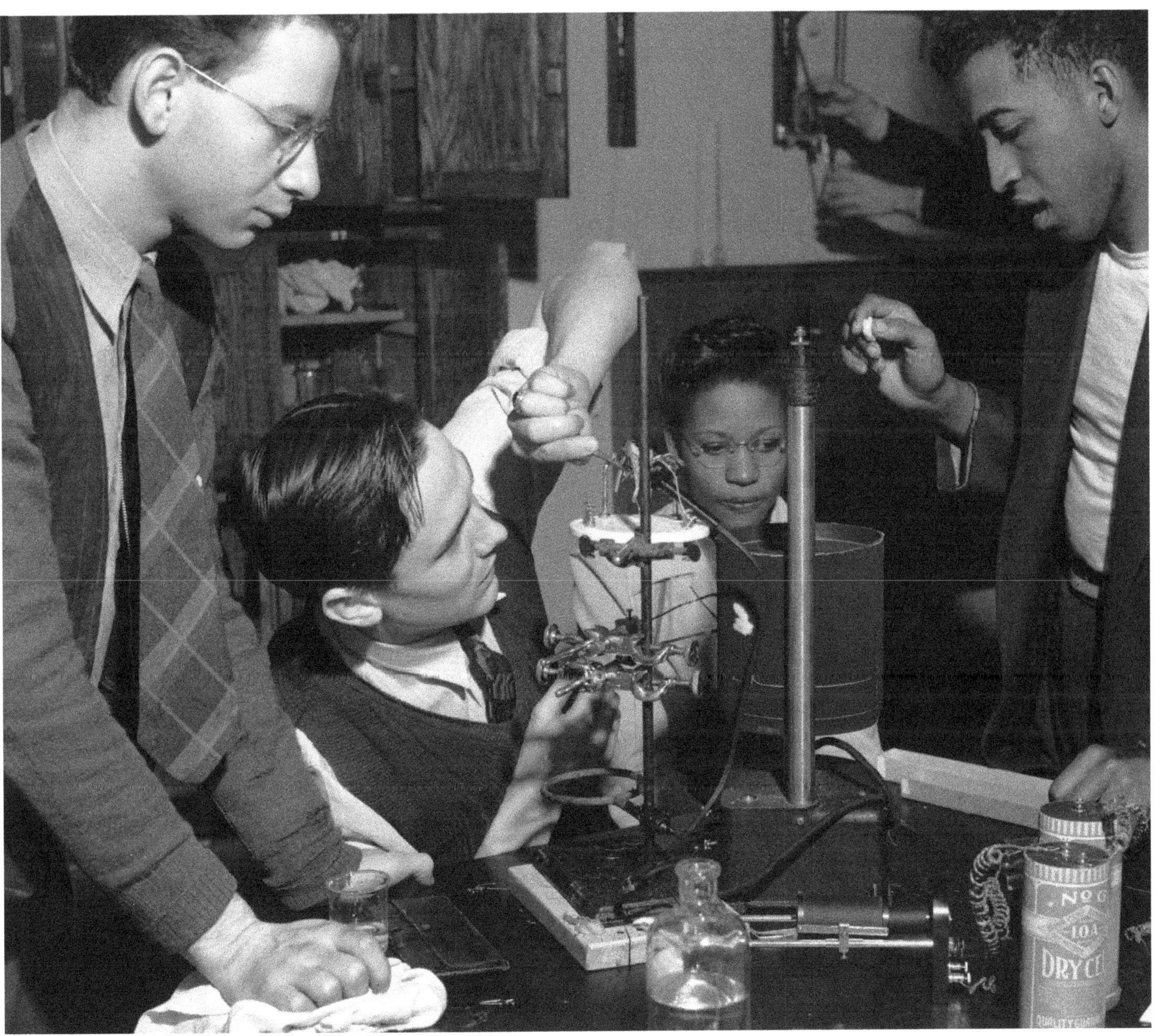

Postgraduate students perform an experiment to study the physiology of the muscle, around the 1940s. The experiment uses frog muscle tissue. Pictured are, left to right, J. S. Newcomer of the University of Utah; A. E. Bell of the University of Kentucky; Hiss Trondailer Jones of Lincoln University at Jefferson City, Missouri; and Samuel Massie of Arkansas State University.

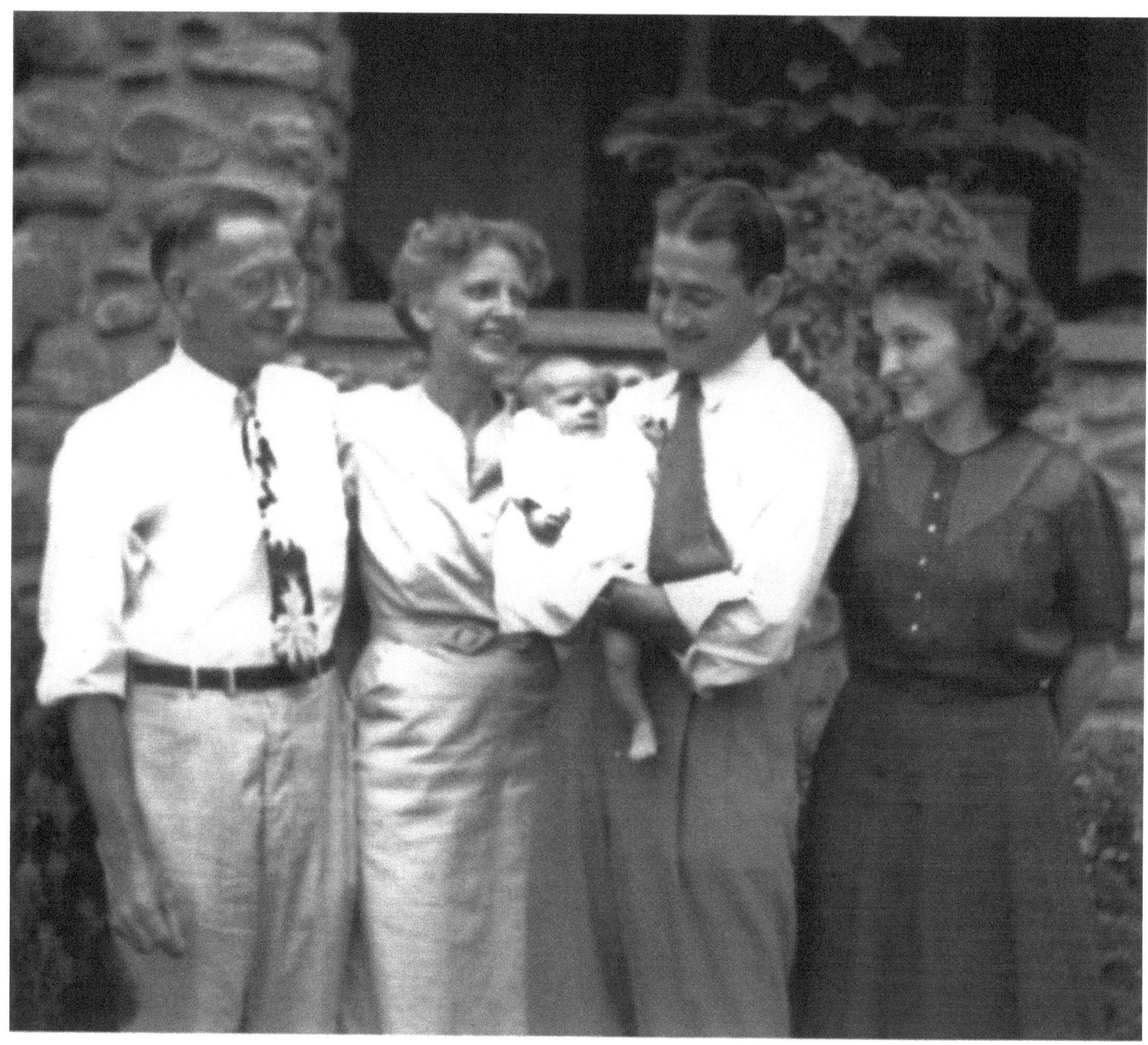

Claude E. McCreight and his family in the summer of 1946

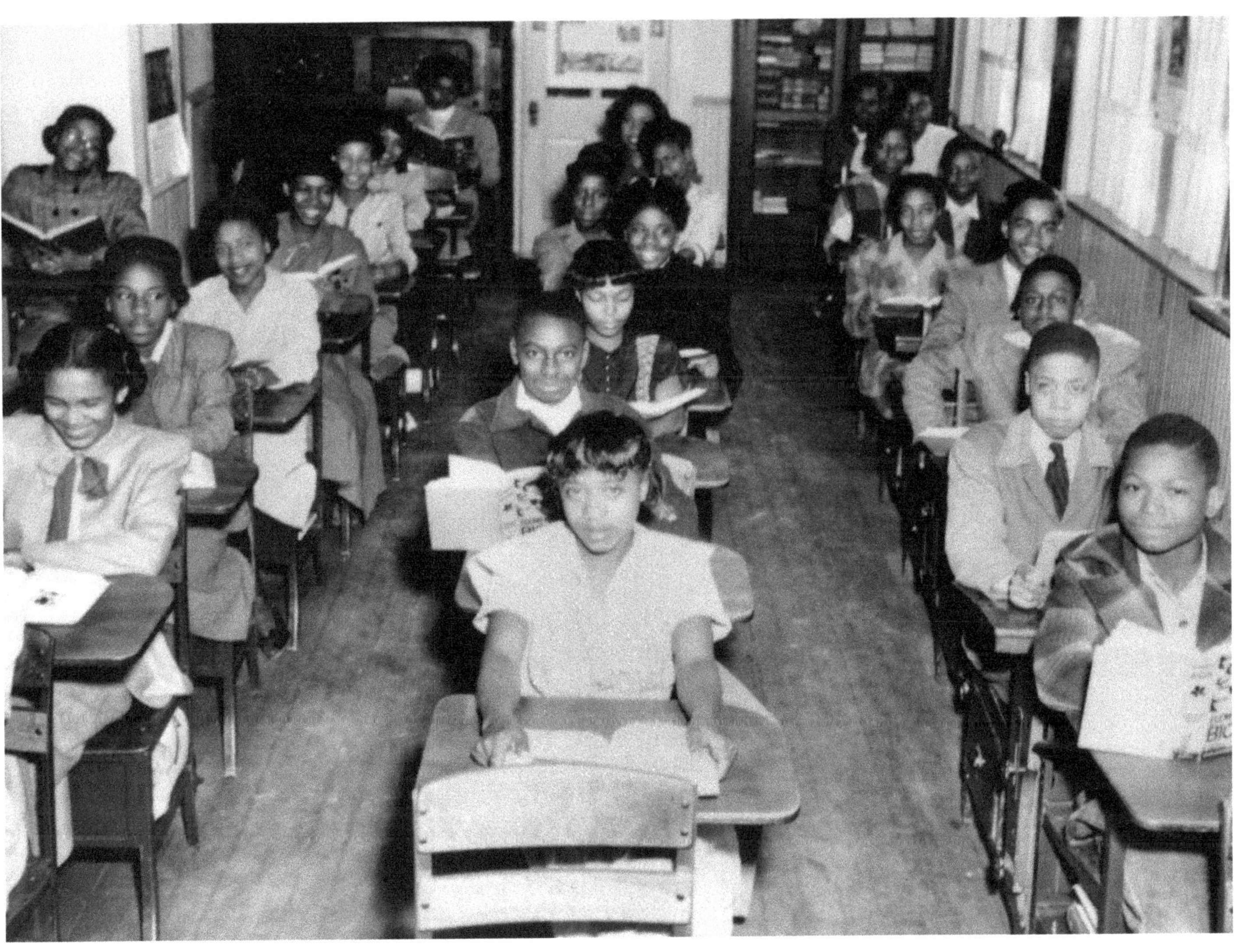

Class is in session at Saint Bartholomew's School in 1949. Saint Bartholomew's School, located at 1617 Marshall Street, was founded by Bishop John B. Morris in 1912 for African-American students. The school closed in 1976.

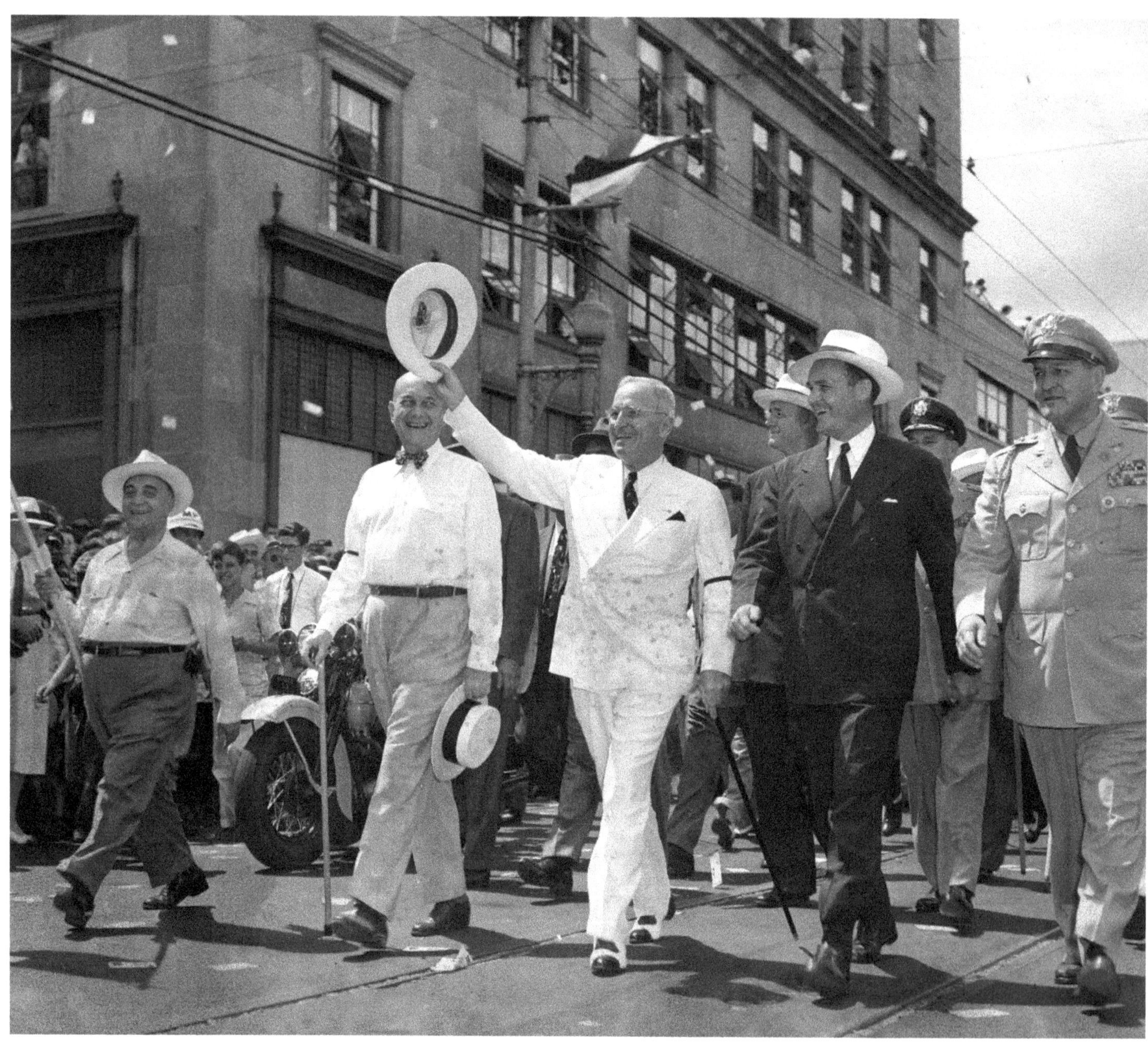

President Truman marches in the 35th Division Reunion parade on June 11, 1949. During World War I, as commander of Battery D, 129th Field Artillery regiment, 35th Division, Truman earned the respect of his men by remaining calm and focused under fire. As president, he made the decision to drop the atomic bomb on the Japanese cities of Hiroshima and Nagasaki, ending World War II.

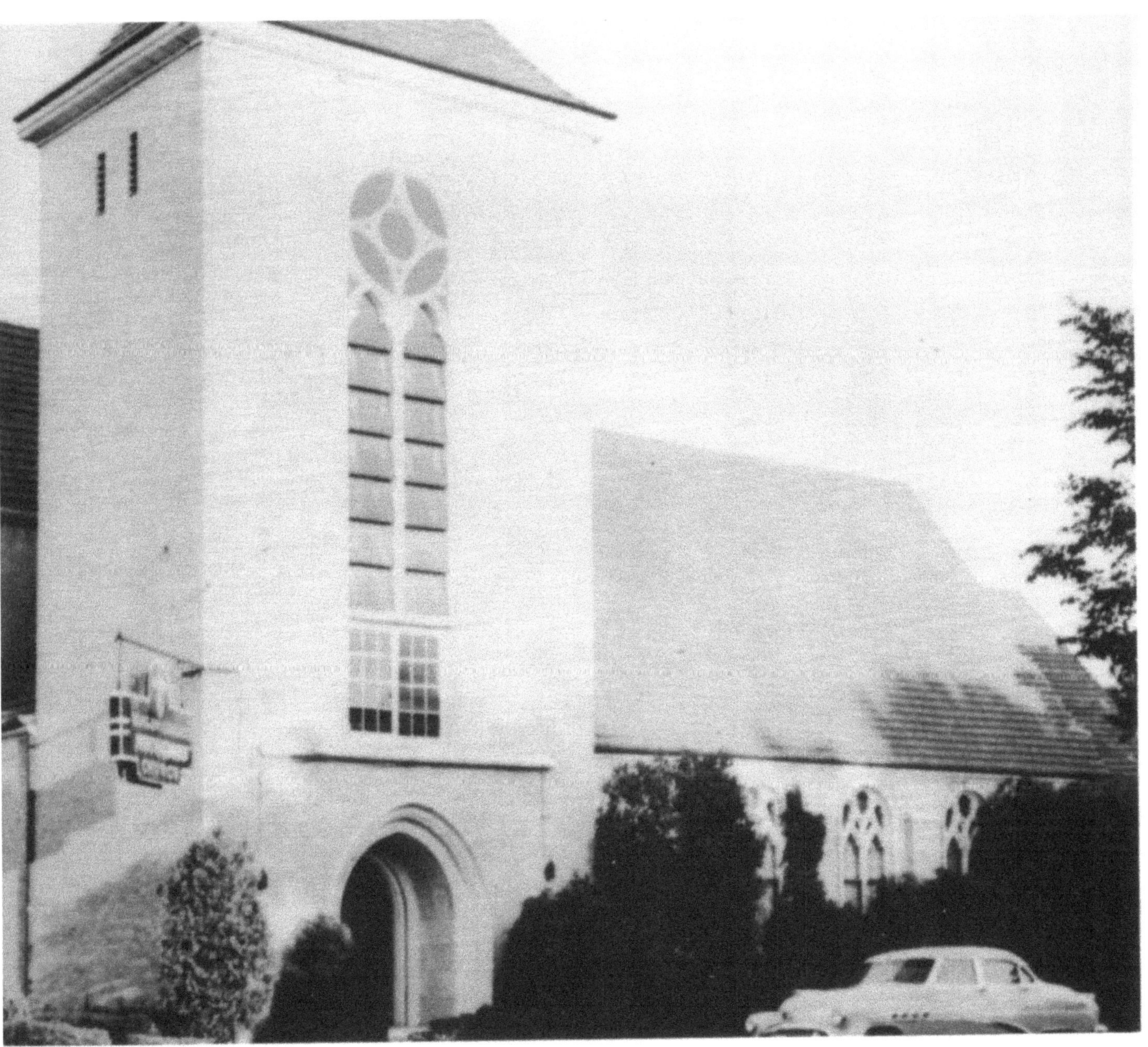

The Wesley Chapel Methodist Episcopal Church (today the Wesley Chapel United Methodist Church), was located at 1109 South State Street, around 1950. By 1853 the members of the Methodist church in Little Rock had outgrown their floor space, so a new facility, called Wesley Chapel, was built near Eighth and Broadway. The church moved again in 1883 to South State Street. The current building was completed in 1927 after fire destroyed the original.

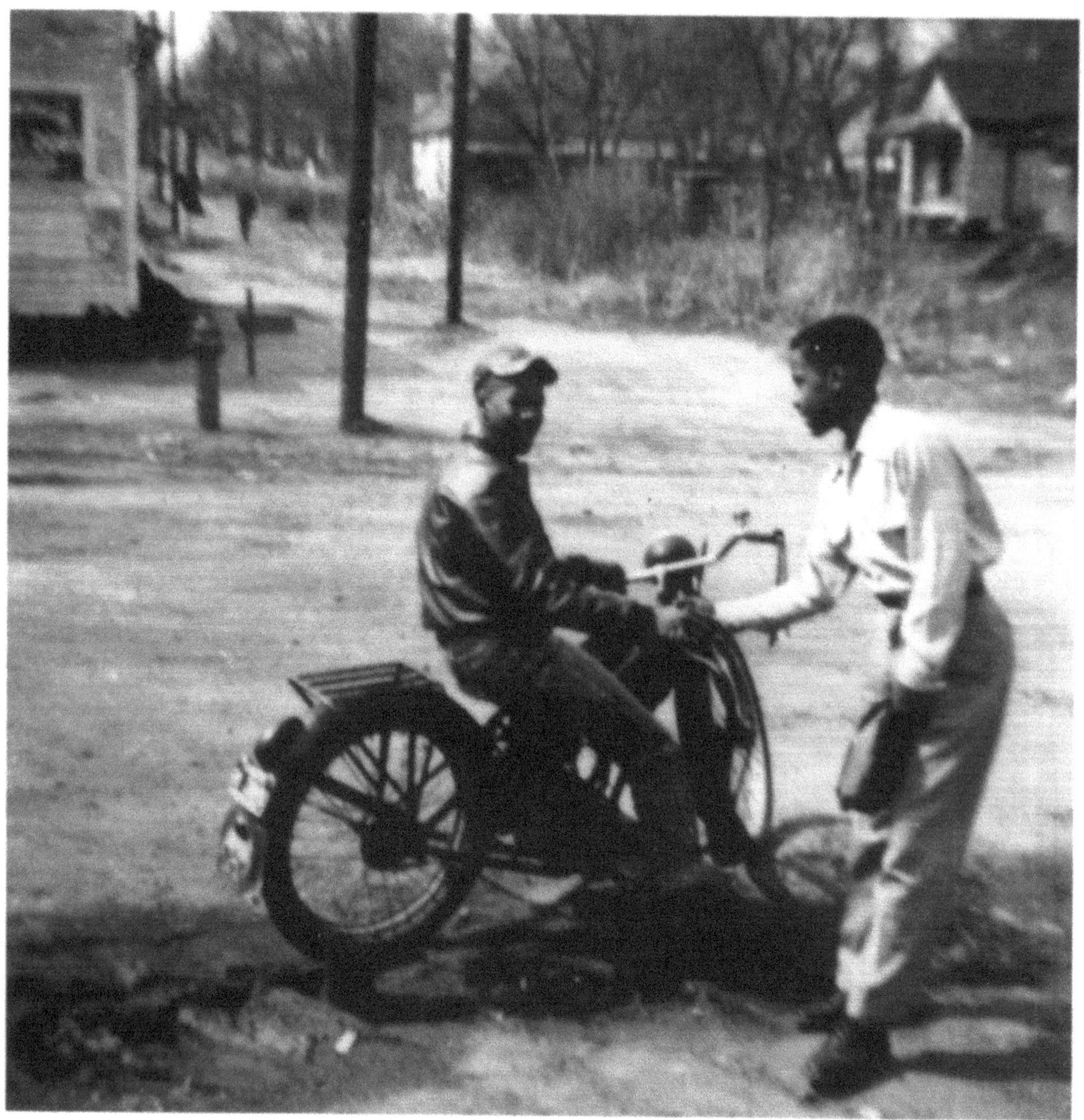

Alfred Russ, Jr., shakes hands with a friend on a motorcycle at Nineteenth and East Commerce streets.

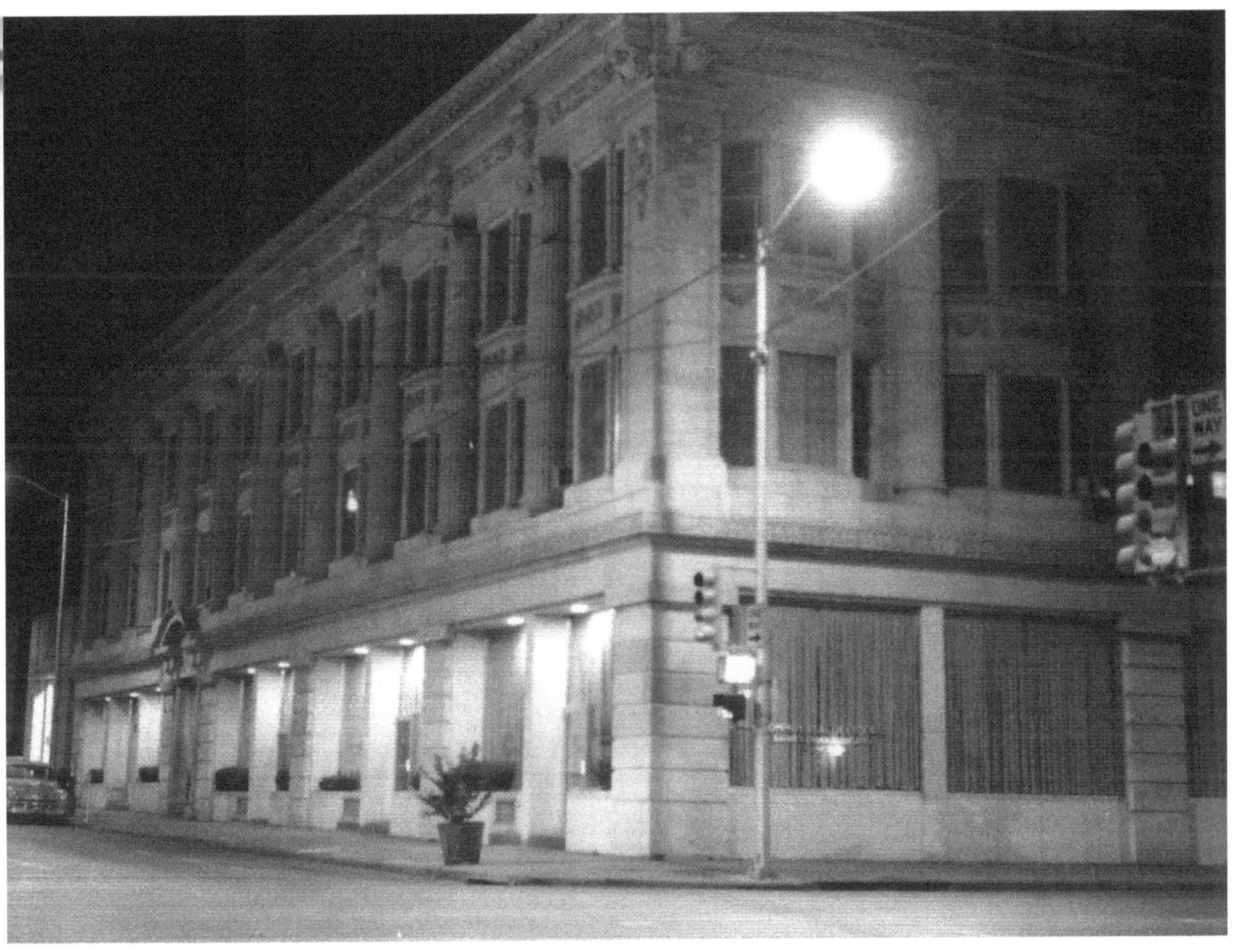

The Arkansas Gazette Building, located at the corner of Third Street and Louisiana Street, was completed in 1908. Founded by William Woodruff in 1820, until its merger with the *Arkansas Democrat* in 1991, the *Arkansas Gazette* was the oldest continuously published newspaper west of the Mississippi. In 1992 the building served as the national headquarters for Governor Bill Clinton's presidential campaign.

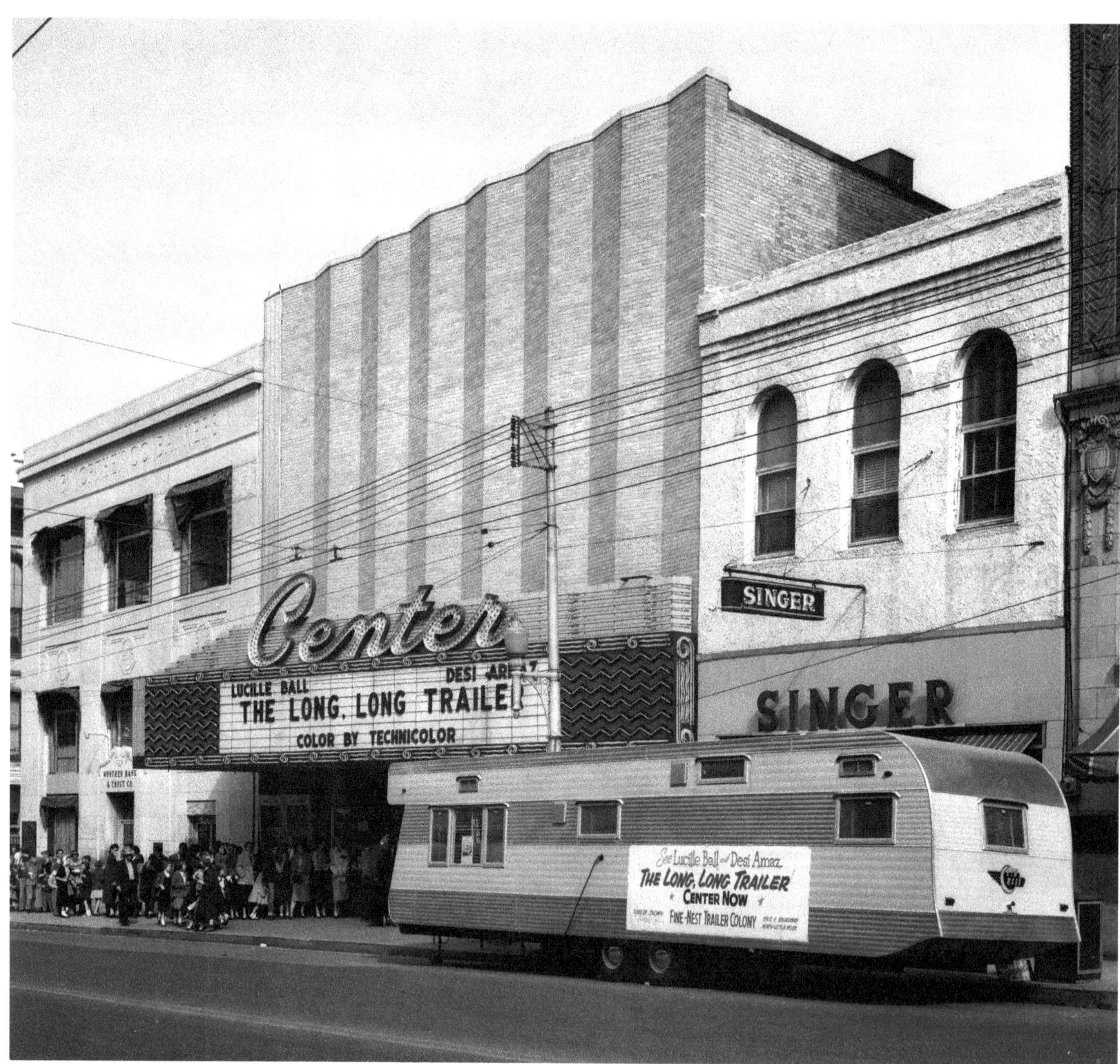

Flanked by Worthen Bank and the Singer Company, the Center Theater was located at East Fourth and Main streets. Little Rockers are queuing up here to see Lucille Ball and Desi Arnaz in the 1954 comedy *The Long, Long Trailer,* about the misadventures of a couple crossing the country to see the sights.

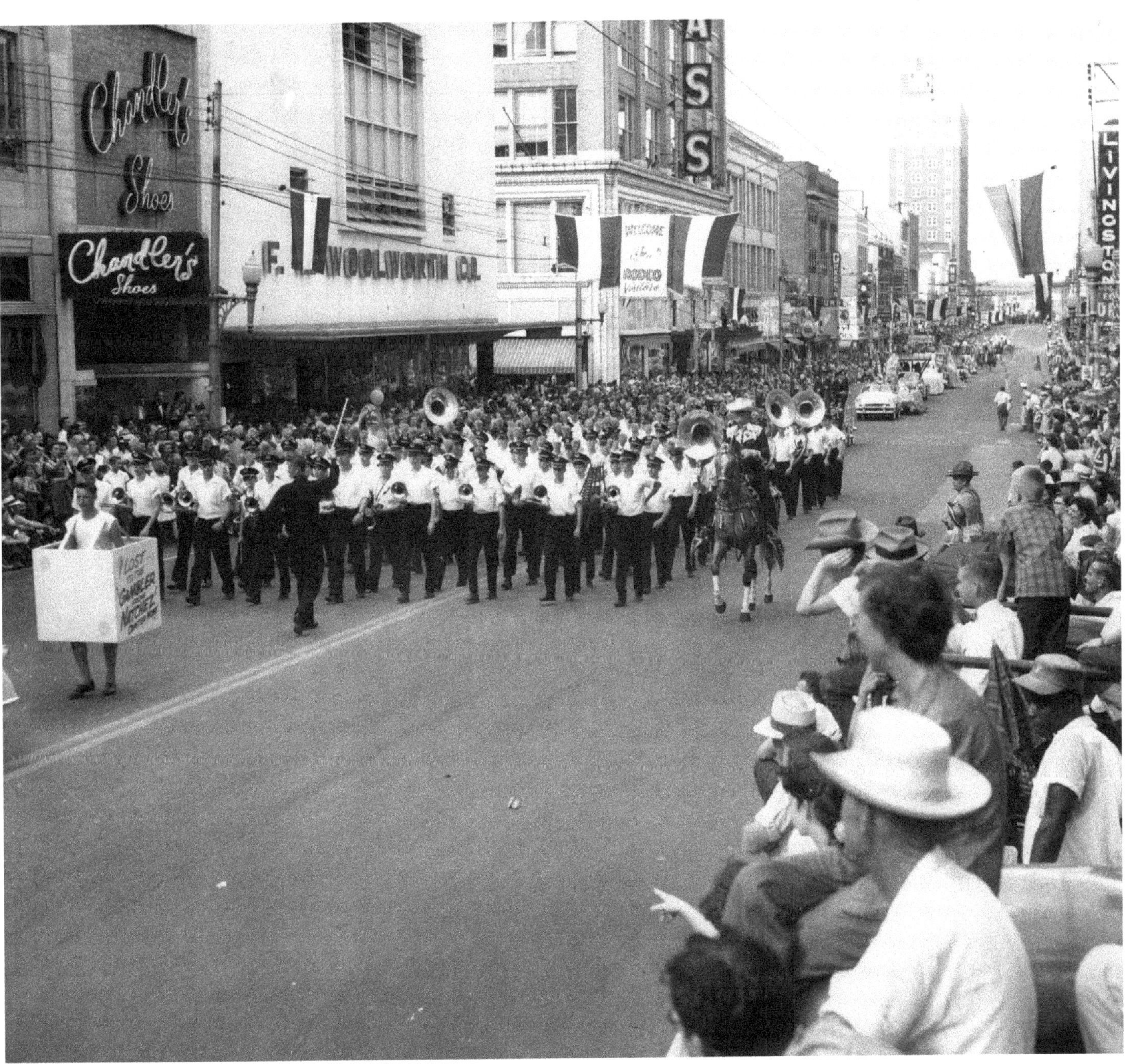

This rodeo parade in downtown Little Rock in 1954 features a man wearing a box sign. The ploy was an ad for *The Gambler from Natchez,* then showing at the Center Theater.

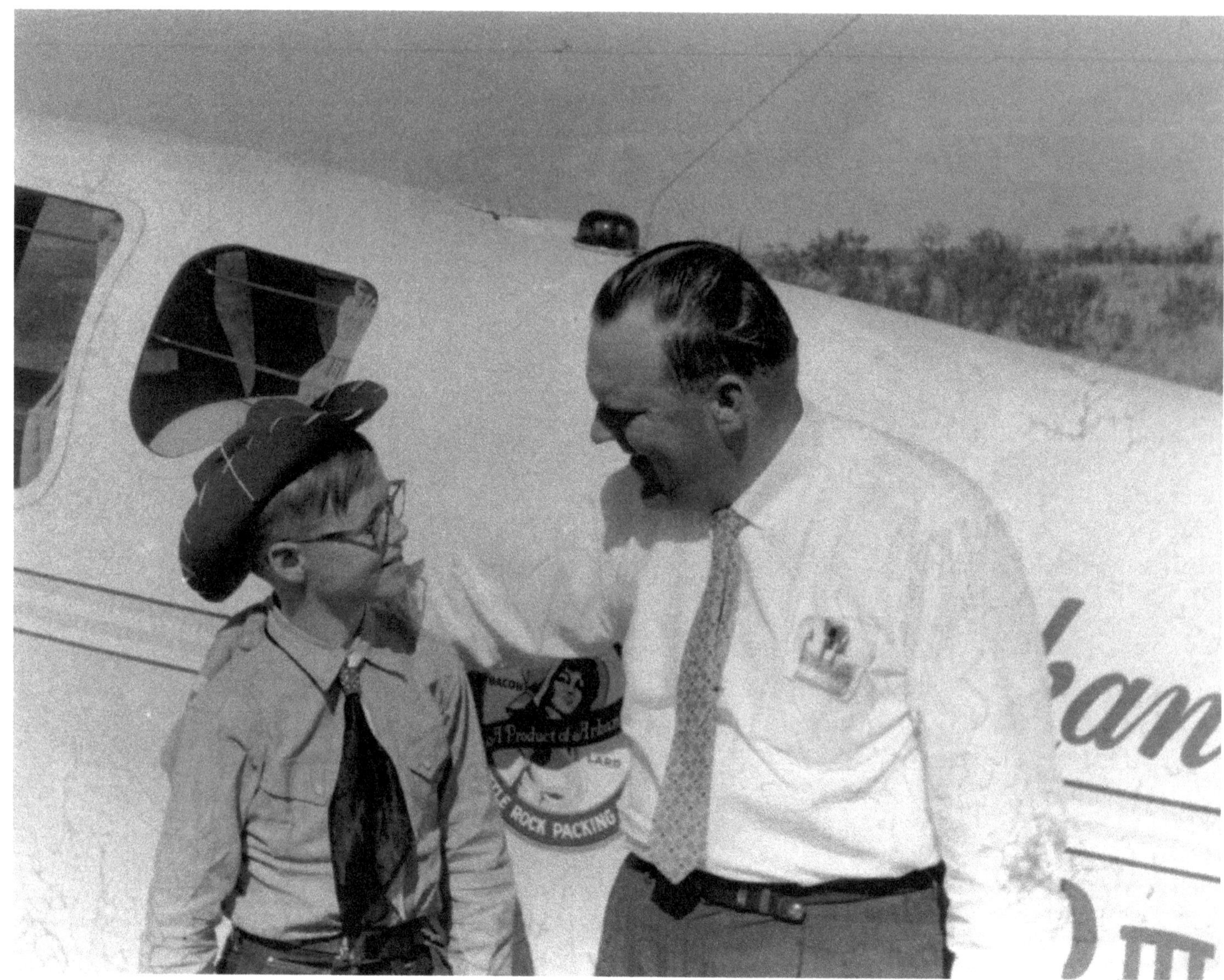

Chris E. Finkbeiner, Chairman of the Board of the Little Rock Packing Company, and James Cobler of Hot Springs, stand in front of Finkbeiner's private plane in June 1956. The two were traveling to the Boy's Ranch in Tascosa, Texas.

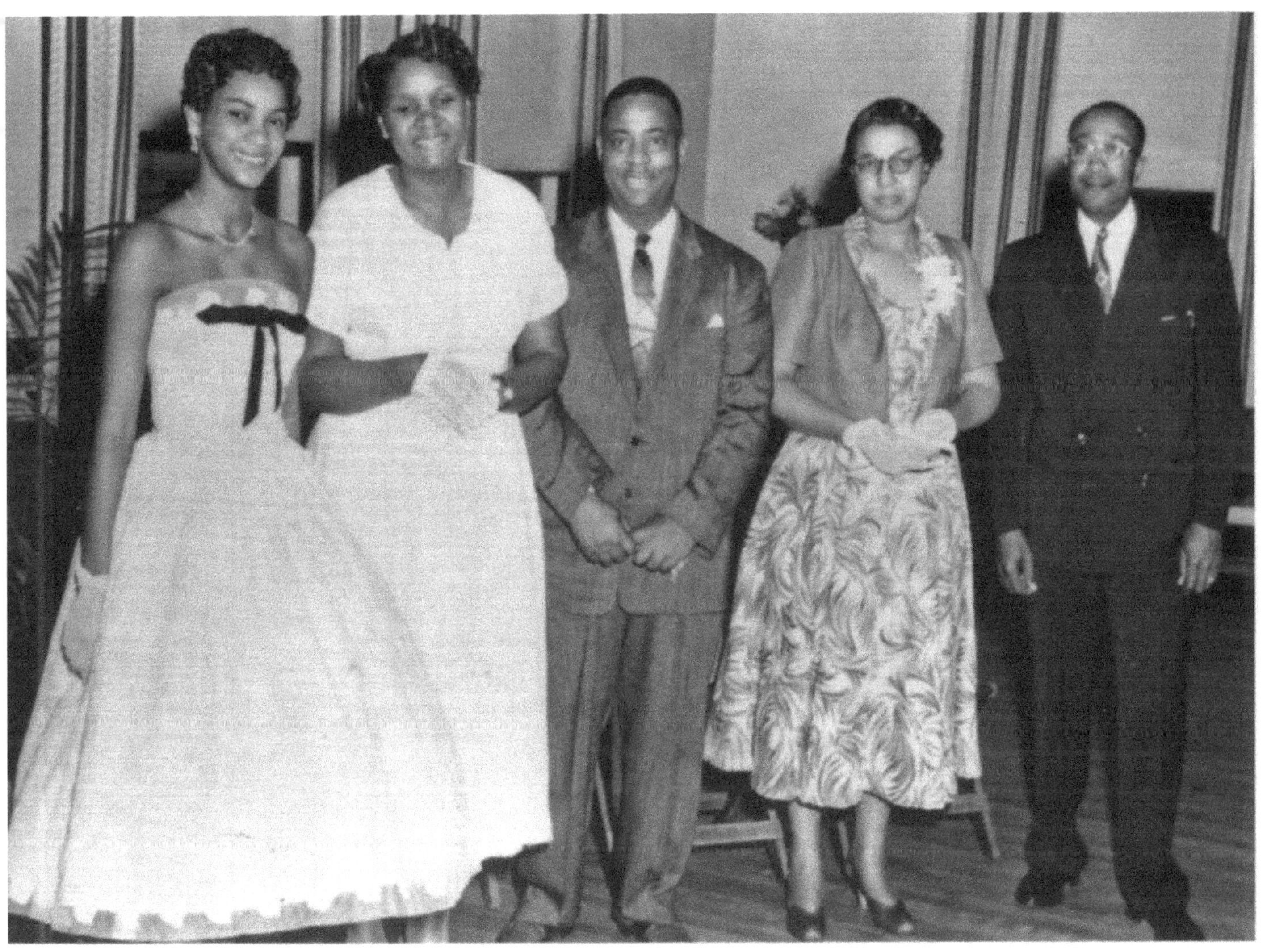

Joyce McClinton and her parents, Edith and Isaiah S. McClinton, stand with Addie and Wesley E. Hayes. Isaiah McClinton was the president of the Arkansas Democratic Voters Association. Hayes was the minister of Mount Pleasant Baptist Church.

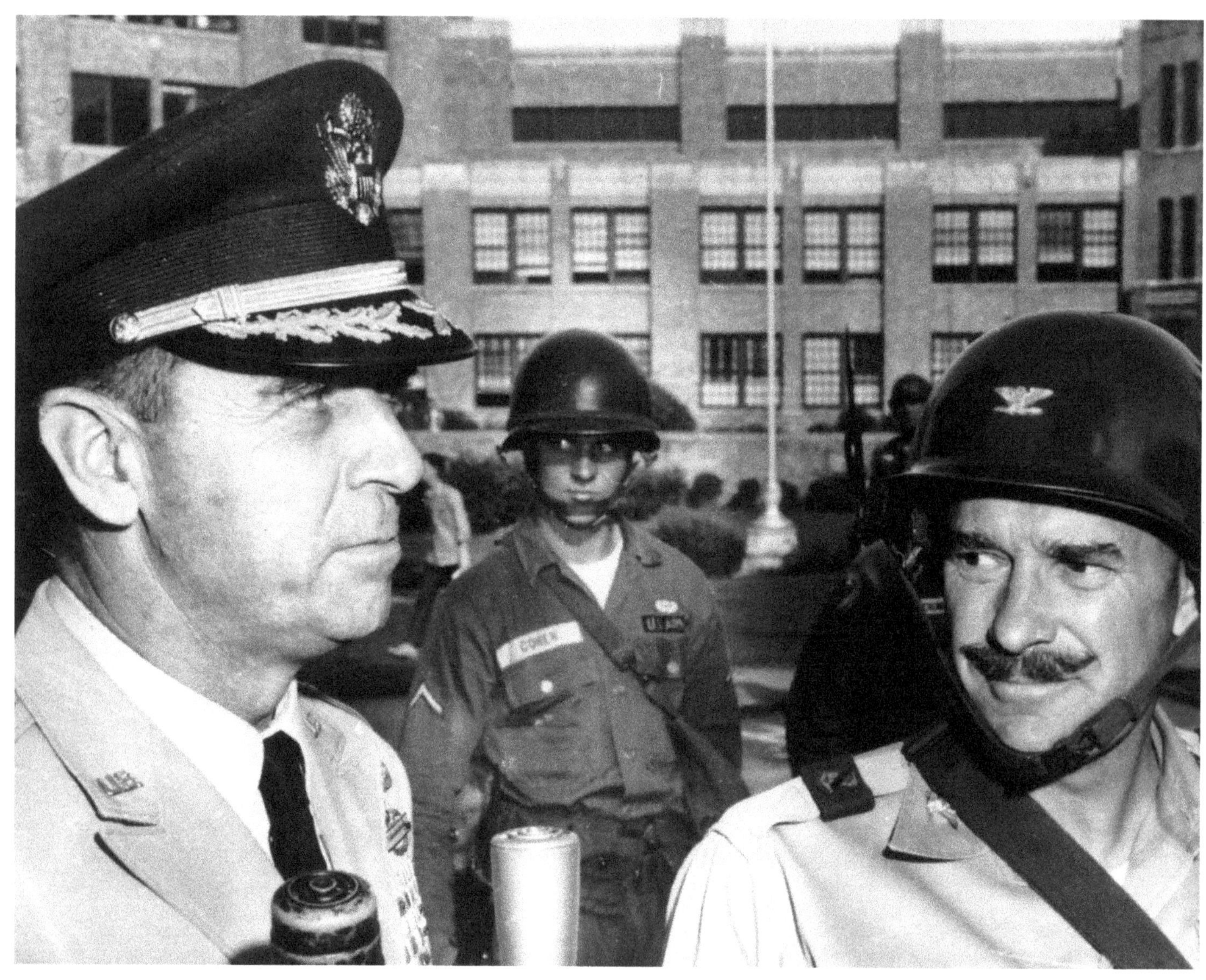

Major General Edwin A. Walker (left) stands with Colonel William A. Kuhn of the 327th Airborne Battle Group outside Central High School on September 25, 1957. The two officers were enforcing integration of the school.

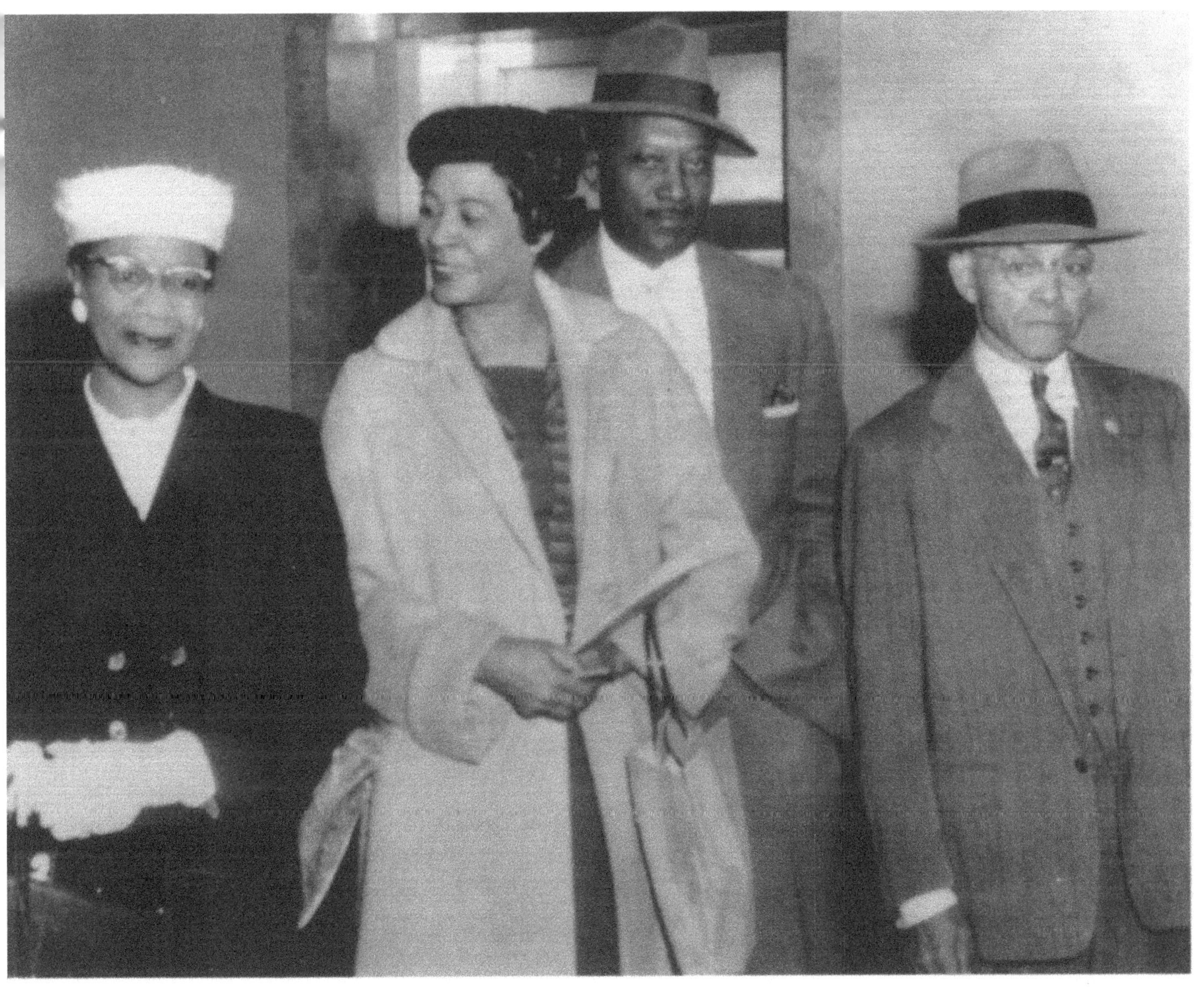

Representatives of the National Association for the Advancement of Colored People, Mrs. Albert Hinkle, Mrs. L. C. Bates, Clarence A. Laws, and P. M. Morgan, arrive in federal court in 1957 to discuss the Central High School integration crisis.

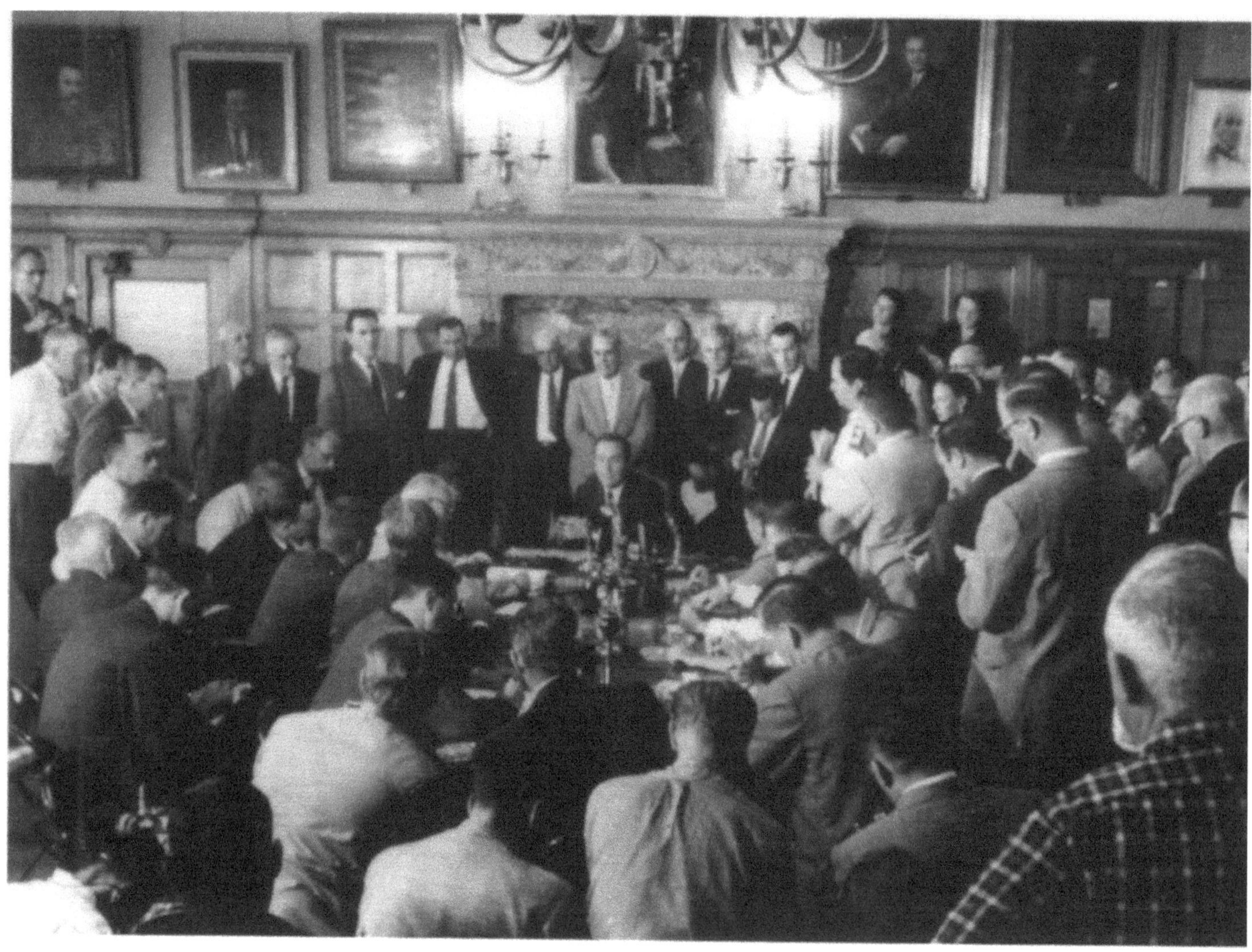

Governor Orval Faubus holds a press conference concerning Central High School integration at the Arkansas State Capitol in September 1957.

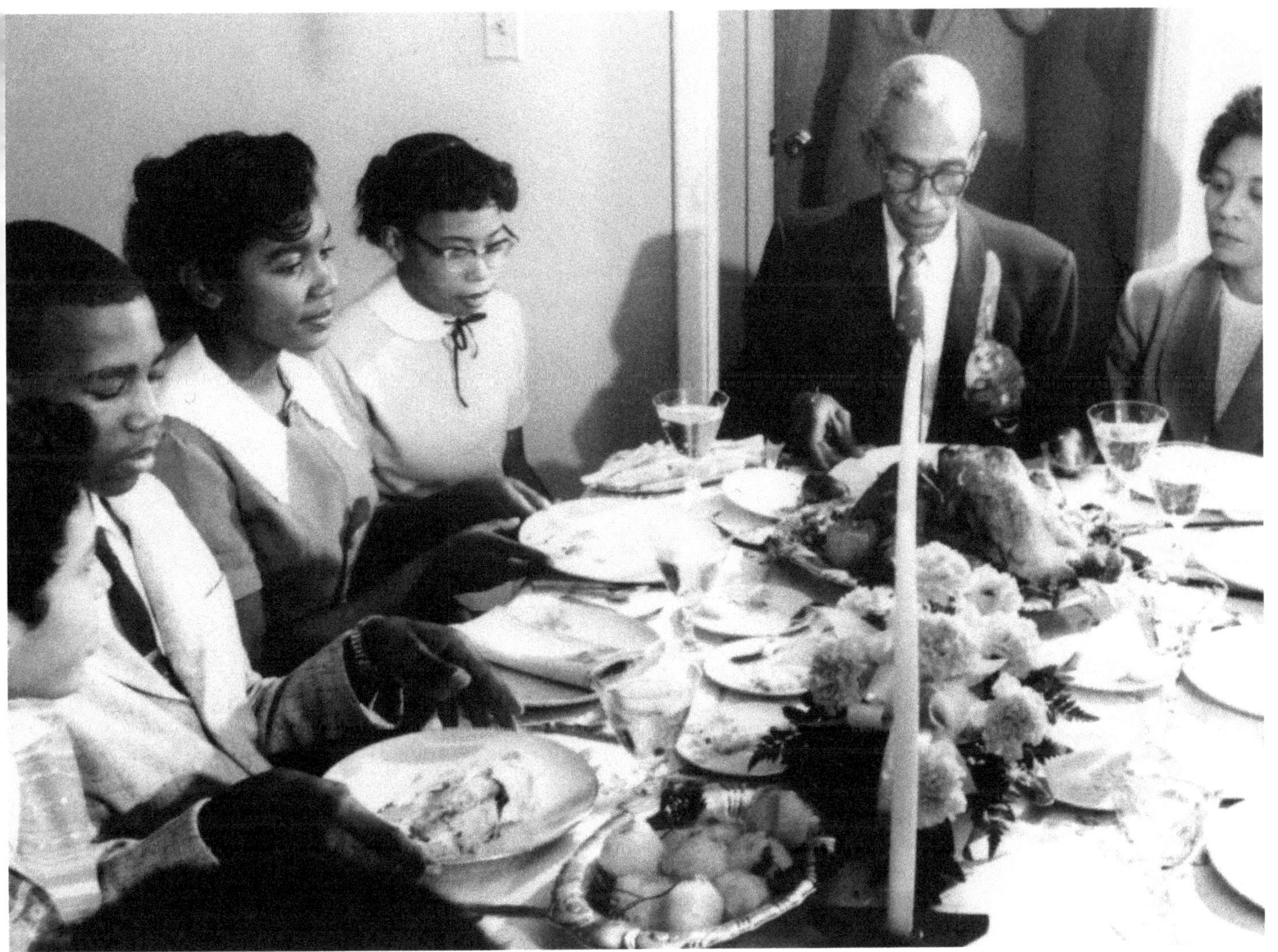

Members of the "Little Rock Nine" share Thanksgiving dinner with Daisy and L. C. Bates in 1957. Pictured left to right are Carlotta Walls, Terrence Roberts, Melba Pattillo, Thelma Mothershed, L. C. Bates, and Daisy Bates.

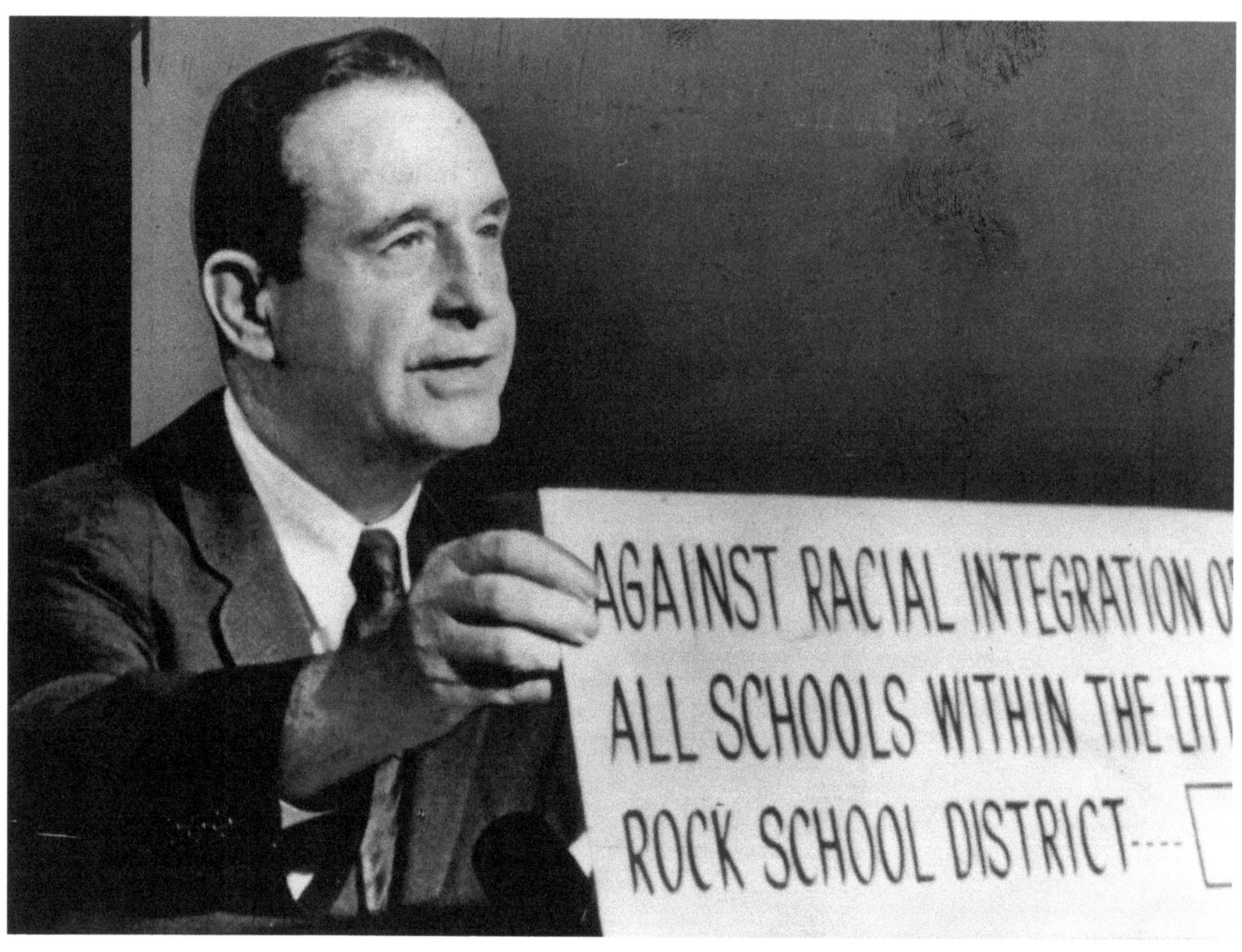

Despite the stance taken by Governor Faubus against desegregation of Little Rock's public schools, he was elected to six terms as governor, receiving 81 percent of the black vote in his 1964 bid against Republican challenger Winthrop Rockefeller.

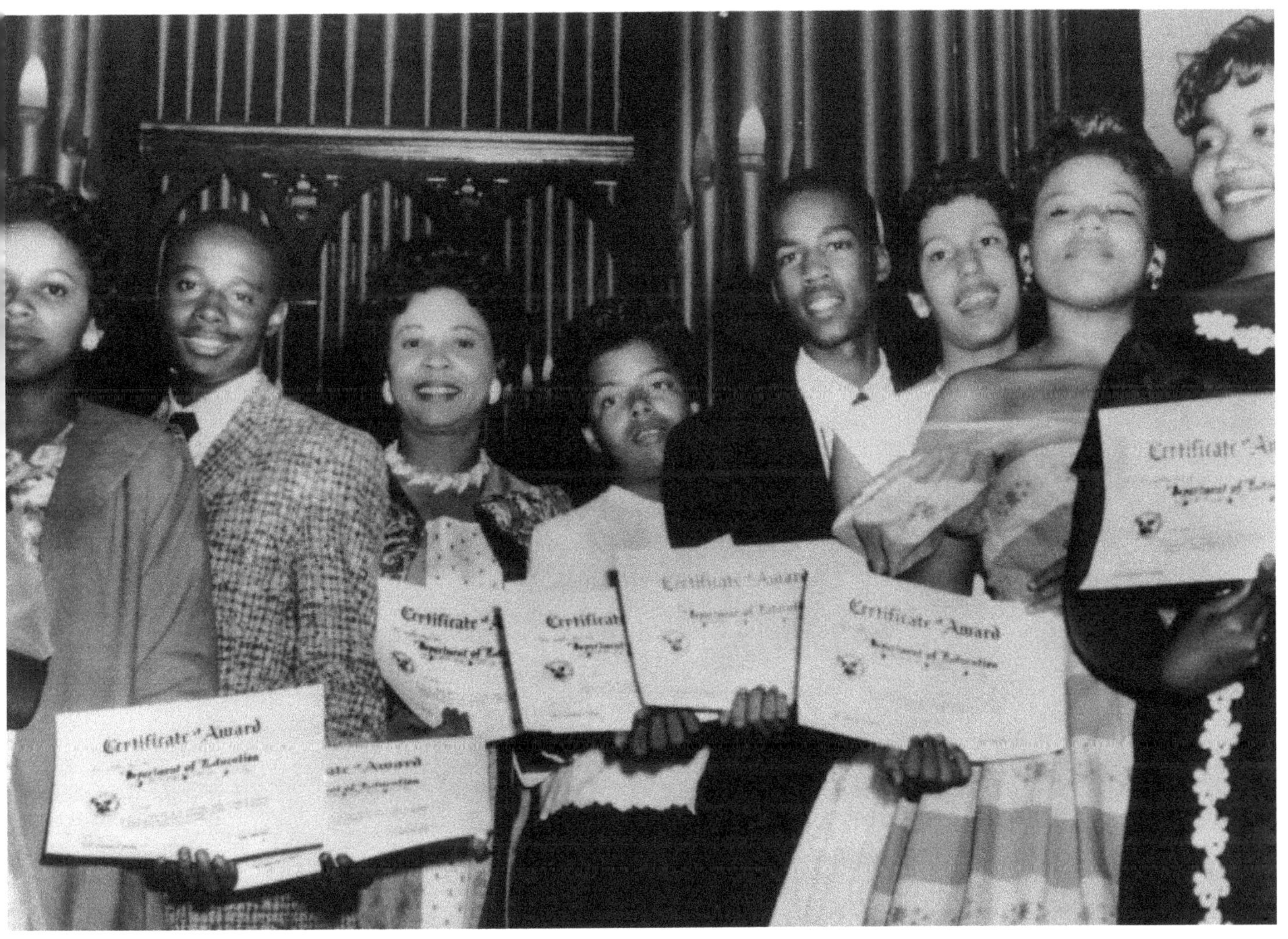

Members of the "Little Rock Nine" receive $1,000 scholarships from the National Negro Elks Convention in 1958. In view left to right are Gloria Ray, Jefferson Thomas, Daisy Bates, Elizabeth Eckford, Terrence Roberts, Carlotta Walls, Minnijean Brown, and Melba Pattillo.

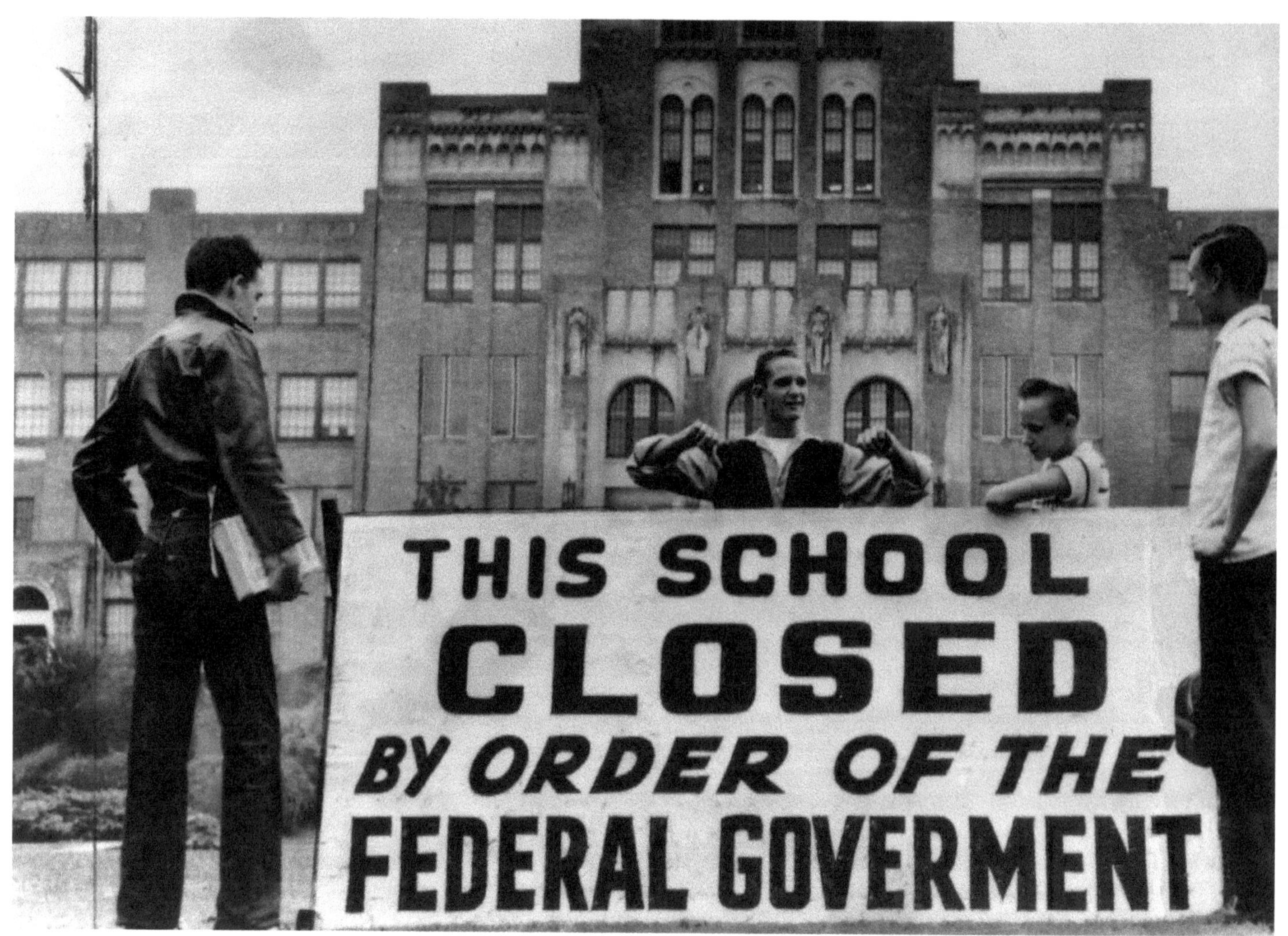

Students stand around a sign proclaiming "This School Closed by Order of the Federal Government" in front of Central High School in 1958. To outmaneuver Faubus, President Eisenhower would federalize the Arkansas National Guard, thus removing them from the governor's control.

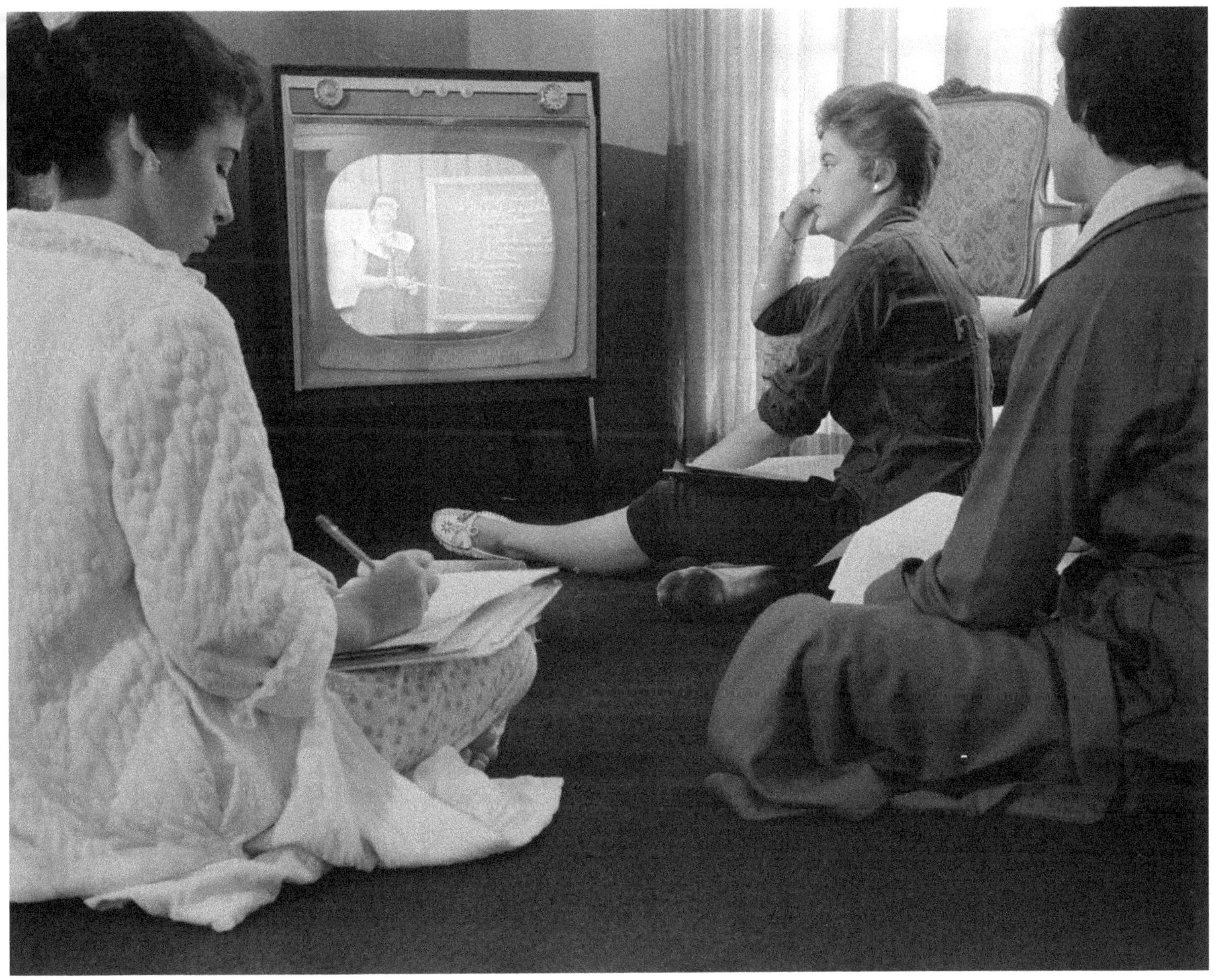

In September 1958, three girls attend lessons by way of television while Little Rock schools were closed. Public schools did not reopen until August 1959, and the intervening year became known as the "Lost Year."

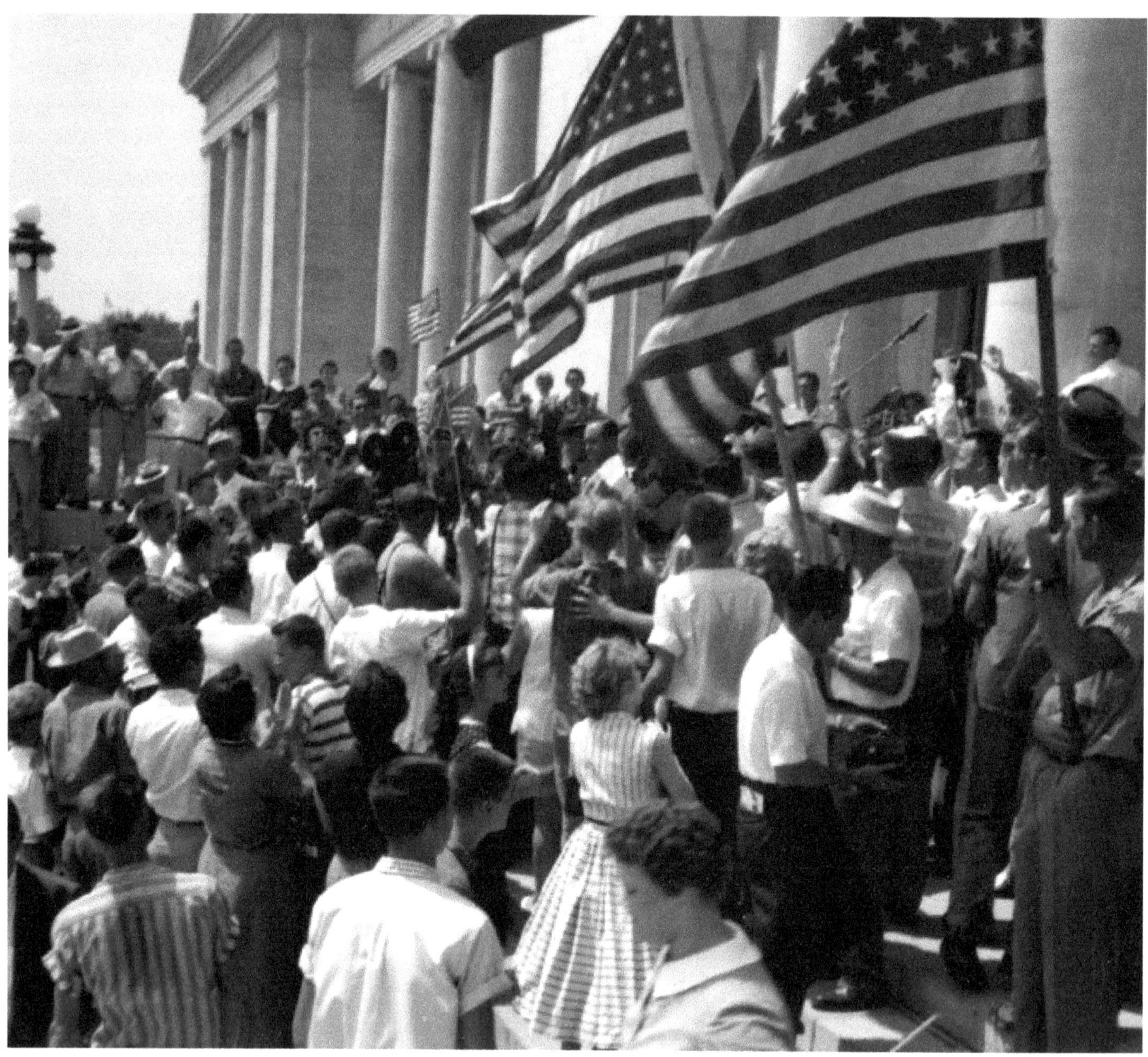

A group of protesters gather on the front steps of the Arkansas state capitol on August 20, 1959, to protest the integration of Central High School.

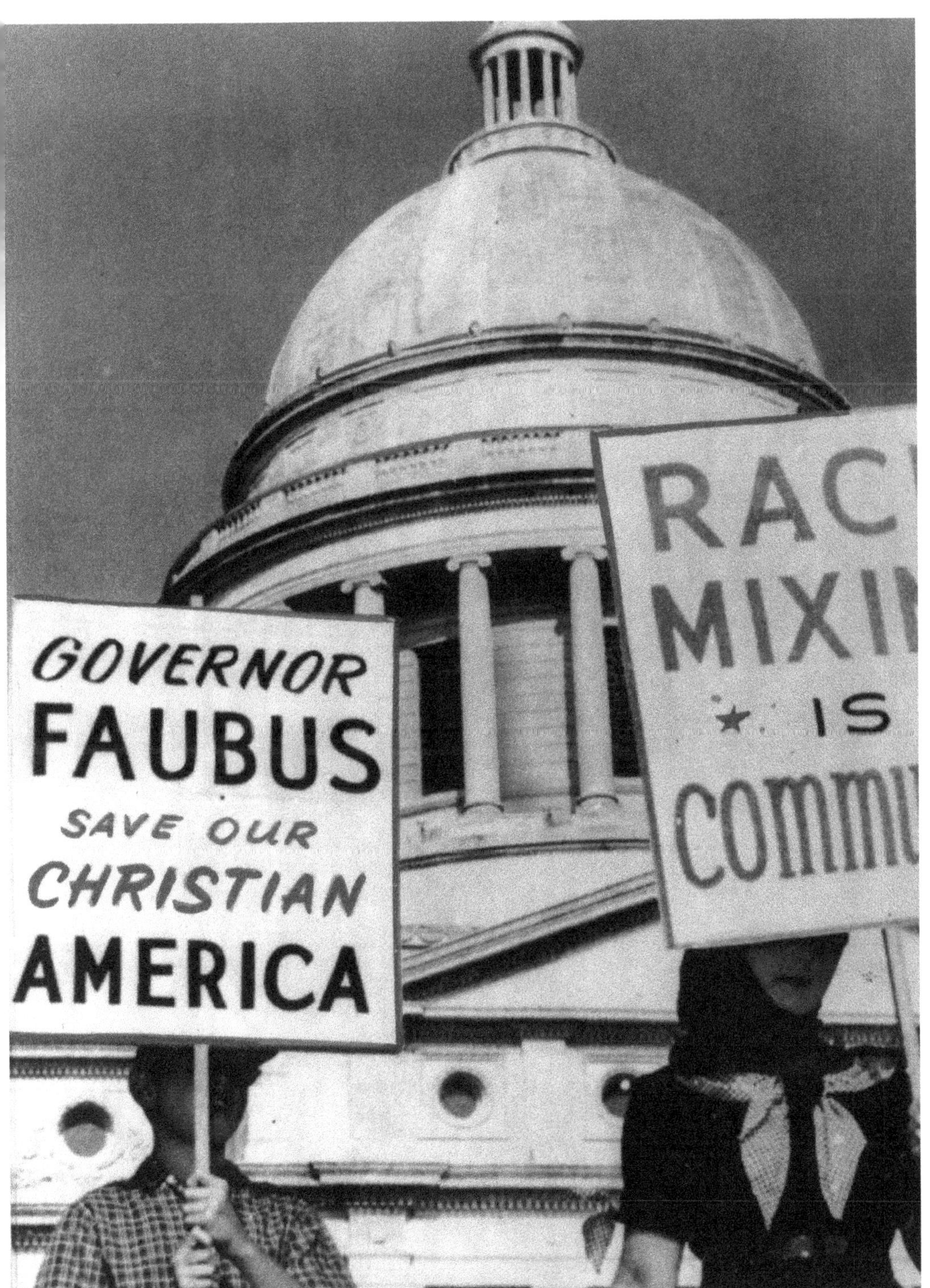

Two citizens stand in front of the Arkansas state capitol to protest the integration of the state's high schools in 1959.

Following Spread: September 17, 1958, was a typical day on Capitol Avenue in downtown Little Rock.

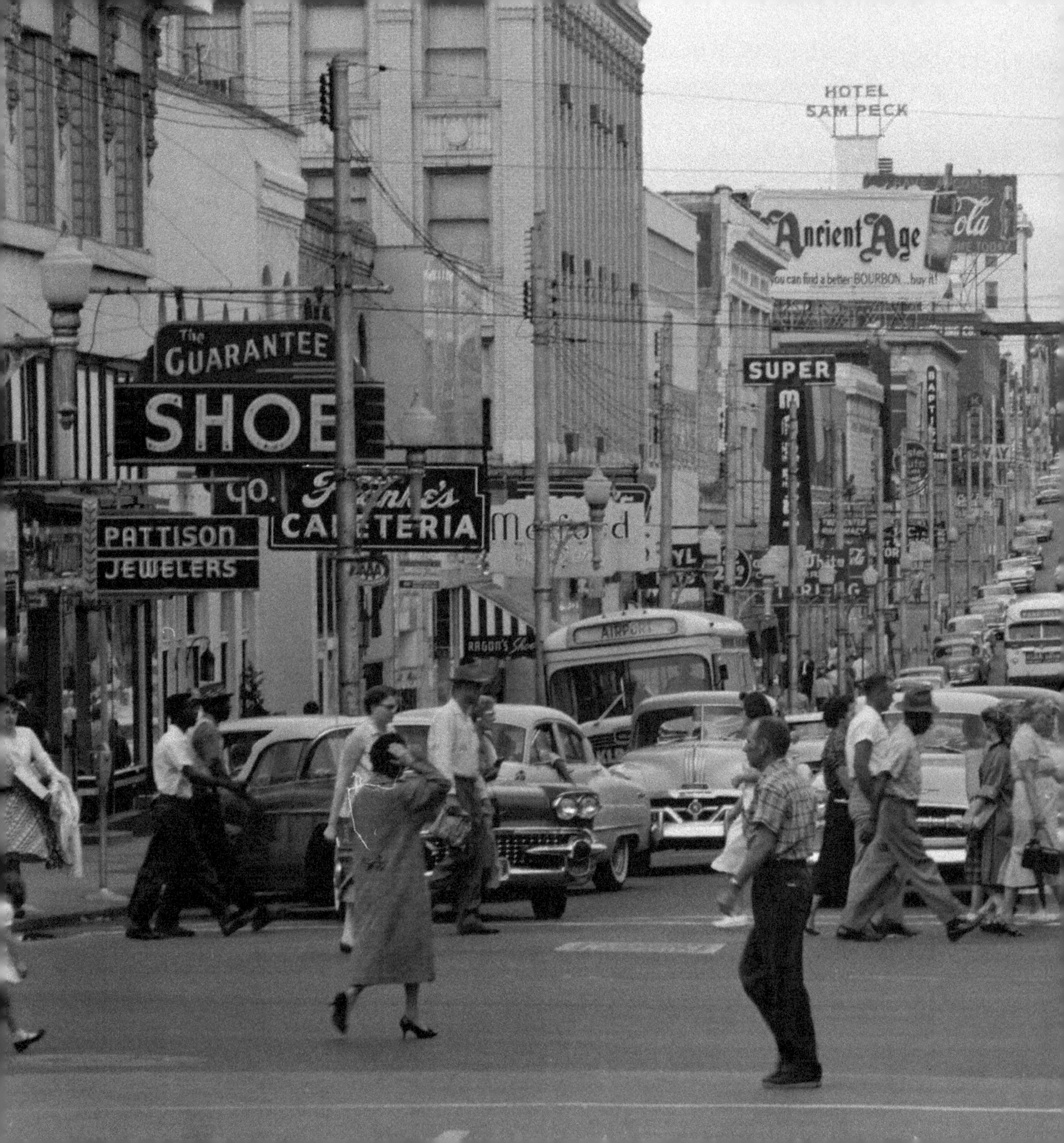

HOTEL
SAM PECK
Ancient Age
You can find a better BOURBON... buy it!
Cola
The
GUARANTEE
SHOE
CO.
Franke's
CAFETERIA
PATTISON
JEWELERS
SUPER
AIRPORT

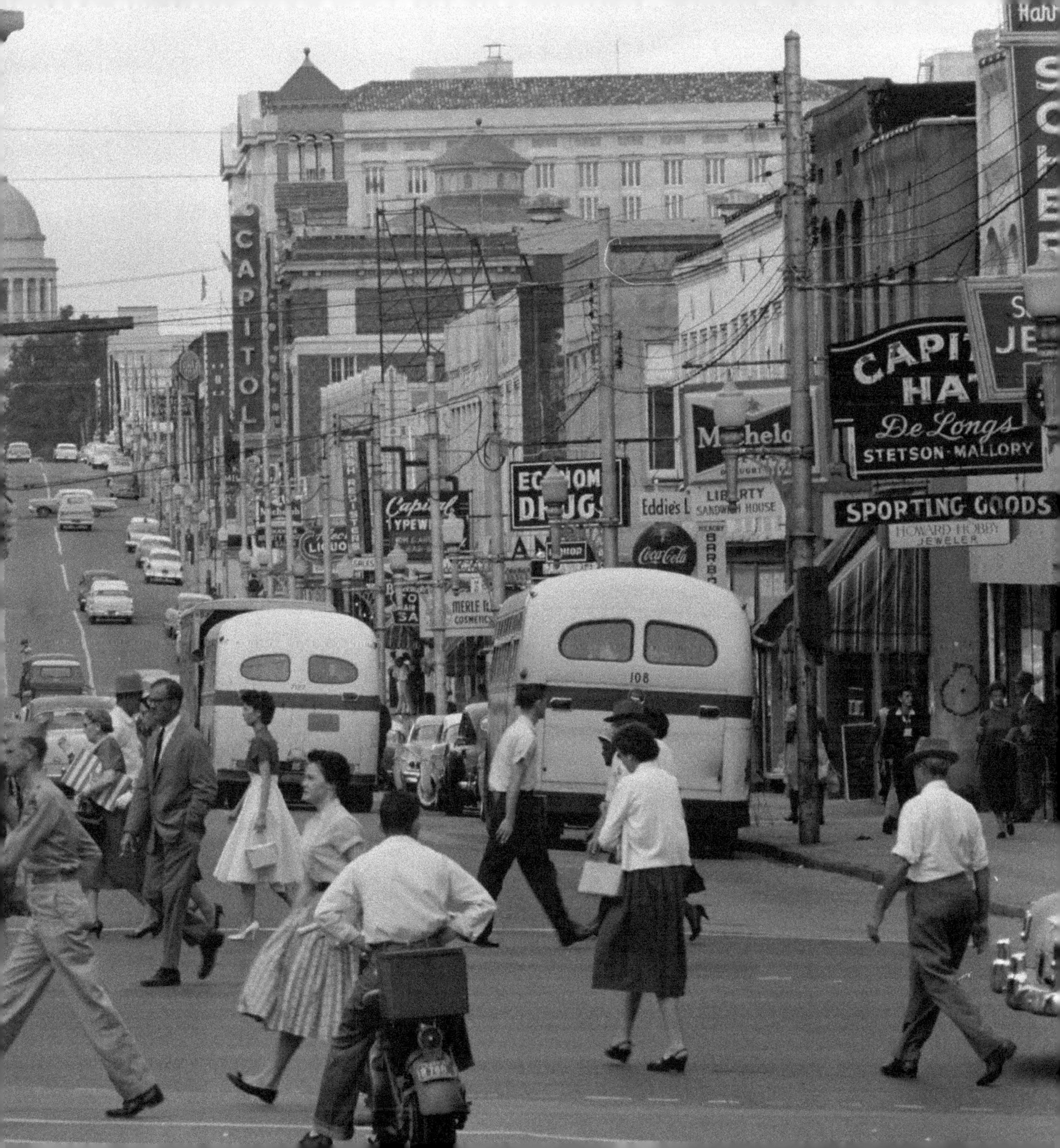

CAPITOL
De Longs
STETSON-MALLORY
SPORTING GOODS
HOWARD HOBBY
JEWELER
LIBERTY
SANDWICH HOUSE
Coca-Cola
MERLE
COSMETICS
108

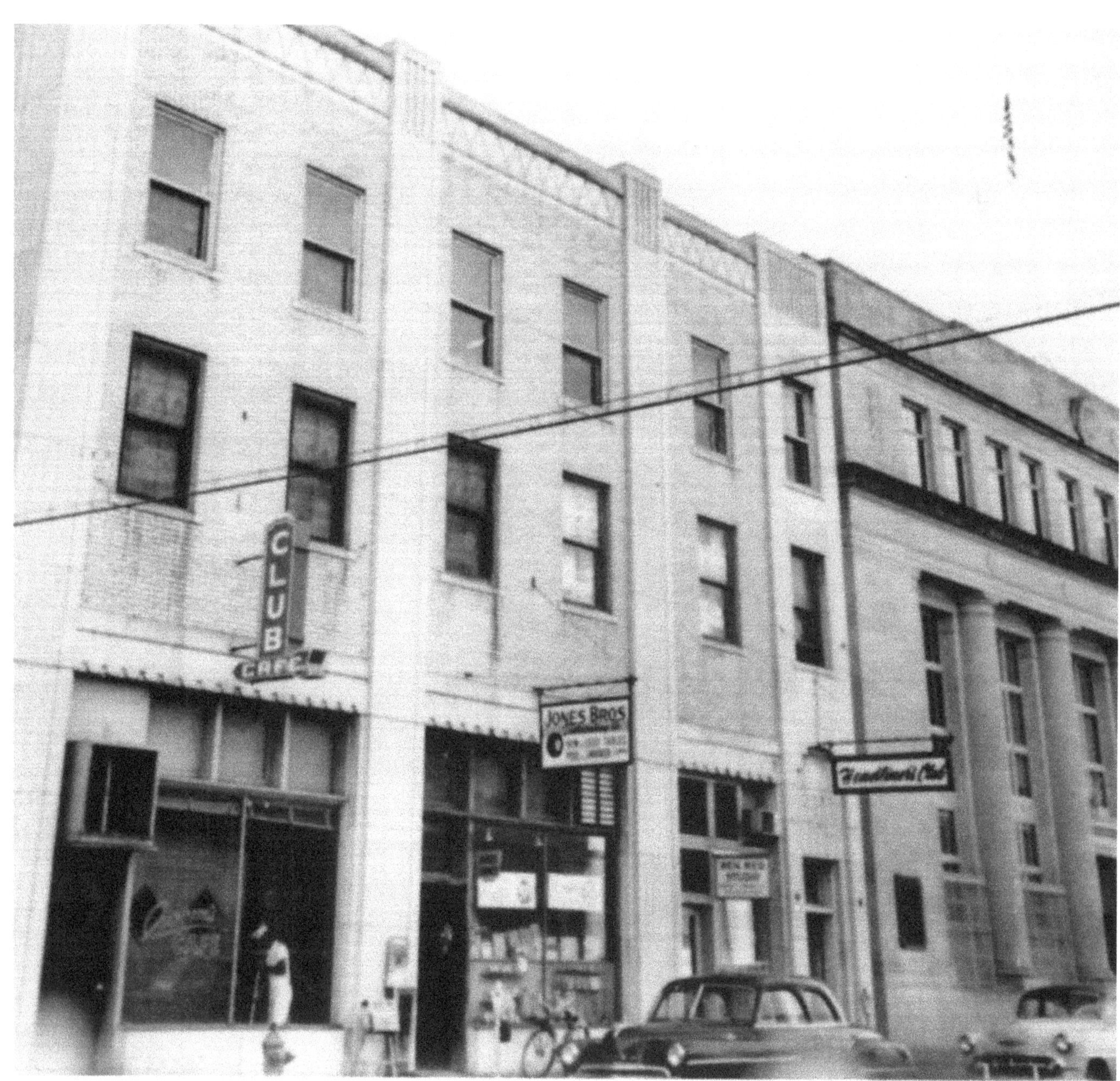

The Gem Building was located at 117½ West Third Street.

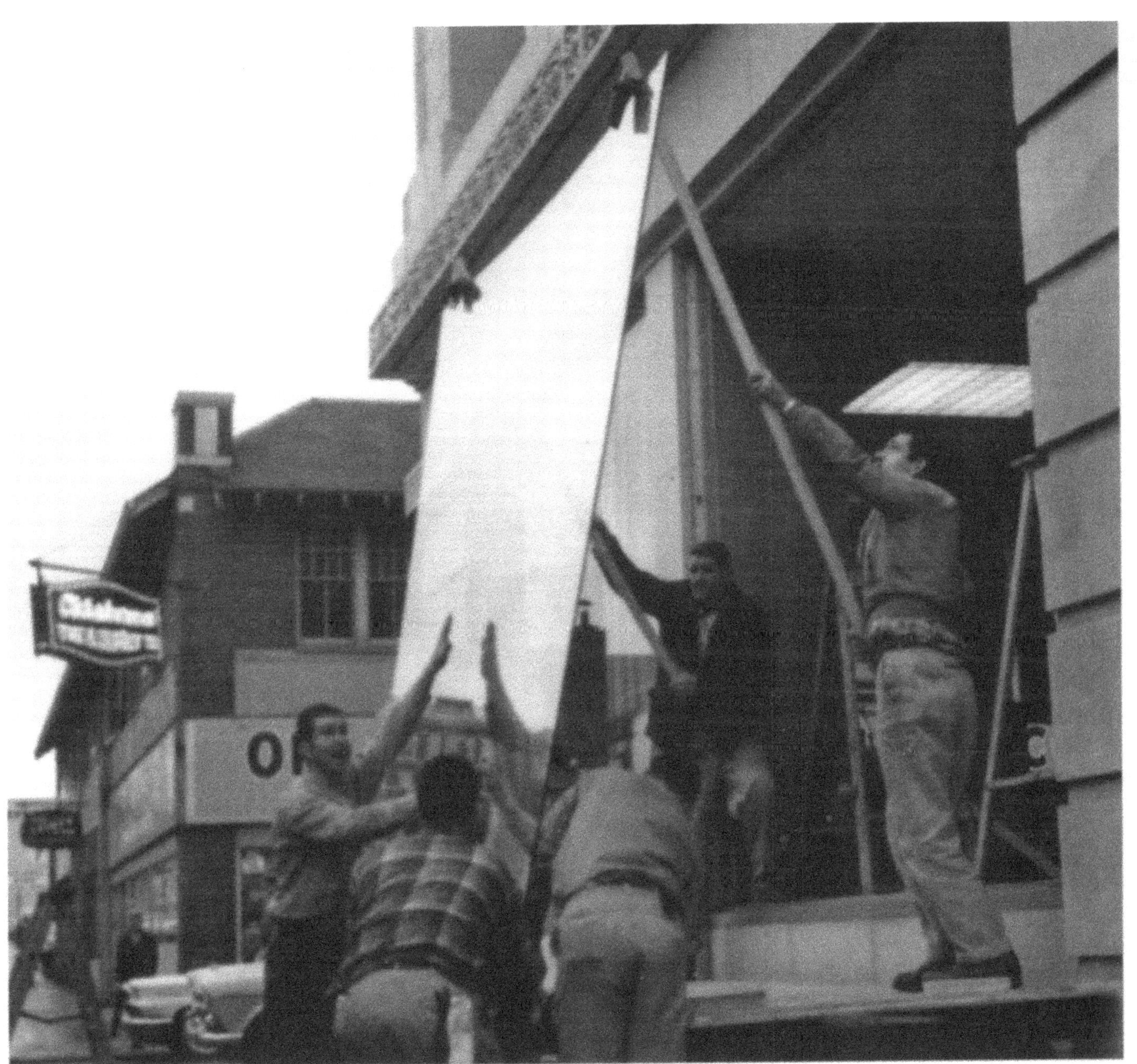

Workers mount a plate-glass window on the Arkansas Gazette Building.

Mary Alice Pickens and Floy Jeanne Cash check new arrivals to the Little Rock Library in February 1958. The Little Rock Library Commission mailed books to people throughout the state of Arkansas. The primary recipients were those with no access to libraries or bookmobiles.

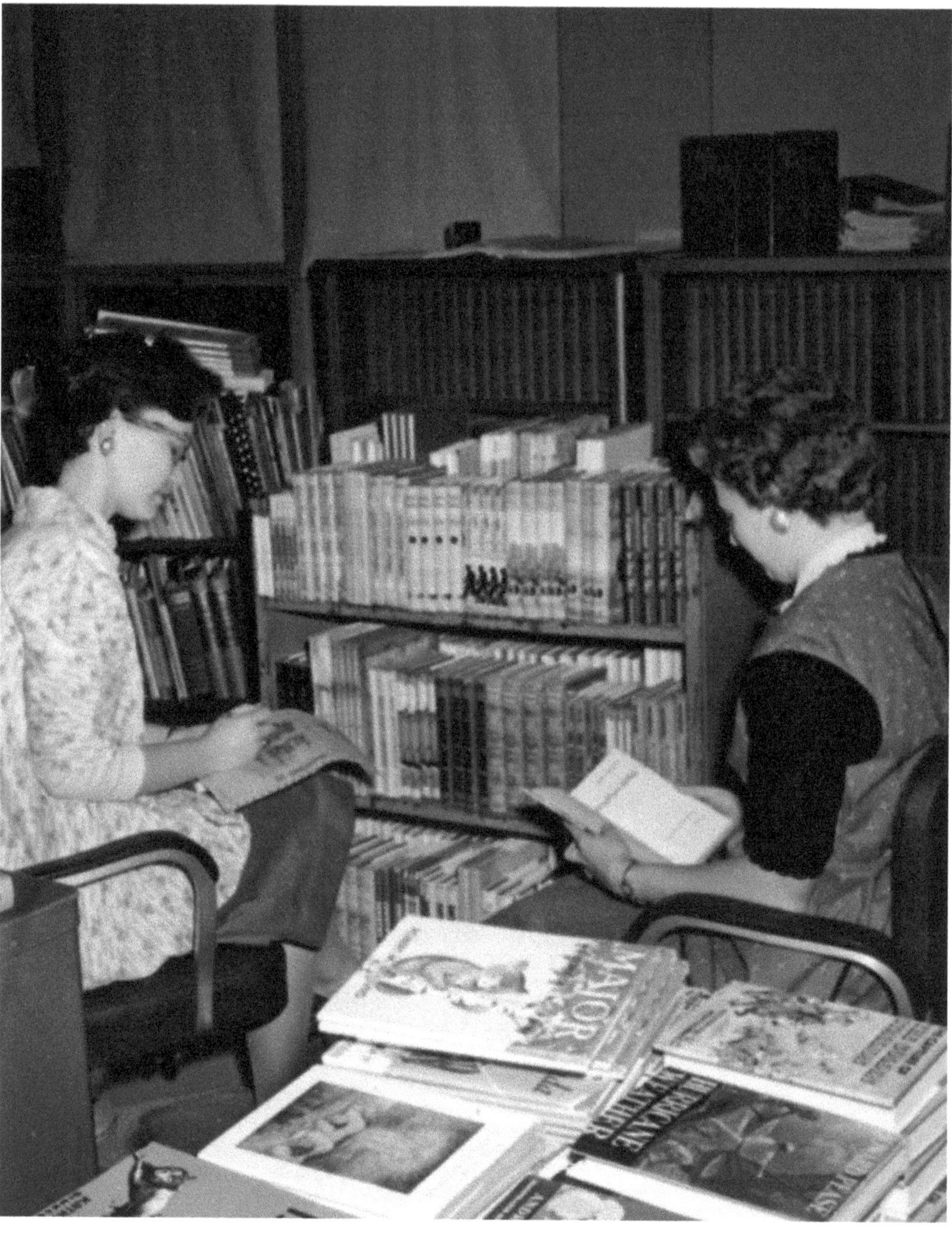

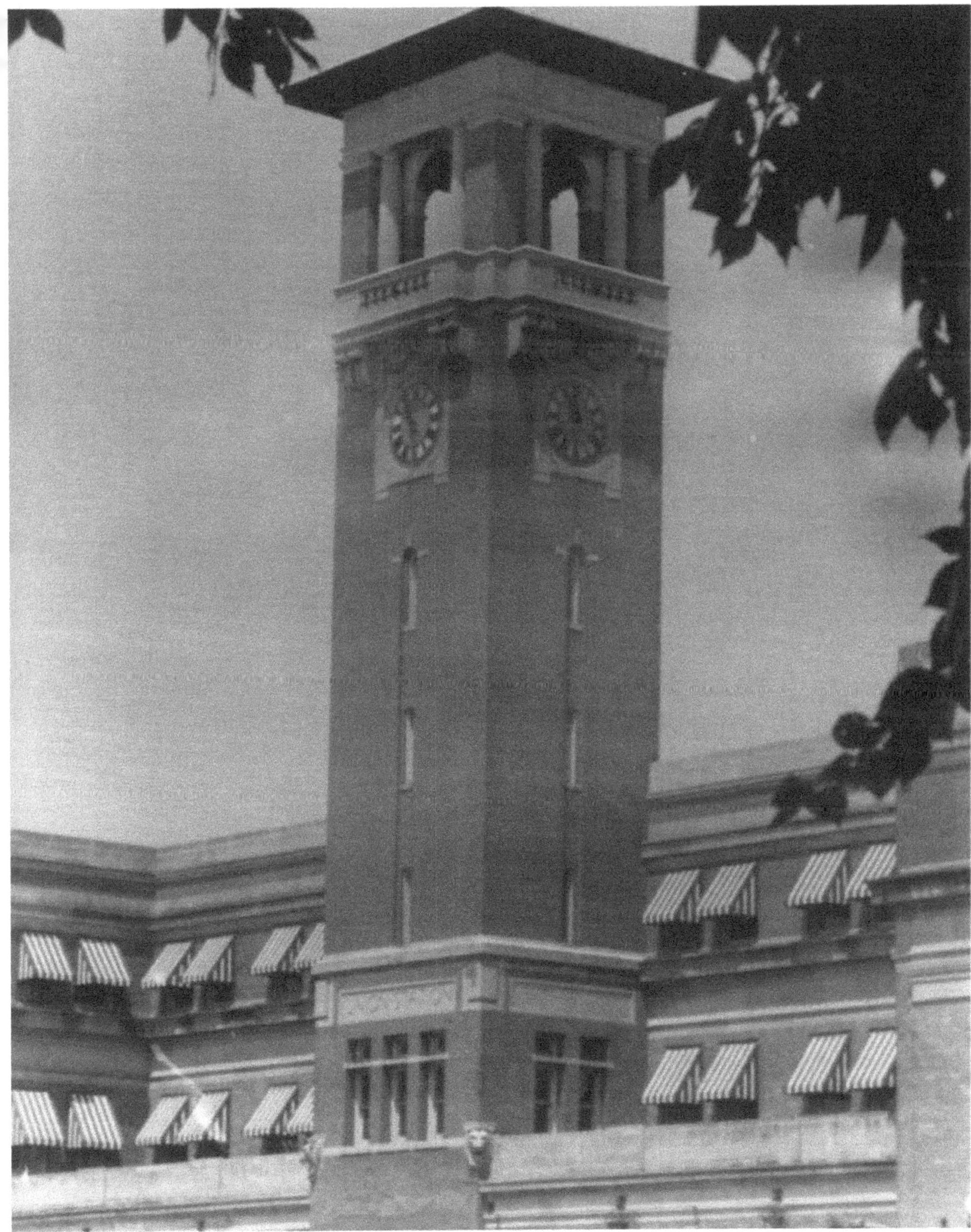

The clock tower of the Missouri Pacific Railroad terminal, built in 1921, is shown here as it appeared in August 1960. Union Station still stands today, emblematic of the nation's railroad heritage.

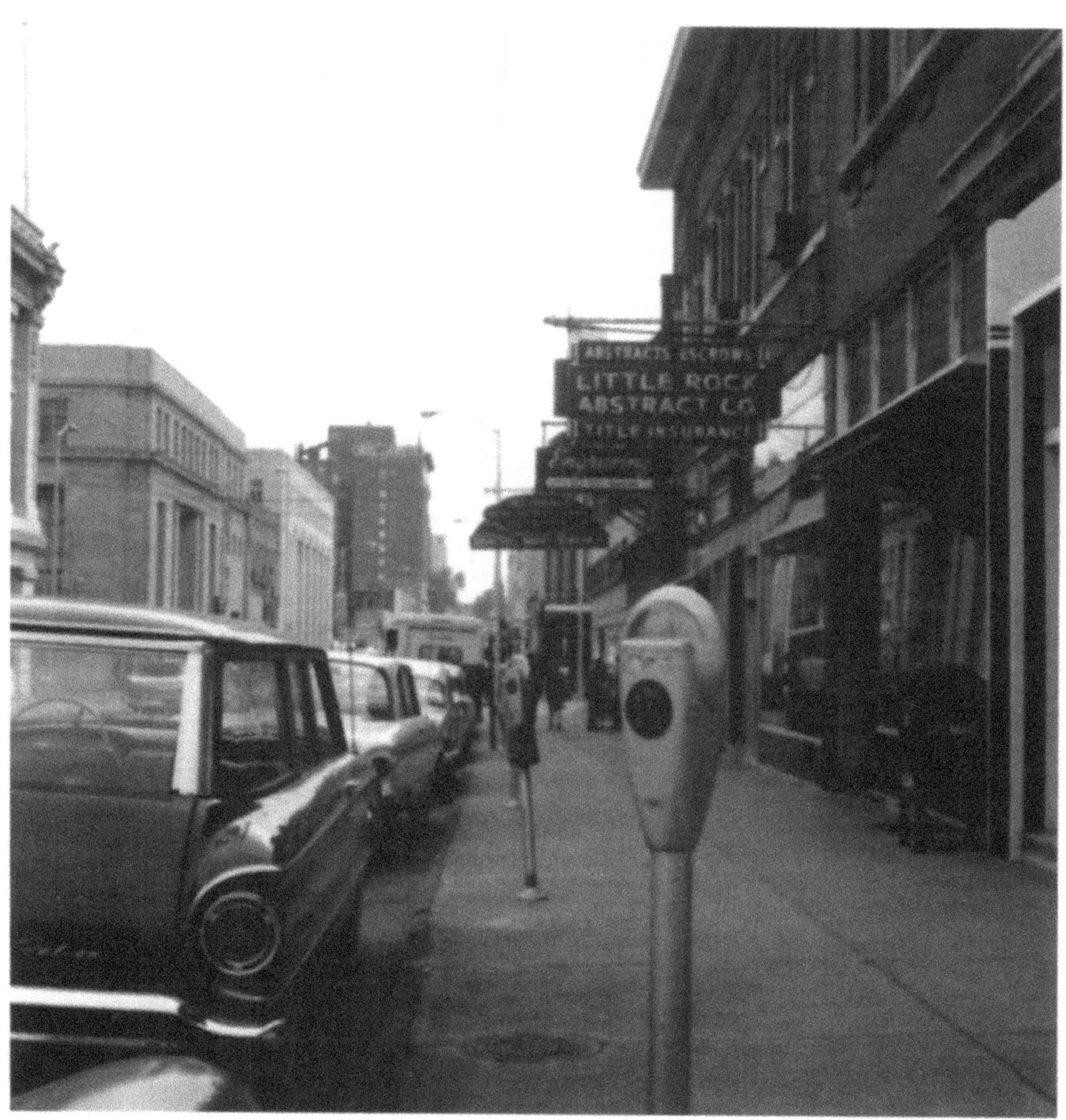

A 1960s view of Louisiana Street, from near the Arkansas Gazette building. When the Ford Falcon (at left) debuted in 1960, Henry Ford's Model T was considered ancient history, at least by those too young to remember the Model T. Parking meters, on the other hand, never seem to go out of style.

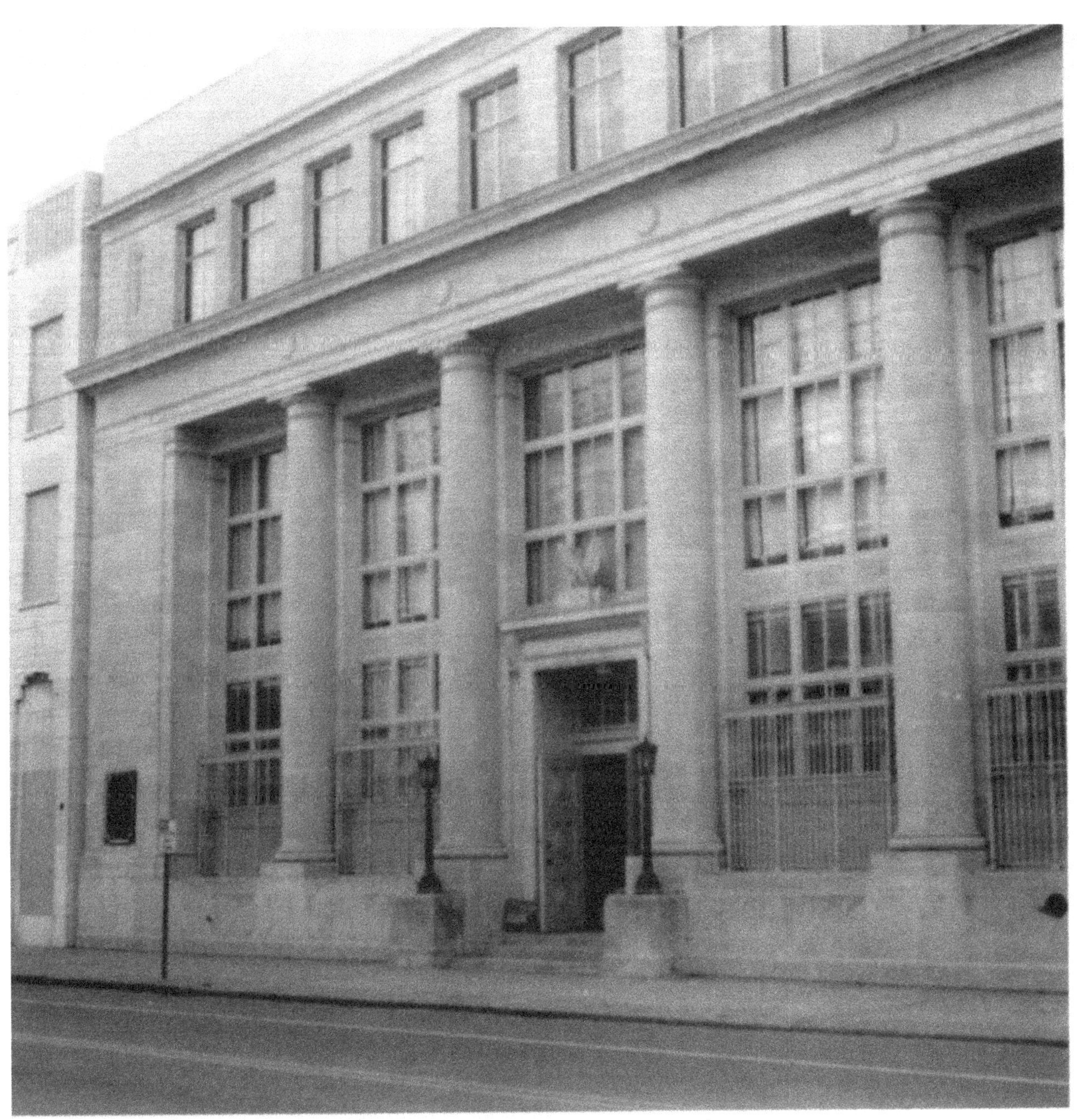

The headquarters of the Little Rock branch of the Federal Reserve Bank of St. Louis, located on the corner of Third and Louisiana streets. The bank is shown here as it appeared in October 1960.

Checks are sorted and wrapped inside the Little Rock branch of the Federal Reserve Bank.

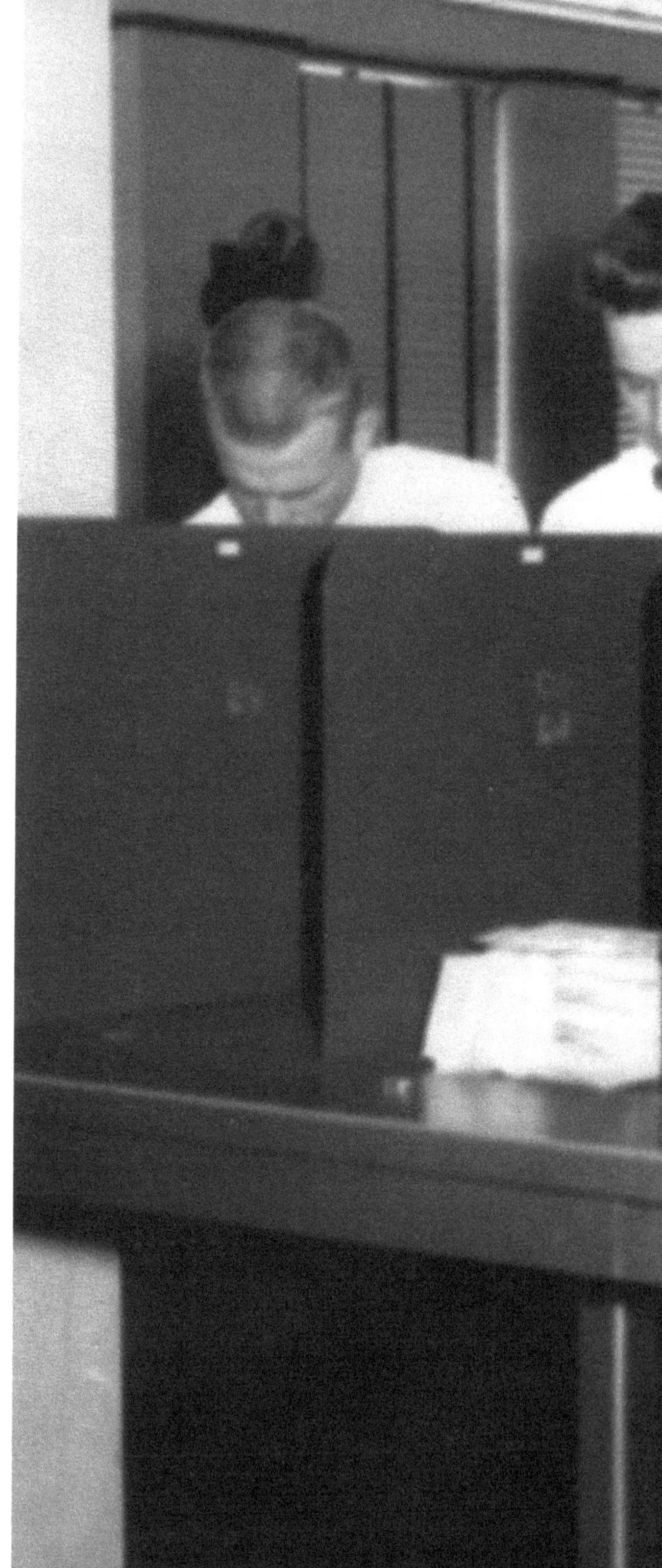

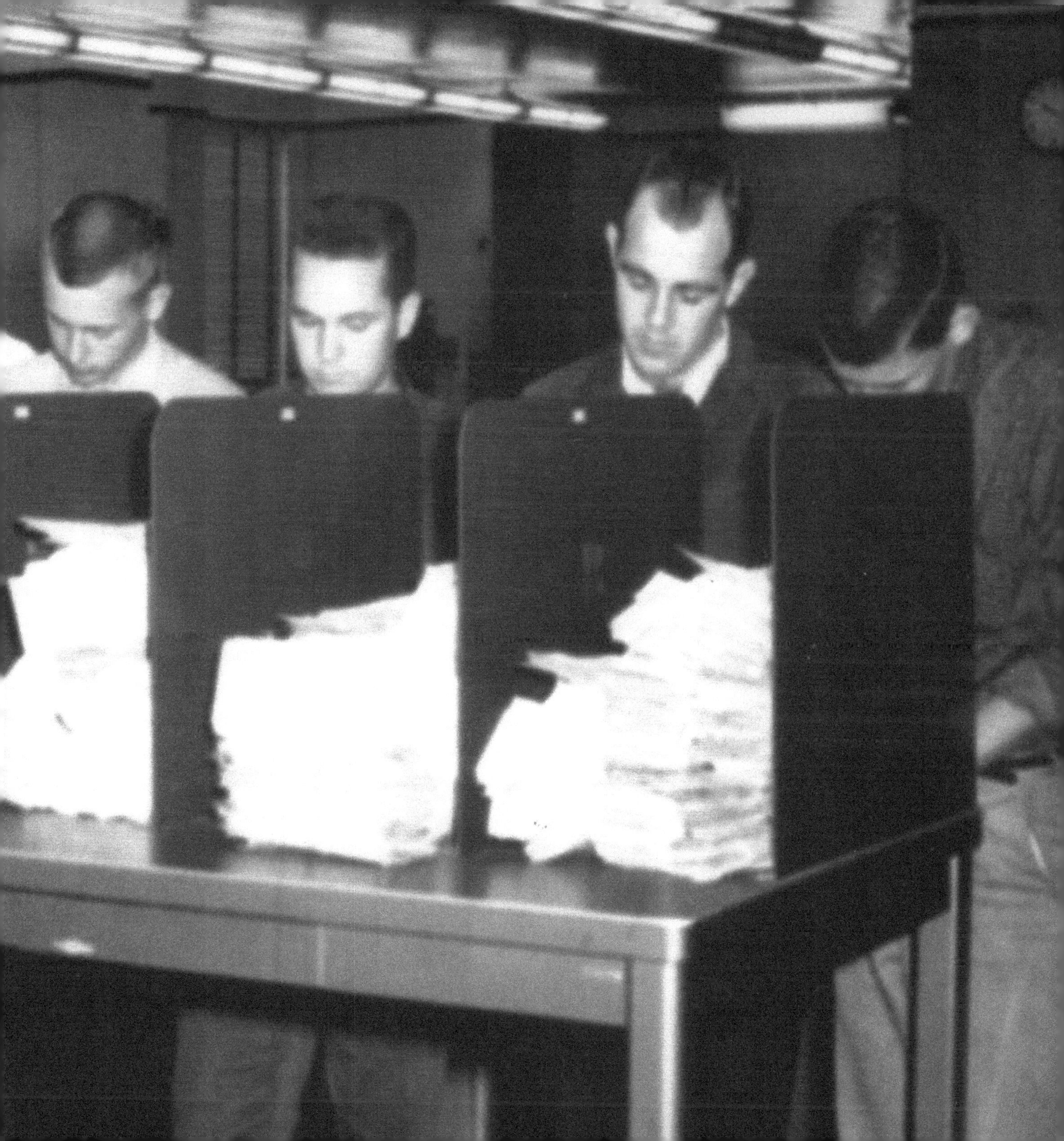

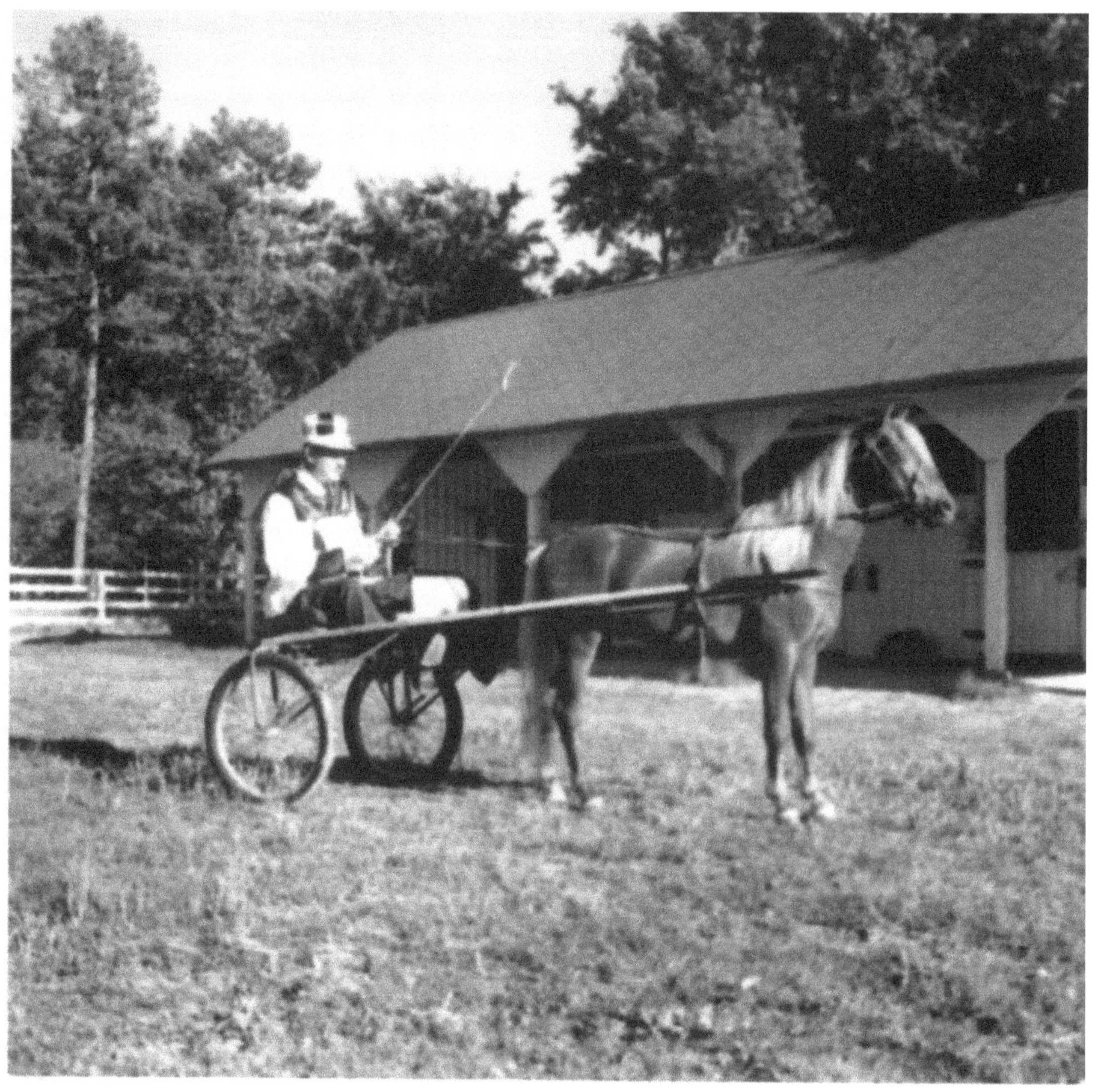

Charles M. Taylor shows off one of his Welsh ponies seated in a harness-racing trotter in May 1961. Harness racing remains a popular sport today in some areas of the nation.

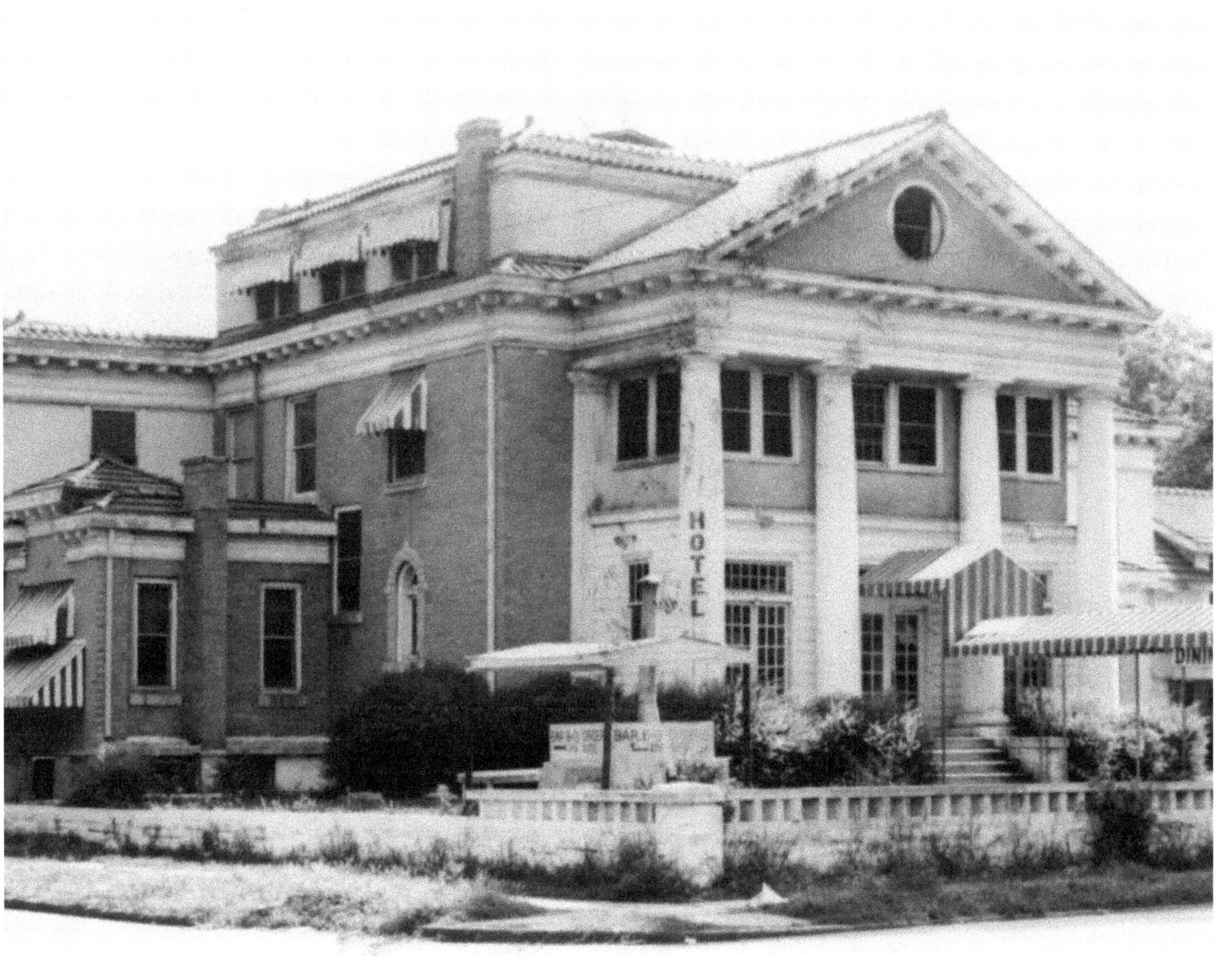

The exterior of the Hotel Charmaine, located at 820 West Fourteenth Street, in June 1961. The hotel, originally a hospital, was purchased by H. L. Johnson in 1949 and remodeled, becoming Little Rock's leading African-American hotel and hosting celebrities like Jackie Robinson and Fats Domino. The hotel was razed the same year this image was recorded to make way for the expansion of Philander Smith College.

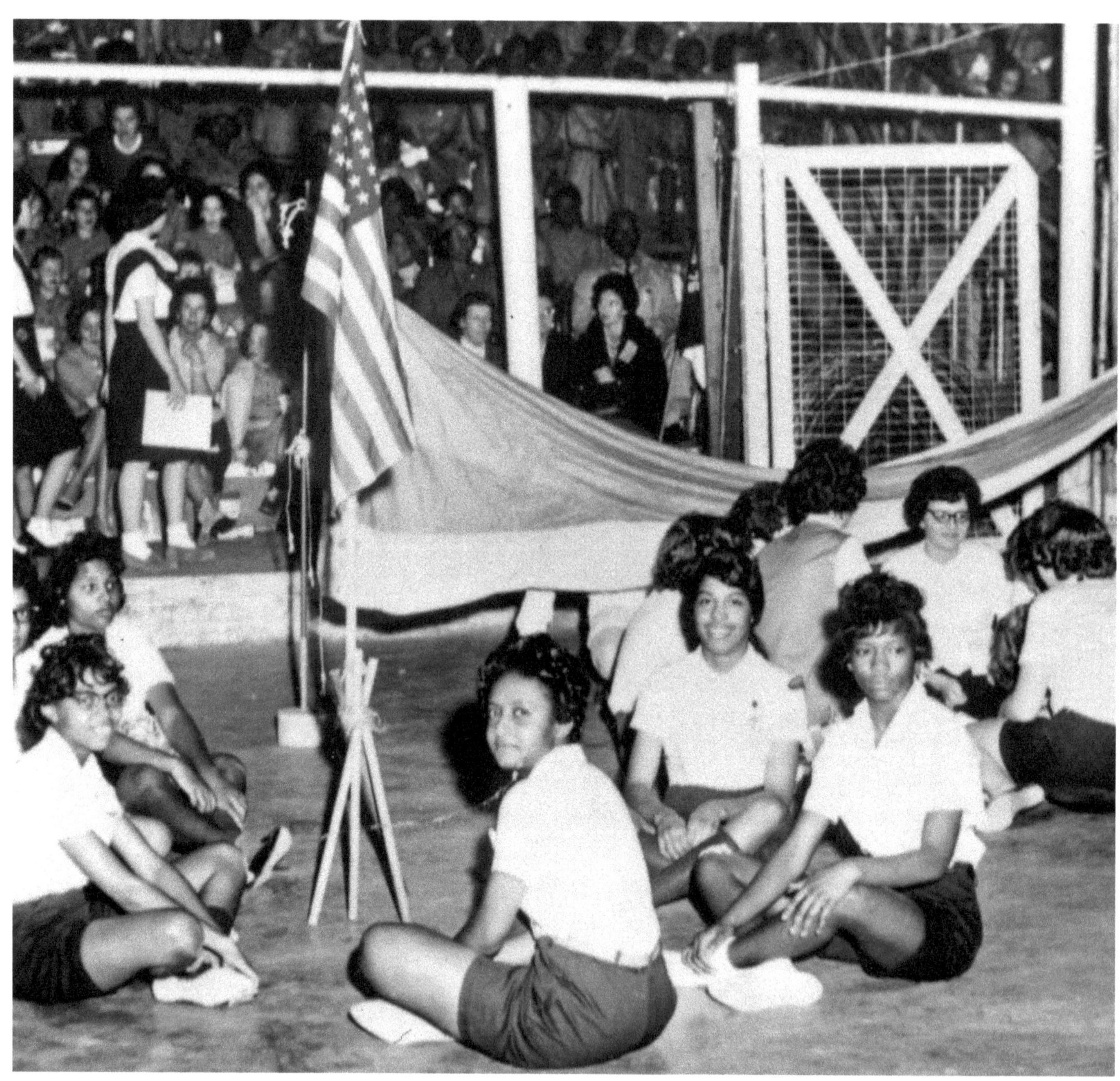

Members of Girl Scout Troop 248 prepare for a jamboree in 1961.

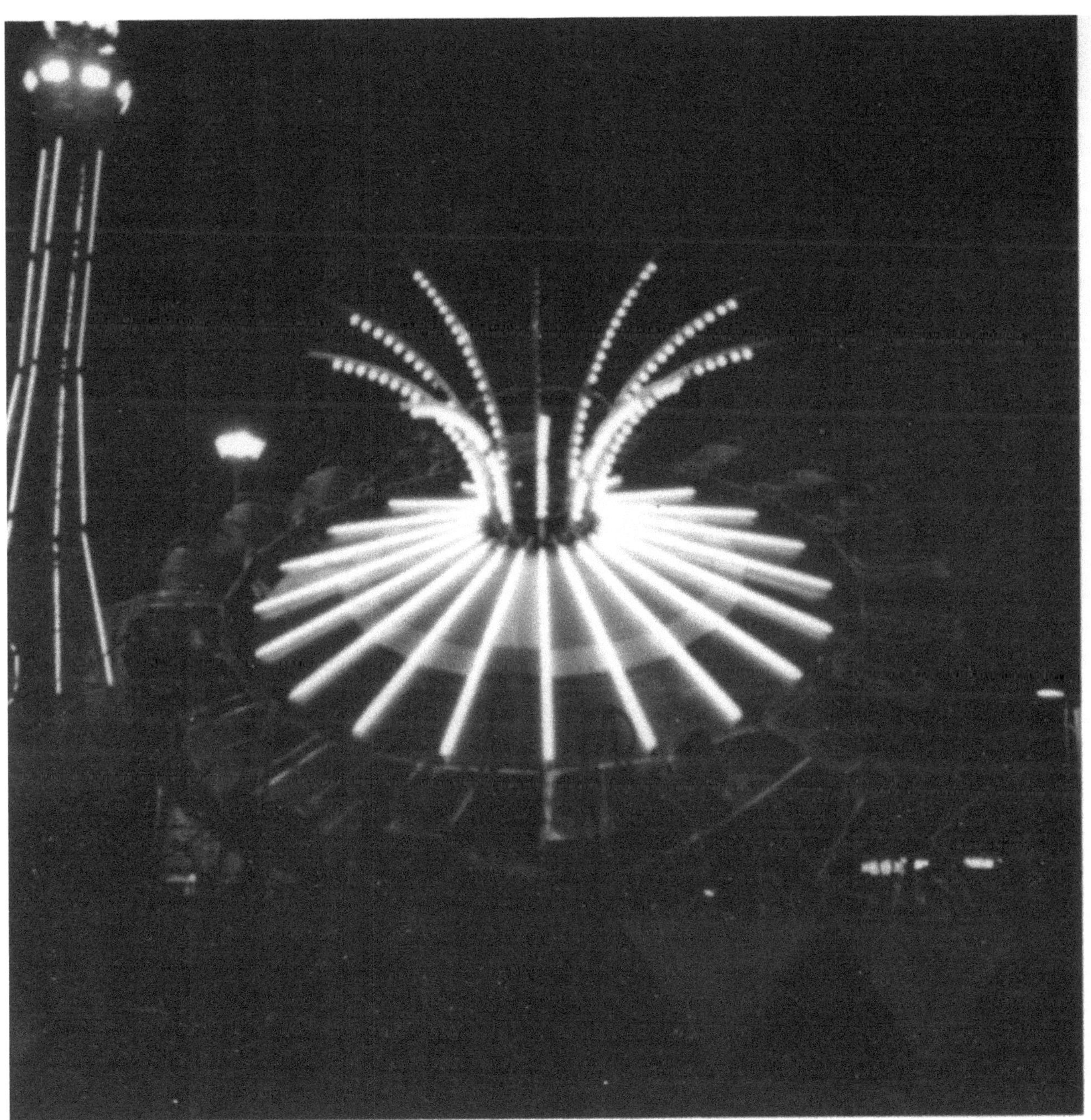

Thrill seekers enjoy an amusement ride at the annual Arkansas Livestock Show in October 1965.

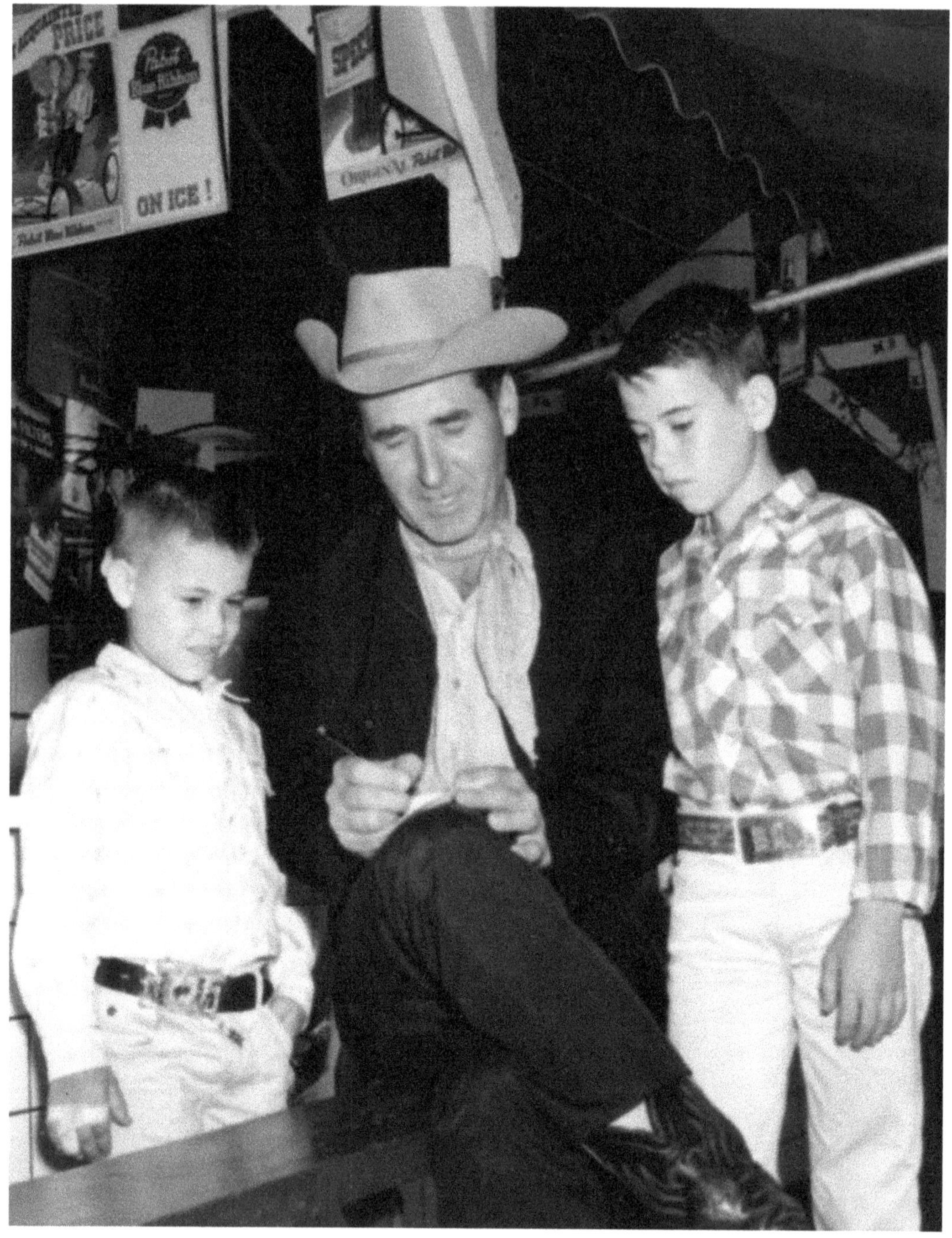

Sheb Wooley, a star from the TV show *Rawhide,* signs autographs for two youngsters in front of Barton Coliseum at the Arkansas Livestock Show in October 1962. Wooley also wrote the hit song "Purple People Eater," wrote the theme song for the TV show *Hee Haw,* and acted in western movies including the classic *High Noon.*

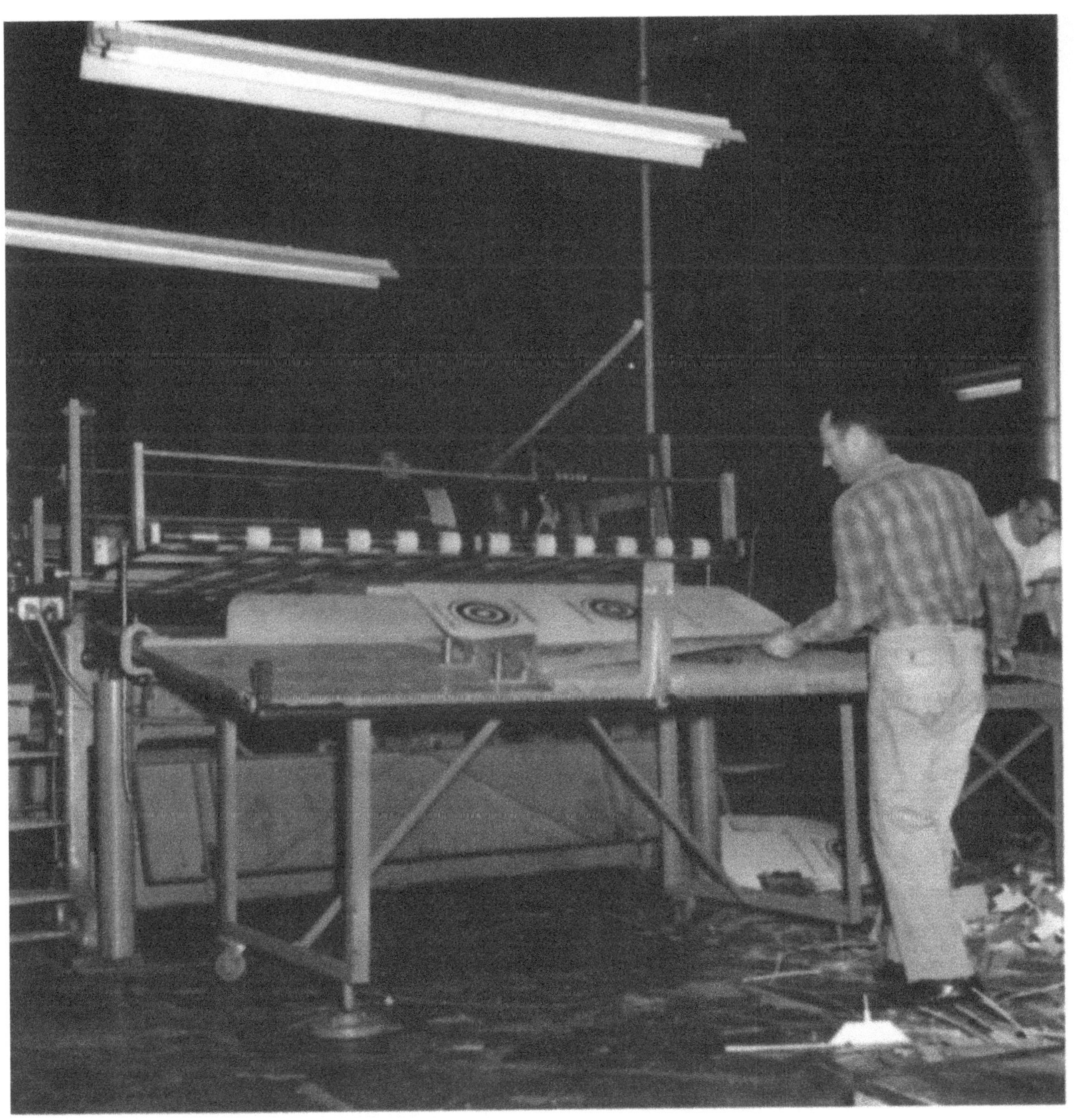

Workers at Hoerner Boxes make boxes from corrugated fiberboard in February 1962. The fiberboard itself was made by gluing together three layers of heavy paper: two smooth outside sheets and an inner, corrugated layer.

The lobby stand in the Arkansas Gazette Building in May 1964.

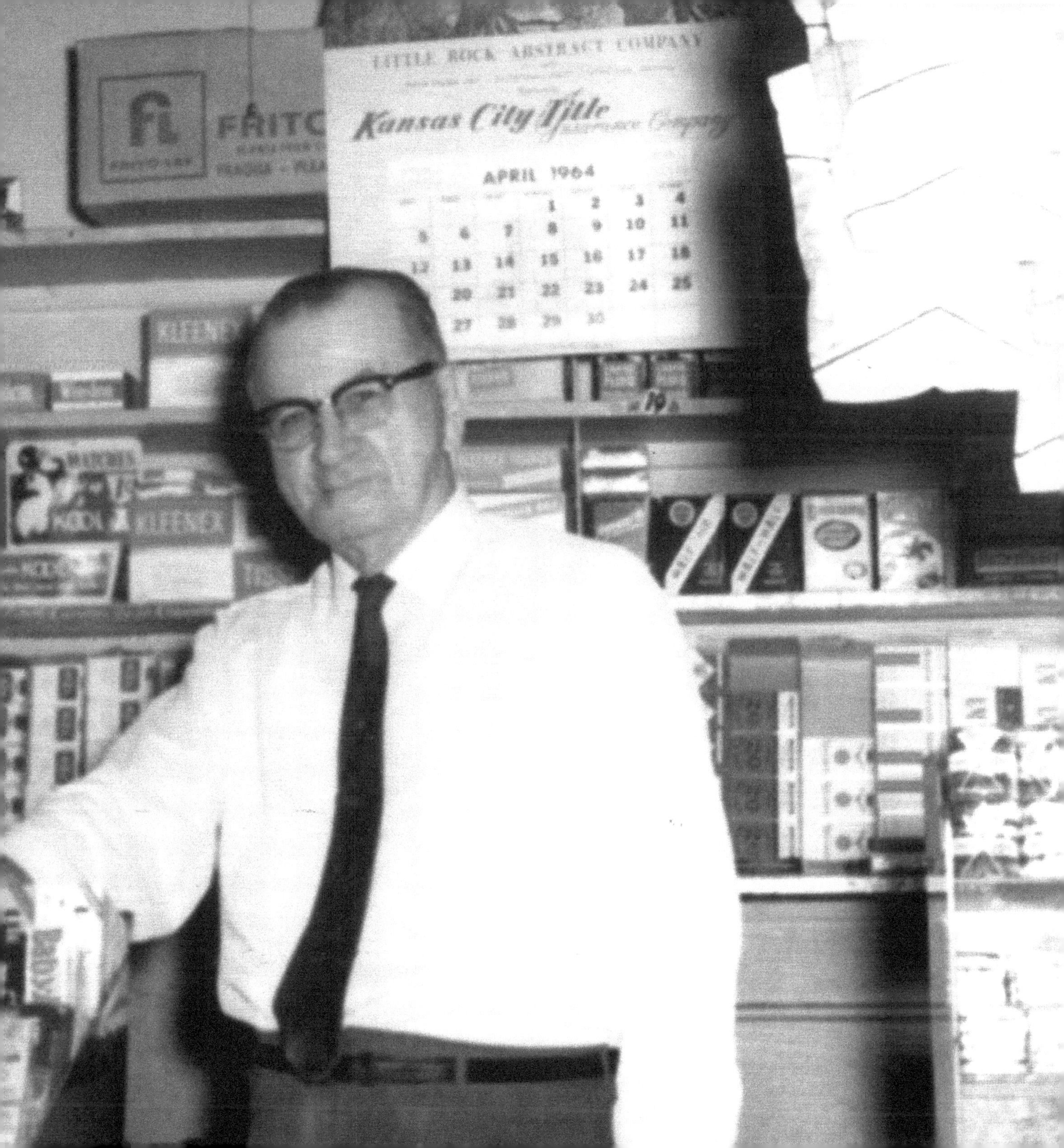
LITTLE ROCK ABSTRACT COMPANY
Kansas City Title
APRIL 1964
1 2 3 4
5 6 7 8 9 10 11
12 13 14 15 16 17 18
20 21 22 23 24 25
27 28 29 30

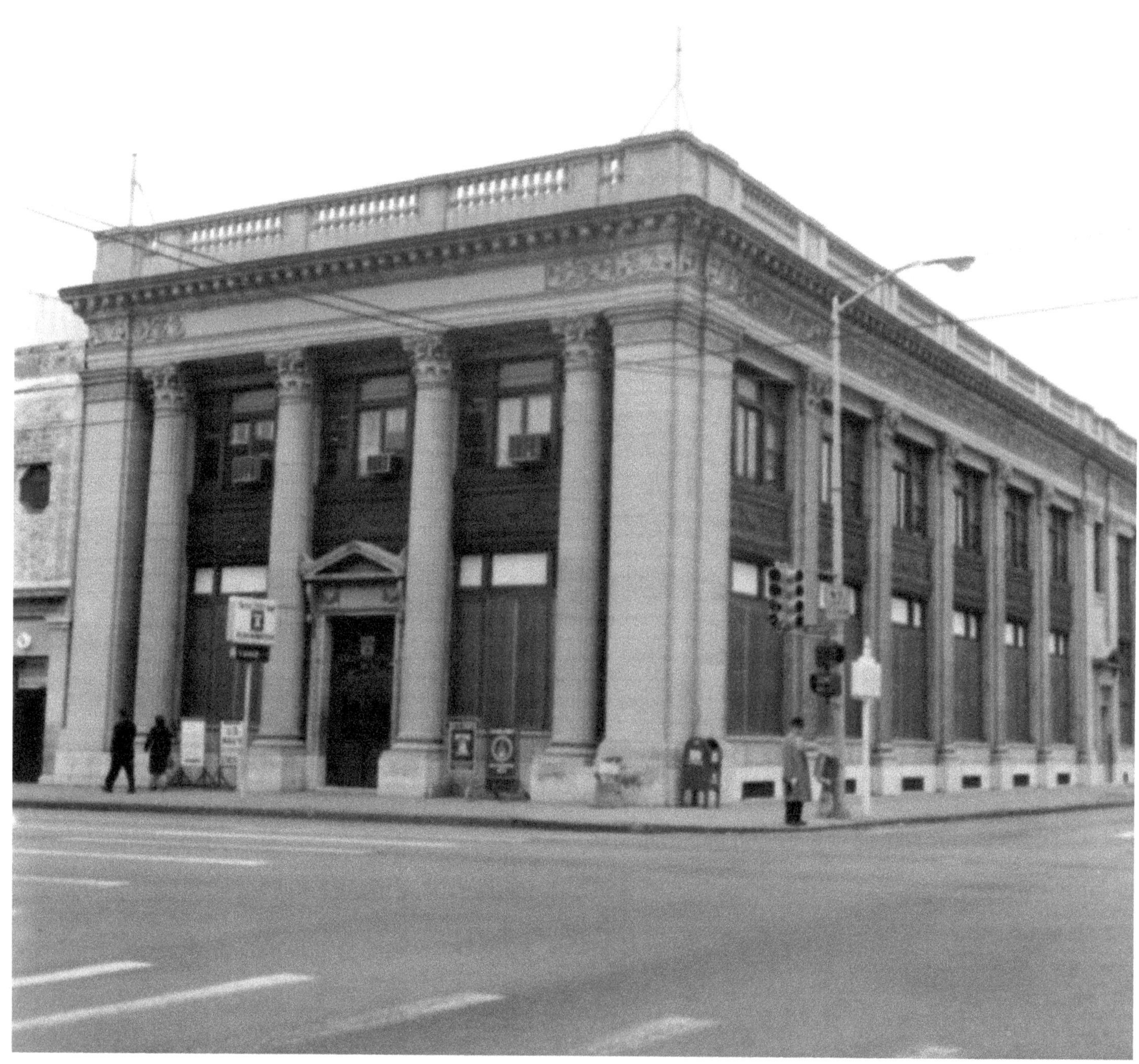

The World War II Soldier Service Center at Third and Main streets. During World War II, the building housed recreational services for thousands of soldiers and their families. By February 1964, it was serving as a recruiting headquarters for all four branches of the American military.

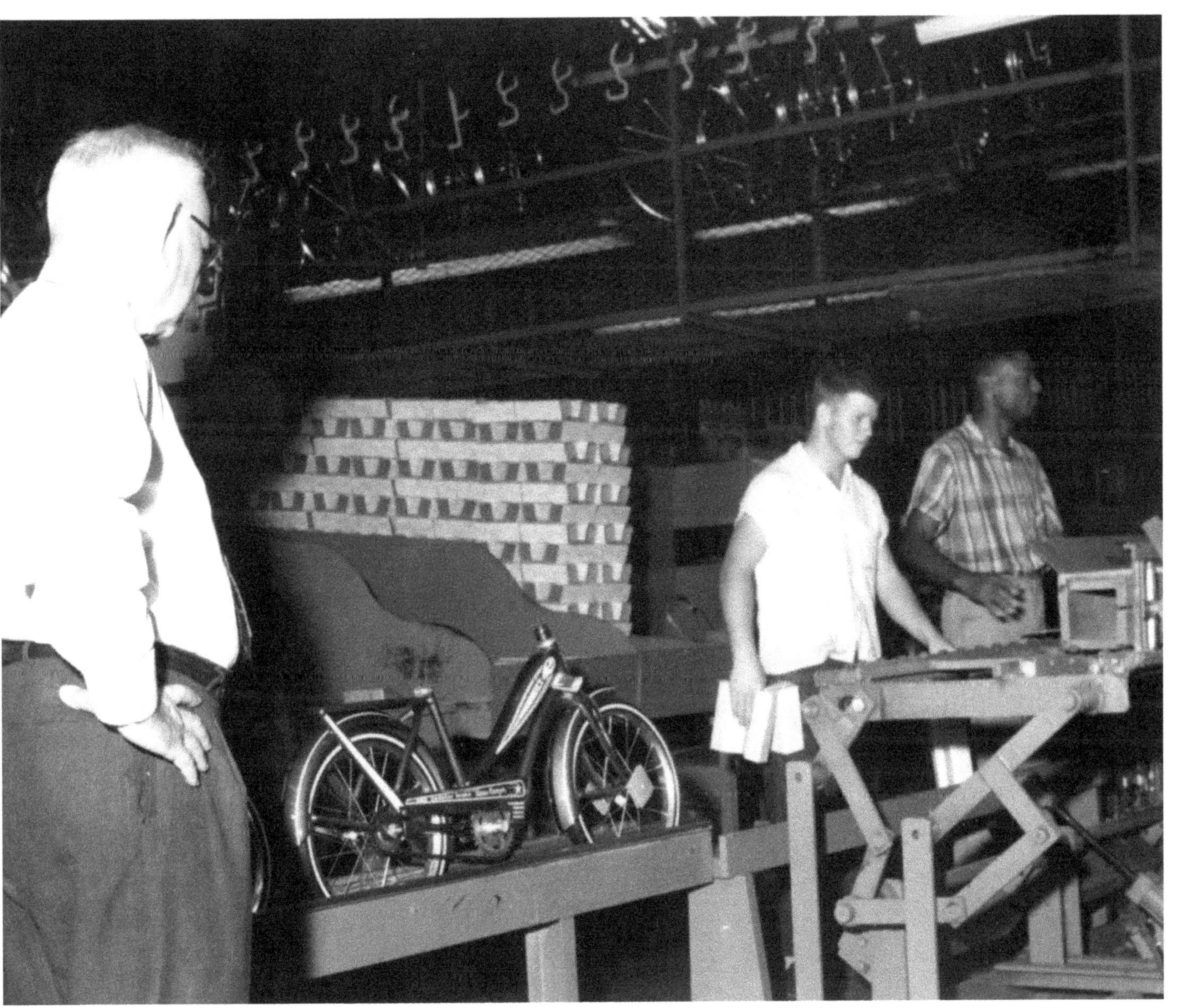

A man supervises workers on an assembly line in June 1963 at the American Machine and Foundry Bicycle Factory, located at West 65th and Patterson streets.

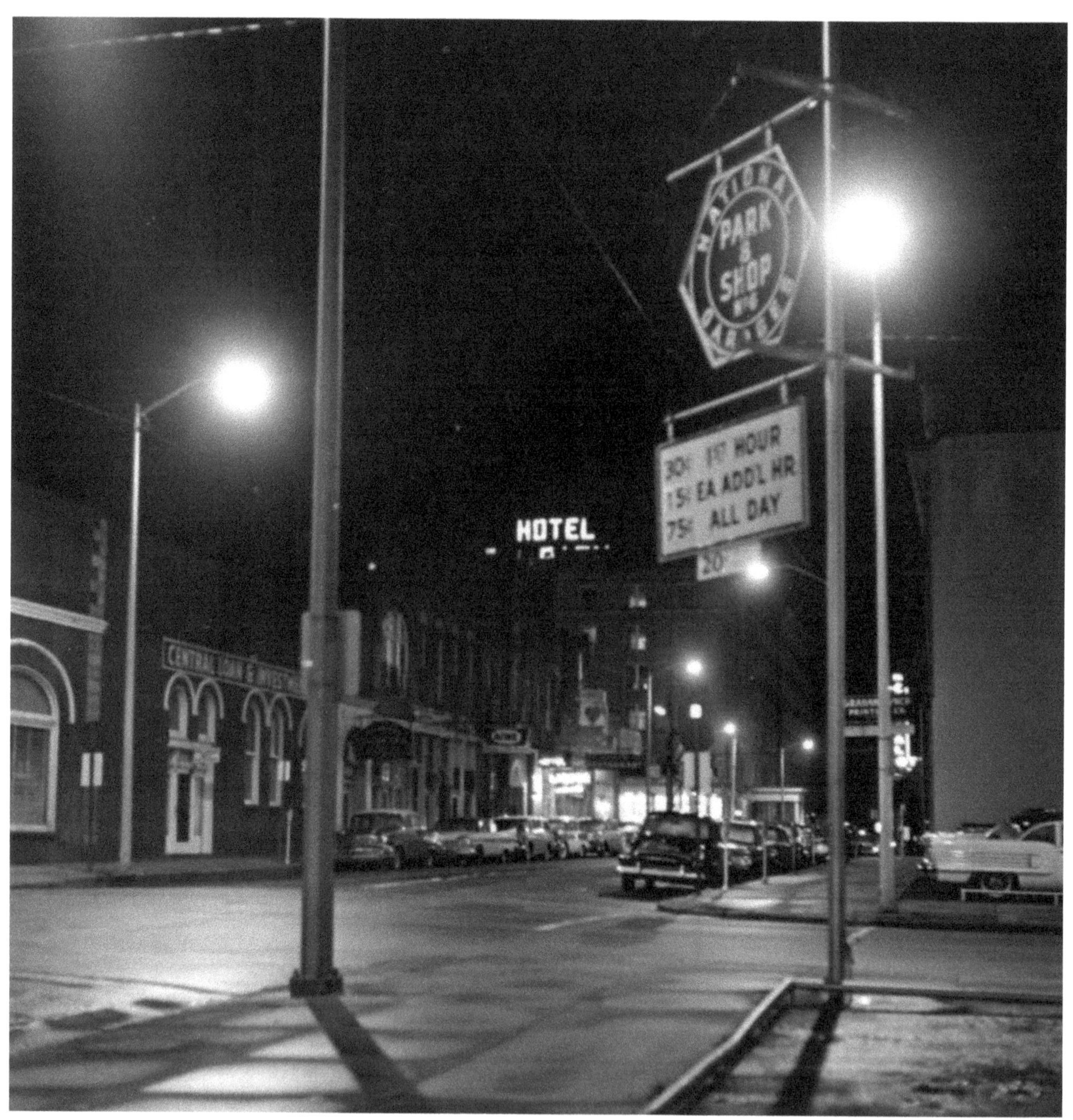

Louisiana Street at night in 1960.

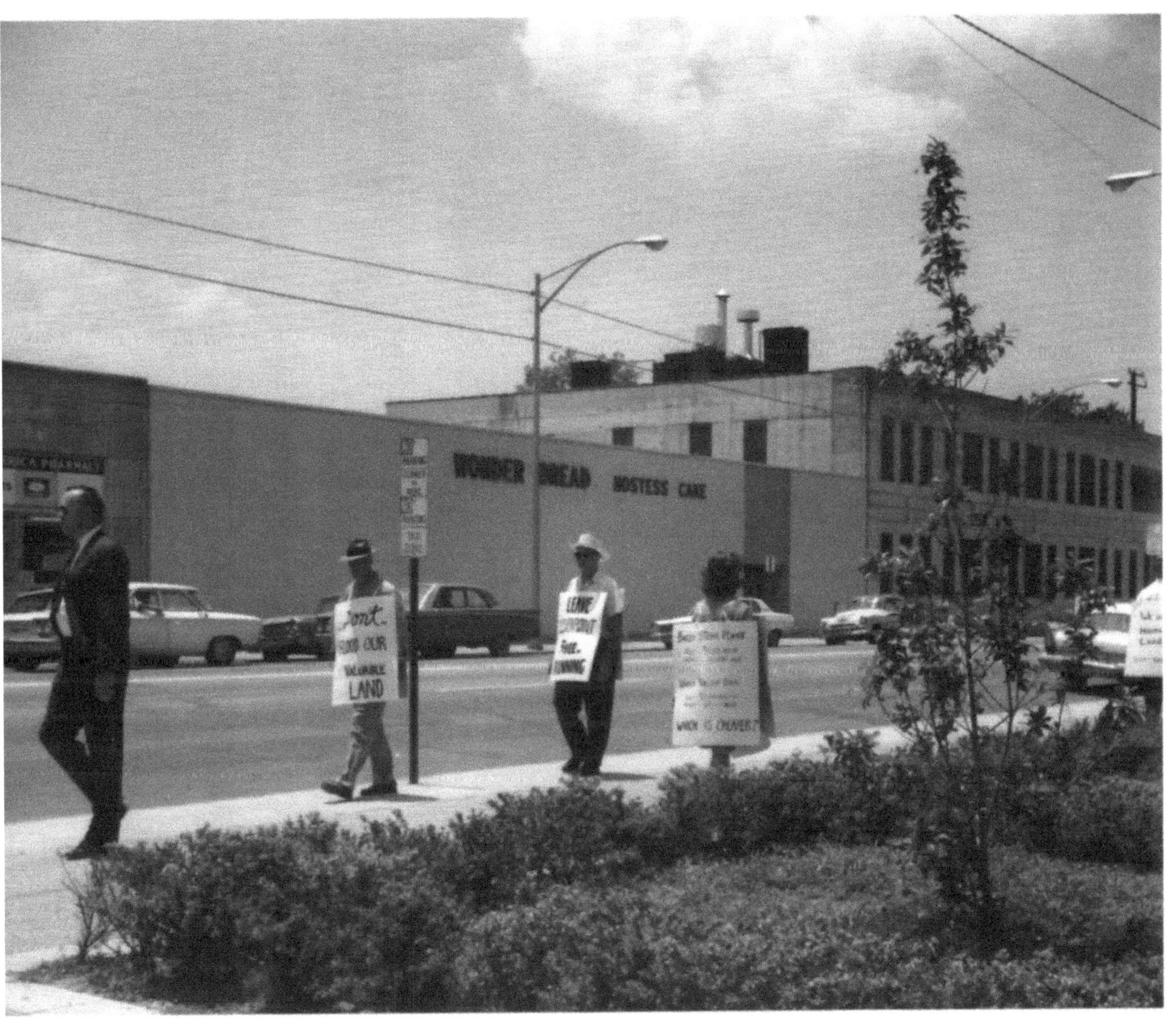

Picketers file past the Federal Building to protest a proposed dam on the Eleven Point River in July 1964. The Eleven Point flows from Missouri, through the Ozark Mountains, and into Arkansas. The dam was not built.

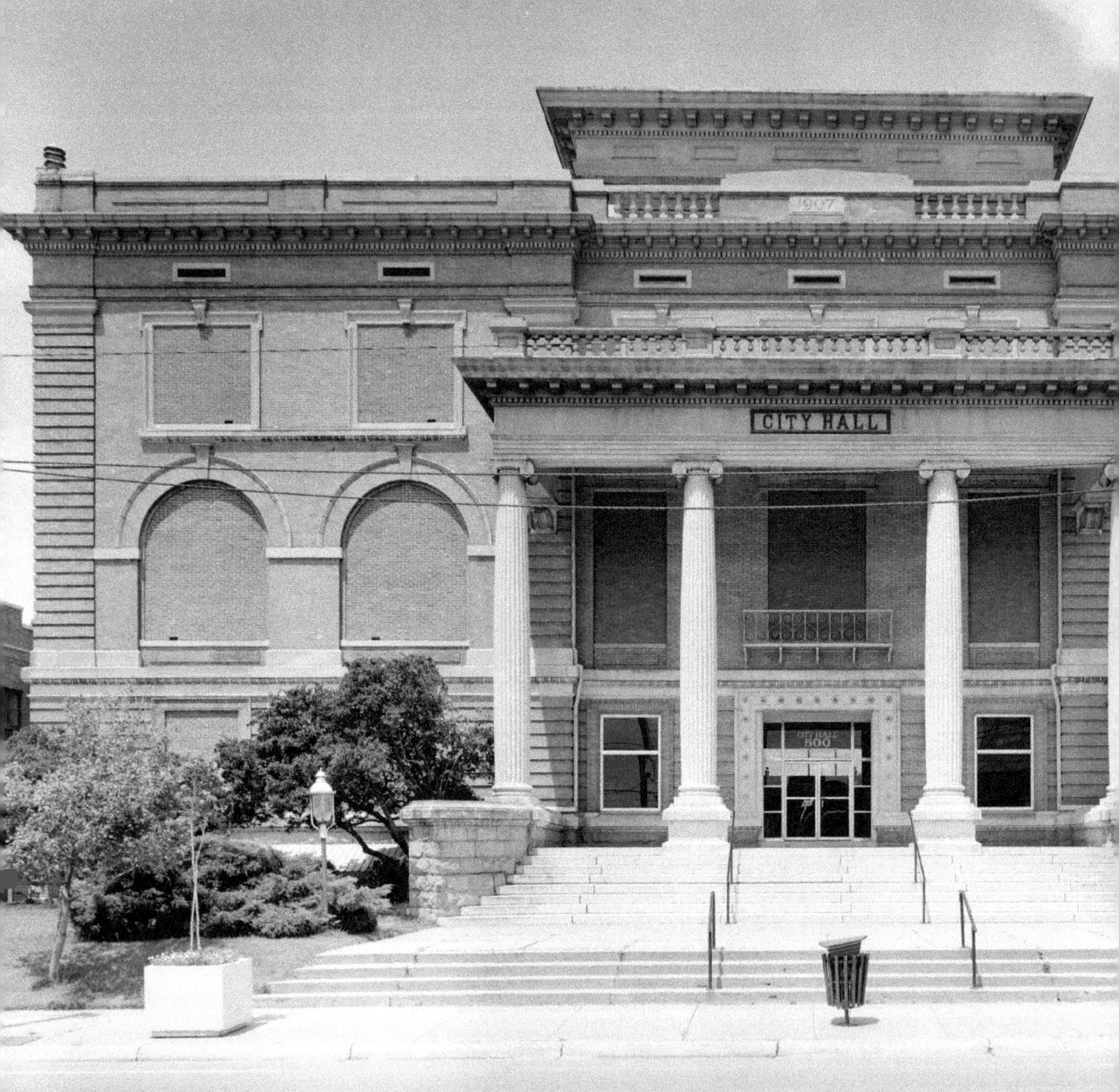
1907
CITY HALL

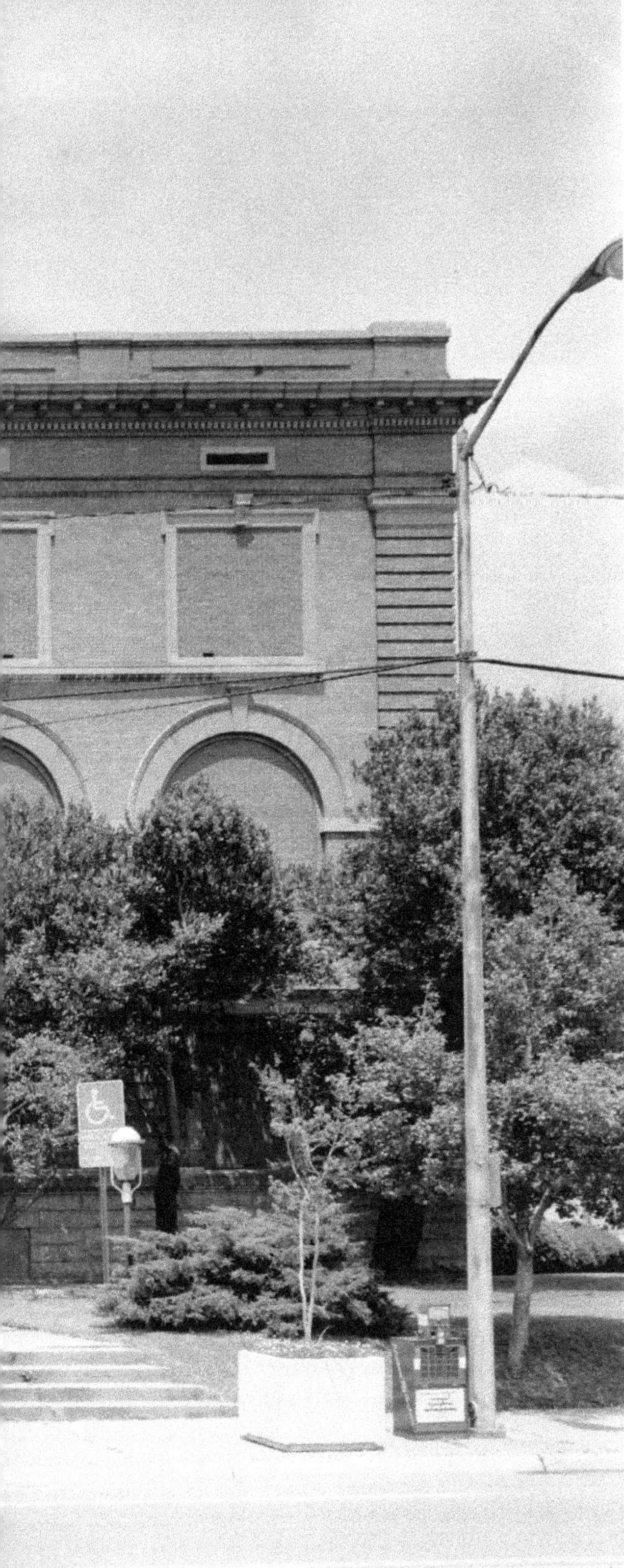

Little Rock City Hall as it appeared in the more recent past.

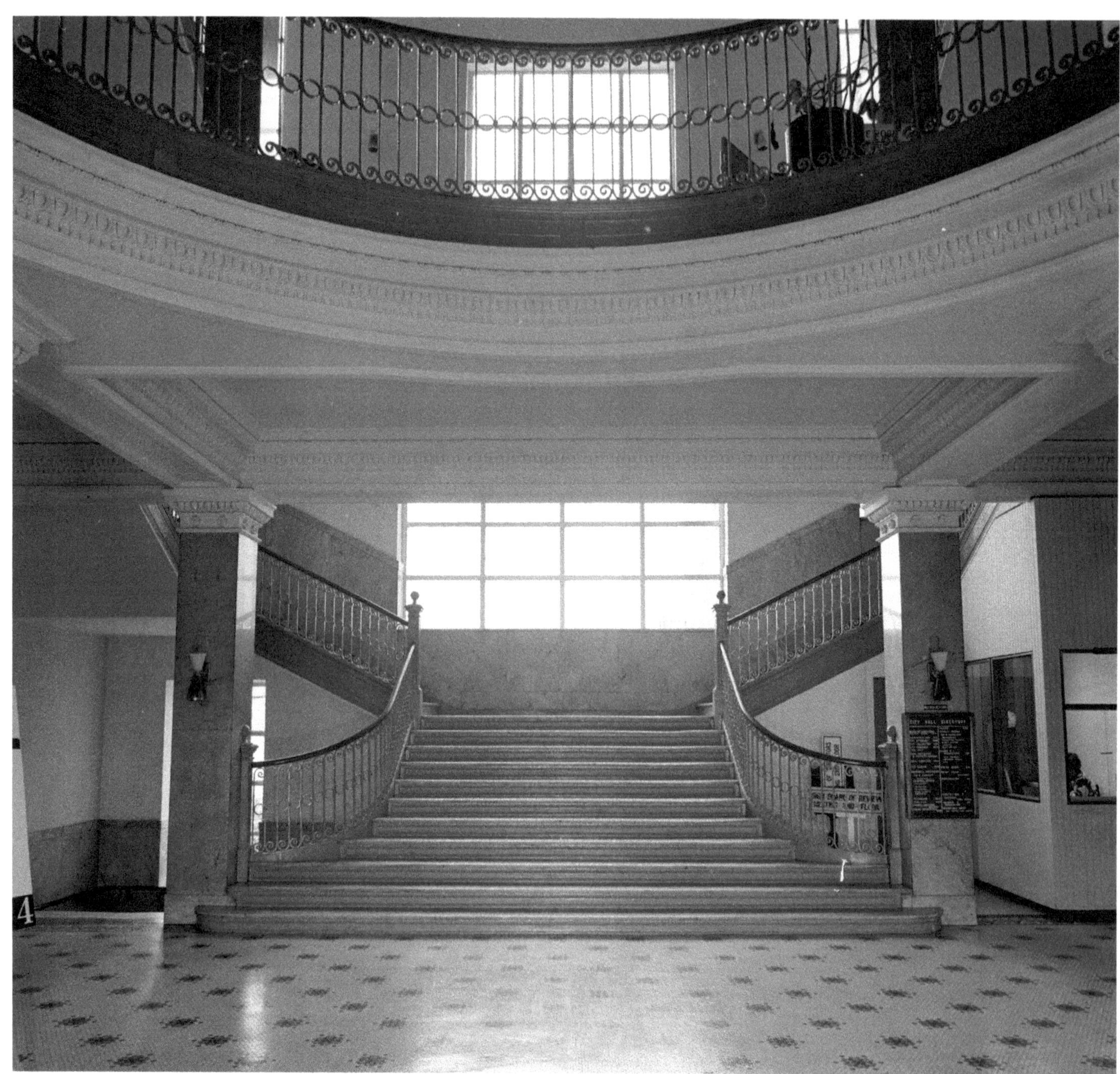

The Main Staircase of Little Rock City Hall.

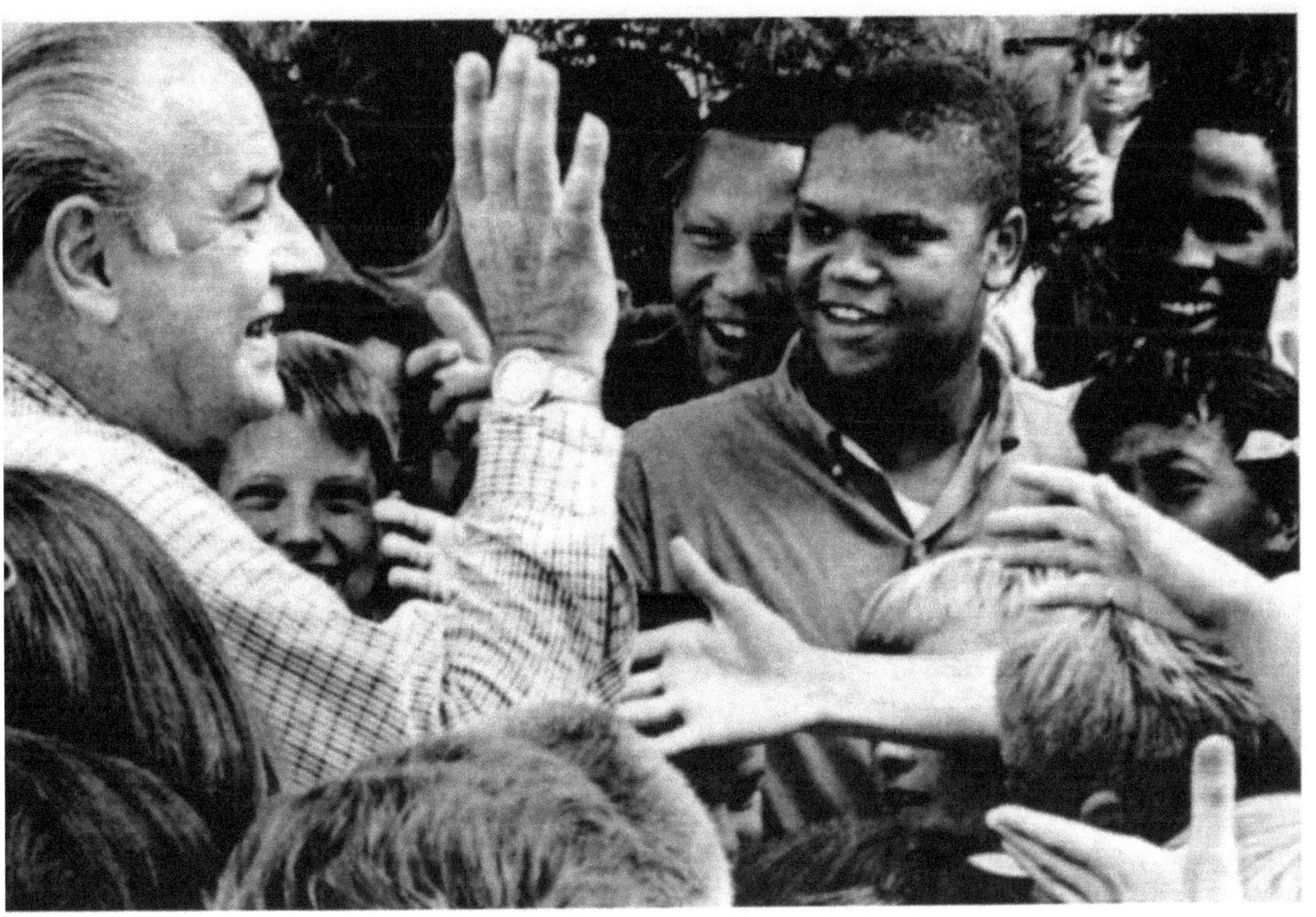

Winthrop Rockefeller greets a crowd of youth around 1968. Rockefeller was a farmer and entrepreneur who established Winrock Enterprises and founded Winrock Realty Company and the Arkansas Realty Company, which built the first skyscraper in Little Rock, the Tower Building. In 1967, he was elected governor of Arkansas and served for four years, becoming the first Republican governor of Arkansas since the Civil War.

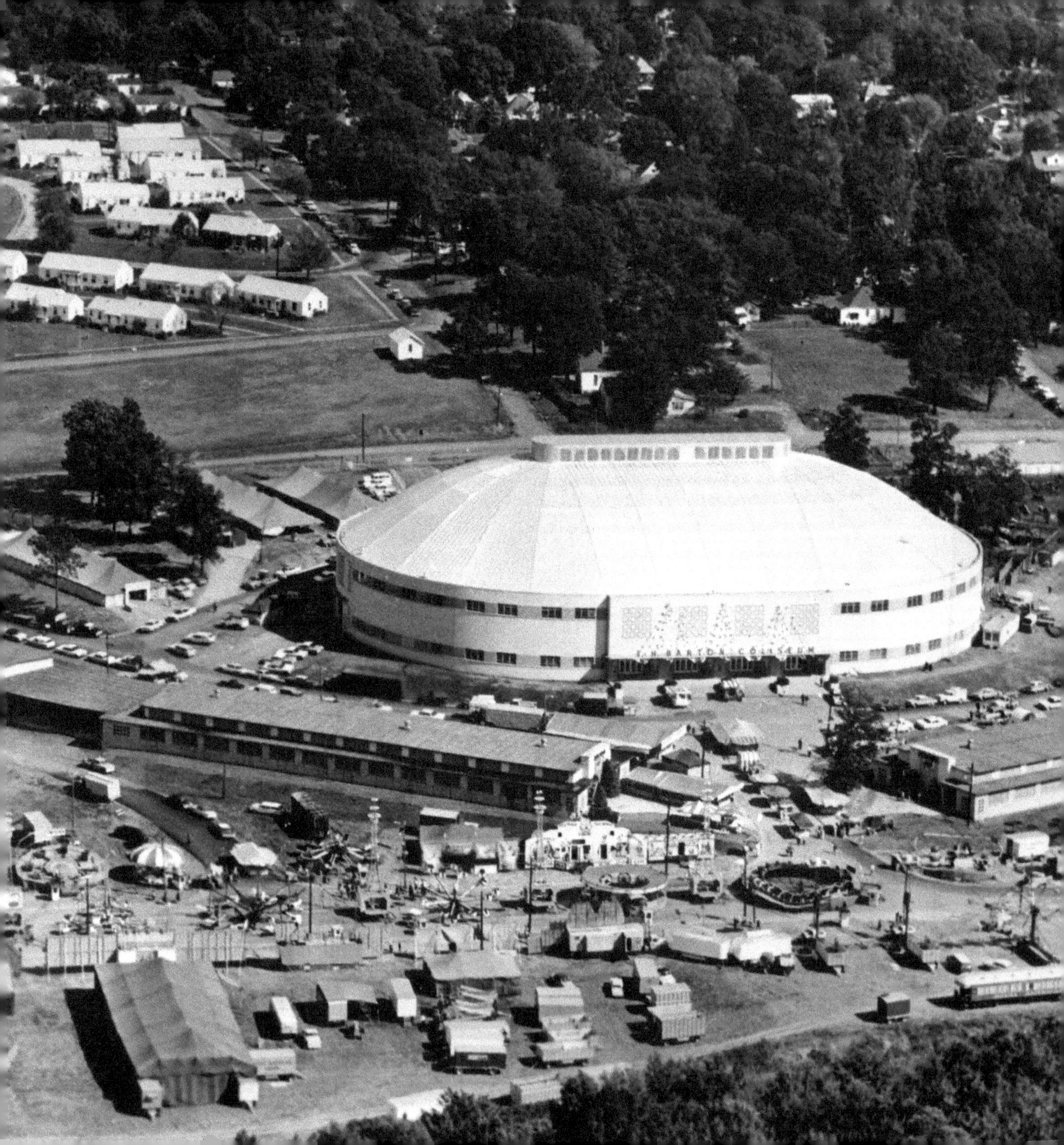

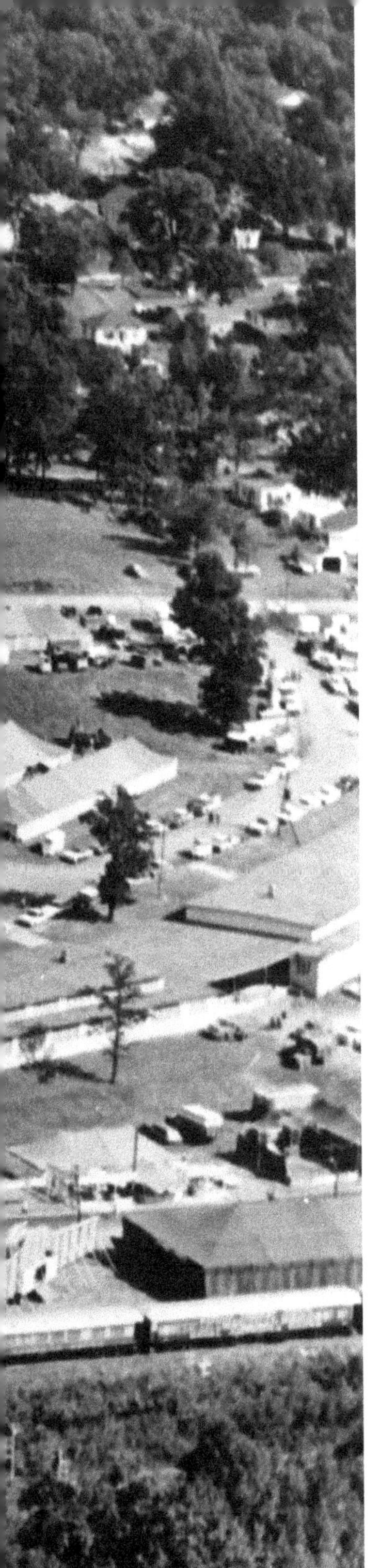

An aerial view of Barton Coliseum, a 7,150-seat multi-purpose auditorium located on the State Fair grounds.

The Old State House in August 1967. The structure was aging gracefully.

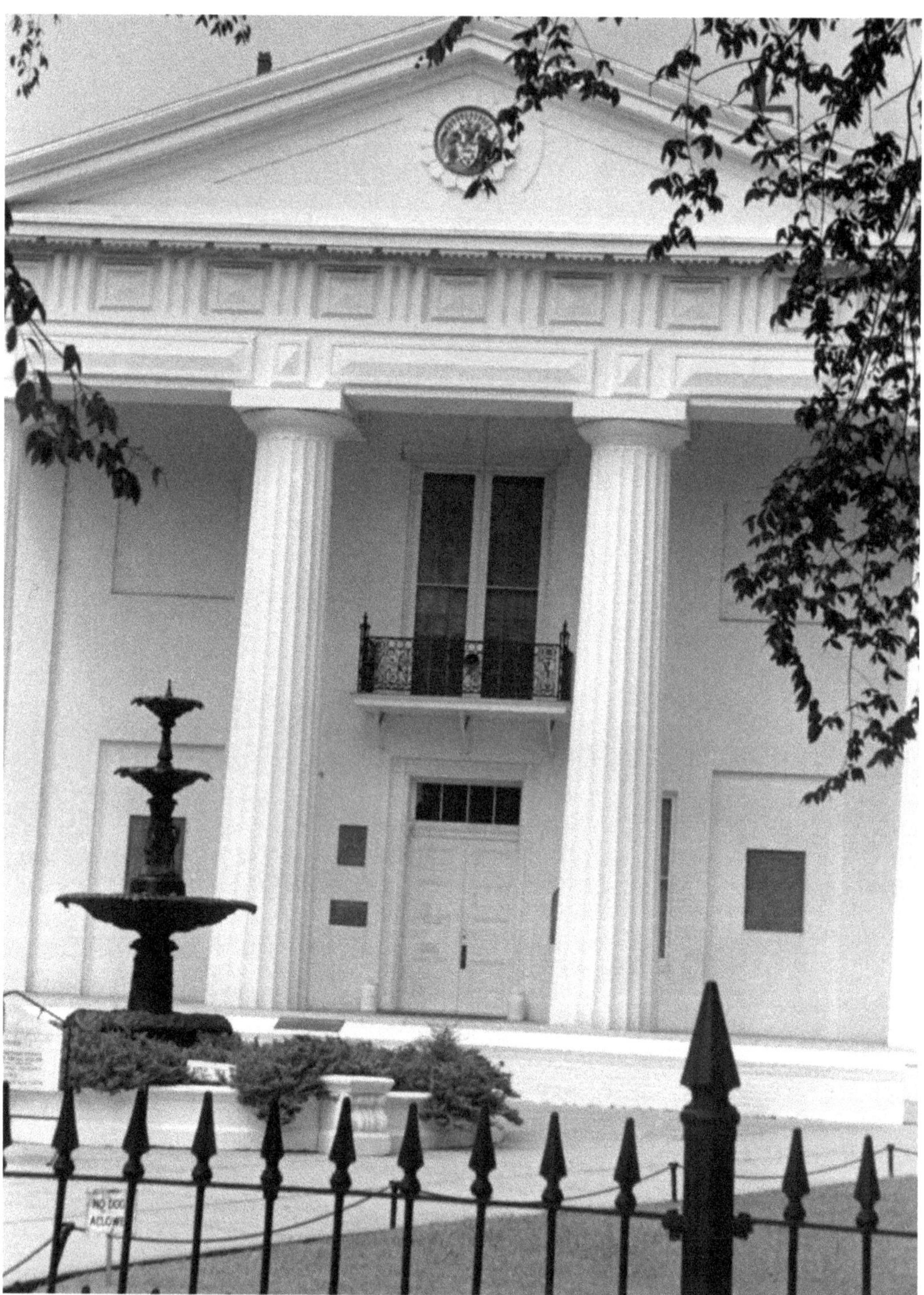

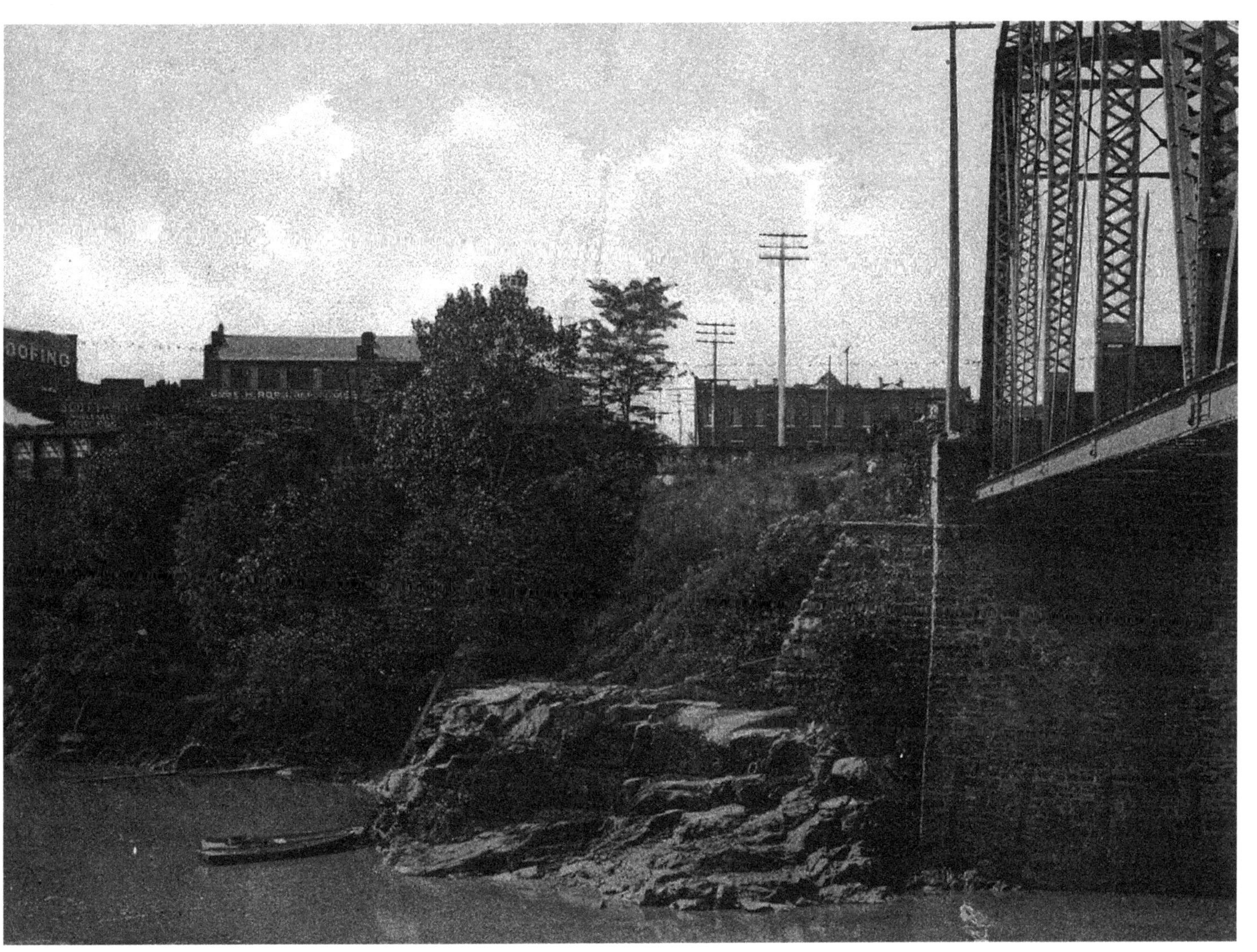

"La Petite Roche," for which the city was named, was discovered by Jean-Baptiste Benard de la Harpe in 1772. The rock was partially destroyed in the early 1900s during the construction of a railroad bridge. During the 1980s, the rock was cleaned and preserved as part of a riverfront redevelopment plan.

Notes on the Photographs

These notes, listed by page number, attempt to include all aspects known of the photographs. Each of the photographs is identified by the page number, photograph's title or description, photographer and collection, archive, and call or box number when applicable. Although every attempt was made to collect all data, in some cases complete data was unavailable due to the age and condition of some of the photographs and records.

I **West on Markham Street**
University of Arkansas
UALR Photo Coll. 79.AR.57

VI **General Steele Headquarters 1865**
University of Arkansas
UALR Photo Coll. 79.AR.60

X **Big Rock Mountain**
Courtesy, Arkansas History Commission
G1730

2 **Main and Markham 1863**
University of Arkansas
UALR Photo Coll. 79.AR.40

3 **Ottenheimer and Levy Goods**
University of Arkansas
UALR Photo Coll. 79.AR.41

4 **Old State House 1863**
University of Arkansas
UALR Photo Coll. 77.MN.02

5 **57th Regiment Infantry**
University of Arkansas
UALR Photo Coll. 77.USCT.01

6 **Arkansas River Railway Bridge**
Courtesy, Arkansas History Commission
G2406

7 **Markham Street**
Courtesy, Arkansas History Commission
G1815-03

8 **Torrent Fire Company**
University of Arkansas
UALR Photo Coll. 10.020

9 **Bowman Block**
University of Arkansas
UALR Photo Coll. 37.005

10 **Cotton Warehouse**
Courtesy, Arkansas History Commission
G1876

11 **City Wood Yard**
Courtesy, Arkansas History Commission
G1891

12 **Stoddard's Bank and Drugstore**
Courtesy, Arkansas History Commission
G1815-02

13 **Inauguration of Mule-powered Streetcars 1877**
Courtesy, Arkansas History Commission
G1895

14 **Post Office Construction**
Courtesy, Arkansas History Commission
G1772

15 **Frozen Arkansas River 1876**
Courtesy, Arkansas History Commission
G1704-2

16 **Denckla Block**
Courtesy, Arkansas History Commission
G1853

17 **McAlmont and Gibson Drugstore**
Courtesy, Arkansas History Commission
G1780

18 **Arkansas Deaf Mute Institute**
Courtesy, Arkansas History Commission
G1916-02

19 **Equitable Block**
Courtesy, Arkansas History Commission
G1920

20 **Stoddard's**
Courtesy, Arkansas History Commission
G1816

21 **Little Rock Catholic Church**
Courtesy, Arkansas History Commission
G1701

22 **Arkansas River Riverbanks**
Courtesy, Arkansas History Commission
G1769-02

23 **Piney Point 1880**
Courtesy, Arkansas History Commission
G1872

24 **Old State House 1880s**
Courtesy, Arkansas History Commission
G4712

25 **Mount St. Mary's Academy**
University of Arkansas
UALR Photo Coll. 67.114

26 **McDonald-Wait-Newton House**
Courtesy, Arkansas History Commission
G2976-48E

27 **Milton Rice House**
Courtesy, Arkansas History Commission
G2976-50B

28 **First Christian Church**
Butler Center for Arkansas Studies
PHO 2-A-12-17 Box 3

29 **Hotel Richelieu**
University of Arkansas
UALR Photo Coll. 37.002

30 **Metropolitan Hotel 1870s**
Courtesy, Arkansas History Commission
G2490

31 **Post Office and Courthouse**
Butler Center for Arkansas Studies
PHO 2-A-6-51 Box 1

32 **Junction Railroad Bridge**
University of Arkansas
UALR Photo Coll. 37.012

34 **Masonic Temple**
Butler Center for Arkansas Studies
PHO 2-A-6-83 Box 2

35 **First German Evangelical Lutheran Church**
Butler Center for Arkansas Studies
PHO 2-A-12-44 Box 1

36 **Steamboat Choctaw**
Courtesy, Arkansas History Commission
ECD2190

37 **Little Rock and Memphis Railroad Company**
Butler Center for Arkansas Studies
PHO 2-A-20-112 Box 3

39 **B. Heine Confectionery**
Butler Center for Arkansas Studies
PHO 2-A-10-64 Box 3

40 **Pulaski County Courthouse**
Library of Congress
LC-USZ62-59893

42 **Post Office and Courthouse**
Courtesy, Arkansas History Commission
ECD1807-09

43 **John Jacobs**
University of Arkansas
UALR Photo Coll. 37.89

44 **W. Siders with Rig**
Courtesy, Arkansas History Commission
PS67

45 **Mosaic Templars Headquarters**
Courtesy, Arkansas History Commission
PS16-03

46 **Gus Blass Company**
Butler Center for Arkansas Studies
PHO 2-A-6-104 Box 2

47 **Ceremony at St. Edward's**
Butler Center for Arkansas Studies
PHO 2-A-12-93 Box 4

48 **View of Main Street**
Library of Congress
LC-D4-71727

49 **View of Main Street No. 2**
Library of Congress
LC-D4-39505

50 **Bear Pits in Forest Park**
Library of Congress
LC-D4-39506

51 **City Park Memorial Fountain**
Library of Congress
LC-D4-71738

52 **Little Rock Travelers Baseball Team**
Butler Center for Arkansas Studies
PHO 2-A-16-38 Box 3

53 City Stables
Butler Center for Arkansas Studies
PHO 2-A-20-124 Box 3

54 Post Office Workers Group Portrait
Courtesy, Arkansas History Commission
PS17-01

55 The Post Office 1910
Library of Congress
LC-D4-39508

56 Forest Park Theater
Library of Congress
LC-D4-39507

57 View of Main Street no. 3
Butler Center for Arkansas Studies
PHO 2-A-7-16 Box 1

58 Little Rock High School
Library of Congress
LC-D4-71745

59 City Hall
Library of Congress
LC-D4-71743

60 The Fred Kramer School
Butler Center for Arkansas Studies
PHO 2-A-5-1 Box 1

61 Arkansas School for the Blind
Courtesy, Arkansas History Commission
ECD1807-24

62 Visit by Theodore Roosevelt
Butler Center for Arkansas Studies
PHO 2-A-18-47 Box 2

63 Thomas Cox and Sons Machinery Company
Butler Center for Arkansas Studies
PHO 2-A-6-6 Box 1

64 Egner's Bakery
Butler Center for Arkansas Studies
PHO 2-A-6-13 Box 1

65 Ehrman's Livery Stable
Butler Center for Arkansas Studies
PHO 2-A-10-16 Box 1

66 Southwestern Telegraph and Telephone Operators
Butler Center for Arkansas Studies
PHO 2-A-10-22 Box 2

67 University of Arkansas Medical School Class Portrait 1908
Butler Center for Arkansas Studies
PHO 2-A-23-46 Box 1

68 Field Trip to Pulaski Heights
Butler Center for Arkansas Studies
PHO 2-A-5-67 Box 1

69 Mount St. Mary's Academy 1909 Basketball Team
Butler Center for Arkansas Studies
PHO 2-A-12-100 Box 4

70 State Capitol Construction 1910
Butler Center for Arkansas Studies
PHO 2-A-15-162 Box 4

71 Construction of Capitol Dome
Butler Center for Arkansas Studies
PHO 2-A-15-161 Box 4

72 Early 1900s Street Scene
Courtesy, Arkansas History Commission
ECD1807-23

73 George Reichardt House
Butler Center for Arkansas Studies
PHO 2-A-6-243 Box 4

74 C. J. Kramer and Company Interior
Butler Center for Arkansas Studies
PHO 2-A-10-120 Box 4

75 The Million Dollar Fire 1911
Courtesy, Arkansas History Commission
ECD1807-27

76 Panorama of the City
Library of Congress
6a17392u

78 Chapple Grocery Delivery Rig
Courtesy, Arkansas History Commission
PS36-02

79 Ramshackle Little Rock Building
Courtesy, Arkansas History Commission
PS36-01

80 Donaghey and Bryan Dining Car Interior
Courtesy, Arkansas History Commission
GO204-18

81 Arizona Hot-air Balloon
Courtesy, Arkansas History Commission
G2678-01

82 City Park Monument-unveiling Ceremony
Courtesy, Arkansas History Commission
G5178-09

83 Confederate Veterans' Reunion
Courtesy, Arkansas History Commission
G2678-11

84 Confederate Veterans' Reunion no. 2
Courtesy, Arkansas History Commission
G5178-02

85 Confederate Veterans' Reunion no. 3
Courtesy, Arkansas History Commission
G2678-05

86 Confederate Veterans' Reunion no. 4
Courtesy, Arkansas History Commission
G5178-30

87 Confederate Veterans' Reunion no. 5
Courtesy, Arkansas History Commission
G5178-22

89 Confederate Veterans' Reunion no. 6
Courtesy, Arkansas History Commission
G2678-04

90 Arkansas Baptist College
Courtesy, Arkansas History Commission
PS44-14

91 Joseph Booker Family
Courtesy, Arkansas History Commission
PS44-23

92 Seventh Street Y.W.C.A.
Courtesy, Arkansas History Commission
ECD1807-33

93 City Park Barracks Cannon
Library of Congress
LC-D4-71739

94 West Second Street Early 1900s
Library of Congress
LC-D4-71729

95 Saint Bartholomew's Church
Courtesy, Arkansas History Commission
PS51-32

96 Little Rock Carnegie Library
Library of Congress
LC-D4-71740

97 Second Baptist Church
Library of Congress
LC-D4-71737

98 Laying Streetcar Track
Courtesy, Arkansas History Commission
PS19-2

99 The Free Bridge
Library of Congress
LC-D4-71732

100 The Capital Hotel
Library of Congress
LC-D4-71734

101 Suffrage Day Rally
University of Arkansas
UALR Photo Coll. 67.128

102 Little Rock Police Patrol
Butler Center for Arkansas Studies
PHO 2-A-21-7 Box 2

103 Hotel Marion
Library of Congress
LC-D4-71735

104 Aerial View 1918
Courtesy, Arkansas History Commission
G4594-41

106 New Union Depot 1921
Library of Congress
LC-D4-71733

107 Youngsters and Nursemaid on Rice Street
Courtesy, Arkansas History Commission
PS48-04

108 W. T. Grant Company Storefront
Butler Center for Arkansas Studies
PHO 2-A-6-229 Box 4

110 David O. Dodd Memorial
Butler Center for Arkansas Studies
PHO 2-A-15-140 Box 3

111 The McHenry House
Library of Congress
HABS ARK, 60-____, 1-1

112 Wallace Building
Butler Center for Arkansas Studies
PHO 2-A-6-99 Box 5

113 Flood of 1927
Butler Center for Arkansas Studies
PHO 2-A-11-8 Box 1

114 Flooded Street
University of Arkansas
UALR Photo Coll. 8.035

115 Flood of 1927 at Bridge
Library of Congress
LC-USZ62-129438

116 New Baring Cross Bridge Construction
Butler Center for Arkansas Studies
PHO 2-A-20-114 Box 3

117 Jamlin Stave Company Operations
University of Arkansas
UALR Photo Coll. 29.006

118 The Shrine Temple
University of Arkansas
UALR Photo Coll. 13.005

119 Old State House 1934
Library of Congress
HABS ARK, 60-LIRO,1-4

120 Checking Cotton
Library of Congress
LC-DIG-fsa-8a16149

121 Red Cross and KLRA Drought Relief Effort
Library of Congress
LC-USZ62-101938

122 Sharecropper Family
Library of Congress
LC-USF3301-006025-M3

124 Sharecropper Children
Library of Congress
LC-USF33-006026-M4

125 Henderliter Place 1934
Library of Congress
HABS ARK, 60-LIRO,2-1

126 Typical October Sunday
Library of Congress
LC-USF3301-006025-M5

127 United States Arsenal
Library of Congress
HABS ARK,60-LIRO,3-1

128 Trapnall Hall
Library of Congress
HABS ARK,60-LIRO,4-1

129 State Hospital 1930s
Courtesy, Arkansas History Commission
ECD2178

130 Soft Drink Summit
Library of Congress
LC-USF34-0182590-C

132 Pike-Fletcher-Terry House
Library of Congress
HABS ARK,60-LIRO,5-1

133 Mount Holly Cemetery
Butler Center for Arkansas Studies
PHO 2-A-22-40 Box 1

134 El Dorado Delegation
Courtesy, Arkansas History Commission
ECD1585-3

135 El Dorado Delegation no. 2
Courtesy, Arkansas History Commission
ECD1585-2

136 State Capitol 1941
Library of Congress
LC-USZ62-59643

137 Red's Pool Hall and Gem Theater
Butler Center for Arkansas Studies
PHO 2-A-4-116 Box 3

139 World War II Parade
Butler Center for Arkansas Studies
PHO 2-A-18-104A Box 1

140 Signs of the Times
Library of Congress
LC-USW3-009375-D

141 World War II Billboard
Library of Congress
LC-USW3-009431-D

143 Arkansas Air Tour Members
Courtesy, Arkansas History Commission
ECD1636-4

144 Shiloh Baptist Church Group Shot
Courtesy, Arkansas History Commission
PS13-03

145 Emergency Gas Pipe
Library of Congress
LC-USW3-009308-D

146 Welding Sections of the Pipeline
Library of Congress
LC-USW3-009247-D

147 Pipeline Crewman on Break
Library of Congress
LC-USW3-009253-D

148 City Hall Signage
Library of Congress
LC-USW3-009432-D

149 Postgraduate Experiment
Library of Congress
LC-USW3-002671-D

150 McCreight Family
Courtesy, Arkansas History Commission
ECD1393-2

151 Saint Bartholomew's Class
Courtesy, Arkansas History Commission
PS51-29

152 President Truman in Parade
Butler Center for Arkansas Studies
PHO 2-A-18-101 Box 3

153 Wesley Chapel Methodist Episcopal Church
Courtesy, Arkansas History Commission
PS09-19

154 Friends at Nineteenth and East Commerce
Courtesy, Arkansas History Commission
PS01-04

155 Arkansas Gazette Building
Courtesy, Arkansas History Commission
ECD0032

156 The Center Theater
University of Arkansas
UALR Photo Coll. 50.003

157 Rodeo Parade 1954
University of Arkansas
UALR Photo Coll. 50.008

158 Chris Finkbeiner and James Cobler
Courtesy, Arkansas History Commission
ECD0217-8

159 Prominent Citizens
Courtesy, Arkansas History Commission
PS09.20

160 Enforcing Integration
Library of Congress
LC-USZ62-135290

161 NAACP Involvement
Library of Congress
LC-USZ62-125613

162 **Governor Faubus Press Conference**
Courtesy, Arkansas History Commission
G1775-07

163 **Little Rock Nine at Thanksgiving Dinner**
Courtesy, Arkansas History Commission
G1775-12

164 **Opposing Integration**
Library of Congress
LC-USZ62-126829

165 **Scholarships for the Little Rock Nine**
Library of Congress
LC-USZ62-126833

166 **School Closing**
Library of Congress
LC-USZ62-126828

167 **Lessons by TV**
Library of Congress
LC-U9-1525Q-35

168 **Protesters at the State Capitol**
Courtesy, Arkansas History Commission
G1775-20

169 **More Protests**
Library of Congress
LC-US62-127043

160 **Capitol Avenue 1958**
Library of Congress
LC-U9-1523A-26

172 **The Gem Building**
Courtesy, Arkansas History Commission
PS15-02

173 **Plate Glass for the Gazette**
Courtesy, Arkansas History Commission
ECD0031-1

174 **At the Little Rock Library**
Courtesy, Arkansas History Commission
ECD00694-04

175 **Union Station Clock Tower**
Courtesy, Arkansas History Commission
ECD1347-03

176 **Louisiana Street 1960s**
Courtesy, Arkansas History Commission
ECD0714-3

177 **Federal Reserve Bank Branch**
Courtesy, Arkansas History Commission
ECD2073-7

178 **Federal Reserve Check Sorting**
Courtesy, Arkansas History Commission
ECD2073-08

180 **Charles Taylor Harness-racing Trotter**
Courtesy, Arkansas History Commission
ECD1028-03

181 **Hotel Charmaine Before Demolition**
Courtesy, Arkansas History Commission
PS14-02

182 **Girl Scout Troop 248**
Courtesy, Arkansas History Commission
PS01-03

183 **Livestock Show Thrill Ride**
Courtesy, Arkansas History Commission
ECD1127-3

184 **Sheb Wooley and Youngsters**
Courtesy, Arkansas History Commission
ECD1104-3

185 **Workers at Hoerner Boxes**
Courtesy, Arkansas History Commission
ECD0698-2

186 **Arkansas Gazette Lobby Stand**
Courtesy, Arkansas History Commission
ECD0030-1

188 **World War II Soldier Service Center**
Courtesy, Arkansas History Commission
ECD0697

189 **Bicycle Factory Operation**
Courtesy, Arkansas History Commission
ECD00008-8

190 **Louisiana Street at Night**
Courtesy, Arkansas History Commission
ECD0714-1

191 **Eleven Point River Dam Picketers**
Butler Center for Arkansas Studies
PHO 37-A-276

192 **City Hall in Recent Past**
Library of Congress
HABS ARK,60-LIRO,6-2

194 **City Hall Staircase**
Library of Congress
HABS ARK,60-LIRO,6-5

195 **Governor Winthrop Rockefeller**
Courtesy, Arkansas History Commission
PS46-04

197 **Aerial of Barton Coliseum**
Butler Center for Arkansas Studies
PHO 2-A-6-202 Box 5

198 **Old State House 1967**
Courtesy, Arkansas History Commission
ECD1530-4

199 **La Petite Roche**
University of Arkansas
UALR Photo Coll. 37.85

HISTORIC PHOTOS OF LITTLE ROCK

After the first sighting of "la petite roche" on the banks of the Arkansas River by French explorer Bernard de la Harpe in 1772, Little Rock grew from a few families living in small log cabins into a thriving capital city with a population of more than 184,000. The city has weathered everything from catastrophic floods to a school integration crisis, yet through good times and bad retains its small-town charm, Southern hospitality, and connections to the past.

From the Civil War to Central High School, *Historic Photos of Little Rock* follows life, government, education, and events throughout the city's history. Published in vivid black-and-white, more than a hundred images communicate historic events and the everyday life of a century of people building a unique and flourishing metropolis, which is today the governmental and cultural center of the state of Arkansas.

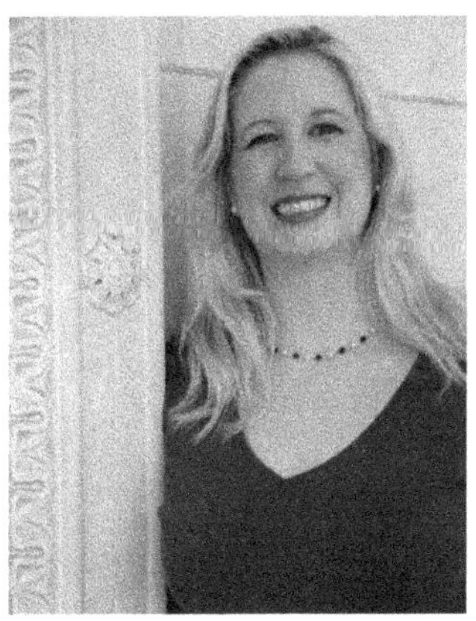

Kimberly Reynolds Rush was born and raised in the Little Rock area. She received a degree in dance management from Oklahoma City University and a master's degree in history from Louisiana State University. She is a former member of the faculty at Southeastern Louisiana University and is currently a member of the adjunct faculty at the University of Arkansas at Little Rock. After several years out of state, she has returned to Arkansas to call the state her home. Kim and her husband, Ryan, live in England, Arkansas.

WWW.TURNERPUBLISHING.COM

www.ingramcontent.com/pod-product-compliance
Lightning Source LLC
LaVergne TN
LVHW060610110826
845154LV00003B/66
* 9 7 8 1 6 8 3 3 6 9 6 6 0 *